A Buddhist Theory of Semiotics

BLOOMSBURY ADVANCES IN SEMIOTICS

Semiotics has complemented linguistics by expanding its scope beyond the phoneme and the sentence to include texts and discourse, and their rhetorical, performative, and ideological functions. It has brought into focus the multimodality of human communication. *Advances in Semiotics* publishes original works in the field demonstrating robust scholarship, intellectual creativity, and clarity of exposition. These works apply semiotic approaches to linguistics and non-verbal productions, social institutions and discourses, embodied cognition and communication, and the new virtual realities that have been ushered in by the Internet. It is also inclusive of publications in relevant domains such as socio-semiotics, evolutionary semiotics, game theory, cultural and literary studies, human-computer interactions, and the challenging new dimensions of human networking afforded by social websites.

Series Editor: Paul Bouissac is Professor Emeritus at the University of Toronto (Victoria College), Canada. He is a world renowned figure in semiotics and a pioneer of circus studies. He runs the SemiotiX Bulletin [www.semioticon.com/semiotix] which has a global readership.

Titles in the Series:

A Buddhist Theory of Semiotics Fabio Rambelli
Introduction to Peircean Visual Semiotics Tony Jappy
Semiotics of Drink and Drinking Paul Manning
Semiotics of Religion Robert Yelle

BLOOMSBURY ADVANCES IN SEMIOTICS

A Buddhist Theory of Semiotics

Signs, Ontology, and Salvation in Japanese Esoteric Buddhism

FABIO RAMBELLI

BLOOMSBURY
LONDON • NEW DELHI • NEW YORK • SYDNEY

Bloomsbury Academic
An imprint of Bloomsbury Publishing Plc

50 Bedford Square
London
WC1B 3DP
UK

175 Fifth Avenue
New York
NY 10010
USA

www.bloomsbury.com

First published 2013

British Library Cataloguing-in-Publication Data
A catalogue record for this book is available from the British Library.

ISBN: HB: 9781441177773
PB: 9781441161963
PDF: 9781441144638
ePub: 9781441154736

Library of Congress Cataloging-in-Publication Data
A catalogue record for this book is available from the Library of Congress.

Typeset by Fakenham Prepress Solutions, Fakenham, Norfolk NR21 8NN
Printed and bound in India

CONTENTS

Acknowledgments vi
Illustrations viii
Abbreviations and conventions ix
Preface x

1 Adamantine signs: The episteme of Japanese Esoteric Buddhism 1
2 Ontology of signs: The pansemiotic cosmos of mandala 37
3 The secrets of languages: Structure of the Esoteric signs 79
4 Inscribing the diamond path: A semiotic soteriology 125
5 The empire and the signs: Buddhism, semiotics, and cultural identity in Japanese history 173

Notes 197
References 222
Index 241

ACKNOWLEDGMENTS

I find it hard to believe that I have been working on and off on semiotic issues for the past thirty years, and that research for this book started more than twenty-five years ago. It all began when, as a freshman in Japanese studies at the Università di Venezia, I attended both Massimo Raveri's lectures on East Asian religions and philosophies and the late Paola Cagnoni's seminar on Japanese performing arts. With Massimo, I discovered first the Zen peculiar attitudes toward language and later Kūkai's thought, whereas Paola exposed me to semiotics and post-structuralism; their classes stimulated me to try to make sense of their respective fields together. In one way or another, avatars of this book have accompanied me for most of my adult life, and during this time I have accumulated a huge debt toward so many people that it would be impossible to acknowledge them all here. But I want to make sure that I duly express my gratitude to people whose help was essential for me. Allan Grapard, for more than words (and signs…) could repay; Massimo Raveri, Adriana Boscaro, Paolo Leonardi, and the late Paola Cagnoni, who guided my first steps into Japanese studies and semiotics; Giusy Montanini, with whom I began my journey into semiotics, hermeneutics, and the philosophy of language; Patrizia Violi, who encouraged me to look at semiotics through Buddhism; Bernard Faure and Ryūichi Abé, who taught me how to look at Buddhism through semiotics; Yamaguchi Masao, without whom Japan would have been different; Richard Payne, Jim Sanford, Charles Orzech, Henrik Sørensen, Ian Astley, and Robert Duquenne, for initiating me into the study of Esoteric Buddhism; Umberto Eco, for his pragmatic and interpretive approach; then, in no particular, order, the late Nino Forte, Max Moerman, Lucia Dolce, Iyanaga Nobumi, Satō Hiroo, Jackie Stone, Silvio Vita, Mark Teeuwen, Susan Klein, Bernhard Scheid, Sueki Fumihiko, Motoyama Kōju, Fujita Ryūjō, Ishizuka Jun'ichi, the late Michele Marra, Roberta Strippoli, Louis Hébert, James Robson, José Cabezón, Akiyama Akira, Tanaka Yūbun, Klaus Vollmer, Eric Reinders, William Bodiford, and Bill Powell. Part of the research for this book, carried out in 2001–3, was made possible by a research grant from the Japanese Society for the Promotion of Science. I am also grateful to the editor of this book, Gurdeep Mattu, and all the people involved in its production. Stephen Wilcox edited the illustrations. Finally, a very special thanks goes to Paul Bouissac: he believed in my Buddhist semiotics project since the very beginning (perhaps, more than

I did), and invited me to write about it in different formats, including an internet course for his Cybersemiotic Institute website and, especially, this very book, published in the series he directs.

Earlier versions of portions of this book have appeared in the following publications:

Rambelli, Fabio (1989), "Il gioco linguistico esoterico. Per una teoria del linguaggio del buddhismo giapponese 'shingon.'" *Versus. Quaderni di studi semiotici*, 54, September–December, pp. 69–96.

—(1991), "Re-inscribing *Maṇḍala*: Semiotic Operations on a Word and Its Object," *Studies in Central and East Asian Religions*, 4, pp. 1–24.

—(1994a), "The Semiotic Articulation of *Hosshin Seppō*: An Interpretive Study of the Concepts of *Mon* and *Monji* in Kūkai's *Mikkyō*," in Ian Astley (ed.), *Esoteric Buddhism in Japan*. Copenhagen: Seminar for Buddhist Studies, pp. 17–36.

—(1994b), "True Words, Silence, and the Adamantine Dance: On Japanese Mikkyō and the Formation of the Shingon Discourse," *Japanese Journal of Religious Studies*, 21/4, December, pp. 373–405.

—(1998a), "Buddhism," in Paul Bouissac (ed.), *Encyclopedia of Semiotics*. London and New York: Oxford University Press, pp. 93–9.

—(1998b), "Daoism," in Paul Bouissac (ed.), *Encyclopedia of Semiotics*. London and New York: Oxford University Press, pp. 173–6.

—(1998c), "Mandala," in Paul Bouissac (ed.), *Encyclopedia of Semiotics*. London and New York: Oxford University Press, pp. 381–2.

—(1998d), "Mantra," in Paul Bouissac (ed.), *Encyclopedia of Semiotics*. London and New York: Oxford University Press, pp. 382–5.

—(1999), "The Empire and the Signs: Semiotics, Ideology, and Cultural Identity in Japanese History," *Versus. Quaderni di studi semiotici*, 83/84, pp. 15–40.

—(2002), "In Search of the Buddha's Intention: Raiyu and the World of Medieval Shingon Learned Monks," in Sanpa gōdō kinen ronshū henshū iinkai (eds), *Shingi Shingon kyōgaku no kenkyū*: *Raiyu Sōjō nanahyakunen goenki kinen ronshū*. Tokyo: Daizō shuppan, pp. 1208–36.

—(2006), "Secrecy in Japanese Esoteric Buddhism," in Mark Teeuwen and Bernhard Scheid (eds), *The Culture of Secrecy in Japanese Religion*. London and New York: Routledge, pp. 107–29.

—(2011), "Sémiotique bouddhiste: perspectives et questions ouvertes," *Protée*, 39/2, Automne, pp. 9–18.

All previously published material, however, has been revised and rewritten (and, in some cases, translated into English) here.

I thank the publishers for their kind permission to reprint copyrighted material in this book.

ILLUSTRATIONS

Tables

3.1 Esoteric semantic isotopies of the name Amida

Figures

2.1 Relations among alloforms
2.2 *Gorin mandara*
2.3 *Gorin mandara*: hierarchy and circularity
2.4 Twofold mandala
2.5 Semiotic square of nondualism
3.1 The five transformations (*goten*) of the graph A
3.2 The *shittan* graph *ban* (Sk. *vaṃ*)
3.3 Semiotic square of semioticity
4.1a and 4.1b Graphs of the five buddhas of the Womb mandala
4.2a and 4.2b Graphs of the five buddhas of the *Vajra* mandala
4.3a and 4.3b Graphs of self-enlightenment
4.4a and 4.4b Graphs of guidance to others
4.5a and 4.5b Graphs of self-enlightenment and guidance to others combined
4.6 The *shittan* graph *hrīḥ* (Jp. *kiriku*)
4.7 and 4.8 Images for incense smoke visualization
4.9 Kakuban's nine-graphs mandala
4.10 The five-element mandala embodied

ABBREVIATIONS AND CONVENTIONS

Ch. Chinese

Jp. Japanese

Sk. Sanskrit

DNBZ *Dai Nihon bukkyō zensho*

KDZ *Kōbō Daishi zenshū*

T. *Taishō shinshū Daizōkyō*

T zuzō *Taishō shinshū Daizōkyō zuzōbu*

Titles of canonical works compiled or translated in China or Korea are cited in Chinese. Chinese names and terms have been romanized according to the Pinyin system (unless when in citations using other systems), the common modified Hepburn system has been used for Japanese, and the standard transliteration system has been used for Sanskrit. Japanese personal names are written in the traditional order, with the family name first.

In dates, years prior to 1873 have been converted to the Western Gregorian calendar.

In order to avoid confusion between Esoteric (Tantric) Buddhism and Western forms of esotericism/occultism, throughout the book the capitalized term "Esoteric" refers to Esoteric Buddhism and is a translation of the Japanese *mikkyō*. It is therefore different from lower-case "esoteric," which denotes something secret or hidden outside of the *Mikkyō* tradition.

PREFACE

Semiotics and Buddhism

In 1970 Roland Barthes, after a trip to Japan, wrote a short but beautifully illustrated book entitled *L'empire des signes*. In this collection of semiotic impressions of "Japan" (Barthes claims that what he is writing about is a "fictive land"),[1] he presented, among other things, an outlook of some semiotic strategies of Zen Buddhism. Barthes argued that Zen Buddhism, which he elevated to the epitome of Japanese culture (and, also, one may argue, of the entire Buddhist tradition), had developed a peculiar semiotics, one that was exclusively concerned with the signifier and ignored, if not completely erased, the signified. Barthes defines "the spirit of Zen"[2] as that peculiar Japanese attitude "which causes knowledge, or the subject, to vacillate: it creates an emptiness of language," it produces "the exemption from all meaning."[3] Barthes's Zen is devoid of center and depth: everything in it is pure surface, mere distinctive feature which does not stand for any meaning, especially because what for Barthes is the central Meaning of Western metaphysics, God, is absent there. As a consequence, Zen culture emphasized surfaces, forms, etiquette, rituals—a play of forms without content and surfaces without depth. This religious and intellectual system without meaning is a paradoxical paradise of the semiotician.

Barthes's treatment of Zen Buddhism was deeply steeped in Orientalism. Certainly not the imperialistic and degrading form of Orientalism stigmatized by Edward Said, but a benign Orientalism, deeply fascinated with cultural differences in a quest for a different theory and practice of culture. It goes without saying that Barthes, however, far from proposing a highly original interpretation of Zen Buddhism, was simply revamping in a (post-?) semiotic fashion received modernist understandings of it, put forth by, among others, Daisetz T. Suzuki, Alan Watts, and the Beatniks. In different words, Barthes's originality consisted in covering these modernist representations with a semiotic patina. It is difficult to decide whether Barthes's own intellectual trajectory away from semiotics in his works following *L'empire des signes* was informed by such knowledge of Zen modernism, or rather if his own post-semiotic ideas resonated with the rhetoric of Zen modernism.[4]

Either way, D. T. Suzuki had already pointed, albeit implicitly, to semiotic issues in Zen thought and practice. Without ever using the term semiotics or any of its accepted terminology, Suzuki stressed that Zen discourse and practice aimed at overcoming the limitations of ordinary language and of signification in general by developing particular strategies, such as the use of paradox (a challenge to thought based on oppositional terms), the exploitation of contradiction (a sort of deconstruction *ante litteram*), repetition (to bring sense-making to a stop), and various other performative methods (exclamation, bodily practices, etc.).[5]

Much before Suzuki, Arthur Schopenhauer had already opened the path, in an indirect way, to Barthes's attitude, by defining the fundamental issues at stake in the supposedly Buddhist semiotic endeavor, namely, the role of intentionality ("will") and the status of signs ("representation")—or rather, to be more precise, the need to quell one's will in order to overcome representations and attain true reality (salvation).[6]

Barthes's book is significant as perhaps the first instance in which Buddhism had aroused the interest of a leading semiotician. Barthes's reconstruction of Zen semiotics has been influential in several respects. It brought to the attention of semioticians all over the world the existence of different semiotic paradigms, in particular, the one constituted in Japan by Zen Buddhism;[7] it laid the ground for several Japanese semioticians' understanding of their own culture; and it also reinforced among Western intellectuals received ideas of Zen, and Buddhism in general, as a form of mysticism that avoided rational discussion and understanding. Thus, Barthes's rejection of meaning and his emphasis on the signifier turned out to be a more fashionable—and perhaps also a more politically correct—way to formulate received stereotypes about Oriental cultures (as unintelligible, formalistic, ritualistic, irrational, etc.).

At first sight, nothing would seem more distant from semiotic concerns than Buddhism. As it is commonly known in the West, at least, Buddhism is essentially a spiritual technique aimed at bypassing thought and signification to produce an experience—enlightenment—that supposedly consists in transcending rationality and language and attaining a state of direct and pure awareness of reality.[8] D. T. Suzuki wrote:

> The basic idea of Zen is to come in touch with the inner workings of our being, and to do this in the most direct way possible, without resorting to anything external or superadded . . . When Zen is thoroughly understood, absolute peace of mind is attained, and a man lives as he ought to live.[9]

That explains the anti-intellectualistic stance proposed by the most influential proponents/vulgarizers of Buddhism: there is no space for such things as philosophical speculations and critical reflection; what really matters is "practice," which is in and of itself productive of such an experience of liberation. This presupposes a radical separation between experience and conscious thought; by transcending (shutting off) thought one can attain a pure, unconditioned experience, which is defined as enlightenment and liberation from reincarnation and suffering. But in spite of its explicit lack of concerns for semiotics, isn't this a veritable semiotics in itself? Such interpretation of Buddhism—and Japanese Zen Buddhism in particular—is heavily influenced by a modernist, Western religious discourse. As Robert Sharf explains, "Suzuki began to render any and all Zen cultural artifacts—from *kōan* exchanges to dry-landscape gardens—as 'expressions of' or 'pointed toward' a pure, unmediated, and non-dual experience, known in Zen as *satori*."[10] However, in modernist theories of religion the sacred is the transcendent, the absolute which manifests itself paradoxically within the profane, whereas in Zen modernism the sacred is what we could call the "pre-transcendental," that is, a cognitive and existential dimension in which reality is putatively experienced directly without the mediation of the mental-categorial apparatus—what Kant defined as the "transcendental." However, as Bernard Faure[11] and Sharf have shown, Suzuki's interpretation of Zen, partly based on Nishida Kitarō's philosophy, is mostly unrelated to the history of the Zen tradition in East Asia. Still, it is possible to find references to a semiotics of pure experience, of immediacy, in the Buddhist tradition of the past. As Bernard Faure has made clear, Zen Buddhism struggled with the impossible task of "constructing" a "direct experience" of the Buddha-mind, and ended up developing what he calls the "rhetoric of immediacy."[12]

Other forms of Japanese Buddhism well known in the West, such as those related to the thought of the thirteenth-century monk Nichiren (CE 1222–1282), focus on the recitation and study of a particular scripture, the *Lotus Sutra*. They claim that the scripture itself is a condensation of the wisdom and the powers of the universe, and as such is productive of salvific effects. This is also an interesting semiotic theory, as it presupposes a connection between text, cosmic structure, and salvation.[13]

Setting aside these issues related to specific sectarian denominations, it is obvious that semiotic concerns are deeply ingrained in the Buddhist teachings dating back to a very early stage. In particular, we find the idea, widespread in ancient Indian thought, that the world is not what it looks, but it is covered by the veil of illusion (*māyā*), which needs to be removed if we want to face the world as it is. This fact generates the need for better, more accurate understanding of the self and of reality—not as a mere epistemological quest, but as directly related to soteriology. Thus, for Buddhism, semiotics is directly relevant to salvation; this is a key point that is often ignored even by Buddhologists. Throughout the ages, Buddhist schools have devised several strategies to provide a more adequate representation of reality aimed at the attainment of enlightenment. These strategies include the following:

- *Specialized terminology*: common to all is the ample use of specialized terminology, as to de-familiarize users from ordinary language and the perception of reality it generates. (Indeed, excessive use of jargon has now become a major obstacle for the understanding of Buddhism among the general public even in traditionally Buddhist countries in Asia.)
- *Estrangement effects*: estrangement seems to be one of the primary effects aimed at by many Buddhist scriptures, such as the *Wisdom (Prajñā-pāramitā) sutras* (with their paradoxical and self-denying language), the *Lotus Sutra* and *Vimalakīrti Sutra* (with their stunning visual imagery), and the *Flower Garland Sutra* (with its surprising understanding of reality).
- *Relativization of ordinary language*: this is carried out through multiple negations (the Madhyāmaka tradition with its emphasis on emptiness or *śūnyatā*), paradoxes (Zen), proliferation of sense (Tantric Buddhism), or emphasis on devotional formulae (Pure Land Buddhism).
- *Detailed explanations of the relational nature of reality*: these range from the twelve chains of causation to complex phenomenologies such as those of the Abhidharma and Yogācāra schools. Such understanding of the relational nature of everything is supposed to foster a different understanding (and perhaps, different representations as well) of things.
- *Doctrines on the absolute language*: Tantric Buddhism developed ancient Indian notions of the cosmic sound into a sophisticated doctrine of mantra as an absolute and unconditioned language, devoid of the problems and limitations we have seen in ordinary language.
- *Doctrines on the non-arbitrary, motivated nature of language and signs*: these were developed especially within the Tantric tradition. This is an important element that deserves further attention as it is related to several semiotic strategies, for instance, semantic isotopies, employment of rhetorical figures (metonymy rather than metaphors), and production of polysemic texts.
- *Widespread use of rituals*: these normally involve multisemiotic symbolism (ways to convey a complex representation of reality in forms that are not possible either to ordinary language or more specific Buddhist terminologies).
- *Textuality and exegetical strategies*: Buddhism has developed throughout the centuries a staggering amount of different kinds of texts composed in several languages. What is less known, however,

is the fact that Buddhism also developed doctrines about textuality (nature, role, and functioning of texts), as well as methods and strategies for text production and exegesis, which were connected to pedagogical philosophy and education methodologies. Scriptures were analyzed on different levels ranging from discussions of their titles, word-by-word commentary, chapter summaries, synthetic exegesis, and intertextual readings in which citations on similar topics from different sources were collated, to allegorical or figural readings (Mahayana texts were read in an Esoteric fashion, while secular texts were read as figurations of Buddhist religious truths).[14]

- *Non-hermeneutical dimension*: Buddhism paid particular attention to this aspect of texts. For instance, Buddhist scriptures, despite their complex meanings, narrative contents, and subtle imageries, are normally used in many ways that bypass their meaning (their hermeneutical dimension); they are worshiped, copied and chanted (even without understanding the words copied), decorated with golden buddhas, inscribed on rocks, exposed to the wind (as in Tibetan prayer wheels). This nonhermeneutical dimension poses interesting challenges to the semiotician, because despite its name it does result in generation of sense; still, it is significant that the inscribed meanings of entire texts are bypassed in favor of different meanings not directly relying upon linguistic expressions.[15]

Buddhism also developed a specialized semiotic terminology, which is unfortunately not well understood in its semiotic specificity, as it tends to be studied in terms of linguistics, philosophy of language, or more general doctrinal scholasticism. In the Japanese case, which is the subject of this book, we find, among others, the concepts of signifier and signified (respectively, *nōsen* and *shosen*), isotopic levels of meaning (superficial meaning or *jisō* and deep meaning or *jigi*, the four levels of meaning or *shijū hishaku*), multiplicity of sign systems (materially based in the objects of sense), and ideas of performative functions of language and signs. All these will be discussed in depth in the book.

Although much has been written on Buddhist linguistic doctrines, theories of mind, representation and meaning, and ritual, a systematic study of Buddhist semiotics has yet to be undertaken; this book is, perhaps, the first attempt in this direction. Of course, a number of other authors have written fine works on semiotic issues pertaining to Buddhism, and I will refer to many of them.[16] To make things clear at the outset, this book is not a semiotic interpretation of certain Buddhist teachings or texts. Rather, it presents a number of themes and methodologies, explicitly semiotic in nature and content, as they have been developed from within the Buddhist tradition. I am aware that the term “Buddhist semiotics” can refer, sometimes ambiguously, to both “semiotics as it developed from within the Buddhist tradition" and "semiotic study of Buddhism," but those two meanings of the term are not necessarily in contrast with each other. In fact, a semiotic study of Buddhism—which, as a semiotic endeavor, needs to be informed by the principles and developments of contemporary semiotic disciplines—should necessarily employ conceptual tools drawn from within the Buddhist tradition itself after they have been elucidated and re-contextualized.

In a sense, semiotics is a rather unfortunate discipline. Its name alone, with its obscure meaning, is enough to turn people off. Semioticians have not improved the situation with their endless proliferation of distinctions, use of the same terms to refer to very different things, and esoteric jargon. To try to make things easier, and simplify a bit, I see semiotics as an open field of problematics, a network of approaches and theories that can shed light on basic issues concerning signification and discursive formations. I agree with James Boon, who considers semiotics "less an integral theory than a clearinghouse of issues in the complexity of communicational processes."[17] To me, semiotics is essentially a conceptual arena to discuss issues related to the production, storage, transmission, and transformation of meaning; of course, operations on meaning also require sensory, material entities (signifiers) to convey it, and rules (codes) to associate these entities with their meanings.

Before I begin, however, a disclaimer is in order. Buddhism is a vast and fluid tradition, spanning about twenty-five centuries across Asia and, for more than a century now, the entire world. It is not a unified religious and intellectual system, and has interacted in many creative ways with the cultures in which it spread (including India, China, Tibet, Japan, Korea, and Southeast Asia). As there is no single and all-encompassing semiotic theory in Buddhism even within the same tradition, it is virtually impossible to describe a normative "Buddhist semiotics;" all there is are several local semiotics (a situation which is somewhat similar to the contemporary semiotic field) addressing issues such as epistemology, the nature of signs, language, visual and artistic representation, semantic systems, and performative aspects.

Because of this general situation, I have chosen to focus for this book on one Buddhist tradition that presents a particularly developed and interesting semiotic discourse, namely, Japanese Esoteric Buddhism (*mikkyō*, lit. "secret teachings" of the Buddha), especially in the variant developed within the Shingon tradition. Esoteric Buddhism, the East Asian form of Tantric Buddhism, was established at the beginning of the ninth century and became one of the dominant intellectual and ritual discourses of pre-modern Japan; and even though Tantric Buddhism is often associated in popular imagination with enhanced sexual techniques,[18] one of the main characteristics of Japanese Esoteric Buddhism is actually its sustained attention for semiotic problematics. The term "esoteric" in the Shingon tradition has very little to do with the range of neo- or pseudo-gnostic positions that developed in the West and are at the basis of Western occultism. As Umberto Eco and others have shown, Western esotericism is founded on an "empty secret" and the endless (and useless) quest to find it. In contrast, Japanese Esoteric Buddhism (*mikkyō*) is based on a particular semiotics not of hiding but of disclosure. The first character *mitsu* in the term *mikkyō*, commonly traslated as "secret" or "esoteric," suggests, rather than an empty secret, density and superimposed layers of meaning (the second character, *kyō*, means "teachings").

In this book, I present a range of philosophical discussions from within the Shingon tradition of Japanese Esoteric Buddhism concerning semiotic themes and practices, based on primary materials composed in Japan between the ninth and the seventeenth centuries (many of which have never been studied outside of Japan) and, when relevant, on their Indian and Chinese sources. Now, the linguistic dimension of Shingon Buddhism has already been studied by Ryūichi Abé in a magisterial work;[19] in the present book, I attempt to outline a larger and more systematic semiotic discourse by focusing primarily, not on mantra, but on signs in general.

To place Tantric Buddhism in a somewhat more familiar context, we can say that differently from Zen Buddhism, with its "rhetoric of immediacy"[20] attempting to bypass semiosis in a rarefaction of signs with its stress on direct, immediate, and sudden enlightenment in which one would be able to break their veil covering the Real, Tantric Buddhism proliferates semiotic systems by creating complex, polysemic texts (best typified by the mandala), with the goal to re-represent reality "as it is" in all its multifarious complexity. It should be emphasized that these two approaches are conceptual tendencies rather than separate and clearly defined semiotic discourses. Thus, in both Zen and Tantric Buddhism we find ambivalent attitudes toward representations of the sacred (images, icons, texts, relics). Some authors treat them as pointers to something else, something that cannot be expressed directly in other ways; others treat them as presences and embodiments of the sacred endowed with autonomous agency and salvific power.[21] In the most radical cases, the entire universe was envisioned as a meaningful text—a mystical (but also lucidly controlled) pansemioticism that still eludes a Western semiotic approach; as far as I know, the only attempt thus far to theorize pansemioticism is Pier Paolo Pasolini's semiotics and ontology of cinema.[22]

Before we begin investigating its semiotics, an outline of Esoteric Buddhism's fundamental doctrines is perhaps in order. These doctrines concern the status of the Buddha, the nature of the universe, the kind of rituals to be performed to attain salvation, and the content of enlightenment.

Esoteric Buddhism claims to be a separate transmission proceeding not from the historical Buddha, Śākyamuni, but from a different and more powerful Buddha, called Mahāvairocana (Ch. *Mohepilushena*, Jp. *Makabirushana*); in Japan, Mahāvairocana is best known as Dainichi (lit. "great sun"), often followed by the honorific attribute Nyorai (Sk.

Tathāgata, lit. "thus-come"). I will be using both names in the text. Now, Esoteric Buddhism explains the relation between Mahāvairocana and Śākyamuni through a reinterpretation of the classical Mahayana doctrine of the three modes of existence of the Buddha. Accordingly, Śākyamuni is understood as a provisional manifestation of the Buddha in this world in a form that was understandable to human beings (Sk. *nirmaṇakāya*, Jp. *ōkejin*, "conditioned manifestation body"); bodhisattvas have access to a loftier form of the buddha, called *saṃboghakaya* (Jp. *hōjin*) as a retribution of their spiritual achievements. Mahāvairocana is identified with the *dharmakāya* (Jp. *hosshin*, lit. "Dharma Body"), the ultimate source of the two previous bodies. Whereas in Mahayana doctrines the *dharmakāya* is an abstract and a-semiotic concept beyond thought and representation, Esoteric Buddhism considers it the ultimate source of all possible signs, thoughts, and representations as personified by the cosmic Buddha.

Furthermore, Esoteric Buddhism considers the Buddha Mahāvairocana coextensive and identical with the entire universe (Sk. *dharmadhātu*, Jp. *hokkai*, lit. "dharma realm"), so that everything that takes place in the universe, either on a macrocosmic or a microcosmic (individual) level, is something done by, and part of, him. This doctrine is the result of a systematic and coherent pantheism. In more concrete terms, however, a personalized form of Mahāvairocana (perhaps, his core), is said to reside in a precise geographical location, namely, the Dharma Realm Palace (Jp. *hokkaigū*) in Akaniṣṭha heaven. Akaniṣṭha heaven is the supreme Buddhafield; it is located far above Mount Sumeru, the cosmic mountain at the center of Buddhist cosmography, at the top of the Realm of Pure Forms (Sk. *rūpadhātu*, Jp. *shikikai*).[23]

It is important to emphasize, though, that Mahāvairocana is *not* a *spiritual* entity permeating the material universe, but envisioned instead as co-substantial with the universe itself. In fact, since the twelfth century, some Japanese scholar monks proposed the doctrine that the Dharmakāya (and thus also Mahāvairocana) is composed of the six elements of the universe (Jp. *rokudai*, i.e. earth, water, fire, wind, space, and consciousness or mind), just like human beings—or, for that matter, any other entity in the cosmos. Everything (including gods, spirits, goblins, but also rocks and trees) is a combination of material elements and mental/conscious potentiality (the six elements); these six elements, in turn, are the results of aggregations of atoms (Jp. *mijin*) moving at random. Thus, Esoteric Buddhist ontology is essentially materialist—it has no place for fuzzy spiritualist substances and forces.

The Esoteric world was also characterized by another feature, namely, systematic correlations among phenomena. Since all things were part of a single totality (the Dharmadhātu-Dharmakāya-Mahāvairocana), and this totality was composed of the same multiple substance (ultimately made of atoms), all things shared substance, qualities, and functions—each thing was a microcosm (a condensation of totality), and at the same time, it was interrelated with all other things. This brought Esoteric Buddhist authors to develop a systematic correlative thinking on the basis of Indian and Chinese precedents.

Next, Esoteric Buddhist authors argued that Mahāvairocana, as the fundamental and ultimate Buddha, continuously preaches the Dharma (Jp. *hosshin seppō*) and is engaged in activities aimed at universal salvation involving his entire body, i.e. the entire universe itself: everything that exists (including human beings, and on a smaller scale, the author of this book, its readers, and the book itself...), is not only part of the Dharmakāya, but also of its ongoing cosmic sermon. As a consequence, in this vast cosmic discourse, not only utterer and receiver, but also signifiers, signifieds, and referents, all coincide—they are all Mahāvairocana, the Dharmakāya and the Dharmadhātu. This is a full-fledged semiotic doctrine that was developed to fit a materialistic, pantheistic universe, and presents a clear interest for the semiotician.

Another important consequence of this world view is that, since all that exists is the Dharmadhātu (the "Dharma Realm," which is also the cosmic Buddha), there is no distinction between the realm of suffering and transmigration (Sk. *saṃsāra*, Jp. *rinne*) and the realm of liberation (nirvana); suffering and salvation must be one and the same (as in the Japanese formula *bonnō soku bodai*, "afflictions are the enlightenment"), and they must occur together in this world. This fact forced Esoteric Buddhist authors to develop and give a concrete shape to a form of nondualist knowledge. Nondualism (Sk. *advaita*, Jp. *funi*) is indeed one of the main features of East Asian Buddhism in general, and Esoteric Buddhism in particular. A nondual perspective is a way of looking at the world that presupposes neither a single unifying principle (monism) nor a struggle between opposite principles (dualism); in contrast, things are seen as the result of different and irreconcilable perspectives, one of difference and the other of identity. The ideal knowledge should be able to accommodate both perspectives when grasping phenomena; as this mode of knowledge overcomes "discrimination" (Sk. *vikalpa*, Jp. *funbetsu*), that is, the ordinary way of thinking based on oppositional categories, nondualism was considered equivalent with Buddhist enlightenment.

In this context, another point worth emphasizing is that enlightenment (Jp. *kakugo*, *bodai*, *tōshōgaku*, or *satori*) was not envisioned as a mystical and ineffable event, but the result of rituals and visualizations based on the ontology and epistemology (and semiotics) I just outlined; it was a way to see every entity as multiple and interconnected, yet singular in its specificity. It brought medieval Japanese Buddhist intellectuals to affirm each phenomenon as both a microcosm and a part of several series of connected elements.

After this general overview of the main tenets of Esoteric Buddhism, let us now take a look at the structure of this book.

Chapter One, "Adamantine signs: The episteme of Japanese Esoteric Buddhism," is a general introduction to the themes of this book. After outlining the general features of Japanese Esoteric Buddhism, it focuses on the main components of the Esoteric episteme, such as its fundamental epistemological model, the nature of signs, the orders of meaning, and the intellectual world of the medieval scholar monks, who were the main authors of this semiotic discourse.

Chapter Two, "Ontology of signs: The pansemiotic cosmos of mandala," deals with the fundamental structure of the Esoteric universe and its semiotic articulations, and identifies a form of correlative thinking as its main logic. The chapter also discusses various aspects of *mandala* as the fundamental model of the universe.

Chapter Three, "The Secrets of languages: Structure of the Esoteric signs," concerns the complex ways in which Esoteric Buddhism envisioned its own signs. After a short discussion of the most influential Buddhist theories about language, the chapter focuses on mantras and *shittan* graphs, as, respectively, phonetic and graphological signifiers of the Esoteric signs. Next, it describes their semantic universe, with special attention to orders of meaning and interpretive strategies aimed at remotivating the signs in order to turn them into microcosm endowed with soteriological power.

Chapter Four, "Inscribing the diamond path: A semiotic soteriology," interprets the soteriology of Esoteric Buddhism from the point of view of its semiotic doctrines and strategies. It begins with the role of vision/visualization as a way to transform perceptual reality according to established doctrinal models. Once the everyday world is envisioned as conforming to these models, it becomes possible for the practitioners to enact semiotic strategies (various forms of manipulations of signs and texts) to simulate a soteriological process; the chapter analyzes in depth the ritual and semiotic manipulations of mantras and the use of mandalas in this process. Next, I argue that many Esoteric Buddhist texts are produced and interpreted as simulations of specific practices—and, at times, of the entire salvation process; when textual practices are not possible, Esoteric signs are used for their pragmatic and performative aspects. Finally, the chapter discusses the ways in which semiotic practices affect (at least, in principle) the body-mind complex of the practitioners and contribute to shaping Buddhist subjectivities.

Finally, the last chapter, "The empire and the signs: Buddhism, semiotics, and cultural identity in Japanese history," shifts the focus from a synchronic reading of doctrinal and ritual texts, to a diachronic overview of some of the ways in which semiotic ideas, largely based (more or less directly, more or less consciously) on the Esoteric Buddhist episteme discussed thus far, concurred in shaping images and representations of Japanese cultural identity, both in Japan and abroad.

In this book we will see that Esoteric Buddhism tried to give a systematic shape to its pantheistic semiotics, rooted not in spiritualism but materialism, without transcendence, in which everything was connected with everything else and had therefore multiple identities. Esoteric Buddhism is particularly interesting for the semiotician, because it challenges old and widespread received assumptions: its pantheism is not confused and spiritualist, but systematic and materialist; far from being a vague and ineffable mysticism, it developed a highly articulated semiotic system; enlightenment is not the unpredictable outcome of experience-based asceticism, but the result of semiotic manipulations of representations. This unusual combination of pantheism, materialism, semiotics, and soteriology brought Esoteric Buddhist intellectuals to argue that each phenomenon has an absolute value in itself (principle of *sokuji nishin*, "each phenomenon is the truth"), *not* because of its "spiritual" essence but because of its very materiality (principle of *tōtai jishō*, "each specific material body is unconditioned"); this is a challenge for our received understanding of Buddhism, but also a fascinating potentiality for contemporary thought.

This book is built on the fine line between debunking and credulity. I am personally agnostic, and I have no interest in proving or disproving anything about Buddhist enlightenment or salvation. Rather, I take the texts seriously for what they say—not necessarily about belief, worship, or salvation, but primarily about their own semiotic concerns and strategies. Yet, whereas my own interests and methodology are based on contemporary semiotics, I attempt to let the original texts speak for themselves, as it were, refraining as much as possible from projecting onto them foreign, anachronistic categories. Of course, in order to make premodern ideas relevant to a contemporary semiotic approach, they have to be, at least to a certain extent, disentangled from their original contexts as sectarian doctrinal discussions and recontextualized as instances of an ongoing semiotic discourse. I am conscious of the fact that contemporary Shingon scholars and priests are unfamiliar with, and perhaps even suspicious of, such recontextualization attempts; however, my goal is not to alter sectarian debates, but to make their intellectual content available to a larger audience.

While writing this book, I have also tried to establish a common ground where scholars of Buddhism (and, of course, more in general, Japanese studies scholars) and semioticians (and perhaps also Buddhist practitioners) could meet and discuss shared intellectual issues. This proved to be a daunting task; the times when leading Western intellectuals were finding inspiration in translations and studies on Asian thought are long gone.[24] Buddhism (and Esoteric Buddhism in particular) has a subtle and complex terminology, and so does semiotics. Combining both would have made this book totally unreadable, but I could not have written it if I had avoided both completely. I have consistently tried to explain all terms and doctrines I introduce in the book—to the extent that this is possible without turning it into a Buddhist encyclopedia; however, there might remain the need to acquire a certain amount of background information and contextualization on both sides of the semiotic-Buddhological divide. While some readers (on each side of the divide) will certainly complain that the book is not specialized enough and others that it is overly infested by jargon, I do hope that enough readers will find it a useful bridge, at least to begin to think about certain issues, as an occasion for further joint inquiries into the fascinating realm of Buddhist semiotics.

Further steps in the study of Buddhist semiotics, particularly as it was developed in premodern Japan, would involve the investigation of specificities proper to various denominations (Pure Land, Zen, etc.); considerations on the existence or not of specific Shinto semiotics and interpretive strategies; the evaluation of the impact of Chinese philosophical systems; and analyses on the ways in which semiotic considerations affected the production and use of sacred objects, as well as representations of sacredness and cultural identity.

Given the growing interest for semiotic issues among scholars of Buddhism, time has come to carry out in a systematic fashion studies of the general semiotics of Buddhist cultures (that is, their general *episteme* or fundamental semiotic attitudes); this would in turn facilitate studies of more specific semiotic subjects within Buddhism such as allegoresis; metaphorical structure of texts, rituals, and artifacts; textuality; text analysis; general rhetorics; translation theories and practices; and the nonhermeneutical dimension and its significance. More on the side of cultural semiotics, research on awareness of linguistic and cultural specificities and cultural self-understanding in historically Buddhist cultures could also benefit from a systematic semiotic approach that addresses different epistemes in various cultures. Buddhism is particularly significant in this respect, because of its sophisticated semiotic apparatus, but also because it spans many different cultures and involves critical discussions with several important religious and philosophical systems. Of course, it would be necessary that semioticians and Buddhist study scholars collaborate closely together in order to develop such research trends. An obvious obstacle to these possible research endeavors is terminology: a project of Buddhist semiotics would employ specialized jargon from both Buddhism and semiotics, thus making it unapproachable but to a small number of initiates... A serious interpretive effort aiming at a wider cultural relevance would require a sort of "de-specialization" and "de-jargonization" of both Buddhist studies and semiotics; globally, both disciplines are too important to be left to semioticians and Buddhologists alone.

My hope is that this book will contribute, even just a little, and in its own idiosyncratic way, to a better understanding of the intellectual dimensions of Esoteric Buddhism on the one hand, and encourage further investigations on non-Western semiotic discourses on the other hand, within the framework of a closer, more proficuous collaboration among Western theoretical disciplines and area-based research.

CHAPTER ONE

Adamantine signs: The episteme of Japanese Esoteric Buddhism

Buddhism is often understood primarily as a monastic tradition concerned with ultimate salvation. However, Buddhism is a cultural system far more complex than a monastic organization, its doctrinal apparatus, and its soteriology. A useful way to understand Buddhism as a cultural system has been proposed by Melford Spiro when he posited three dimensions in Burmese Buddhism, that he calls, respectively, nibbanic, kammatic, and apotropaic. The nibbanic level refers to the quest for ultimate salvation; historically, this has been the concern of a rather small group of practitioners. Kammatic Buddhism refers to merit-making and is primarily concerned with improving the material existence in this world (including the next reincarnations), also as a means for spiritual betterment. Finally, apotropaic or magical elements deal with securing protection from evil forces and natural disasters—aspects that are commonly, but incorrectly, referred to today as "superstitions."[1]

Spiro's framework can, with a few minor modifications, be proficuously generalized to Buddhism as a whole. Thus, we have a sphere concerning ultimate salvation (be it extinction into nirvana, deliverance into a Pure Land, or becoming a buddha in the present body), a sphere related to material and spiritual existence in this world envisioned as processes of merit-making, and a sphere of magical operations. It is important to stress that these three spheres are mutually interrelated. Magical protection allows one to lead a more secure life, which can thus be dedicated more easily to merit-making. Merit-making, in turn, is more or less directly related to ultimate salvation, which is often envisioned as the final result of the accumulation of good karma. Envisioning Buddhism as the field of complex and varying interactions among these three spheres enables us to go beyond the limitations intrinsic to received emphasis on soteriology and to recognize that the impact of Buddhism has always been extensive and profound (and beyond the realm of religion narrowly conceived) on many aspects of the cultural traditions in which it spread. Among the cultural elements that have been influenced by Buddhism in Japan we find literature and the arts, scientific discourses (astronomy, conceptions of the body, etc.), political theory, and, especially, philosophical speculation about language and signs—the main subject of this book.

This chapter describes the discourse of Japanese Esoteric Buddhism (particularly the Shingon tradition) as it developed in conjunction with the emergence of a distinctive form of philosophical reflection on signs and the formation of a corpus of practices relating to the production of meaning. My basic hypothesis is that Esoteric Buddhism (Jp. *mikkyō*, "secret [Buddhist] teachings") can be understood as a discursive formation that presupposes a particular cosmology, a particular attitude towards reality, and a particular episteme, understood here as "the attitude that a sociocultural community adopts in relation to its own signs."[2] It can be seen, in other words, as an ensemble of knowledge and practices concerned with the interpretation of reality as well as the production, selection, conservation, and transmission of knowledge. These things, in turn, are implemented through interpretive strategies, repertoires of metaphors, and a general structuring of knowledge. Like every discourse, that of Esoteric Buddhism determines (and is determined by) distinctive institutions, ideologies, rituals, and power relations. The semiotic paradigm of Esoteric Buddhism was extremely influential in Japan for centuries and still operates today (albeit in a marginalized and nonorganic fashion) in certain aspects of culture such as popular religious beliefs and practices and in popular culture (in addition, of course, to the doctrines and liturgies of the Shingon school). An understanding of this paradigm is thus essential for the study not only of premodern Japanese religiosity and culture but also of Esoteric ceremonies, magic rituals, traditional forms of divination, and aspects of popular culture still present in contemporary Japan.[3] The reconstruction of the Esoteric Buddhist discourse and its underlying episteme should, ideally, begin with a consideration of the Tantric-Daoist syncretism that occurred mainly, but not exclusively, within the Chinese Zhenyan lineage during the Tang (seventh to tenth centuries) and Song dynasties (tenth to thirteenth centuries), and then trace its development and transformations in Japan. In this book I confine myself, however, to the Japanese Shingon tradition as it developed between the ninth and the sixteenth centuries, even though I believe that the basic epistemic assumptions, discursive practices, and rhetorical strategies discussed here reflect traits common to all the multifarious forms assumed by Esoteric Buddhism in Japan.

The Tantric revolution

In East Asia, Tantric Buddhism is commonly referred to as "Esoteric Buddhism" (Ch. *mijiao*, Jp. *mikkyō*). Here, "Esoteric" does not refer to a discursive formation analogous to Western esotericism and spiritualism, but to a form of Mahayana Buddhism that explicitly developed multiple interpretations of reality and of the Buddhist teachings, and attempted to connect them to multiple ritual systems. It should be noted, however, that over the past few years, scholars have begun to call "Tantric Buddhism" certain forms of East Asian Esoteric Buddhism, as a way to emphasize their continuities with Indic religious formations; at the same time, Ronald Davidson has referred, provocatively, to "Indian Esoteric Buddhism" in order to deflect stereotypes about Tantrism and focus instead on doctrinal, ritual, and social aspects of Tantric Buddhism.[4]

Tantrism is the general term for a religious and intellectual movement that developed in India between the fifth and the thirteenth centuries. It is not clear from within which religious tradition it originally arose, but in due time Tantric ideas and practices were present in the entire spectrum of Indian religiosity; thus, we find Tantric forms in Buddhism, Hinduism, and even in Jainism. Tantrism also spread over most of Asia, together with the diffusion of Indic religions and cultures, and played important roles, at various historical periods, not only in India and Nepal, but also in China, Mongolia, Tibet, Korea, Japan, and Southeast Asia. The term Tantrism refers to a group of texts, containing ritual instructions of a more or less secret, initiatory nature, known as *tāntra*. Buddhist Tantrism, in particular, was also known variously as Tāntrayāna (the Tantra Vehicle), Mantrayāna (the Mantra Vehicle), and Vajrayāna (the Diamond Vehicle)—in these cases, "vehicle" designates a system of doctrines and practices for salvation. These terms all refer to some of the distinctive features of Tantrism, namely, its emphasis on the use of mantras and similar ritual languages of potency; its focus on various and complex ritual activities as described in tantric texts; and the idea that it was the supreme form of attainment and salvation, a feature often described through the metaphor of the *vajra*, a term referring to the diamond (the most precious and indestructible substance), the lightning (symbol of divine power), and a supreme weapon (symbol of authority and, within this context, of spiritual attainment). The specificity of Tantric Buddhism is also indicated by the fact that it claims to be a separate transmission not from the historical Buddha, Śākyamuni, but a different Buddha, known as Mahāvairocana (Jp. *Dainichi*), who is considered the supreme and unconditioned modality of existence of the Buddha (Sk. *dharmakāya*, Jp. *hosshin*) and is envisioned as being coextensive with the entire universe (Sk. *dharmadhātu*, Jp. *hokkai*).

James Boon writes: "'Tantrism' is a nineteenth-century European coinage based on an 'exotic' term. The 'ism' part makes shifting fields of oppositions, differentiations, and plural relations sound substantive, doctrinaire, and uniform."[5] Tantrism, from its very beginnings on the Indian subcontinent, has constituted a complex heterology, an attempt, often successful, to confer centrality to a heterogeneous ensemble of elements that were culturally marginal and were as such excluded from institutionalized discourses. In fact, as Boon suggests, "Tantrism" is merely "a name for a polymorphous reservoir of ritual possibilities, continuously flirted with by orthodoxies yet also the basis of countering them"; it defines a field of possibilities against which "more orthodox positions and transformations become shaped and motivated."[6] Interestingly, Boon sees "a Western parallel" of Tantrism in "that range of hermetic heterodoxies, a murmur of Gnostic, Neoplatonist, crypto-liturgical positions: from freemasons to Bohemians, from counter-culture to *poètes maudits*."[7]

Tantrism was in origin a heterology of what Michel de Certeau calls an "untiring murmur" at the background of Buddhist cultures involving a "consumption" and displacement of "high" culture products and discourses by marginalized individuals and social groups.[8] Tantrism can be characterized as a complex magico-ritual apparatus that systematically reverses the renouncement ideals proper to religious institutions, especially Buddhism,[9] although it does not necessarily conceive of itself as an opposition ideology. In this sense, at least, Tantrism was parasitical upon existing normative forms of Buddhism, which it reversed and/or subverted. However, one of the most striking components of Tantrism (its emphasis on visualization and control over invisible forces as a way to speed up the attainment of supernatural powers, known as *siddhi*, and salvation), has been emphasized by Michel Strickmann: "The practitioner propitiates a deity, with whom he then proceeds to identify himself or otherwise unite;" eventually, "in the course of performing Tantric rituals, the officiant actually became the Buddha."[10] What Michel Strickmann called the "Tantric revolution" refers to the fact that many people in many parts of Asia began to claim that they could visualize all kinds of demonic, supernatural powers; that such a controlled visualization was also a way to subjugate and control these forces; and that a control could have a soteriological import.[11] It is obvious that the Tantric revolution also had a semiotic significance, because it provoked deep discussions on the nature of the images visualized, their relation with the deities or buddhas they reproduced, and the status of the power attained in this way.

Esoteric Buddhism in Japan: the Shingon tradition and the exo-esoteric system

Tantric Buddhism interacted in Japan with other Buddhist movements, religious traditions, and philosophical systems to create a new organism, called by historian Kuroda Toshio the "exoteric-esoteric establishment" (*kenmitsu taisei*), with its own ideology (*kenmitsushugi*, exo-esotericism).[12] In this terminology, "esoteric" (*mitsu*) refers to Esoteric Buddhism in all its forms (thus not limited to the Shingon tradition), whereas "exoteric" (*ken*) is the general name for the other Buddhist denominations existing in Japan at the time. Kuroda's concepts, formulated to describe the complex Buddhist institutional system in medieval Japan, have opened the way for a new understanding of Japanese Buddhism as a general cultural system related in multiple ways to other religious and cultural systems. Kuroda's views have undergone various adjustments, but on the whole they are useful tools for portraying what is an ideological, political, and economic organism. Kuroda stresses the fact that what underlies the entire exo-esoteric system is not a particular sect, but Esoteric Buddhism as a whole as a common substratum of ideas and practices concerned with the ultimate meaning of reality and the supreme goals of Buddhist cultivation.[13] This system was not just a religious logic and ideology, but was so closely connected to Japanese political authority that it acquired the status of an official ideology and gradually esotericized the state apparatuses.[14] It constituted the hegemonic system of thought and practice in medieval Japan and was the reigning orthodoxy and orthopraxy.[15] Shinto (Japanese local cults) was fitted into this framework as a local and concrete manifestation of Esoteric Buddhism.[16]

Some scholars have resisted Kuroda's sweeping interpretation of the religious world of medieval Japan, variously opposing to it sectarian-based histories, localized counter-examples, and different cultural factors.[17] It is possible to bypass some of these criticisms, however, by envisioning the exo-esoteric system not as the entire institutional and ideological apparatus of Japanese medieval Buddhism, but as something akin to a generative scheme of multiple cultural interventions, an open framework that the various Buddhist schools and traditions could actualize on their own terms. In fact, all Buddhist schools offered the same range of "products" and "services," such as simple formulae for salvation and rebirth in some Buddha's paradise, easy practices, relations with local "Shinto" cults, Esoteric doctrines and practices, political ideologies, and rituals for the protection of the state and the ruling lineages (*chingo kokka*); these were then personalized through peculiar doctrines and practices. In this respect, the schools formed a type of trust controlling the religious market, and Esoteric Buddhism was their common religious, epistemic, and ideological substratum. However, whereas Kuroda and other scholars are concerned primarily with the social, institutional, and ideological aspects of the medieval exo-esoteric system,[18] this book will focus especially on its epistemic aspects. In particular, I see the Esoteric Buddhist discourse as an important component of what I call the "exo-esoteric episteme," by which I mean the basic epistemic features of Kuroda's "exo-esoteric" establishment and ideology.[19] In this way, by shifting the interpretation of the term "exo-esoteric" to the episteme of Esoteric Buddhism, it is possible to extend its application beyond the middle age to subsequent periods of Japanese religious history.

The need to articulate distinctions between Esoteric Buddhism and other "exoteric" forms was introduced by the monk Kūkai (774–835), the founder of the Shingon sect, in the early ninth century as a means to define the relations between the Shingon Esoteric system and preexisting teachings, which he considered superficial and provisional. Kūkai reversed traditional hermeneutical criteria,[20] turning what was "evident" (*ken*, teachings that are clear and self-evident without problems of interpretation) into something "superficial," and what was "hidden" or "not immediately evident" (*mitsu*, teachings related to a certain intention of the Buddha and therefore apparently unclear and requiring interpretation) into something "profound and true." Kūkai's understanding of the term *kenmitsu* came to be widely accepted, and after the late Heian period (twelfth century) it was commonly used to designate the entire Buddhist system. Kūkai opened the way for a definition of the Esoteric Buddhist discursive field as comprising what the other doctrines do not teach, what the other schools ignore and leave unsaid. Thus, the silence of the Buddha marked the boundaries of Shingon intervention.

Esoteric Buddhism played another important role, functioning as a relay in the circuit between cultural center and marginality; this made the exo-esoteric system an important instrument of power. Through the symbolic and ritual control and integration of negative forces that threatened the cultural center from the "outside,"[21] and by providing central institutions with an efficacious cosmology and a distinctive epistemic field, Esoteric Buddhism became the dominant paradigm of Japanese medieval culture and played an important role in subsequent periods as well. Moreover, monks belonging to Esoteric lineages were closely related to the imperial court and the ruling families, so that the Tendai and Shingon schools exerted a veritable cultural hegemony. Esoteric Buddhism succeeded in reformulating on its own terms and from its own perspective the main concepts and practices of Japanese culture. In the systematic esotericization of Japan and its culture that was carried out during the middle ages, geographic space was conceived of as a mandala, the Japanese language was identified with the absolute language of mantras (Jp. *shingon darani*), and literary production was assimilated to sacred texts dealing with Esoteric truths.

Japanese Buddhism already contained numerous Esoteric (Tantric) elements before Kūkai's intervention, mainly relating to ritual. It is nevertheless possible to trace a distinction between early Tantrism and post-Kūkai Esoteric Buddhism. In the latter one finds an attempt to develop a systematic discourse, different from, and sometimes antithetical to, "normal" Buddhist discourse. Although a very few differences can be detected with regard to cosmology and soteriology, post-Kūkai Esoteric Buddhism does present a more systematic aspect and devotes a large amount of attention to semiotic and discursive problems—usually connected, again, with its need to establish its own orthodoxy. Esoteric elements in pre-Heian Japan constituted a literary and ritual genre, whose products are assembled in a loose corpus of Indian mantric formulae called the *darani-zō* (*dhāraṇī* repository), one of the five sections of the Buddhist Canon;[22] these esoteric formulae, variously called in Japan *darani* ("*dhāraṇī*"), *ju* ("spells"), and *mitsugo* ("mysterious words") formed a heterogeneous field not organically integrated within the preexisting Buddhist traditions.[23] (Mantras will be discussed more in depth in Chapter Three.)

According to the account of the development of dharanic thought in China and Japan provided by Ujike Kakushō,[24] spells originally designed to facilitate the understanding and use of Mahayana doctrines turned into instruments of sacred power, which would enable their practitioners to become buddhas in their present bodies (Jp. *sokushin jōbutsu*)—the soteriological ideal of Tantric Buddhism. Ujike points out that, after the age of the great Indian masters of Esoteric Buddhism in the early Tang Dynasty (seventh to eighth centuries),[25] increasing attention to linguistic problems together with a new vision of salvation caused the transformation of the *dhāraṇī* repository into the Shingon tradition.[26] Just as mysticism separated from theology in Europe in a process studied by Michel de Certeau,[27] so the ideas and practices of the Dhāraṇī repository detached themselves from the Mahayana corpus to form an independent discourse.

Tantrism was also concerned with the operations performed on the terms it invested with meaning. It thus possessed pragmatic and metalinguistic significance: it specified both how to use and how to interpret its expressions. It specified, in other words, ways to *practice* language. These linguistic and semiotic practices concerning mantras, when they became complex and explicit enough, established a field of their own: Esoteric Buddhism proper.

Semiotic innovations in the Shingon tradition

Kūkai (774–835) is considered to be the founder of the Shingon sect of Japanese Buddhism. One of the most fascinating figures of Japanese history, he was a subtle philosopher, an endowed artist, an ascetic, and a shrewd politician who was able to gain the imperial support for his new sect. His numerous accomplishments have become the source of countless legends about his life, and for many centuries Kūkai, commonly known with his posthumous honorific name of Kōbō Daishi ("the great master who has spread widely the Buddhist teachings"), has been the most venerated saint in Japanese Buddhism. A large part of his philosophical and religious production is animated by semiotic concerns, and focuses especially on the nature and functioning of the absolute language of mantras. Kūkai was actually the first Japanese thinker to explicitly outline the fundamentals of Esoteric Buddhist semiotics. He authored several texts dealing with semiotic issues, such as the status of language and its relations with reality, the structure of the Esoteric semantic system, and the role of ritual practices consisting in the manipulation of Esoteric objects and symbols to attain liberation. The soteriological goal of the Shingon school, defined by Kūkai as "becoming buddha in this very body" (*sokushin jōbutsu*), is a transformation of the body/speech/mind of the practitioners in a way that enables them to acquire a Buddha-body in the present lifetime; this goal was achieved mainly by semiotic manipulation of images and objects. By "semiotic manipulation" I mean the processes that took place in text production, exegesis, and rituals, in which concepts, images, and objects were subjected to various kinds of manipulations—among which semantic analyses and visual transformations played an important role—that turned them into direct instruments of salvation.

Kūkai found an interesting and productive way to overcome the limits of classic Mahayana philosophy of language, according to which linguistic expressions are related arbitrarily to their meaning and cannot signify the content of enlightenment. As Etienne Lamotte puts it, "The letter indicates the spirit just as a fingertip indicates an object, but since the spirit is alien to syllables... the letter is unable to express it in full."[28] (In this passage, "spirit" refers to meaning.) Systematized for the first time by Kūkai in the early ninth century, Shingon semiotics maintains instead that languages and signs are fallacious and sources of ignorance and suffering only to those who do not understand their origin and their real meaning. Kūkai wrote that only if language and reality are closely and deeply related to each other is the Buddha able to show the way to salvation through his teachings.[29] Kūkai further developed this idea in a doctrine known as *hosshin seppō* (the preaching by the Dharmakāya). According to it, the Buddha is neither silent nor uses language as a mere provisional tool, but instead manifests his teachings as the cosmic Buddha Mahāvairocana (Jp. Dainichi) in his absolute modality of existence known as Dharma-body (Sk. *dharmakāya*, Jp. *hosshin*). In other words, the entire universe, as the supreme body of the Buddha, preaches the Dharma and leads beings to salvation. While classical Mahayana schools describe the Dharma-body as devoid of signs and forms, Esoteric Buddhism conceives of it as the totality of all possible signs. The Dharma-body is thus able to "speak" and explain its own enlightenment to all beings; an absolute language exists that in some way is able to convey the ultimate reality, and a particular semiotics governs such absolute language. According to Shingon philosophy, thus, the cosmic Buddha as *dharmakāya* is engaged in an endless and universal semiotic activity; each single thing in the universe is part of this ongoing self-referential and cosmic speech act called "preaching by the *dharmakāya*" (*hosshin seppō*). (I will discuss this pansemiotic vision in the next chapter.) This doctrine is based on the identity of language and reality. Nevertheless, in order to acquire a direct salvational value, that is, in order to actually contribute to the attainment of the goals of Esoteric Buddhism (becoming Buddha in this very body—*sokushin jōbutsu*—and obtaining worldly benefits—*genze riyaku*), it is not enough to simply postulate the deep identity of language and reality: such identity must be self-evident from the structure of language itself, as a way for Tantric practices to result really as efficacious and instantaneous as they claimed to be. For this reason, Tantric Buddhism devoted major efforts to the rearticulation and remotivation of its signs.

Shingon semiotics, initially outlined by Kūkai on the basis of Indian and Chinese doctrines, was further developed by numerous scholar monks, both inside and outside the Shingon sect, throughout premodern Japanese history; we will meet several of them in this book. Eventually, mantric expressions were spun into a complex network of correlations. Sanskrit letters were correlated to natural elements, parts of the human body, stars, orients, seasons, and so on. Meditation on these microcosmic letters produced a "symbolic" assimilation of the whole cosmos within the ascetic, making each linguistic unit a minimal mandala.

Exo-Esoteric doctrine

Let us now look at the basic doctrinal framework of the exo-esoteric (*kenmitsu*) intellectual system, based on a number of representative texts on the subject.[30] This brief and synchronic account of the core of the Esoteric Buddhist teachings, despite its neglecting of subtle doctrinal distinctions, sectarian debates on controversial themes, and important historical developments, will describe the general landscape of the Shingon epistemic field. As explained above, Esoteric Buddhism divides the Buddhist teachings into two general kinds: superficial and secret. Superficial teachings are the provisional doctrines taught by the Buddha Śākyamuni, or, more generally, by conditioned manifestations of the Buddha, i.e. the *nirmaṇakāya* and the *samboghakāya*;[31] the meaning of these teachings is supposed to be clear and easy to comprehend. In contrast, secret teachings are "the most profound doctrines beyond the faculties of sentient beings, dealing with the ultimate secrets of all buddhas' enlightenment."[32] As an unconditioned discourse spoken by the Dharma-body to itself (*hosshin seppō*) for the pure pleasure of listening to the Dharma, these teachings are permanent and immutable and transcend the doctrine of the decline of the Law (*mappō*).[33] They are composed of "truth words" (*shinjitsugo*) free from all communicational, pragmatic, and contextual constraints.[34] In this way, these teachings are not limited by their listeners' expectations and circumstances.

Ken and *mitsu* also show different attitudes towards principle (*ri*) and phenomena (*ji*).[35] This is particularly important for the present discussion, because these two ontological categories possess a deep semiotic relevance. According to standard (exoteric) Mahayana, *ri* can be seen as the ideal *type* of a sign, while *ji* defines its *tokens*, a type's actual and manifold occurrences.

This distinction between *ri* and *ji* establishes two separate levels of reality, namely, Dharma-essence (*hosshō*) and its multifarious dharmic aspects; *ken* thus fails to attain true nondual knowledge (the non-discriminatory form of awareness that characterizes enlightenment). Esoteric Buddhism, in contrast, states that both *ri* and *ji* are absolute and unconditioned; every single dharma entity, with all its particularities, displays true reality (*jissō*). According to the Esoteric tradition, the modalities of existence of the Dharma-body (*shishu hosshin*), its activities (*sanmitsu*), and its wisdom (*gochi*) are not different from the elements of ordinary human cognition (sense organs, objects, mind apparatus).[36] As a consequence, the Esoteric absolute principle (*ri*) is in a nondual relation to phenomena (*ji*). Being articulated in substance (*taidai*), signs (*sōdai*), and dynamic manifestations (*yūdai*), it does not transcend human intellective faculties, and the world of enlightenment—the ultimate result of religious practice (*kabun*)—can be described and explained in the absolute language of the Dharma-body.[37]

In Esoteric Buddhism individual phenomena do not differ from the supreme principle; an individual entity is no longer a mere token (*ji*) of a type (*ri*), but is itself an absolute, a microcosm. There is ultimately no distinction between the mind of each ascetic and that of the Buddha. Salvation is thus close by and easy to attain: who performs Esoteric Buddhist rituals will "become a buddha instantaneously" in their present "body generated by father and mother." The Esoteric cosmos is an immense salvific machine in which everything is absolute.

The nature of Buddhist signs

Issues of representation, involving vision and images, are deeply ingrained in the Buddhist teachings since a very early stage. Indeed, one of the fundamental presuppositions of Buddhism, quite common in ancient Indian thought, is that the world is not what it looks like, but is covered by the veil of illusion (*māyā*), which needs to be removed if we want to face the world as it is. This fact generates the need for better, more accurate understanding of the self and of reality—not as a mere epistemological quest, but as directly related to soteriology. Vision (in the sense of correct understanding of the world) is particularly relevant to Buddhism; this involves the development of images to figure the aspect of the true reality behind the veil of illusion. Thus, for Buddhism, a theory and a practice of representation are directly relevant to salvation.

The earliest representations of the Buddha are striking because of the absence of their subject; the Buddha himself is never shown, his place taken by certain objects such as his feet, an empty parasol, an empty throne, the *bodhi* tree (under which he attained enlightenment), or the Wheel of Dharma or *dharmacakra* (which represent his teachings). Scholars have argued that this form of representation indicates an aniconic stance that is peculiarly Buddhist.[38] In this context, aniconism is defined as an "aversion to depicting spiritual entities of the very highest order" due to the fact that, in Buddhism, "the most crucial spiritual insights lie beyond the power of human imagination to describe or depict"; thus, "the visual arts can allude to them only obliquely, through omission or the use of non-iconic figures."[39]

From a semiotic perspective, this aniconism simply refers to the fact that early Buddhists chose to avoid anthropomorphic representations of the Buddha on the one hand and visual renderings of certain concepts such as emptiness (Sk. *śūnyatā*, Jp. *kūshō* or *kū*) and nirvana on the other—concepts that were nonetheless represented copiously in texts. However, it is important to emphasize that, even at this early stage, Buddhism did not deny the possibility of representation. In fact, early Buddhist images do give shape to something that the scriptures define as beyond representation, namely, the radical difference of Buddha's ontological status: these images represent both the Buddha's absence (Buddha extinguished himself into nirvana) and his provisional presence (his traces) in this world. Thus, these images represent fairly well both Buddha's extinction and his existence in this world. Absence of representation is therefore not an absence of signification; far from it, the meaning of the early Buddhist teachings could be conveyed adequately only by "emptying" and "absenting" the Buddha. In this case, absence and invisibility do not point to mystical ineffability, but to its opposite: visual representations are perfectly adequate to their textual counterpart. It should be noted that for the early Buddhists, nirvana itself constituted the proof of the truth and validity of the teachings of the Buddha; it is from within this context that these images were produced and worshiped. It is only in a second phase, roughly connected with the emergence of Mahayana, that Buddha's enduring presence—and his continuing salvific activity—in this world, rather than his extinction into nirvana, acquire preeminence; this doctrinal shift generated a change in iconography that resulted in the production of anthropomorphic representations of the Buddha. (This shift occurred towards the first century BCE, and with increasing frequency after the first, and especially the second centuries CE.)

Early representations of the Buddha are based on the principle of metonymy, as they are either metonymies proper (the parasol, the empty throne, the *bodhi* tree, but also the Wheel of Dharma as an attribute of the Buddha) or synecdoches (the Buddha's feet, his relics); metaphorical renderings seem to have been avoided by the first Buddhist artists.[40] The invisibility of the Buddha after his nirvana was conceptualized in different terms by different forms of Buddhism, which resulted in different modalities of representation: one emphasizing absence and invisibility, the other emphasizing presence and visibility. However, both modalities share the same kind of signs (ostensive signs) and employ the same metonymic logic.

The existence of a fundamental relation of metonymy in the Buddhist representations of the sacred seems to find a confirmation in a doctrine on the objects of worship from an early scripture, the *Mahā-parinibbāna-sūtta*.[41] According to this doctrine, there are three categories of objects worthy of worship, namely, bodily relics (Sk. *śarīraka*) of the Buddha or a saint, such as bones, hair, teeth, but also footprints and handprints; objects used by saints (*paribhogika*), such as the Buddha's alms bowl, clothes, seat, and the *bodhi* tree; and memorial objects (*uddeśika*, literally "objects that suggest, illustrate or explain"), such as representations of the Three Jewels (*triratna* or *triśūla*),[42] the Dharma Wheel (symbol of the Buddha preaching), and the *stūpa*. Now, each sacred object can be classified according to any of these three categories. For instance, a *stūpa* is *śarīraka* when it contains a saint's bodily relics, *paribhogika* when it contains objects that formerly belonged to a saint, or *uddeśika* when it is a monument marking a sacred space or commemorating a particular event in a saint's hagiography. From the perspective of Umberto Eco's modes of sign production,[43] bodily relics are samples (homomateric signs), footprints are imprints (motivated heteromateric signs), used objects are symptoms (motivated heteromateric signs), and memorial relics are clues (motivated heteromateric signs); these are all instances of motivated signs.

In other words, we are dealing here with a semiotics of motivation with signs that are either heteromateric or homomateric, oscillating between recognition and ostension—perhaps, with an historic-intellectual preference toward the latter. Umberto Eco has defined ostension as a semiotic phenomenon occurring "when a given object or event produced by nature or human action (…) is 'picked up' by someone and *shown* as the expression of the class of which it is a member." Thus, we can interpret a Buddhist sacred image as a *double* of its original model, as when "a cigarette is shown in order to describe the properties of a cigarette"; as an *example*, when an object is chosen to represent its class of objects; or as a *sample* when "only part of an object is selected to express the entire object (and therefore its class)."[44] Sacred icons are *doubles*, i.e. authentic copies, of the Buddha (in accordance with widespread tales on the origin of the first image of the Buddha) and, further, *examples* and *samples* of absolute reality to be grasped after the attainment of enlightenment.

Whereas early representations of the Buddha are based on the principle of metonymy, as we have seen, anthropomorphic Buddhist images can be defined, in semiotic terms, as doubles, copies, samples, or examples. This nature of Mahayana images is well rendered by the Japanese term *funjin* (lit. "splintered bodies," that is, alternative bodies or alloforms; Sk. *vigraha*). What matters here is that both modalities of representation employ ostensive signs: on the one hand, the physical absence of the Buddha in the image is an example (or a sample) of nirvana; on the other hand, the hieratic presence of the Buddha as a sacred image is a double of the realized Buddha. All these signs are not arbitrary, but motivated and closely connected to their referents: in the case of relics (fragments of the very body of the Buddha), they are indeed parts of the referent.

Adamantine signs

After this introduction to the theoretical framework of the discourse of Esoteric Buddhism in its relations to other Buddhist schools, and an outline of Buddhist signs as they are employed in the representation of the sacred, it is now time to turn our attention to the internal structure of the exo-esoteric episteme. A full description of its actual articulation should take into account the diachronic transformation of Buddhist semiotics, the complex epistemic relations within Buddhism as both a "high" culture and a "popular" phenomenon, and the presence of other influential models of semiotics and semiosis (Confucian, Daoist, and later, "Western") that coexisted and interacted in various ways with and within the *kenmitsu* epistemic field. In this book, I present a synchronic approach based on premodern texts on the subject.

On a superficial, immediate level, the most evident feature of Esoteric Buddhist texts is their phonetic and graphic exoticism, in which the foreign is considered to be more authentic. This is reflected in the large number of Sanskrit terms and in the use of Indic characters called *siddhaṃ* (Jp. *shittan*). It could be said that the core of Esoteric texts is formed by mantras (Jp. *shingon*) and *siddhaṃ* (*shittan*), and that everything else exists only to create a context so that they might be correctly practiced.[45] This reflects an idea of language and signs typical of Tantrism.

Tantrism transformed language from its status as expedient means (Sk. *upāya*, Jp. *hōben*), employed in order to convey meaning or induce certain actions, to an absolute and unconditioned entity, something that could not be translated without losing its essential character. Kūkai believed that the Indian phonemes and script were endowed with a unique nature. He wrote: "Mantras, however, are mysterious, and each word is profound in meaning. When they are transliterated into Chinese, the original meanings are modified and the long and short vowels confused."[46] Correct interpretation and use depend upon correct transmission. Kūkai mentions that the great Tantric master Amoghavajra (Ch. Bukong, Jp. Fukū; 705—74), aware of the limits of translations, taught his disciples by using only Indian words.[47] He thereby gave epistemic relevance to the Esoteric concept of an unaltered transmission based upon an original ostension (see Chapter Two).

In more general terms, Esoteric Buddhist soteriology presupposes a pansemiotic universe in which everything is organized in a systematic way and endowed with meaning. This general view is based on three postulates: (i) the entire cosmos (Sk. *dharmadhātu*, Jp. *hokkai*) is the Buddha in his unconditioned modality (Sk. *dharmakāya*, Jp. *hosshin*); (ii) the Dharmakāya is constituted of the six cosmic elements (Jp. *rokudai hosshin*, i.e. earth, water, fire, wind, air, space, and consciousness/mind); and (iii) the Dharmakāya preaches incessantly the Dharma to itself and to all, in all possible signs and languages, in a pleasurable and salvific monologue (*hosshin seppō*).

Within a pansemiotic universe every thing is a multiple entity, with different aspects, and interrelated with other things. As in the case of sacred objects discussed previously, in Esoteric Buddhism too, each entity can be a *double*, an *example*, and a *sample* of any other entity, within a semiotic system based on ostension. Thus, each component of the mandalic cosmos is both related to any number of other entities and equivalent to the totality itself. Relations between entities are based on either their inner structure (as in correlations based on the five cosmic elements) or phenomenal configurations (associations of different phenomena on the basis of other criteria). Either way, these relations are based upon selected aspects/components of the signifiers and the signifieds of the entities involved. Esoteric Buddhism carried out a radical reformulation of signs through processes of "remotivation" aimed at overcoming the arbitrariness of language and signs by finding a special "natural" relation between expressions, meanings, and referential objects. Remotivation involves the reorganization of a sign's semantic field to make meaning (the signified) "similar" to its expression (signifier). Signs thus become reproductions of their objects and inscriptions of soteriologic processes; language dissolves into a network of polymateric signs, veritable minimal mandalas able to represent/manifest the absolute, as explained by doctrines about mantras (polymateric signs in themselves) as Mahāvairocana's absolute language of supreme enlightenment.

The logic of these relations derives from both Indian Tantric and Chinese systems of correlative thought; in both systems, elements were organized in closed series regulated by a rigorous combinatory logic. Correlative thinking makes the entities "consubstantial" and "interchangeable" with each other; they become "each other's signs"—as we have seen, doubles, samples, or examples of each other and the totality. In this way, the Sanskrit letter *A* does not just "signify" or "represent" wood, spring, or the liver (as in a common set of associations); these three items are, to borrow Bruce Lincoln's definition, *alloforms*, that is, "alternative shapes of one another."[48] Open-ended clusters of *alloforms* (composed of objects, actions, states, and qualities—as distinct occurrences of the different modes of the cosmic substance), constitute peculiar Esoteric semiotic entities that can be defined as *microcosmic macrosigns*. A macrosign is not just a representation, but a "sample" or double of the absolute reality, of which it presents all fundamental features and functions. Correlative series condense in a macrosign elements organized according to theleological processes (as in the stages in the path towards salvation),[49] hierarchical modes (the levels of beings, and the five buddhas with Mahāvairocana at the center/top), or by circular arrangements (as in the five agents of Chinese cosmology and in the cycle of seasons). Thus, the correlative deep structure of the universe is reflected in its superficial appearances; as each object embodies the totality, also Indian, Chinese, and Japanese entities are all alloforms of each other. Relations were developed along two vectors: one centrifugal, emphasizing one entity's lateral connections with other entities in a type of unlimited semiosis; and one centripetal, emphasizing the absolute nature of each single phenomenon as a condensation of the totality. These two directions were unified in the interpretation of the semantic structure of each entity.

Semiosophia, semiognosis, semiopietas: Esoteric Buddhist orders of meaning

Indeed, it is possible to recognize within Esoteric Buddhism three different modes of semiotic knowledge and interpretive practice of reality, which I will call, respectively, semiosophia, semiognosis, and semiopietas.[50] *Semiosophia* refers to the exoteric forms of knowledge of signs (*sō*), according to which language and signs are considered to be arbitrary and illusory, but nevertheless usable as expedient means (*upāya*) in order to indicate the truth. I use here the term semiosophia instead of *semiotics* in order to distinguish it from both semiotics as common sense and semiotics as a metalanguage.[51] Various exoteric types of semiotics can be classed as semiosophia, including those based on doctrines such as Abidharmakośa (Jp. Kusha), Yogācāra (Jp. Hossō), Mādhyamika (Jp. Sanron), Tendai, and Kegon. Although there seem to be three fundamental epistemological models (Abhidharma, Mādhyamika, and Yogācāra), each school developed its own concept of the sign in relation to its view of ultimate reality and its hermeneutic strategies. A comprehensive study on these matters is still waiting to be undertaken. In the exo-esoteric paradigm, *mitsu* semiotics presupposes *ken* semiotics;[52] semiosophia thus constitutes the superficial level (what is called by exegetes *senryakushaku*, lit. "abbreviated interpretation") on which the Esoteric interpretive structure (*jinpishaku*, lit. "profound interpretation") is built. Next, *semiognosis* denotes Esoteric semiotic doctrines and practices as

> something akin to a type of soteriological knowledge (i.e. leading to salvation) that is gained through specific ... practices of a predominantly ritual or mystical character ... [B]oth [semio]sophia and [semio]gnosis are connected with systems of symbolic representation, but their epistemological frameworks and intentionality differ.[53]

Semiognosis refers to specific knowledge and practices that are

> claimed to have been extracted from [signs themselves], to correspond in mysterious ways to sacred scriptures and to divine rule, and to lead either to mystical achievement or to religious salvation.[54]

The initiatory knowledge concerning structure, function, and power of the Esoteric symbols (especially mantric expressions and their graphic forms, the *siddhaṃ* script) is considered the kernel of enlightenment and the key to becoming a buddha in the present body (*sokushin jōbutsu*). Kūkai equates the signs (*monji*) of the "preaching by the Dharma-body" (*hosshin seppō*) with the three secrets (*sanmitsu*, the three factors at the source of salvation, i.e. the body, speech, and mind) pervading the Dharma-realm; thus language and signs (*sōdai*) cannot exist separately from the cosmic substratum (*taidai*) of original enlightenment. Kūkai then adds: "Therefore, the Buddha Mahāvairocana, by expounding the meaning of [the relations between] language and reality, arouses sentient beings from their long slumber." Esoteric Buddhist semiotics thus has a direct soteriological relevance: "Those who realize this are called the Great Enlightened Ones, those who are confused about this are called 'ordinary beings.'"[55]

As a consequence, one of the fundamental activities of Esoteric Buddhist exegetes is a work on language and signs aimed at "re-motivating" them—that is, overcoming the arbitrariness of language and signs by finding a special "natural" relation between expression, meaning, and referential object. Remotivation is accomplished by reorganizing each expression's semantic structure and thereby making the expression "identical" to its meaning. In this process an Esoteric symbol becomes a kind of replica of its object, and the practice in which it occurs is deemed to be identical to its goal. The salvific practices in Esoteric Buddhism consist mainly in visualization and manipulation of mantric expressions (*shingon darani* and *shittan*) and other complex symbols of various kinds, whose very structure, organized on three deeper levels (*jinpi* "profound," *hichū no jinpi* "secret within the profound," and *hihichū no jinpi* "most secret within the profound"), appears to the initiated person as the inscription of the path to salvation and to the attainment of supernatural powers (*siddhi*).[56] I would like to emphasize here that by signs I do not mean only linguistic expressions, but any form of representation (icons, ritual implements, etc.).

The relation between semiosophia and semiognosis is represented by the two-level semantic structure of Esoteric signs. The superficial level is called *jisō*, and the deep, Esoteric level is called *jigi*. *Jisō* refers to a signification based on appearances, the shape of a sign: the primary meaning at this level is usually a term that begins with the same sound as its expression. For example, the *jisō* of the Sanskrit expression *va* is *vāc*, that is, "word, language." In this way, the syllable *va* is treated as the condensation of another sign it stands for, namely, *vāc*, whose meaning is illustrated according to mainstream exoteric teachings.

The Esoteric Buddhist episteme, in its more conscious and systematic manifestations, was essentially a "high" culture phenomenon. Nevertheless, it is important to trace the dissemination of Esoteric doctrines and practices among the general populace, and to analyze their transformations and the counter-practices they produced. This dissemination was extremely important for the establishment, which saw the "Esotericization" of the lives, activities, and environment of ordinary people as a powerful device for controlling them. In general, "popular" texts dealing with Buddhism (performances, sermons, vernacular literature, and narratives) were not directly concerned with Esoteric doctrines—one must recall that, because of its peculiar belief that it expressed the absolute point of view of the perfectly enlightened Buddha, it was not easy for Esoteric Buddhism to translate its own doctrines into everyday language and practices. There is a literary genre, however, known as *engimono* (origin narratives), in which Esoteric Buddhism succeeded in transposing its absolute logic of the unconditioned (*jinen hōni*) into a narrative of karmic events that occurred at specific historical moments in particular places.[57] The same can also be said for medieval commentaries on classical *waka* poetry, which attempted to anchor the Japanese language and its poetic forms in the absolute language of mantras and *dhāraṇī*. These materials were vehicles for the diffusion of Esoteric ideas outside of temple specialists.

The diffuse beliefs and non-specialized practices of the uninitiated concerning such Esoteric entities as sacred images, texts, amulets, and talismans, constitute *semiopietas*, "a primarily religious mood of relation to sacred [semiotic forms]."[58] Semiopietas is the Esoteric Buddhist "easy path" (*idō*) to salvation, represented mainly by Esoteric worship of the Buddha Amida (*himitsu nenbutsu*) and practices related to the Mantra of Light (*kōmyō shingon*).[59] For most of these practices no formal initiation was required; all that was needed was a transmission with simple explanations, called *kechien kanjō* ("initiation establishing a karmic tie [with a deity or a mantra]"); furthermore, practices pertaining to semiopietas were in some cases considered to be efficacious even when not correctly performed, provided the intention was right. Since the salvific power of signs is intrinsic to them, the uninformed use of amulets or talismans (use that leaves meaning out of consideration) has its theoretical foundation in semiognosis, and is legitimated by the weight of tradition and the idea of unaltered secret transmission (see also Chapter Three).

Mind, knowledge, and salvation

As is clear from the previous discussion, epistemology (acquisition of a true knowledge of the self and the word) is a central issue for Buddhism. Buddhism recognizes the existence of two radically different cognitive modalities corresponding to two different kinds of semiotics: while one is related to what could be called "ordinary" semiosis (semiosic processes occurring in ordinary states of consciousness—that is, semiosic processes usually studied by semiotics), the other form of Buddhist semiosis refers to the interactions with reality according to different forms of awareness.

Ordinary knowledge (in Sanskrit *jñāna*) is considered fallacious because it mistakes a presumed ontological reality of the universe with ordinary psycho-mental phenomena and processes (modalities and functions of mind) creating such reality. In contrast, true, absolute knowledge, called *prajñā* or *bodhi*, is the product of the performance of religious practices (meditative, devotional, and ritual practices in general), resulting in non-ordinary states of body-mind-language. Usually translated as "enlightenment," it is often confined by scholars among dubious phenomena pertaining to irrationality and mysticism, thus ignoring its semiotic and cultural interest.

Mind is an extremely complex and important subject in Buddhism in general and Esoteric Buddhism in particular.[60] It is partly due to the fact that Buddhism envisions liberation as based on the acquisition of a special wisdom, that is, a different cognitive approach toward reality. Such new cognitive approach is called in the Japanese tradition *satori* or *kakugo*, usually rendered in English as "enlightenment" or "awakening." "Enlightenment" refers to the attainment of "light" as a new, and correct, vision that dispels the "darkness" of ignorance. "Awakening" is closer to the Buddhist original as the realization that ordinary, profane reality is just a dream and therefore is unreal. Here we should stress once more that *satori*/awakening is, contrary to common understanding, a cognitive state, not a mystical experience. Esoteric Buddhism builds up on previous theories of the mind and expands them to connect mind directly to the body on the one hand and to reality on the other. It also tries to develop in more concrete terms the mechanics of the transformation of the deluded mind that is necessary in order to attain awakening. In this respect, it is interesting to note that the sentence from the *Dari jing* "know your mind as it really is" (Jp. *nyojitsu chi jishin*) is considered to be the quintessence of the Shingon teachings.[61] This sentence has generated countless commentaries, including the monumental *Himitsu mandara jūjūshinron* by Kūkai.[62] In this work, Kūkai describes ten stages of awareness, which can also be characterized as ten modes of functioning of the mind, since they describe for each stage the mind's understanding of reality and awareness of itself, its moral outlook, and its soteriological implications.

The basic epistemological model consists in a circulation between the physical (Sk. *rūpa*, Jp. *shiki*) and the mental (*nāma*, *myō*), through perception (*vedanā*, *ju*), ideation (*saṃjñā*, *sō*), and volition (*saṃskāra*, *gyō*). These are the five aggregates (*skandha*, *un*) that constitute all sentient beings (including, but not limited to, human beings). This doctrine was aimed at explaining the fundamental Buddhist tenet of no-self (*anātman*, *muga*), which excludes the existence of a substantial self (or soul). Mahayana Buddhism further developed this theory in two directions: either by denying the substantial and autonomous existence of the five aggregates, or by emphasizing the role of mind.

According to the first interpretation, put forth by the Mādhyamika school originating in India with Nāgārjuna (second to third centuries CE), emptiness (Sk. *śūnyatā*, Jp. *kū*) is the essential condition of all things and beings. In this context, *śūnyatā* is both an ontological and epistemological concept. Ontologically, it refers to the fact that nothing has autonomous existence, everything being the result of a combination of causal factors; epistemologically, it refers to the fact that since everything is relational, the task of language is that of describing both the lack of autonomy and the essential relationality of things.

The second interpretation, which emphasizes the role of the mind, was developed by the Yogācāra school (also known as *vijñaptimātratā*, "consciousness-only"), established in India by Asaṇga (fourth century CE) and Vasubandhu (fourth to fifth centuries). According to it, all things as we perceive and understand them (including ourselves) are the result of mental activities articulating (i.e. giving shape) to an underlying substance/substratum. This substratum, being ultimately ungraspable, is defined as the realm of emptiness (*śūnyatā*)—understood as that which exists as it is (*tathatā*, Jp. *shinnyo*, lit. "suchness"). It should be noted the Yogācāra tradition's different understanding of *śūnyatā*, with respect to the Mādhyamika tradition, and its emphasis on ideation and the role of mind.

Common to both schools, however, is a nominalistic understanding of language as a fundamental tool for the creation of reality as humans understand it.[63] Since beings are by definition unenlightened (at least, before their exposure to Buddhism), their understanding of the world is wrong. Language and the conceptual apparatus it mobilizes articulate reality into discrete entities (a process defined as "discrimination," Jp. *funbetsu*), giving human beings a false sense of things. Because of this, the knowing subjects understand objects as existing independently of them; the subjects also understand themselves as existing independently and autonomously. This is the origin of fundamental ignorance (Sk. *avidyā*, Jp. *mumyō*), which causes in turn desire, frustration, and suffering (*dukha*, *ku*)—the main causes for rebirth. Buddhist soteriology aims at making individuals aware of their fundamental misunderstanding of reality through a complete reformulation of the role of language and its relation with reality; this is also a semiotic issue.

Perhaps, the most influential Buddhist model of semiosis in Japan was the one developed by the Yogācāra School. It emphasized the connections among three different layers of psycho-physical reality: the material world, the mind, and the set of perceptive, intellective, and volitional activities connecting them. As is clear from its most common appellation, "Consciousness-only" (Sk. *vijñaptimātratā*, Jp. *yuishiki*), the basic tenet of this tradition of thought is that only mind "exists," and the world is the result of the mind's activity. External reality as it appears in our ordinary experience is in fact a projection of our deluded (non-enlightened) mind, which articulates what is de facto an unconditioned, absolute substance into objects, events, sensations, thoughts, and so forth. The so-called outside world is devoid of an autonomous existence; it is structured in an organized way according to specific categories (and the ontological status of these categories is a matter of debate in Buddhist thought), but is not independent from the mind articulating them.

The Yogācāra School studies in detail this articulation process that produces our deluded world of suffering in order to reverse it. The goal of this tradition consists in achieving a radical transformation of the mind, so that it no longer produces deluded representations of a fictional external world but reflects passively and accurately the unconditioned entity that constitutes absolute reality (Sk. *tathatā*, Jp. *shinnyo*).[64]

The absolute continuum is first divided into five major categories, encompassing a total of a hundred constitutive entities (dharmas). The five categories are: mind (Jp. *shinnō*, lit. "mind-king"), mental factors (Jp. *shin shouhō* or *shinjo*, lit. "mind's possessions"), matter (Jp. *shikihō*, "entities endowed with form"), immaterial entities independent of the mind (Jp. *shin fusōō gyōhō*), and unconditioned entities (Jp. *muihō*). Mind includes the eight consciousnesses (Jp. *hasshiki*), or sections of the mind. Mental factors include mental faculties such as perception, volition, and ideation, mental functions such as desire, memory, and meditation (Sk. *samādhi*, Jp. *sanmai* or *jō*), good mental states (faith, dedication, patience, etc.), negative mental states (afflictions, Sk. *kleśa*, Jp. *bonnō*: greed, anger, ignorance, arrogance, doubt, and wrong ideas), secondary afflictions, and neutral mental states (such as regret and sleep). Material dharmas include the five bodily sense organs and the corresponding five realms of material objects (respectively, eye/forms, ear/sounds, nose/odors, tongue/tastes, body/tactile perception). Among the independent immaterial entities we find dharmas such as acquisition, life, meditation, names, impermanence, succession, direction, time, and number. Finally, unconditioned entities include space, immobility, the elimination of ideation, and Suchness.

This typology disrupts facile dichotomies such as mind/matter and conditioned/unconditioned, but at the same time points to a complex series of interactions that gesture toward the overcoming of conditioned thought. For example, mental states are bridges between the mind and material objects; some mental states defined as "purer" have the possibility to become a starting point toward the recovery of the original and unrepresentable unconditioned state. This state is represented in this typology by the unconditioned dharmas, but as long as they are envisioned as elements in a typology they are precisely that, representations, and not the "real thing." On the other hand, the catalog of immaterial dharmas provides us with a list of basic entities that are necessary in order to think and act in the world—fundamental categories of thought, distinct from the mind, from mental states, matter, and unconditioned entities.

Semiosis (and resulting knowledge) is a complex process of interaction between various levels and functions of mind with a supposedly "outside" world through the mediation of senses. There are three different cognitive modes or attitudes toward reality, known as the "three natures" (Sk. *trisvabhāva*, Jp. *sanshō*) because the nature of reality changes depending on our interpretive approach. The first mode is delusion: reality is the product of attachment to deluded views (Sk. *parikalpita*, Jp. *henge shoshū*). In this mode, things and events are seen as unproblematic, self-identical, and objectively existing. The second mode is based on the idea of co-dependent origination (Sk. *paratantra*, Jp. *etaki*); here, objects that appear to exist autonomously are in fact the products of causal chains; as a result, everything's existence depends on something else's, and thus everything is devoid of substantial identity. The third mode understands reality as it really is, in its perfect and true form (Sk. *parinişpanna*, Jp. *enjōjitsu*); it is a glimpse of Suchness (Sk. *tathatā*, Jp. *shinnyo*).

There is a deep semiotic awareness in these three cognitive modes. They presuppose a distinction between an entity's mental image (Jp. *omokage*), its external appearance (*gyō*), its semiotic configuration (*sō*), its material substance (*tai*), and its essence or nature (*shō*). Deluded vision focuses only on appearance and signs; the co-dependent outlook goes beyond semiotic configurations to attain the substance; the perfect mode makes one realize the nature of things. A well-known example describes what happens when a person mistakes a rope for a snake. That person thinks that a mental image of a snake corresponds to a real state in the external world; the "snake" is an image, a semiotic configuration, and a material substance. This is the ordinary, unaware semiotic approach to things, according to which images and signs are identical to their referents. In this case, however, the image of the snake is only the product of one's deluded mind and has no substance in itself. The physical object rope, in turn, is the result of a production process based on the manipulation of straw; the rope is the semiotic configuration taken by the straw thus manipulated, and the straw is its essence.[65] This example, however, should not be taken literally because of its limitations. It does not suggest that straw is true reality (in itself beyond ordinary cognitive capacities), but it does indicate that our vision of the world is usually mistaken: there is no material substance, what exists is an unconditioned essence and its semiotic configurations. Quite literally, though, beings live in a world inhabited by "snakes" everywhere—false visions, wrong ideas, misperceptions generating fear and other afflictions that imprison the beings in the cycle of rebirth and suffering.

Yogācāra Buddhism envisions mind ("mind-king") as a type of mental hardware, distinct from its mental states and the mental entities (ideas, categories, words, signs) it manipulates. Mind is structured into eight levels or functions usually rendered into English as "consciousnesses" (Sk. *vijñāna*, Jp. *shiki*): five sense consciousnesses (one for each sense organ), intellect (Sk. *mano vijñāna*, Jp. *ishiki*), self-consciousness (Sk. *mano nāma vijñāna*, Jp. *manashiki*), and store consciousness (Sk. *ālaya vijñāna*, Jp. *arayashiki*). Perceptual data from the five sense organs (preceding the attribution of a name) are elaborated by the first five consciousnesses; the sixth consciousness unifies the data, attributes names and formulates judgments. Incidentally, the intellect is treated as both another sense organ and a sense consciousness: its perceptual realm is the thinkable, and its products are ideas. These six first consciousnesses are based on another consciousness, called *mano nāma vijñāna*, which is the center of self-awareness and creates the distinction between subject and object—thus, it makes knowledge possible. Beyond it there exists a still deeper consciousness, *ālaya vijñāna*, a store of sign-seeds (Sk. *bīja*, Jp. *shūji*), acting recursively on perception and volition, on the interaction of mind with the world. *Ālaya vijñāna* is often interpreted by modern authors as a kind of Freudian, or perhaps Jungian, unconscious, but it would be more accurate to consider it as the mental center of semiosis. It contains the seeds of all perceptions, objects, thoughts, deeds, and volitions accumulated by the subject. Past experiences and their seeds influence the future ones, and future experiences and seeds reorganize in turn the seed deposit; in this way, and interestingly, time and karma have a semiotic foundation. External reality is non-existent, because the objects appearing to ordinary beings are created by consciousness through a complex work of conceptual articulation and organization. Since only mind exists, and the world is the result of the articulating activity of the mind (*vijñaptimātratā*), the image that a person has of the ordinary world is nothing but a transformation of *ālaya vijñāna*. Moreover, the Yogācāra School emphasizes that, from the point of view of enlightenment, also mind and consciousness, themselves products of one deluded mind's discrimination, are ultimately non-existent. In enlightenment, everything is not different from Emptiness—which could be approximately described as semiosic potentiality and mirror-like quiescence. Human beings are not aware of the existence of the store-consciousness and think that their perceptions are direct and true, and that their thoughts correspond to and represent a reality objectively existing "out there."

Of course, our awareness of the external world would be impossible without sense organs. Yogācāra thought posits six sense organs (Jp. *rokkon*), namely, sight, hearing, taste, smell, touch, and the intellect (the latter is considered a sense organ because it perceives dharma or abstract categories, i.e. the thinkable). Each organ perceives specific qualities among six perceptual fields (*rokkyō*) in the "outside" world, respectively, forms, sounds, flavors, perfumes, tactile qualities, and the thinkable. Perceptual data of direct experience (preceding the attribution of a name) are further elaborated by six sense consciousnesses (*rokushiki*) corresponding to each of the six sense organs: eye consciousness, ear consciousness, taste consciousness, smell consciousness, touch consciousness, and the intellect consciousness (*ishiki*). The latter consciousness, in particular, unifies the perceptual data, attributes names, and formulates judgments on things and situations. These six consciousnesses are based on another, deeper consciousness, called *mano nāma vijñāna* (Jp. *manashiki*), which is the center of self-awareness. A still deeper consciousness, the *ālaya vijñāna* (Jp. *arayashiki*), the "store consciousness" is, as we have seen, at the core of Yogācāra epistemology and semiotics.

Thus, knowledge of the external world involves the interaction of several factors. Objects (material entities) stimulate sense organs (perception); sense organs send their raw data to their respective consciousnesses (mind), which transform them into mental entities; mental entities are then synthesized by the intellect to produce ideas, volition (intentionality), and activities in the world (mental factors). In reality, however, the process goes in the opposite direction. Awareness begins when movements in the absolute continuum of Suchness stimulate the store-consciousness (*ālaya vijñāna*), which produces an idea of self and objects as existing separately; ideation (representation) begins with the projection upon the outside of seeds of various kinds from the store-consciousness. The distinctions self/others and subject/object are the sources of ignorance and suffering because it foments desire and anger and the other afflictions (Sk. *kleśa*, Jp. *bonnō*). It is only in religious practice that one can overcome the afflictions and experience the unconditioned (Jp. *muihō*). The discursivization of experiences, desires, and thoughts requires the activation of immaterial entities such as language, time, space, number, etc. It is these immaterial entities that de facto produce our symbolic realm, in the same way as ideation produces the imaginary realm and meditation enables one to attain Suchness.

Yogācāra semiotics actually posits two kinds of signs: signs as characteristics of the objects (*lakśaṇa* and *nimitta*, both rendered in Japanese as *sō*), and signs as cognitive and passional potentialities stored in *ālaya vijñāna* (Sk. *bīja*, Jp. *shūji*). *Lakśaṇa* is the name of signs characterizing the essence of things (such as the thirty-two marks of the Buddha-body), and has positive overtones. *Nimitta* are superficial, external characteristics of things. We could define the former as signs of an entity's essential qualities and the latter as signs of its accidental qualities. The power of *ālaya vijñāna* to create all things, as a kind of virtual reality, depends on the semiotic seeds it stores. There are, in turn, two kinds of seeds: (i) linguistic and karmic seeds; (ii) innate and newly produced *bīja*. The phenomenal existence of the subject and the outside world is closely related to the language that articulates them; language is stored as linguistic seeds. Seeds articulate reality either through words or by indices: in the first case, their activity is called "expressing meaning" (Jp. *hyōgi*), a reference to a distinction between signifier (the expression) and signified (its meaning); in the second case, their activity is called "expressing an object" (*kenkyō*) without the use of words. Linguistic seeds are in turn sown by good or bad actions (one's vision of the world determines one's actions), thus producing what are called "karmic seeds," which affect the subject's karmic becoming. Innate *bījas* are those that determine one's spiritual capacities and potential of attainment in soteriology.[66] Newly produced *bījas* are seeds "sown" (deposited) after an experience, and produce a general transformation of the entire pool of seeds stored. In fact, seeds produce the phenomenal world, but at the same time the phenomenal world affects *ālaya vijñāna* by "sowing" new seeds into it. Production of new *bīja* depends on perceptual and cognitive contact with external signs (*lakśaṇas* and *nimittas*); at the same time, recognition of objects consists in the identification of *lakśaṇas* and *nimittas* through *bījas* already stored in *ālaya vijñāna*.

The production of new seeds is called "perfuming" (Sk. *vāsanā*, *abhyāsa*, or *bhāvanā*, generally translated in Jp. as *kunshū*): as a perfume lingers on a dress, so the impressions of experienced things remain in the consciousness and affect mind and body. The cognitive and affective contents of phenomena perfume, through the power of karma, the knower's *ālaya vijñāna*, thus producing new *bījas*, which in turn give rise to other phenomena. It is this recursive circuit of subject and object that generates the ordinary world. In this way, semiosis, as the discriminatory process articulating the world, is the cause of ignorance, attachment, illusion, and suffering—resulting in further ignorance and rebirth. However, the fundamental teaching of the Buddha is that it is possible to escape from such vicious circle of ignorance—suffering—rebirth.

Yogācāra speculation indicates a method to overcome such cognitive delusion. Since everything is produced by seeds stored in the *ālaya vijñāna*, it is necessary to control the seeds' operations. Yogācāra practice consists precisely in the control and purification of seeds, so that they stop producing a false reality and enable the mind-king to reflect absolute reality as it really is. In short, the ideative action of the seeds is based on two kinds of factors: afflictions (*bonnō*), resulting from attachment to the idea of a self (*gashū*), and cognitive factors (*shochi*), resulting from attachment to the idea of an external reality (*hōshū*). There are two other kinds of seeds as well: pure (*muro*) and impure (*uro*). Impure seeds reproduce the previous two factors of delusion, whereas pure seeds are conducive to enlightenment. Yogācāra practice, based on study and meditation, is meant to reduce the production of impure seeds and their effects while increasing the production of pure seeds. The function of the seeds issuing forth from *ālaya vijñāna* consists essentially in providing designations of portions of the absolute continuum, thus articulating it into distinct entities (again, as separate from the designating and desiring subject). Seeds articulate reality either through words or by indices: in the first case, their activity is called "expressing meaning" (*hyōgi*), a clear reference to a distinction between signifier (the expression) and signified (its meaning); in the second case, their activity is called "expressing an object" (*kenkyō*) without the use of words.

A gradual reduction of seed production results in the decrease of semiotic activity and in the purification of *ālaya vijñāna* and the mind apparatus as a whole. By dismantling the symbolic realm, the imaginary realm also gradually disappears and the Real (Suchness) begins to surface to consciousness. This purification of the mind is called "transformation of consciousness to attain wisdom" (*tenshiki tokuchi*): the eight sections of the mind-king turn into "four wisdoms" (*shichi*), which constitute the mental apparatus of enlightenment—or, in other words, the mind of the Buddha. The five sense consciousnesses turn into the "wisdom that carries out completely what needs to be done" (*jōshosachi*), that is, the ability to bring benefits to sentient beings. The intellect (*ishiki*) turns into the "wisdom to observe the sublime aspect of things" (*myōkanzatchi*)—the capacity to transcend superficial aspects of things and attain their essence. The self-consciousness (*manashiki*) turns into the "wisdom of the undifferentiated nature of all things" (*byōdōshōchi*). Finally, *ālaya vijñāna* becomes the "wisdom of the great, perfect mirror" (*daienkyōchi*), a clear mirror that reflects without alterations the ultimate nature of the Dharma realm. At that point, *ālaya vijñāna* reveals its true aspect as "pure consciousness" (Sk. *amala vijñāna*, Jp. *amarashiki*), envisioned as a clear mirror.

As we can see, the transformation of the mind is a veritable reversal. The former center of delusion becomes a perfect mirror reflecting absolute reality; what was the center of the self now understands the fundamental undifferentiatedness of all things; the previous intellect, which manipulated superficial impressions about things, is now able to reach the essence of things; finally, what functioned as the interfaces between the mind and reality, the five sense consciousnesses, are now the tools to carry out salvific activity in favor of sentient beings.

Once human cognitive apparatus has been transformed, once *ālaya vijñāna* has turned into a supreme mirror-like organ, semiosis (as the activity of creation, interpretation, and transmission of signs) is brought to an end by the attainment of Emptiness. What remains is only the ritual reiteration of cosmic processes and the reflection of the absolute and undifferentiated Dharma Realm. Buddhist texts describe this situation that defies human possibility of comprehension through the metaphor of Indra's Net: each pearl reflects all the other pearls, without interpreting or modifying them. The Buddhist universe in its absolute modality is made of reflections reflecting reflections, in a cosmic interplay of pure light.

The Yogācāra tradition envisions this transformation process as requiring three great kalpas, a non-specified, almost infinite span of time.[67] During that time, the practitioner would perform the preparations necessary to walk the bodhisattva's path, and then proceed along the ten stages of the bodhisattva's career. In the Esoteric Buddhist interpretation, the three kalpas can be overcome in a single moment of enlightened thought (see Chapter Four).

The Shingon tradition accepts the basic structure of the mind as developed by the Yogācāra tradition. However, it also operated a number of changes and additions/deletions to it: the nature of the mind (*shinnō*, mind-king) and its connections with the body and reality in general, the methods to awaken the deluded mind to wisdom, and the time-span required to attain the transformation of the mind. The most striking change is perhaps the radical reduction of the time-span required to attain the transformation of the mind into a wisdom-producing apparatus. As we will see in Chapter Four, the scholar monk Raihō (1279–1330?) interpreted *kalpa* ("aeon") as *vikalpa* ("discrimination"), so that duration is reduced to the instantaneous activity of the mind. Once a practitioner overcomes discrimination, his/her mind is free from conditioning and attains wisdom; this process does not necessarily requires countless aeons—in fact, Shingon claims that through its practices it can be achieved in one or two lifetimes. Analogously, the Yogācāra ten stages of the bodhisattva's path are reduced to the visualization of the deities in the mandala—in this case, time is reduced to space.[68] Of course, Shingon's intervention did not limit itself to claim that its soteriology was quicker than the Yogācāra's, but proposed a set of practices to prove its claim. Ritual and meditation on the mind in particular were supposed to directly enact the transformation of one consciousness. In this respect, an important element is represented by the concept of *bodhicitta* (Jp. *bodaishin*). This key concept, literally meaning "the mind (*citta*) of enlightenment (*bodhi*)," usually refers to the "thought of enlightenment," that is, the initial desire to be saved and to engage in Buddhist practice. This is the very beginning of an individual's process of salvation, and therefore it is a very important moment. In Japan, however, in the context of the doctrines on the original enlightenment (*hongaku*) of beings, *bodhicitta* was often interpreted as "the enlightened mind." In this case, the implication was that one could arouse the desire of enlightenment because the principle of enlightenment is innate to all sentient beings—in other words, we are "always-already" enlightened, we just don't know it. Practice thus becomes a process of self-awareness to one's innate Buddha-nature. Esoteric Buddhism added a further important layer of meaning: in a coherent nondualistic fashion, it stressed that if everyone is innately enlightened, then the initial desire for enlightenment (*bodhicitta*) is already the final goal of practice. This move enabled Esoteric Buddhism to emphasize the possibility to attain salvation in the present life—or, as the well-known Japanese definition has it, to "become a buddha in this very body."[69]

Another important Shingon contribution to the theory and practice of the mind is the identification of the "mind-king," e.g., the mental hardware of sentient beings, with Dainichi Nyorai. The Buddha at the center of the two fundamental mandalas manifests all other beings and entities, in the same way as the mind produces mental states.[70] If the human mind is already the Buddha Dainichi, then each individual's afflictions and other negative states of mind are just illusions—or, more exactly, they are no different from enlightenment. This is another way to express the famous tenet that "afflictions are themselves the enlightenment" (*bonnō soku bodai*). This connection with Dainichi also resulted in the positing of a fifth form of wisdom to be achieved with the transformation of one's mind apparatus: the "wisdom of the substance-nature of the Dharma realm" (*hokkai taishōchi*). In the Shingon epistemology, this is the fundamental wisdom, the real understanding of the nature of reality—something that goes beyond the mere unaltered reflection of the "great and perfect mirror (of the mind)–wisdom" (*daienkyōchi*) that grounded enlightenment in the

Yogācāra tradition. This wisdom is produced by *amala vijñāna*. As we have seen, according to the Yogācāra definition, *amala vijñāna* was not a separate consciousness, but an attribute of *ālaya vijñāna* that emphasized its original purity and therefore the innate possibility to transform itself into a pure mirror of Suchness. Esoteric Buddhism, however, gives an ontological ground to *amala vijñāna* as the real foundation and essence of the mind, as a synonym of original enlightenment (a text defines it the "consciousness of original enlightenment" or *hongakushiki*), Suchness, and Dharma realm. With this move, absolute reality comes to constitute the mind of sentient beings; soteriology (religious practice) consists then in acquiring awareness of this fact.[71]

One of the ways in which the transformation of the consciousness apparatus was believed to occur also involved the manipulation of specific mantras. For example, a ritual commentary by the Pure Land and Shingon monk Shōgei (1341–1420) suggests that the transformation of the mental apparatus from discriminative machinery into a clear and undifferentiated pure mirror usually referred to as the five wisdoms (*gochi*) takes place thanks to the mantra *vaṃ hūṃ trāḥ hrīḥ aḥ*, representing the state of enlightenment associated with the Vajra realm. This mantra stands for the five buddhas (respectively, Mahāvairocana, Akśobhya, Ratnasaṃbhava, Amitābha, Śākyamuni), the five directions (center, east, south, west, north), and other correlative series based on them, in particular the five wisdoms. Let us briefly follow Shōgei's exegesis.

The seed *aḥ* represents the transformation of the five sense consciousnesses into the "wisdom that carries out completely what needs to be done" (*jōshosachi*); *hrīḥ* indicates the transformation of the sixth consciousness (*ishiki*) into the "wisdom to observe the sublime aspect of things" (*myōkanzatchi*); *trāḥ* indicates the transformation of the seventh consciousness (*manashiki*) into the "wisdom of the undifferentiated nature of all things" (*byōdōshōchi*); *hūṃ* stands for the transformation of the eighth consciousness (*arayashiki*) into the wisdom reflecting all things as a perfect mirror (*daienkyōchi*); finally, *vaṃ* represents the ninth consciousness (*amarashiki*). Because of its particular status, *amarashiki* is not subject to transformations, but constitutes the nondual and signless mandala of the Dharma realm or, in another terms, the wisdom of the original nature of the Dharma realm (*hokkai taishōchi*). Shōgei defines the set of these five syllables as the mantric seed of the single mind of sentient beings because it represents the universal, pure, and undefiled mind pervading the Dharma realm (both sentient beings and buddhas) in the form of the five wisdoms.[72]

In this way, enlightenment (the transformation of the consciousness apparatus), which required such a long endeavor according to the Yogācāra tradition, in esoteric Buddhism becomes almost mechanical and, in any case, certain. In Shōgei's case above, even visualization is no longer necessary, since the understanding of the deep meaning of the mantra and of its salfivic effects is enough to trigger its mind-transforming power.

The world of scholar monks

It is now time to take a look at the cultural world of the authors (and recipients) of these discourses, namely, the scholar monks (*gakuryo*, *gakuto*) of the main temples. In medieval Japan, the Buddhist clergy (*daishu*) was divided into several groups hierarchically organized. Whereas the monastic organization differed, at times even conspicuously, from one temple to another, in general it is possible to identify a tripartite structure composed of scholar monks, worker monks, and itinerant or visiting monks.[73] Numerically, the scholar monks were a small minority among the clergy.

Unfortunately, we only have a fragmentary knowledge of the education process of early medieval Shingon scholar monks.[74] In the middle ages there were very few "schools" open to the public, and most of these were affiliated with local temples. Education of noble and wealthy youth was essentially carried out in the family through textbooks of "family instructions" (*kakun*) that were handed down in private, oral transmissions (variously known as *hiden*, *denju*, *menju*). Such texts were often secret (*hisho*, *hihon*).[75] The education of monks ranged from semi-literacy, to memorization (more or less accurate) of scriptures and mantras, to highly sophisticated technical skills and philosophical learning. An example of the education curriculum for children at the Ninnaji temple in Kyto in the late Heian period can be found in the *Uki*, the diary of monk-prince Shukaku (1150–1202). It consisted in worship of the protecting god (*kami*) of the temple, reading short scriptures such as the *Heart Sutra*, and chanting *dhāraṇī* (such as the *Kujaku myōō shingon*) and the invocation to Kōbō Daishi (*Namu Henjō kongō*). Education proper consisted in learning how to read and write, composing prose and poetry, and singing and playing music. Children also learned how to play *go*, *sugoroku* (a board game), *kemari* (a type of soccer), and archery.[76]

One can easily imagine well-known monks such as Kakuban (1095–1143), Raiyu (1226–1304), and Gōhō (1306–62) learning to read and write in this way in their childhood, favored by their affluent background and the vicinity of their residence to a temple of some importance. There they met priests who taught them some basic Shingon teachings and gave them the tonsure. These novices' talent and wealthy backgrounds enabled them to continue their studies at major temples, where they received more specialized training.

It is possible to have a glimpse of that training through the regulations of the Kyōō jōjūin, a center of advanced studies in Esoteric Buddhism funded by retired emperor Go-Uda at Daikakuji in the 1280s. These regulations prescribe three major areas of study, each to be mastered in one year, for a total of three years. These areas were, respectively, the *Jinggang ding jing* (Jp. *Kongōchōgyō*), the *Dari jing* (Jp. *Dainichikyō*), and *shōmyō* Buddhist chanting along with *shittan* Indic writing. Education consisted in listening to lectures by scholar monks for three months, followed by an individual study period of three months, at the end of which the student would receive the consecration (*kanjō*) by an *ajari* (Esoteric Buddhist master) in the discipline.[77] Classes were usually held in a lecture-discussion format. The text constituting the main study material was addressed at the pace of one scroll every ten days. For each scroll, the master first read the text and taught its pronunciation, intonation, and punctuation; he then explained relevant terms and sentences by referring to previous scholarship. Next, beginners followed by more advanced students asked questions.[78] Information also survives concerning the medieval Tendai tradition, according to which one or two lecturers (*nōke*) taught in front of forty to fifty students,[79] in a situation that was probably not too different from that at major Shingon temples at the time.

An important component of the training of Shingon scholar monks was a period of study spent at some important temple in Nara. Usually, Shingon disciples studied Hossō (Yogācāra) doctrines at Kōfukuji and Kegon and Sanron (Mādhyamika) doctrines at Tōdaiji.[80] The Nara Buddhist establishment had traditionally strong ties with Shingon; Tōdaiji in particular even claimed leadership in the Shingon sect.[81]

The fundamental form of higher learning in medieval Japan was a dialogic model known as *dangi* or *rongi*, in which young scholar monks were asked to illustrate a doctrinal theme and respond to questions from senior monks who often upheld unorthodox views.[82] In fact, many medieval texts were written in the context of such educational processes. Commentaries were often directly related to their authors' activities as lecturers. They read a text, wrote a commentary, lectured on it, and then rewrote it by including the comments and criticism they had received during their lectures. Sometimes, they repeated this process several times before putting forth a definitive version. In other words, commentaries were an essential component of the medieval Shingon education system. This system was based on lectures (*kō*) and debates (*dangi*) in which the scholar monks took part. Throughout the year, there were several occasions to listen to, and actively participate in, such events. The most famous monks were also invited to lecture at other temples and, in some cases, even at the imperial court. There were several levels of debates, from intermediate to advanced. Novices probably only listened, or exercised their debating skills with their peers or while receiving instruction from their masters. Interestingly enough, many texts written by scholar monks reproduced the education process in which they were used.

Esoteric Buddhist monks received a specialized training in a number of philosophical issues and ritual matters. When the training in a particular subject was concluded, the student went through a consecration ritual known as *kanjō* (lit. "pouring water on the top of the head"), a kind of anointment, which sanctioned the level of education that had been attained. *Kanjō* rituals were a component of the Esoteric Buddhist semiotic system, and a semiognosis of consecration also developed. The *Keiran shūyōshū*, a fourteenth-century Buddhist encyclopedia, treats the meaning of consecration as being inscribed in its name. Thus, the first character of the term *kanjō*, *kan* ("pouring water"), refers to wisdom attained through practice; the second character, *chō* ("top of the head"), refers to the realm of the eternal principle (*ri*) of original enlightenment. Together, these two characters mean that the wisdom of the past buddhas, in the form of water, is poured on the head of the new buddha in the initiation ceremony;[83] consecration rituals made practice and original enlightenment coincide.

Around the end of the Heian period (twelfth century), and more frequently in the Kamakura period (thirteenth to fourteenth centuries), different forms of *kanjō* began to appear; they concluded secret transmissions (*kuden* or *hiden*) concerning esoteric texts, doctrines, and rituals. Gradually, consecration rituals also came to be performed to transmit knowledge concerning literary texts such as poetry collections and the *Ise monogatari* (*waka kanjō*), performing arts (Nō, music), professional tools and crafts, and so forth.[84] The attainment of secret knowledge transmitted through initiation rituals was a soteriological goal, since it was equivalent to the attainment of salvation (becoming a buddha or, in the case of *shintō kanjō*, identifying oneself with the Japanese gods or *kami*) and involved a promise of worldly benefits (outside of the religious world, this translated as professional and artistic success); it was also a moral obligation as the realization of the essential principles and duties of a specific craft or profession (and, at the same time, the attainment of the "trade secrets" of a specific family lineage). It is not by chance, then, that in medieval Japan *kanjō* became the template for procedures to transmit legitimate knowledge in general as part of certain hierarchical systems, such as family lineages dealing with specific literary and artistic texts, with technologies, and with extra-canonical teachings such as matters related to the gods.

The reason for the development of such a wide range of initiation rituals is not clear. I believe it was a consequence of the systematic "mandalization" that was carried out in medieval Japan by Esoteric Buddhism as a way to establish a type of cultural hegemony among the intellectual elites. In such a framework, each text and each cultural artifact, including non-religious ones, was understood as a potential Esoteric entity endowed with several levels of secret meanings. A particular role was played by texts concerning Shinto issues, with their emphasis on cosmology, cosmogony, and the specificity of Japan, also because they added a layer of localness and concreteness to highly metaphysical Buddhist speculations.

Because of the nature of such knowledge, not everyone was entitled to receive it; consecration rituals, with their strict regulations, functioned as devices to control meaning and limit access to knowledge. They were also means to control legitimacy. Contrary to common understanding, consecrations (also as they are still performed today) do not generally reveal occult doctrines or "esoteric" truths. Those are (and were in the past) relatively easily available in texts studied before the performance of the initiation ritual. What the ritual enacts is the sanctioning of the adept's legitimate belonging to a certain lineage, and his/her capacity to teach certain doctrines and to perform certain rituals. It also guarantees the soteriological attainment of the initiated, which was often related to his (more rarely, her) social position in the hierarchy of religious institutions. For these reasons, what the master reveals at consecration are details such as the order of utterance of a series of mantras, specific pronunciations or intonations, which mudras to perform and when—precisely, the kind of *knowledge* that distinguishes a true certified professional from the amateur. In other words, consecration rituals control the structuring and the reproduction of the Buddhist Esoteric system—a system both of knowledge and of power.

A textualized world

It is possible to find a distant model of the doctrinal discussions, which constituted an important component in the training of Japanese scholar monks, in the Buddhist scriptures themselves; sutras are in fact dialogues between Śākyamuni and his disciples (and opponents). In China this model interacted with another pedagogic paradigm, known in Japan as *sekiten* and associated with the Confucian tradition and its examination system. As a learning methodology, it generated a relentless investigation into the meaning of texts; it was a dialogue with a text and its author, and a conversation with previous masters. The significance of this textual interrogation is however not just speculative, since the understanding of the meaning of a text was directly connected with the understanding of the intention of its author—and, ultimately, of the Buddha—an endeavor with important soteriological consequences. Texts were treated as clues, traces of the intention of the Buddha, but also as "relics" of previous masters, signposts on the itinerary to the Buddha's mind and by extension to one's own salvation. One day, the Japanese scholar monk Raiyu dreamt that the bodhisattva Mañjuśrī appeared to him and praised one of his texts saying that it was the best preparation for rebirth in the Pure Land he could do. Mañjuśrī also congratulated Raiyu's scholarship, saying that his commentaries well represented the intention of the Buddha (*butsui*).[85] Commentaries resulting from this investigation into the intention of the Buddha were considered in turn soteriological instruments to spread the Dharma; as such, they were used as lecturing material to disciples and even to the Japanese gods (*kami*). We find here a close relationship between scholarship and salvation. Texts were used and produced in a ritual dimension. In some cases, they acquired a magic, talismanic status as "relics" of their authors and embodiments of enlightenment.

This elusive and endless quest for the "intention of the Buddha," through extensive analysis of scriptures and commentaries by past masters, seems to have been a primary aim of scholar monks' activity. By discerning this intention, it was theoretically possible to continue transmitting the "lantern of the Dharma." Identifying the "intention of the Buddha," that is, the real meaning of what the Buddha had said and the key to the path of salvation he had opened, was by no means an easy task (Raiyu compared his exegetical activity to picking up a single hair from the hair of nine cows, or to taking up a single drop of water from the ocean).[86] As is well known, the East Asian Buddhist Canon is composed of a large number of scriptures, many of which are in open contradiction with each other. To make matters even more complicated, the two major scriptures of Esoteric Buddhism as they were known to the medieval Japanese scholar monks, that is, in Chinese translation, were believed to be nothing more than a summary of a larger written text, unavailable in this world, which was in turn a short version of a cosmic text constituted by the entire universe. The real intention of the Buddha could be understood only through full access to that cosmic text—something that by definition was only possible to buddhas and bodhisattvas. Medieval Japanese commentators were therefore forced to work by approximation through studying scriptures, classical commentaries, and the work of past masters.

Their production shows a surprising lack of systematicity. Scholar monks primarily composed readings of major texts, descriptions of ceremonies, and notes on doctrinal and ritual matters, but in general they wrote no substantial work on specific doctrinal issues. Most doctrinal themes of medieval Japanese Buddhism were developed in this way, as scattered fragments, side notes, and afterthoughts on previous works.[87] However, it would be wrong to assume that, as frequently has been done, medieval Japanese were not "logical" or "rational." On the contrary, their arguments are clear, linear, and rational. Simply stated, they were operating within a discursive system different from our own. The peculiarities of medieval discourse raise general questions concerning the nature of medieval Buddhist intellectual systems—or, in other words, the *episteme* of exo-esoteric Buddhism.

Scholar monks affiliated with exo-esoteric Buddhist institutions were living in a textualized world. Every phenomenon or event was a potential message from the buddhas and the *kami*; it was thus necessary to be able to read the multifarious "texts" of the world. The world was textualized along two fundamental models, the *sutra* and the *mandala*. They tended to overlap in Shingon semiotic ontology, according to which sutras are instances of mandala (as part of the *hō mandara*, as we will see below). Textual production was generally not a systematic theoretical elaboration, but a continuous accumulation of thought fragments over the years in different texts and for different audiences in different situations. There was no attempt to formulate a complete and closed intellectual system. Instead, scholar monks engaged themselves in never-ending doctrinal interrogations and ritual performances, which amounted to an endless proliferation of scriptural and mandalic signifiers and signifieds.

Their doctrinal texts are usually word-by-word commentaries of other works or sections thereof. This particular interpretive procedure, probably derived from the study of Sanskrit (*shittangaku*), which was essential for understanding the Esoteric canon, aims at identifying the sense of a text not by referring to a unified vision of the totality of the statements it contains, or by placing specific terms and expressions in their context, as is the case with modern textual criticism. Scholar monks generally decomposed a text into its constitutive elements (sentences, words, at times even single characters) and indicated the meaning of each of them. They identified specific doctrinal themes in the text and expanded unevenly on each of them. This procedure is uncannily postmodern, as it fragments texts and deprives them of a unified center of signification. Subjected to this treatment, texts of previous masters acquire a surprisingly rhizomatic flavor. This fact is a consequence of the nature of medieval Shingon episteme. In the case of an Esoteric Buddhist scripture, it makes no sense to talk about its total meaning: first, because that scripture in its Chinese translation is only a minimal fragment of an all-encompassing cosmic text; second, because the total meaning of that scripture is the total meaning of the Dharmakāya and must include everything. The rhizomatic nature of commentaries was reduced by developing categories, classifications, and hierarchies, and by establishing orthodox interpretations. In other words, there was an attempt to impose an order, albeit fragmentary, upon reality (the Dharmadhātu), but this order was never fixed, but fluid, ever-shifting, polymorphous. This order was known only to, and could only be controlled by, scholar monks; this was perhaps their main source of legitimacy and *raison d'être*.

However, it would be wrong to conceive commentarial activity as solely an ontological and epistemological struggle to understand the principles of reality and the mechanisms of salvation hidden in the Buddha's mind. Writing was primarily a practical activity, related to the status and the duties of scholar monks. Learning and writing for scholar monks in general had several functions: in addition to an undeniable component of individual pleasure and satisfaction, these activities were related to salvation as good deeds generating merit for rebirth into the Pure Land; they were essential for educating new generations of priests; and they were also influential in obtaining promotions (on personal, lineage, temple, and sect levels).

The complex relationship between study, writing, and salvation, also connected with legitimacy, authority, and, ultimately, power, helps us understand the role of learned monks in medieval Japan. Social historian Itō Masatoshi, for example, sees scholar monks essentially as Buddhist sophists, whose scriptural knowledge was used to legitimize questionable practices related to the political and economic survival of their own institutions, such as the justification of war and killing (the principle "to kill one so that many may live" or *issatsu tashō*) and the idea according to which material donations to temples were inviolable (the so-called "Buddha-law" or *Butsuda hō*). According to Itō, doctrinal debates prepared scholar monks to master the rhetorical and intellectual skills needed to justify ethically questionable practices that had little to do with religion as the pursuit of ultramundane, soteriologic goals, and instead, everything to do with secular activities. As a support for this thesis, Itō mentions the fact that learned monks were usually not involved in the religious guidance of commoners—a task that was mainly carried out by worker- and itinerant monks.[88]

Itō's argument is undeniably appealing. At least, it offers an explanation as to why learned Buddhist monks in Japan (and perhaps also elsewhere) were able to justify in Buddhist terms acts and ideas that have little to do with Buddhist ethics and practice (homicide, violence, ownership of properties and wealth, but also more generally the systematic violation of the precepts). All of these heterodoxical interventions were, Itō contends, "expedient means" (*upāya*) to protect religious institutions and thus to ensure the prosperity of Buddhism and the sustenance of the political regimes to which it was related. Itō, however, presents medieval religious institutions as realms of ideological false conscience, but when false conscience becomes systematic, it is no longer bad faith, but a system of values in its own right; as such, it cannot be dismissed as "sophistry."[89] Instead, we could argue that the main occupation of medieval scholar monks was the establishment and reproduction of their own lineages (broadly understood to range from their personal line of descendants all the way to their Buddhist sect)—an endeavor that in itself carried a soteriological potential. That endeavor involved study, writing, teaching, and educating disciples. It also involved political and administrative duties necessary for the maintenance and development of the lineages—lineages that were characterized in religious terms as composed of "adamantine Buddha's sons" (*kongō busshi*). As a result of scholarly activities, learned monks could acquire symbolic capital and a sense of distinction (for themselves and their own lineages), both highly valued in medieval Japanese society. This strategically essential position of elite scholar monks explains why they were never eliminated from the major temples, despite the fact that they were increasingly challenged in important political decisions by the more numerous worker-monks. Their survival throughout the middle ages was due not to a generic recognition of the importance of scholarship for Buddhism, but to their role as creators of a sense of identity, social significance, and of ideological scenarios within religious institutions.

Ritual and the adamantine dance

I have claimed that at the background of the various avatars of Tantrism, at least in Japan, lie certain ideas on cosmology and soteriology that possess a semiotic nucleus defining phenomena as manifestations of the Dharmakāya and that, above all, deal with the power of symbolic actions to produce salvation. Esoteric Buddhism envisions the cosmos as a fractal structure, in which each phenomenon is "formally" similar to all others and to the totality. This recursive cosmology is related to a recursive soteriology that attributes enormous importance to ritual practice and visualization.[90]

Allan Grapard points to the existence of an "*episteme* of identity"[91] underlying Japanese mythology and mountain asceticism, an episteme that sees "the world (nature) and words (culture) in the specific lights of similitude, reflection, identity, and communication,"[92] on the basis of rules grounded on "associative linguistic phenomena such as metaphor, paronomasia, and anagogy."[93] In other words, operations on the substance (both graphic and phonetic) of language and meaning governed the Esoteric interpretation of reality.[94] Grapard explicitly refers here to the pre-classical European episteme as reconstructed by Michel Foucault. According to Grapard, these combinatory practices brought about a reduction from plurality to singularity,[95] but one could argue that they also exposed the plural nature of supposed singular entities.[96]

In any case, I suggest that this "episteme of plural identities," at least in its more systematic forms, was first codified on the basis of Esoteric Buddhist doctrines, and that it later assumed a kind of cultural hegemony in medieval Japan. This episteme appears to be characterized by the workings of what Tsuda Shin'ichi calls "logic of yoga," which asserts the substantial non-differentiation of all things on the basis of concepts of analogy and resemblance. This opens the way, in turn, to a kind of "symbolic omnipotence," based on the belief that ritual—indirect, "symbolic" practices—produces numberless powers by virtue of the structure of the signs involved in the ritual process.[97] It should be clear, however, that such epistemic constructs, far from being just simple ritual or meditative escamotages, were directly related to the creation of a ritualized world (closely connected to power and dominant ideology) in which each event, each phenomenon was cosmologically marked and played a salvific function. Moreover, as forms of visualization based on a complex semantic and ritual network, symbolic practices grounded on the logic of yoga produced a cognitive transformation; when seriously performed, Esoteric practices could perhaps disclose a different world.

The basic epistemic framework of the Shingon tradition, with its complex interrelations of cosmology, soteriology, semiotics, and ritual, was shared by virtually all Esoteric lineages in Japan. It should be stressed, however, that the preceding account applies mainly to those scholar monks who attempted make the Esoteric universe manifest through meditation and ritual and who exploited to the utmost degree the power that they attributed to Esoteric (or esotericized) signs—a semiotic power that reinforced, and was reinforced by, economic, social, and political power in the framework of a coherent sociocosmic order. It appears, from diaries and other textual evidence, that these monks and the people in their entourage lived in an esotericized, ritual universe. They shared a common mentality and an ensemble of combinatory beliefs and practices; at the bottom of their way of life was the awareness (rarely discussed explicitly or critically) that the cosmos was an incessant "adamantine dancing performance,"[98] a continuous transformation of shapes similar to the endless movement of waves on the surface of the sea, governed by linguistically grounded combinatory rules. Perhaps, a good model for their basic attitudes was Jinson (1430—1508), the abbot of the Daijōin *monzeki* temple of the Kasuga-Kōfukuji complex in Nara, as portrayed by Allan Grapard:

> To Jinson, the mirror-like relation between the heavenly bureaucracy and the structure of [his religious institution] and of society in general was the manifestation of a preestablished harmony that could never be discussed, even less, called into doubt. Such preestablished harmony, however, grounded though it may have been in myth and supported by ritual, needed another type of reinforcement … provided by economic power.[99]

Medieval Japanese ideals, rituals, and practices of orthodoxy and identity were thus underlain by a combinative episteme of transformation, in itself an avatar of Indian mentality. This epistemic field manifested itself and was actualized in at least two ways: in a fully conscious way through semiognosis, and in a simplified and uninformed way through semiopietas (semiosophia lying outside of the "Tantric" mentality). Both paradigms were aimed at esoterically framing the lives of the people, and functioned as powerful means of social control. But when the incessant "adamantine dance" of shifting forms was properly performed and ritually controlled, the Esoteric cosmos took on the shape of an immense salvific "machine," where all movements were ritualized and oriented to individual self-realization and universal salvation.

CHAPTER TWO

Ontology of signs: The pansemiotic cosmos of mandala

As we have seen, Esoteric Buddhism identifies the Buddha Mahāvairocana (Jp. *Dainichi*) with the Dharmakāya (Jp. *hosshin*, lit. "Dharma Body"), the ultimate source of all possible signs, thoughts, and representations, and envisions it as coextensive and identical with the entire universe (Sk. *dharmadhātu*, Jp. *hokkai*). Furthermore, Mahāvairocana is perpetually engaged in teaching the Dharma on a cosmic scale, in a sermon/performance involving all possible signs and semiotic substances. Kūkai's most important semiotic text, the *Shōji jissōgi*, addresses all these issues while presenting itself as an extended exegesis of a short philosophical poem:

> The five great elements have vibrations;
> Each of the ten worlds has its language;
> The six kinds of objects are signs;
> The Dharmakāya Buddha is the Reality.[1]

This poem describes the pansemiotic nature of the Esoteric cosmos. The first verse indicates the material basis of signs and semiosis; the five great elements (*godai*, in order, earth, water, fire, wind, and space), the substance of the universe, spontaneously produce vibrations that turn into sounds. These sounds are the substance of the languages of all kinds of existence in our world (the ten worlds: buddhas, bodhisattvas, self-enlightened ascetics or *pratyeka-buddhas*, disciples of the Buddha Śākyamuni or *śrāvaka*, gods, humans, demi-gods or *asuras*, animals, hungry ghosts or *preta*, and denizens of hell), with the implication that human beings, animals, deities, and so forth, all have their own language. Next, the totality of reality as subject of perception and intellection is articulated into signs (*monji*). The

Buddha Mahāvairocana as Dharmakāya is the entire universe, and signs of all sense objects are the components of his ongoing cosmic sermon. Interestingly, Kūkai indicates "signs" with a term used to refer to "writing" but also decorative patterns: visual, design elements are envisioned as the fundamental elements of Esoteric semiosis.

In this chapter, I outline the fundamental Esoteric Buddhist ideas about the world, which also constitute the framework of semiotic doctrines and practices. We will see the materialistic ontology that lies at the basis of the Esoteric universe and its pansemiotic nature as it is expressed in the doctrines on Mahāvairocana's cosmic sermon (*hosshin seppō*). Next, in this connection, I will discuss the semiotic articulation of reality and the correlative thought that characterizes it. Finally, I present the mandala, perhaps the most important semiotic model of Esoteric Buddhism, with its definitions, functions, and the semiotic operations it involves.

Pansemiotic ontology: the three modalities of the universe

The Shingon tradition developed a sophisticated materialistic cosmology according to which the Buddha-body in its absolute aspect (Sk. *dharmakāya*, Jp. *hosshin*) is constituted by the six elements that compose the universe, namely, earth, water, fire, air, space, and consciousness or mind; material substance, being the stuff of which the body of the Buddha is made, is not essentially different from animate, sentient matter. As a consequence, Kūkai envisioned a type of universal sentiency.[2] Furthermore, the six elements are all constituted by atoms (*mijin*), that come together to form entities and then separate to dissolve them in seemingly random processes (although karma seems to be the basic factor in the atoms' operations).[3]

This universe is not an inert, chaotic substance; it is a pansemiotic universe in which everything is organized in a systematic way and endowed with meaning. All entities in the universe are parts of the same macro-entity, the Dharmadhātu, which is in turn coextensive and identical with the Dharmakāya.[4] The ontological foundation of Shingon pansemiosis is provided by the doctrine of the *sandai* (the "three greats," i.e. the three modalities of the universe), which concerns the three modalities of existence and manifestation of the cosmos. The *sandai* are, respectively, material substance (*taidai*), semiotic manifestation (*sōdai*), and operations (*yūdai*).[5] The *sandai* doctrine is an original reformulation of the classical Buddhist distinction between substance/essence (*shōtai*) and manifestation/operations (*sōyū*), often used as a hermeneutic device contrasting the way a thing is to the way it appears. In Kūkai's treatment, such a hermeneutic device became the ontological structure of the universe, a clear move toward a pansemiotic theory.

Taidai, the substance of the universe, is the collective name of the six elements (as we have seen, earth, water, fire, wind, space, and consciousness), the cosmic substance that produces the phenomena and their characteristics; it is variously equated with Suchness (Sk. *tathatā*, Jp. *shinnyo*), emptiness, and the Dharmadhātu (*hokkai*). In a way, *taidai* is a kind of pre-semiotic continuum constituting the stuff of signs and signification. The Japanese scholar monk Raihō wrote:

> The six elements pervade sentient and nonsentient beings. Their substance [Jp. *taishō*, Sk. *ātmakatva* or *dharmatā*] is so immense that there is no larger mundane or supramundane entity. This is why they are called six great [elements]. They are the foundation of everything, from the buddhas down to all living beings: all beings are constituted by them. This is why they are called "Great substance." According to the exoteric teachings, Suchness [*shinnyo*] and Dharma-essence [*hōshō*, Sk. *dharmatā*] are mere principles, colorless and formless. According to Shingon, the [universal] substance [*tai*] is made of the six great elements. Endowed with colors and forms, substance fully encompasses all powers and virtues. Being immense and unlimited, it is called Dharma realm [*hokkai*] ... Karma and the myriad virtues are grounded on this Dharma-essence, called Dharma of Self-Enlightenment [*jishōhō*].[6]

The six elements are endowed with intrinsic and essential qualities (hardness, humidity, heat, mobility, unobstructedness, understanding), which manifest themselves in visible and perceivable forms (activities, geometrical forms, colors, mantric seeds, deep meanings, and so forth).[7] In other words, *taidai* is not a chaotic and a-semiotic matter. It is so to speak "always-already" semiotically organized: the material/mental stuff is naturally and originally articulated in forms and contents. Moreover, qualities and characteristics are originally correlated to each other. This explains the peculiar nature of the Esoteric cosmos, at the same time singular and plural, as the totality of meaningful and structured differences, which in turn lies at the basis of the correlative kind of semiotics proper to Shingon. In it, every sign is actually a macro-sign, a combination of several semiotic orders, and a microcosm in its own right. By its nature, *taidai* appears as a complex combination of semiotic structures, known as *sōdai*.

Sōdai, the semiotic configuration of the universe, refers to the countless alterations and transformations of *taidai*. Such transformations are perceived on an ordinary level of consciousness as independent from *taidai* and therefore as differentiated forms—the superficial characteristics appearing on the six elements. The term *sō*, as the Sino-Japanese rendition of the Sanskrit *lakśaṇa* and *nimitta*, is usually translated as "characteristics," "aspects," "marks," or "shapes." However, Esoteric Buddhist exegesis in general, not only Shingon, attributes to this term an explicit semiotic value. A Tendai text defines *sō* as "that which through analysis produces meaning,"[8] a definition not too distant from that of modern Western semiotics, according to which a sign is interpreted and can be invested with meaning on the basis of systems of expression and content. For Kūkai, too, differential traits are systematically organized in coherent structures, and possess both a form (an abstract position within a structure) and a substance (a set of elements that fill that abstract position).[9] Therefore, *sōdai* constitutes a semiotic system; it is a mandala or, rather, the mandalic structure of the universe; as such, *sōdai* is coextensive to *taidai*. The Shingon exegesis distinguishes between the unconditioned and spontaneous mandala (*hōni mandara*), i.e. the esoteric cosmos as the absolute and supreme Mandala, and the conditioned mandala (*zuien mandara*), i.e. mandala as it is reproduced or represented.[10] In a way, this is a difference between an abstract model and its concrete manifestations, although these two different categories of mandala are posited as ultimately identical, each being the reflection of the other.

In addition to *sōdai*, *taidai* also manifests itself as endless movements and activities, known as *yūdai*. *Yūdai*, the endless salvific activity of the universe, refers to the incessant transformation of differentiated forms in which *taidai* manifests itself. This unceasing operativity aimed at universal salvation is represented by the three secrets (*sanmitsu*) of body, language, and mind, which are the three foci of ritual practice according to Shingon soteriology. The three secrets are the deep aspect of the three karmic activities (*sangō*), the sources of rebirth and suffering. As a consequence, every activity in the universe is an act of Mahāvairocana aimed at the salvation of all beings; the Shingon universe is an enormous recursive soteriological machine, in which everyone is endlessly engaged in the salvation of everyone else; moreover, everything has meaning as part of an ongoing cosmic "sermon" by the Dharmakāya (*hosshin seppō*).

In contemporary semiotics, only the Italian film director, writer, and cultural critic Pier Paolo Pasolini (1922–75) tried to outline a theory of pansemiosis. In several essays on the semiology of cinema, Pasolini presented his project of a "semiology of the language... of reality."[11] According to Pasolini, reality, the world "out there" perceivable by the senses, is the fundamental structure of communication and meaning, to the point that "*all of life in the entirety of its actions is a natural, living film*,"[12] and cinema is "*nothing more than the 'written' manifestation of a natural, total language, which is the acting of reality*."[13] More explicitly, "the 'phenomena' of the world are the natural 'syntagmas' of the language of reality."[14] In other words, it is "not that 'nomina sunt res,' but 'res sunt nomina.'"[15] Pasolini recognized that human language is itself part of reality,[16] one of the means through which reality itself speaks. Thus, linguistic signs merely *translate* the signs of the language of Reality.[17] How does such a language of reality operate? According to Pasolini, "Reality doesn't do anything else but speak with itself using human experience as a vehicle";[18] actually, "there is no 'signified': *because the signified is also a sign.*"[19] As we shall see later, this intuition is useful to understand an important category of Esoteric semiotics that I call "macrosign."

In the late sixties and early seventies, Umberto Eco judged Pasolini's ideas as "of a singular semiological naïveté," for they were "in contrast with the most elementary aims of semiology, which is to eventually reduce the facts of nature to cultural phenomena, and not to bring the facts of culture back to natural phenomena."[20] Pasolini replied to Eco that his own aim was precisely "*the definitive transformation of nature into culture*,"[21] a clear pansemiotic project. He then criticized Eco for his refusal to deal with the metaphysical issues of semiotics, such as the ontological ground of meaning, signification, and communication. According to Pasolini, such an ontological basis of semiosis and meaning could only be found in a pantheistic entity. Pasolini argued in his characteristic half-mocking and provocative style:

> Let us therefore suppose, "per absurdum"... that God exists [...] [L]et us limit ourselves to calling God Brāhma, and let us shorten this to B. The existence of B. (whose character is Vedic-Spinozian) causes the statement "reality is a language" to no longer be apodictic and unmotivated, but [to be] in some way sensible and functional: "reality is the language of B." With whom does B. speak? Let us assume with Umberto Eco. [...] Let us assume that in this moment B. speaks with Eco, using as sign, as ultimate sign, the hair of Jerry Malanga [an actor whom Pasolini liked]. But what difference is there between the hair of Jerry Malanga and the eyes of Umberto Eco? They are but two organisms of reality, which is a *continuum* without any break in continuity; a single body... The hair of Jerry Malanga and the eyes of Umberto Eco therefore belong to the same Body, the physical manifestation of the Real, of the Existing, of Being; and if the hair of Jerry Malanga is an object that "reveals itself" as "sign of itself" to the receptive eyes of Umberto Eco, it cannot be said that this is a dialogue; [it is] a monologue which the infinite Body of Reality has with itself.[22]

Significantly, Pasolini refers to such a supreme entity as "Brāhma" or "B.," and explicitly calls reality "the language of B.," in a move that closely resembles classical Shingon theoretical positions clarified for the first time in Japan by Kūkai in his *Shōji jissōgi* with respect with the semiotics and ontology of Mahāvairocana. In Pasolini's words the underlying idea here is one of the "universe as a Body which signifies to itself";[23] according to this view, "reality speaks with itself since perception is a response to signification that reality addresses to itself in the shape of a perceiving subject."[24] However, Pasolini was not aware of the semiotics of Tantric Buddhism. He wrote: "In the long history of cults, every object of reality has been considered sacred: this has never happened with language. Language has never appeared as hierophant."[25] Pasolini's image of "the language of

B." echo Kūkai's doctrine of the *hosshin seppō*, according to which the Dharmakāya as the Dharmadhātu continuously speaks the Dharma to itself in a pleasurable and salvific monologue—a monologue spoken in all possible languages and sign systems, i.e. through reality itself, and perceived by itself, as the totality of reality, in the shape of a perceiving subject.

The Esoteric Buddhist pantheistic and pansemiotic universe was not a vaguely conceived mystic substance in which all phenomena were blurred in a universal soul, a type of *anima mundi*. On the contrary, premodern Japanese authors emphasized its materialistic component and were aware of the interplay of differences and indifferentiatedness that characterized such a complex formation. To better describe such complexity, the scholar monk Raihō (1279–1330?) introduced the concepts of singular Dharmadhātu (*ichi hokkai*) and multiple Dharmadhātu (*ta hokkai*).[26] The singular Dharmadhātu represents the principle of essential undifferentiatedness (in which all phenomena appear as manifestation of a single, unifying principle), whereas the multiple Dharmadhātu represents the principle of differentiation (in which all phenomena appear as absolute entities).[27] He argued that exoteric teachings reduce everything to the unity of the singular Dharmadhātu, because they treat individuality and multiplicity as provisional distinctions, there being no autonomous entity; the multifarious aspects that characterize the dimension of the provisional truth (*zokutai*) are reduced to the single principle of the supreme truth (*shintai*). As a consequence, "one" and "many" are relative terms and the Truth transcends them both, since the "pure one" (*jun'itsu*) is just a provisional term referring to emptiness and nirvana, and multiplicity is a mere phenomenal occurrence, a trace left by causation. In contrast, Esoteric Buddhism posits a multiple Dharmadhātu, in which all things transcend conditioned and relative existence; in it, each element of multiplicity is autonomous and all-pervading. The individual nature (*jishō*) of each being, a combination of matter and mind (*shikishin*), is not dissolved in a transcendental nondualism (*funi*) or in absolute identity (*ichinyo*), which characterize the singular Dharmadhātu. All dichotomies (ignorance and enlightenment, pure and impure, cause and effect, self and others, etc.) preserve their individual nature and do not get confused with each other. The substance of the twofold mandala (the Womb and the *Vajra* mandalas) is nondual, but there is no unity apart from dualism; the one is the two. However, since singular Dharmadhātu and multiple Dharmadhātu are perfectly interpenetrated, there is awakening in ignorance and ignorance in awakening.[28]

The cosmic Buddha as the origin of signs

Classical Mahayana maintained that the various buddhas are manifestations, in the form of *nirmaṇakāya* or *samboghakāya*, of a higher spiritual principle, the Dharmakāya, that remains beyond the reach of the senses and the intellect of sentient beings. Kūkai argued, against traditional Buddhology, that Mahāvairocana, the main Buddha of the Shingon school, is neither *nirmaṇakāya* nor *samboghakāya*, but is himself the Dharmakāya. Furthermore, he contended, the Dharmakāya is not silent and signless, but the source of all signs and languages. As a consequence, signs and languages are not conditioned, but are absolute entities that have the power to give both worldly benefits and supramundane salvation to their rightful users. *Hosshin seppō* refers to the idea that the preaching of the Dharma is made by Dainichi, the Dharmakāya Buddha himself and not just by the *nirmaṇakāya*, his provisional manifestation. This concept is stated for the first time in the *Ben kenmitsu nikyōron* (814), where it constitutes a powerful doctrinal justification of the salvational supremacy of the Esoteric teachings.

The idea that the Dharmakāya, eternal and immutable, keeps preaching the Dharma in some way, even after the nirvana of Śākyamuni, was already circulating in Japan also at a popular level before Kūkai's Esoteric doctrines became the predominant Buddhist paradigm. For example, the *Nihon ryōiki*, a collection of Buddhist tales compiled around 822, was not written under the influence of Kūkai's Esoteric Buddhism,[29] but includes stories about *rihosshin* (Dharmakāya-as-principle, that is, the Dharmakāya in its absolute form) as an entity manifesting itself in the world through signs and various kinds of "messages" (not just verbal ones) for the salvation of sentient beings.[30] Obviously, it would have been difficult to explain to non-Buddhists or even to a general Buddhist audience that the Dharmakāya was an absolute entity without attributes. Anyway, it is likely that a relatively organic theory of the "Dharmakāya's preaching" (*hosshin seppō*), grounded on the identification of Dainichi with the Dharmakāya (Jp. *hosshinbutsu*) originated in Tang China Esoteric circles and subsequently was developed in Japan by Kūkai, in the light of pre-existing conceptions widespread among his contemporary itinerant religious specialists and mountain ascetics.[31] As Yoshito Hakeda explains,

> Kūkai expanded the meaning of the word 'preaching.' He interpreted it as the acts of communication of the Dharmakāya Mahāvairocana. Oral preaching is only one of the means of communication [...] Kūkai's speculation along this line culminated in [the *Shōji jissōgi*, where he] asserts that the Dharmakāya Mahāvairocana is Reality and reveals himself through all objects of sense and thought [...] All phenomena point to the underlying Reality, Mahāvairocana, and at the same time are expressions of that Reality.[32]

Mahayana texts describe the preaching of the historical Buddha as a complex and polymateric act of communication, for Śākyamuni made use of various semiotic substances: verbal language, silence, gestures, colors, lights, and smells.[33] These manifold dimensions of Buddha's preaching may well have fascinated Kūkai, according to whom the senses and the sensible world were not only causes of delusion and suffering, but privileged vehicles of the Dharmakāya's messages. *Hosshin seppō* seems then to refer to that vast *bruit de fond*, a cosmic sea of never-ending communication, described by Michel Serres.[34]

Kūkai's interpretation of the Dharmakāya, considered as orthodox by the Kogi branch of Shingon, was challenged in the thirteenth century by the scholar-monk Raiyu (1226–1304) with his "empowerment body" doctrine (*kajishin setsu*), which later became the doctrinal trademark of the Shingi Shingon tradition. According to Raiyu, the Dharmakāya (Mahāvairocana), that is, the absolute and unconditioned Buddha-body, is essentially signless and speechless. The Dharmakāya is, however, endowed with a particular modality of existence, called the "empowerment body" (*kajishin*), which constitutes its semiotic aspect, and in particular its preaching faculty.

The starting point of the issue is the opening passage of the *Mahāvairocana Sutra* (*Dari jing*): "At one time, the Bhagavat abode in the great palace of the adamantine Dharma-world produced by the empowerment of the Tathāgata."[35] Śubhakarasiṃha and Yixing, in their commentary, made a distinction between the meanings of "Bhagavat" ("venerable one") and "Tathāgata" (lit. "Thus-come"), both in origin honorific appellations of the Buddha. According to the authors, "Bhagavat" refers to "Vairocana as the Dharmakāya in its essence" (*Birushana honji hosshin*), whereas "Tathāgata" indicates "the empowerment body of the Buddha" (*butsu kajishin*).[36] The *Commentary to the Mahāvairocana Sutra* (*Dari jing shu*) thus makes an initial distinction between these two modalities of the Buddha-body, based on the distinction between the pure mind of the Buddha (*shinnō*) and its mental functions (*shinjo*), which in turn suggests a difference between the Buddha as he really is and the Buddha as he appears, even to himself. The "faculty of empowerment" (*kajiriki*), in particular, seems to refer to the faculty of self-awareness. The *Commentary* further argues that the essence of Mahāvairocana's spontaneous enlightenment (*jishō sanbodai*), as the realization of the original unproduced nature of all things (*shohō honsho fushō*), transcends all mental states (*shukka issai shinji*). As such, it is beyond language (*gongo jinkyō*) and thought (*shingyō yaku jaku*). However, the authors (Śubhakarasiṃha and Yijing) suggest that the Buddha is aware that from such a state he could not save the beings. Accordingly, he enters the *samādhi* (meditative state) of the empowerment of supernatural powers (*jizai jinriki kaji-zanmai*) and manifests himself to all beings in an infinite variety of shapes.[37] This second passage from the *Commentary* seems to reinforce the previous distinction between an original state beyond thought and representation, and a state of empowerment in which the Buddha manifests himself and teaches the way of salvation to all beings.

With these statements as his starting point, Raiyu developed a theory of this elusive empowerment body. Raiyu begins by arguing that the Baghavat contains both an essential body (*honjishin*) and an empowerment body (*kajishin*). The essential body is signless (*musō*) and therefore transcends language,[38] since in the absolute and unconditioned realm of self-presence (*jishō*) that characterizes this modality of the Buddha there are neither true words (*nyogi go*) nor visualization (*kan*).[39] However, the essential body, while abiding in the "land of self-presence (*jishōdo*)," manifests the empowerment body and preaches the *Mahāvairocana Sutra*. This preaching took place only for Mahāvairocana's own pure pleasure of the Dharma (*hōraku*), and not in order to address a real audience. As Raiyu explains, the empowerment body corresponds to the *saṃbhogakāya* (*hōjin*); at this stage, the empowerment body is an epiphenomenon in the Buddha's mind related to the acquisition of self-awareness, described as "pleasure of the Dharma." The empowerment body is the author of the *Mahāvairocana Sutra* and corresponds to Mahāvairocana as represented in the central lotus of the mandala.[40]

The empowerment body is a form of the Buddha's pleasurable self-awareness that in turn generates other manifestation bodies for the benefit of sentient beings. We find here the idea of an entity or a process that turns the stasis of the unconditioned Buddha into movement, his silence into language, and his undifferentiatedness into signs. Such a change, produced by a specific activity, empowerment (*kaji*), is related to the Buddha's acquisition of a sense of self-awareness—and, as a consequence, of awareness of the existence of other beings as well.

At any rate, the entire universe is an ongoing, multimedial sermon/performance of the Buddha. As such, it can be envisioned as a text to be interpreted in order to find instructions about salvation. The idea that the entire universe is a sutra appears in India in the *Buddhāvataṃsaka sūtra* (Ch. *Da fangguang fo huayan jing*).[41] Kūkai developed on this idea and applied it to the *Mahāvairocana Sutra* and other Esoteric scriptures:[42]

> There are three versions of this sutra [*Mahāvairocana Sutra*]. The first is the spontaneous and unconditioned (*hōni*) and permanent text, that is, the Dharma mandala of all buddhas. The second is the large version circulating in the world, that is, the sutra in a hundred thousand verses transmitted by Nāgārjuna. The third is the abbreviated text of some three thousand verses. Even though it contains three thousand verses in seven fascicles, this abbreviated version embraces the larger ones as the few contains the numerous. One character contains unlimited meanings; one single stroke of the brush contains innumerable truths.[43]

As we can see, for Kūkai, the original and complete text of the scripture is the entire universe; Kūkai considers this scriptural modality of the universe as the Dharma mandala, one of the four kinds of mandala that structure the Esoteric universe, the one which manifests its linguistic and graphic modality of existence. Kūkai conceived of this cosmic text as "spontaneous and unconditioned (*hōni*) and permanent"—a veritable absolute entity coextensive with the Dharmakāya. Next, the second version of the scripture is the written text supposedly transmitted by the mythological figure Vajrasattva to the philosopher-bodhisattva Nāgārjuna inside the Iron Stūpa in south India; this is an abridged translation in human language of the cosmic text.[44] Finally, the third version of the sutra is a further abbreviation transmitted to East Asia and translated into Chinese by Śubhakarasiṃha (Ch. Shanwuwei, Jp. Zenmui, 637–735), the founder of Chinese Esoteric Buddhism. What unites these three versions is a logic not "of abridgment but of condensation";[45] the three versions, in fact, are not separate entities but "three mutually inclusive levels of the same sūtra."[46]

In these statements we find a correlation between scripture and mandala, each being a translation of the other in a different semiotic system (linguistic versus visual) and support (paper versus silk brocade). The fact that the entire universe can be envisioned as a text implies that it is a semiotic entity and, therefore, it is always-already articulated in expressions and contents; the semiotic articulation of reality is, in fact, one of the main subjects of Esoteric Buddhist semiotics.

The origin of language

Doctrines about Mahāvairocana's sermons, their actual utterer, and the textual dimension of the universe were also related to Esoteric Buddhist ideas on the origin of language and signs. Are they spontaneous, unconditioned entities that appear to be present in the world and are used by the Buddha in his cosmic sermon? Or, instead, are they artificial, conditioned entities created by someone for some specific purpose? We find both positions in Japanese Esoteric Buddhism. According to one interpretation, language was created by a deity (usually the Indian god Brāhma) or a semi-divine being. The second interpretation presents language as an absolute, unconditioned, and non-created entity.

The *Mahāvairocana Sutra* gives us an account of Mahāvairocana's *samādhi* in which language originates:

> In order to fulfill his original vow to save sentient beings, Mahāvairocana practiced [the recitation of] this mantra [the letter *A*]. Immersed in the *samādhi*, from all his voice organs he uttered the mantra in sounds resembling the voices of all living beings. With this utterance, new karmas rose and ripened in the beings in accordance with their original nature. As a result of these karmas, all kinds of letters of different colors and shapes, all kinds of language, and concepts corresponding [to these signs] manifested themselves. By means of these letters, language, and concepts, Mahāvairocana expounded the Dharma for the sake of all beings and they rejoiced.[47]

As Ryūichi Abé explains, "This appears to be the sūtra's mythopoetic depiction of what Kūkai has referred to as the generative process of signs (...), at which the primordial, protosemantic voice transforms itself into signs via letters."[48] We have here a clear connection between soteriology and linguistics, as languages and signs appear to be a manifestation of Mahāvairocana Buddha's "original vow to save sentient beings." The description of this process of manifestation is particularly interesting. First of all, Mahāvairocana chants the sound *A*—which presumably exists spontaneously and in an unconditioned fashion. As a karmic consequence of this primordial utterance, letters, languages, and concepts appear. The *Mahāvairocana Sutra* continues:

> No sooner had [Mahāvairocana delivered his teaching of the Dharma] than he came to issue forth from his pores all his transformation bodies [of buddhas and bodhisattvas], immeasurable as empty space. Amidst this boundless world, he pronounced the single syllable [*A*] indicative of his permeation in the universe, a syllable heard by his audience as a verse, the "procreation of Tathāgatas."[49]

Here we find several important elements: the universe is created by Mahāvairocana immersed in *samādhi*; the tool he employs in his mythopoetic act is the mantric seed letter *A*; and creation is the result of semiotic articulation, what Ryūichi Abé calls "semiogenesis."

Let us now turn our attention to the Sanskrit letter *A*. Why is it so important in Esoteric Buddhism? As Abé explains, the letter *A*

> is the origin of all the alphabet's letters, yet it stands at their origin only as a mark of absence—that is, the negation of unconditioned identity, immediacy, and permanence. The letter A is the origin of no origin. It is, quintessentially, the originally nonarising. In other words, the letter A ... stands for the very movement of differentiation.[50]

The Esoteric meaning of the letter *A* is based on two factors, namely, its position in the Sanskrit alphabet as the first letter, and its privative, negative value when used as a prefix (similar to the English "a-" in "ahistorical"). Thus, *A* is taken as referring to origin and unfolding, and at the same time, to uncreatedness (*honpushō*) that expresses the unconditioned nature of all things. In fact, the *Dari jing* further defines mantras as "spontaneous and unconditioned" (*hōni jinen*) entities, independent even from the Dharmakāya itself;[51] the Dharmakāya merely uses them to "express" or "represent" its own enlightenment. The movement of differentiation articulating language and the world is, at the same time, a centripetal movement toward homogeneity and undifferentiatedness—interrelated trajectories that are at the basis of the doctrines on the original condition of the Dharmakāya and its empowerment body (*kajishin*).

Mantras, in turn, gradually transform themselves (through a degenerative process) into the world's everyday languages; language outflows from the Dharmakāya. As Kūkai wrote,

> The origin of names is in the Dharmakāya. They all issue forth from him and turn into the languages circulating in the world. If one knows [the words'] true meanings those words are called mantras (*shingon*); if one does not know [the words'] ultimate origin, those are called false words [*mōgo*][52]

Kakuban also describes the origin of language in the following way:

> When we investigate into the origin of names and things, [we find that] they all come from mantras [...] Even though unenlightened beings, including the god Brāhma, do not understand true reality, at least they understand words and names. Thus, the Tathāgata, out of compassion, taught them the *brāhmī* script (*bonji*). Brāhma learned it first and then transmitted it to the other beings. Humans, gods, demons, and animals, all use those sacred words (*shōgo*).[53]

In this passage it is striking that Kakuban does not distinguish between the "language of Brāhma" (*bongo*, i.e. Sanskrit) and "Brāhma's writing" (*bonji*, i.e. the writing system of Sanskrit known as *brāhmī*); thus, it is not clear whether the Tathāgata taught Brāhma a written or a spoken language. In any case, "secret words" (mantras) were, according to Kakuban, the first language used by sentient beings. Other accounts explain that, while supernatural beings have preserved their original mantric language, human beings, because of their delusion, have turned it into a degenerated form of communication—the various languages spoken in the world today. Among them, only Sanskrit was able to preserve some connection with the original "sacred words."

The Tendai scholar monk Annen (841–895?) adds that Sanskrit "was originally taught by the buddhas of the past to give religious instructions." However, "after the buddhas left this world, Brāhma sent his three children to the realm of desire [our world]" and spread the three writing systems.[54] Several centuries later, a text entitled *Bonkan taieishū*, written in 1581 by the Buddhist priest Ryōjō, presents an interesting synopsis of several accounts about the origin of language:

> According to master Bodhiruci, characters were first written by Brāhma, the king of the gods, who inscribed them on *tāla* tree leaves. It is also said that the bodhisattva Fugen [Sk. Samantabhadra] appeared as Brāhma [and created the writing system]. [According to yet another account,] at the beginning of the present *kalpa* [cosmic cycle] Brāhma and Viṣṇu got married and gave birth to three children, namely, Brāhma, Kharoṣṭha,

> and Cangjie. Brāhma created the *brāhmī* script in India—the forty-seven syllables [of the Sanskrit alphabet] still used today. Kharoṣṭha went to the Dragon Palace and created the *kharoṣṭhi* alphabet, written left to right. Finally, Cangjie was Iśāna/Maheśvara, that is, the Lord of the Sixth Heaven; he later flew to China where he invented the Chinese characters written vertically.[55]

This citation refers to an unknown text by Bodhiruci (d. 527), a monk from northern India who translated several Buddhist scriptures into Chinese. The leaves of the *tāla* tree were used in ancient India as a support for writing letters and documents; Mahayana scriptures were also written on those leaves. Kharoṣṭha is the name of a legendary Indian ascetic; some sources attribute to him the creation of the *kharoṣṭhi* alphabet, a form of writing used in north-western India and parts of central Asia between the fourth century BCE and the fourth century CE. This alphabet was written from right to left, not from left to right as Ryōjō writes; but the citation passage probably refers to other alphabets, more exotic to the Japanese, from further west, written from left to right. (European missionaries had already arrived to Japan when Ryōjō was writing.) The Dragon Palace (*ryūgū*) is a mythological place located at the bottom of the sea where Buddhist scriptures and magical objects are kept. Cangjie is a Chinese legendary figure: as a minister of the mythological Yellow Emperor, he is attributed with the invention of Chinese characters.[56]

Several medieval texts also emphasize that the language of India (Jp. *bongo*, that is, Sanskrit) is the "correct language" (*shōon*), as opposed to that of China which is a "marginal language" (*bōon*)—a theme that recurs in many medieval discussions on the subject. In other words, medieval Japanese scholars thought that Sanskrit was the true language, as the language created directly by the buddhas and the gods; Chinese was a kind of secondary language created through imitation of nature and therefore was unable to tell the ultimate truth about things.[57] This opposition between Sanskrit and Chinese was based on the fact that esoteric Buddhism and Confucianism had different ideas about the origin of language. Kūkai wrote that "the Confucian teachings are presented through natural patterns drawn on the backs of tortoises and on dragons."[58] More specifically,

> When [the ancient rulers] had observed the changing of the seasons in the sun, moon, and stars, and the process of transformation at work on the nine continents, then with the sounds of metal and jade, of pipes and reeds, they forged their patterns (Ch. *wen*, Jp. *mon*) in order to nurture the common man.[59]

In contrast, Kūkai wrote that the "Buddhist truth is transmitted through letters [*mon*] which spontaneously appeared in the sky and among men."[60] This passage refers to the appearance in the sky of the Sanskrit letter *A* as the result of Esoteric practice.[61] As we have seen, according to a different Indian doctrine, reported in the *Mahāvairocana Sutra*, Sanskrit letters are not the product of conditioned causation, but spontaneous and autonomous (*hōni jinen*) entities.[62]

In this way, Buddhism—and Esoteric Buddhism in particular—is intrinsically superior to other teachings because of the ontological status of the linguistic medium that transmits it. While non-Buddhist teachings are based on conventional sign systems derived from the imitation of natural patterns and regularities, Buddhism is conveyed by an unconditioned and spontaneous language. While non-Buddhist languages are "marginal" and fallacious, Buddhist language is able to speak and manifest the truth. In particular, that of mantras is the true language because, as Kūkai wrote, "it alone can designate infallibly the reality of objects as they truly are."

The semiotic articulation of reality

Kūkai also began to study the way in which the cosmic discourse of the Dharmakāya was organized, and especially its signs. He wrote:

> The Buddha [Mahāvairocana] reveals his teachings (*seppō*) necessarily by means of signs (*monji*). These signs are constituted by the six kinds of objects, whose origin lies in turn in the three secrets of the Dharmakāya.[63]

Here Kūkai envisions the signs (*mon*, *monji*) of Mahāvairocana's discourse (*hosshin seppō*) as constituted by the particularities to be found in the sense objects (the material and mental components of reality); from these particularities people can grasp the characteristics of each entity. Kūkai added that "differences are signs (*monji*), because every particularity is a pattern (*mon*); each pattern (*mon*) has its own name, that is why it is called *monji*."[64] These signs are multi-semiotic like divination diagrams:

> in the sermons delivered by the Buddha, a single syllable [...], like the signs on the back of a tortoise and the diagrams of the *Yijing*, bears the endless multiplicity of reality; like Indra's net and Śakradeva's grammar text, it contains countless meanings.[65]

Chinese divination was able to explain the complexity and the integration of the universe through a limited repertory of discrete expressions, because it presupposed the existence of isomorphisms among the phenomena (and also of codes of transposition). Kūkai's identification of the divination signs of the *Yijing* with the mantric expressions and with Indian references to Indra's net (a metaphor for the interrelated nature of all phenomena) and Śakradeva's putative original grammatical text, is most telling, as an attempt toward the integration of the Indian Tantric world-view with the Chinese correlative one.

The concepts of *mon* and *monji* play an important role in Kūkai's *Shōji jissōgi*; they appear as many as forty-three times in that text, and yet their meanings remain rather elusive. There is an almost total agreement among contemporary scholars that Kūkai's *mon* and *monji* refer to linguistic entities, even though some interpret them as "writing, written language, script," and others as "verbal language." Others yet are aware of the semantic breadth of Kūkai's terms and try to explain them as "words in the broadest sense," or as "language in a broad sense," in a vague gesture toward a language that would encompass virtually everything—including objects most different from ordinary linguistic units, such as phenomena of reality.[66] Current interpretations are clearly inadequate.

The matter is made even more complicated by the fact that in modern Japanese language, *mon*, read *bun*, refers to written sentences, and *monji*, read *moji*, designates written characters; but Kūkai's use of the terms does not coincide with contemporary usage. In fact, *mon/monji* appears to be the equivalent in the visual and grammatological fields of another term, *shōji*, which refers instead to the phonic-linguistic nature of reality.[67]

It is possible to divide the meanings of Kūkai's *mon/monji* into four main semantic fields: (i) linguistic elements, such as tones and inflections of spoken language, phonemes and syllables, and words; (ii) semiotic elements, such as visual patterns (synonym of *aya*, "pattern"), differences and particularities of visual objects (*shikihō*), differences and particularities of all six kinds of objects (*rokujin*), and more generally phenomena (as a synonym of the contemporary terms *araware* or *genshō*, lit., "phenomena"); (iii) writing, such as graphemes, ideographs, and pictograms; and (iv) written texts. Fields (iii) and (iv) are the most common meanings today: (i) is mostly peculiar to Buddhist philosophical texts; and (ii) was developed primarily by Kūkai as a way to clarify the nature of the preaching of the Dharmakāya (*hosshin seppō*).

One of Kūkai's definitions of *monji* considers them particularities and differences (*shabetsu*) in the six kinds of objects (*rokujin* or *rokkyō*), even though in his work he dealt almost exclusively with the audible and the visible realms—perhaps because Esoteric practices in general are based on chanting and visualization, and the other senses have a secondary role. In addition to his theories on linguistic signs, Kūkai examined in detail also the visual objects (*shikihō*), i.e. the material objects of our world. He applied the Yogācāra epistemology (discussed in Chapter One) to explain how objects are perceived and understood:

> All perceptions of sight (colors, shapes, and movements) result from the operations of the eye and form the field of visual entities. [At the same time,] they are the result of the operations of the eye-consciousness, constitute the field of entities pertaining to the eye-consciousness, and are

> caused by the eye-consciousness. [At the same time,] they are the result of the operations of the mind-consciousness [Jp. *ishiki*; Sk. *mano-vijñāna*], constitute the field of entities pertaining to the mind-consciousness, and are caused by the mind-consciousness.[68]

Next, he defined "differences" (*shabetsu*) as the conceptual entities resulting from this cognitive process: "Such differences are signs (*monji*), because each individual aspect is a semiotic pattern (*mon*)."[69] As examples of visual objects Kūkai indicates paintings, decorative patterns on textiles, colors, and every particularity of visible forms;[70] these are not what Japanese authors call "words in a broad sense" (a very vague expression anyway), but, rather, *signs*.[71] Kūkai further outlines three kinds of visual objects and their semiotic aspects, namely, colors (*shiki*), forms (*gyō*), and movements (*hyō*);[72] later commentators further discussed this doctrine for which Kūkai only provided a brief outline. For example, the scholar monk Dōhan (1184–1252) wrote that colors are signs (*monji*) of visual objects (*shikijin*); sounds are signs of aural objects (*shōjin*), the smell of incense is a sign of smell objects (*kōjin*); types of flavors (strong, light, etc.) are signs of taste objects (*mijin*); tactile smoothness and roughness are signs of touch objects (*shokujin*); and mental factors and states (*shinjo*) are signs of mental objects (*hōjin*);[73] a more detailed list was developed by Raiyu.[74]

In an explicitly semiotic perspective, *monji* can be defined as *particularities, characteristics, modalities of the material dharmas, determined by the discriminative activity of consciousness on the basis of general categories.* This definition can be further articulated as: (i) synonym of *sō* (*lakśaṇa* or *nimitta*), aspects and particularities of the objects, patterns identified on, the things (according to the state of consciousness of the interpreter), and (ii) representations of the above material patterns, images produced by the activity of consciousness on the basis of abstract categories (semantic fields such as "colors, forms, and movements"[75] and semantic axes such as high/low, to go/to come, etc.).

The concept of *mon/monji* is thus a general label for many different phenomena, ranging from the semantic markers of the objects (marks of the properties making it possible to discriminate between phenomena), to the semantic axes and fields in which these marks are structured. These are the most elementary levels of the series of orders and codes in which the Esoteric cosmos is articulated. According to the Yogācāra epistemology, which played a very important role in conceptual framework of Kūkai's *Shōji jissōgi*, there is in practice no distinction between (i) and (ii), i.e. the patterns on the objects and their representations, both being visual phenomena and, therefore, material entities.

Another aspect of signs is their connection with the mind as the source of meaning. For instance, Kūkai wrote: "All signs (*monji*) issue forth from the mind. Mind is the root, the signs are the branches [...] the mind is internal, signs are external."[76] In other words, signs are not just mimetic representations of the external reality (things); signs are also externalized doubles of the mind, which is their internal origin. In this way, Esoteric semiosis is a mimetic continuum centered on signs (written signs in particular) connecting reality and mind. This is not at all surprising, given the fact that the dominant form of Buddhist epistemology stated that everything is a product of the mind.

And yet, Kūkai's *monji* are not just elements in a semiosic process resulting in fallacious representations. The human mind is a condensation of the cosmic Mind of the Dharmakāya Mahāvairocana Buddha, in turn coextensive with the Dharmakāya's body (Dharmadhātu, that is, reality). As articulations of reality, *monji* are also articulations of the Dharmakāya's cosmic sermon (*hosshin seppō*) and are endowed with an ontological value. Kūkai refused to consider the words uttered by the Buddha and the signs of his multimedial sermon as mere expedient means and gave them instead an absolute value, thus opening up the way for the transformation of the universe in a hierarchy of structured salvific messages, and of the Dharmakāya in a colossal semiotic machine in which everything was interrelated with everything else.

Correlative thinking

We have already seen that Esoteric Buddhism envisions the universe as the body of the cosmic buddha, and everything within it is meaningful and part of a never ending salvific activity. An influential text in the Japanese Buddhist canon states:

> in Mahāvairocana's body-and-land, environment and beings are interpenetrated, essence and signs are identical; Suchness pervades the Dharmadhātu and the body-speech-mind of the Supreme Self [Mahāvairocana] are undifferentiated, like cosmic space. Space is a sacred place, and the Dharmadhātu is the practitioner's residence.[77]

Shingon exegetes engaged themselves in a constant theoretical labor to define the principles and practical consequences of this vision, which goes beyond specialized religious practice to potentially affect all aspects of everyday life. It was necessary to show how Mahāvairocana and sentient beings are interpenetrated, how essences and signs are identical, and what this all means in practical terms. The most powerful model available to the premodern Japanese for explaining the regular and foreseeable interactions of macrocosm (Mahāvairocana's Dharmadhātu), microcosm (each individual sentient being), and mesocosm (society) was the Chinese correlative cosmology, which came to be integrated with Indian Tantric thought.

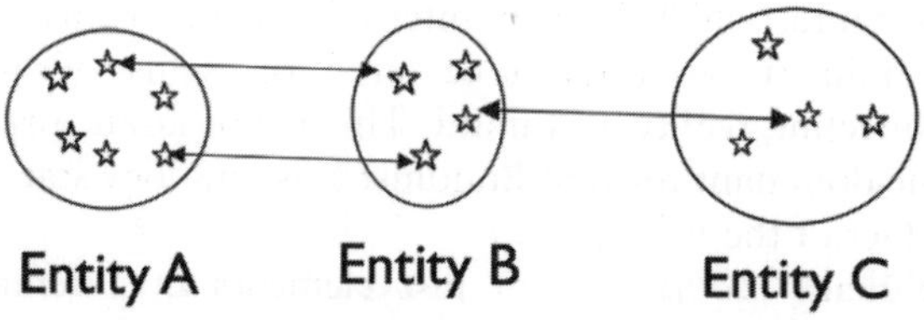

FIGURE 2.1 *Relations among alloforms*

Criteria of correlation, however arbitrary, were not purely conventional. Elements were associated analogically on the basis of metaphorical and metonymical relations through processes that have never been exhaustively studied. In general, once a contact point between two elements was found, a total transfer of their properties takes place, in order to confer to each one of both terms *all* attributes of the other. (See Figure 2.1.)

As we have already seen, Allan Grapard has identified an "episteme of identity" in premodern Japanese Buddhism; in light of Tsuda Shin'ichi's suggestions, we can identify three related elements in this epistemic field: the "logic of yoga," the principle of "symbolic omnipotence," and symbolic practices.[78] None of these was peculiar to Esoteric Buddhism; nevertheless, they concurred, together with other postulates and corollaries, in determining the originality of its system. According to the logic of yoga, which appears in various forms in most Esoteric texts, every object is: (i) part of or reducible to one of several cosmic series (natural elements, seasons, directions, colors, internal organs of the body, stages in the process leading to salvation, and so forth), which constitute multiple microcosmic orders; (ii) correlated to homologous objects in every other cosmic series (earth=spring =east=yellow=liver=arousing the thought of enlightenment, and so on); and (iii) substantially identical to the totality of the enlightened universe. As a matter of fact, according to the Esoteric teachings, all cosmic series are nothing other than transformations of the same substance and substratum-space, defined in various ways (*hokkai*, *isshin*, *shinnyo*); for this reason, the parts and the whole share the same characteristics. The direct precedent for this conceptual system in Japan was the Chinese correlative thought based on the interactions among the five fundamental constituents of reality (Ch. *wuxing*, Jp. *gogyō*, i.e. earth, water, wood, fire, and metal) and their transformations.[79] Chinese five agents form a closed set, regulated by a rigorous combinatory logic. According to Léon Vandermeersch, the elements in each series "respond to each other within the same structure and reveal the orderly unity of the universe. Through inexhaustible correspondences, phenomena… appear very easily… as each other's signs."[80] However, we are dealing here with more than semiotic resonances. As Bruce Lincoln points out, describing the correlative mechanisms in ancient Indo-European cultures,

> The... items in any such correlation are thus placed in homologic relation, a fundamental consubstantiality and interchangeability being posited between them. Each item in such a homology is thus seen to consist of and derive from the material substance of the other. The... items are thus what I call *alloforms*—that is, alternative shapes of one another.[81]

In this way, earth does not just "stand for" spring or the east; these three items are "alternative shapes of one another," particular occurrences of the different modes (elemental, seasonal, directional, and so forth) of the underlying cosmic substance (*taidai*). Such a substantial identity was always counterbalanced by phenomenal, actual differences: similarity, as already suggested by James Boon for the Tantric culture in Bali, never means absolute identity,[82] but is always stipulated within conflicting positions of identity/difference in a coherent nondualistic logic. Such logic neither establishes a relation between pairs of objects, as Tsuda Shin'ichi believes, nor reduces differences to a uniform and undifferentiated substratum; on the contrary, the Dharmadhātu is described as a complex combination of different entities. What Allan Grapard has called "episteme of identity" can in fact be reformulated as an episteme of "multiple identities" or "identical multiplicities"; this situation was elaborated by premodern Japan authors in the doctrines of singular and multiple Dharma Realm previously discussed.

This correlative and combinatory episteme allowed for the possibility to control objects and states of the world through the manipulation of certain symbolic entities connected to them (principle of symbolic omnipotence). Here lay the conceptual nucleus of the so-called magical practices in medieval Japan, which, far from just being instances of superstition, were on the contrary also supported by a sophisticate intellectual system centered on systematic correlation. The principle of symbolic omnipotence in turn generated practices based on the actual manipulation of symbolic entities. This episteme operated on various levels of sense, the most relevant of which were semiosophia and semiognosis, on a theoretical and initiatory level, and semiopietas, on an uninformed level of everyday praxis (see Chapter One). Together, they generated a common mentality, whose core was a combinatory and transformative nebula of beliefs and practices, and the idea that the cosmos was a continuous transformation of shapes. In addition, within the closed and orderly yin-yang cosmos, realm of sympathy and resonance, "signs, conceived of as a clue of a hidden reality, are also instruments for action upon reality: they give rise to events, as well as they express or foretell them."[83] It is in this sense that everyday actions, in so far as they are actualization of correlative series, are part of a large cosmic soteriological design. This system was coherent and systematic, but also open to new additions, which made it singularly dynamic and resilient to opposition—to the extent that even medieval heretical movements such as the Ichinengi and the Tachikawa-ryū also employed correlations.[84]

One Japanese text is particularly important to understand the dynamics of premodern Japanese correlative thought, the *Gorin kujimyō himitsushaku* by Kakuban (1195–1147). This text and its sources present a combination of Indian Tantric teachings and practices and Chinese doctrines and rituals, mainly drawn from medicine and alchemy (especially from texts such as the *Huangdi nei jing su wen*) and Daoism, with a strong emphasis on correlative systems.[85] These ideas, especially after the treatment by Kakuban and others, became the template of Japanese Esoteric Buddhism and also influenced various aspects of cultural life in medieval Japan, such as music, linguistics, and poetry.

The practices these texts describe consist mainly in visualizing the universe as a *stūpa* in five elements representing the five fundamental shapes (a square/cube, circle/sphere, triangle/pyramid, crescent/half section of a sphere, and sphere/water drop). It gradually develops into Mount Sumeru, the Buddhist cosmic mountain,[86] and later comes to coincide with the ascetic himself. By becoming a *stūpa*, that is, the mystic and cosmic body of the Buddha, the practitioner is able to become a buddha himself. This ritual is based on visualizations of three sets of five-syllable mantras, respectively: *a va ra ha kha; a vaṃ raṃ haṃ khaṃ;* and *a vi ra hūṃ khaṃ.* As Kakuban explained, the five-syllable mantra is

> the general substance of the six elements and the four kinds of mandala, the differentiated aspects of the four Buddha bodies and the three secrets, the goal of the four saintly beings and the six destinations, the true form of the five paths and the four kinds of birth; therefore, it [this mantra] subjugates the four kinds of demons and produces liberation from the six paths.[87]

The underlying idea is that these mantric seeds develop into a number of cosmic orders, all organized in quinary series. Mantras, that is Mahāvairocana's absolute and unconditioned language, is thus presented as the starting point of the Esoteric cosmos.

Next, these texts establish systematic correlations between the five-syllable mantras and the five buddhas of the mandala of the two realms (*ryōbu* or *ryōkai mandara*), the five supreme wisdoms associated with each of them, the five phases of Shingon soteriology, the five cosmic elements (both Indian and Chinese) and their primary colors, seasons, directions, the human body (internal organs and their superficial protrusions), and the human cognitive apparatus. Kakuban expands this system by adding correlations to include planets and Indian and Chinese deities. Later authors further developed Kakuban's synthesis by providing even more complex series of correlations, thus expanding enormously the potential impact of mandalic thought and practices. For example, the Tendai/Zen monk Yōsai (or Eisai, 1141–1215) understood space-time and cosmic matter as the physical substratum of salvation, and beings as mental entities (*shinjū*) in Mahāvairocana's original mind; he also established a series connecting the entire universe as a combination of correlations, Mahāvairocana's mind, Mahāvairocana's Dharmadhātu Palace (Hokkaigū), and the body-mind of sentient beings.[88] He further developed his views in another text he wrote towards the end of his life, *Kissa yōjōki*, in which he extolled the virtues of tea drinking for the maintenance of the cosmic balance within one's psycho-physical complex.

The delicate and dynamic balance between differentiation and centralization is also present in other texts devoted to Shingon correlative thought.[89] Open-ended clusters of alloforms, objects, actions, states, and qualities—distinct occurrences of the different modes of the cosmic substance, form those peculiar esoteric semiotic entities I call microcosmic macrosigns. A macrosign, the matrix of the Esoteric system of meaning, is always unconditioned for it transcends any definition that is not a mere list of some of its elementary components. These components can indifferently be signifiers or signifieds to each other: as Pier Paolo Pasolini wrote, "in reality there is no 'signified': *because the signified is also a sign*."[90] Every object or image in visualization represents, as Umberto Eco put it, "an organic *imago mundi*, an image of the world that is the result of a divine textual strategy."[91] The best example of macrosign is perhaps the five-element *stūpa* (Jp. *gorintō*, also known as five-element mandala or *gorin mandara*) (see Figure. 2.2).

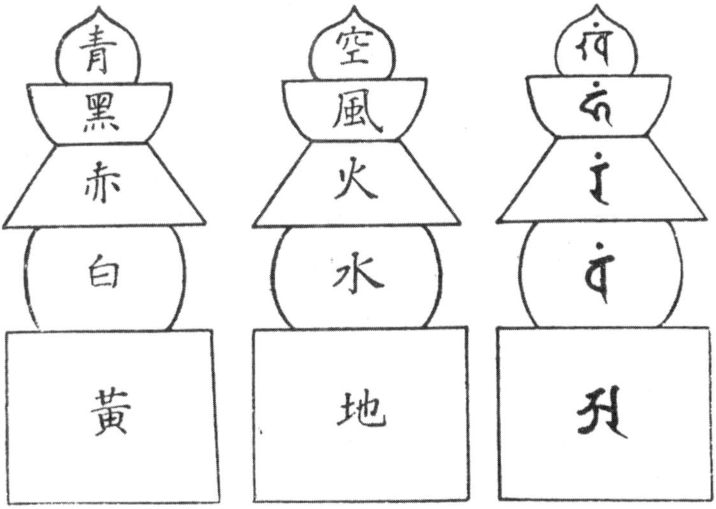

FIGURE 2.2 Gorin mandara. Left: the primary colors (bottom to top: yellow, white, red, black, and blue); center: the five cosmic elements (bottom to top: earth, water, fire, wind/air, and space); right: the five-syllable mantra *a vaṃ raṃ haṃ khaṃ*. *From* Gorin kujimyō himitsushaku *by Kakuban. In T. 79, p. 12c.*

This materialistic correlative cosmology generated a philosophical problem concerning the ontological status of the various differentiated elements. Yōsai attempted to explain differentiation by emphasizing the "static and permanent" (*jōjū*) aspect of absolute reality and the fact that all differences were only superficial attributes of beings who are, after all, part of Mahāvairocana.[92] The Shingon scholar-monk Raihō wrote a tract dealing with the nature of differentiation, entitled *Shohō funbetsushō*, where he developed Shingon ideas about the absolute nature of the five (and six) elements as the unconditioned material body of the Dharmakāya. Raihō argued that the five-element *stūpa*, as the innate shape of the Dharmadhātu—what he calls "Dharmadhātu *stūpa* (*hokkai tōba*),[93] is the origin of all body-mind complexes of the universe; it is also the place where beings return to after death.[94] In this way, Raihō opened the way for the systematic adoption of the five-element *stūpa* as the model for funeral monuments and ancestor tablets in Japan. Raihō further introduces a distinction between two kinds of five-element *stūpa*: while one is "unchangeable" (*fuhen*), the other is "conditioned" (*zuien*). The unchangeable *stūpa* is the absolute and unconditioned, plural and at the same time undifferentiated, substance of the Dharmadhātu, whereas the conditioned *stūpa* is the product of the combination of such absolute multiple substance. This distinction is also present within the human body.[95] In this text, Raihō uses systematic correlations to develop Shingon materialistic cosmology and ontology in a way that recognizes the multiplicity of the real and the absolute value of profane phenomena without sacrificing the centralizing power of the *stūpa*.

The *stūpa* (Jp. *sotoba*; also called *seitei* from the Sanskrit *caitya*) has a rich symbolism: it is cosmic axis, body of the Buddha, container of Buddha's relics, funeral monument, memorial tablet for the ancestors, but also symbol of the place where initiation to Esoteric Buddhism takes place.[96] The five-element *stūpa* has some iconic aspects, in that it reproduces the original shape of the five elements, i.e. the material substance of the Dharmadhātu; as such, it offers the image of the subtle body of both the buddha and the practitioner. However, as with most Esoteric signs, this *stūpa* is not just a reproduction, an image, but a "sample" of the absolute reality, of which it presents all fundamental features and functions. Correlative series constituting the *stūpa* macrosign contain elements organized according to directional processes (as in the stages in the path toward salvation), hierarchical modes (the levels of beings, or the buddhas with Mahāvairocana at the top), or by circular arrangements (as in the five agents of Chinese cosmology, or in the cycle of seasons). Accordingly, the five-element *stūpa* presents a twofold (or rather, nondual) deep structure (see Figure. 2.3).

The five-element *stūpa* represents the Dharmadhātu both in its appearance (verticality, hierarchy, difference), and in its recursive deep structure (undifferentiatedness)—a clever image of the nondualism (*funi*) lying at the basis of the Esoteric episteme. This *stūpa* was also interpreted in light of

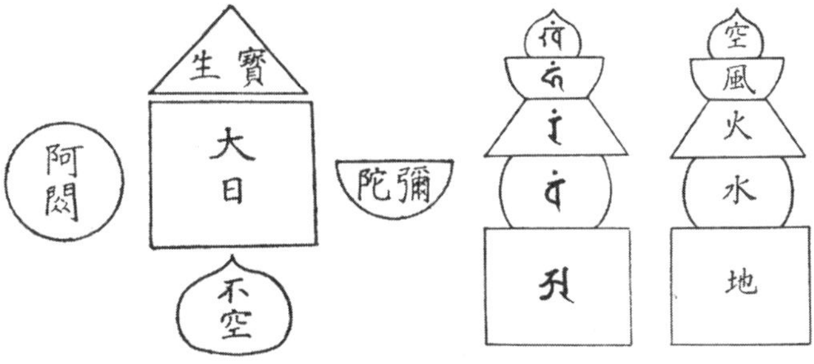

FIGURE 2.3 Gorin mandara: *hierarchy and circularity*. Left: the five central Buddhas of the mandala (*gobutsu*; center: Mahāvairocana; left: Akśobhya, bottom: Amoghasiddhi; right: Amitabha; and top: Ratnasambhava). Center: the five-syllable mantra. Right: the five cosmic elements. *From* Gorin kujimyō himitsushaku *by Kakuban. In T. vol. 79, pp. 12c–13a. Tokyo: Daizō shuppan.*

dominant combinatory paradigms associating elements drawn from Indian, Chinese, and Japanese lore and texts. For example, an early fourteenth-century Tendai encyclopedia presents this *stūpa* not just as an abstract model of the cosmos and the individual practitioner, but as concrete objects and places,[97] such as the Iron Stūpa in South India (*Nanten tettō*) where the Indian Budhdist philosopher Nāgārjuna was believed to have received the initiation to the *Jinggang ding jing*;[98] with the *stūpa* built by king Kinzoku in northern Indian near which the Womb mandala appeared in the sky to the Esoteric Buddhist patriarch Śubhakarasiṃha; with the Treasure Tower described in the *Lotus Sutra*;[99] and with the cavern in which the Shinto sun goddess Amaterasu hid herself tired of her brother Susanoo's mischief.[100] When the components of the five-element *stūpa* came to include canonical and extra-canonical sources, especially Japanese mythology, this macrosign could be used as a symbol of the triumph of order over chaos (Amaterasu's story) as a metaphor for the attainment of enlightenment.[101] Even though all Esoteric texts stress that afflictions (*bonnō*) are identical with enlightenment (*bodai*), and that enlightenment is the realization of this principle—often described as Nāgārjuna entering the Iron *Stūpa* to receive the initiation into the Esoteric teachings,[102] still enlightenment was presented as a form of compliance with authority and obedience to rules and protocols.[103]

Mandala: the fundamental model of the universe

As we have seen, the entire universe of Esoteric Buddhism is an immense mandala, produced by the Dharmakāya during meditation through manipulation of semiotic substances that are already preexisting as unconditioned entities; the cosmos is always-already structured on a deep level and semiosis is the manipulation of this underlying structure. Moreover, Esoteric semiosis coincides with soteriology: on the one hand, everything the Dharmakāya does, thinks, or speaks, is for his pure pleasure of the Dharma (*hōraku*); on the other hand, all this is for the benefit of sentient beings who can thus attain enlightenment. Enlightenment is defined by Kūkai and later exegetes as a knowledge concerning the functioning of languages and signs and their relations to the absolute reality of the enlightened universe. Let us now take a closer look at mandala and its semiotic principles.[104]

Definitions

Mandala is a visual object (in Sanskrit *maṇḍala* means "circle") representing a symbolic matrix of the universe, often depicted as a complex icon with many deities; it plays a central role in Esoteric Buddhism as both the underlying structure and perceptible apparition/representation of the cosmic substance and its endless salvific activity. In practical terms, mandala is a Buddhist sacred space inside or before which rituals and various kinds of religious practices are performed. Its primal models are the area surrounding the *pippalā* tree under which Śākyamuni attained nirvana, the ritual platform (Jp. *dan*), and the temple. A space structured around a center is probably "based on the prescientific experience of a human being observing the horizon and the celestial vault of which he occupies the center."[105] Pictorial representations of sacred space, today's best-known mandala, probably developed out of ritual platforms. Gradually, a mandalic vision was applied also to the ascetic's body and to the world.

The most common mandalas are two-dimensional; drawn on paper or cloth, they are hung on temple walls or spread out on altar tops as focal points for Buddhist ceremonies and ritual actions (mainly, veneration and contemplation). As Elizabeth ten Grotenhuis explains, "A two-dimensional mandala, however, is meant to be transformed into a three-dimensional realm, usually a palatial structure, by means of contemplation and ritual. In their two-dimensional form, these mandalas often look like architectural ground plans, seen from an aerial perspective."[106]

Among the many definitions of mandala, one of the most suggestive has been proposed by Giuseppe Tucci, who called it a "psychocosmogram"[107]—a graphic representation of the cosmos and the individual spirit of the ascetics. According to Yamasaki Taikō, "the esoteric *mandala* illustrates enlightenment, and so the true self ... [It] symbolically represents the 'universal form' of all things and beings."[108] More recently, Ryuki Washio, Chief Abbot of the Tōji temple in Kyoto wrote in the catalog of an exhibition of mandalas:

> The term mandala is a transliterated Sanskrit word meaning "a thing with an essential value." The "essential value" is the Dharma or universal truth which governs all laws and phenomena. However, we have forgotten this essential value and as a result suffer from anxiety and confusion in our daily lives. The mandala is the concrete symbol of this essential value which is hidden in the innermost recess of our hearts. In other words, we have mandalas in our minds which are blessed by the Buddha's wisdom and mercy. When we realize this, we will understand the nature of our real existence. The universe depicted in the mandala is the same universe which exists in our minds.
>
> I hope that this exibition will give everyone an opportunity to understand this universe and lead them towards an encounter with their true being.[109]

It would be easy to dismiss this as just another form of New Age obscurantism presenting "our real existence" as something separate from our daily life, since "our true being" is to be "encountered" in the understanding of and subjection to the "universal truth which governs all laws and phenomena." However, mandala is not (or not just) the arrangement of mystical visions and enlightenments guided by a universal and mysterious inner necessity of human spirit, as suggested by Giuseppe Tucci under the influence of Carl Gustav Jung. Received definitions such as these raise interesting problems: which are the codes of this representation? What is its underlying semiotic system? Usual psychological and iconographic approaches ignore these questions and fail to explain the epistemic nature of the relations connecting the Esoteric cosmos with the mandala. In fact, mandala is the result of a more or less conscious material (and semiotic) effort to create a definite object as an answer to doctrinal, historical, and cultural impulses.

If we interpret the catalog citation above not as a description, but rather as a normative statement, an entire discursive field unfolds before us: that of the ideological functions of mandala. In this new perspective, statements such as "We have mandalas in our minds" or "The universe depicted in the mandala is the same universe which exists in our minds" should be read as attempts to convince us that our mind innately (and probably "unconsciously") understands and reflects a certain cosmic order, in spite of "anxiety and confusion" that plague "our daily lives" as a consequence of our "forgetting" the "universal truth." We can detect here a complex set of issues concerning self-identity (opposing our daily selves to our mandalic minds), semiotics (mandala as a representation of a mental universe which "is the same" as the external universe governed by the Dharma), and power (the delineation of a supreme and unchangeable cosmic order).

This ideological approach to mandala is not just a personal agenda animated by contemporary concerns. Kūkai had already raised similar issues in a memorial to the Japanese imperial court describing the items he had brought back to Japan after his study trip to China:

> The Dharma is beyond speech, but without speech it cannot be revealed. Suchness transcends forms, but without depending on forms it cannot be realized. [...] The Buddha's teachings are indeed the treasures that help pacify the nation and bring benefits to the people.
>
> Since the Esoteric Buddhist teachings are so profound and mysterious as to defy expression in writing, they are revealed through the medium of painting to those who are yet to be enlightened. The various postures and *mudrās* [depicted in mandalas] are products of the great compassion of the Buddha; with a single glance [at them] one becomes buddha. The secrets of the sutras and commentaries are in general depicted in the paintings, and all the essentials of the Esoteric Buddhist doctrines are set forth therein. Neither masters nor students can dispense with them.[110]

As these words by Kūkai make clear, mandalas are complex systems of representation that try to overcome the limitations of signs to express the Buddhist Dharma in its fullness: paintings that express through forms that which is formless. Here lies the epistemological paradox of mandala—and perhaps, of sacred art in general as well. Mandalas are not just pictorial translations of speech; they are maps of Suchness. As a systematic model of the cosmos, a mandala is a powerful device for absorbing heterogeneous elements, providing them with well-defined status within the Buddhist Esoteric tradition. At the background of every mandalic object lay one or more texts, a set of doctrines, a certain cosmological and soteriological outlook, knowledge of religious and ritual practices, and social and political ideas. Furthermore, mandalas are not merely pointers, "fingers pointing at the moon" easily mistaken with the moon itself, but are envisioned as endowed with an intrinsic salvific power generated by the compassion of the Buddha; as Kūkai wrote, "with a single glance [at them] one becomes buddha." The practice of mandala consists in manipulating signs in order to affect reality and to produce in the practitioner a different perception of reality.

Typologies

There are several kinds of mandala, each kind being very different from all the others, and whose only common ground seems to be the fact that they represent a sacred realm and its inhabitants in various visual formats. We have the mandala proper, as it is defined in Esoteric Buddhism; mandala representing specific deities (*besson mandara*); paintings of the Pure Land; and images of Shinto-Buddhist combinatory cultic centers and their deities (*suijaku mandara*, *sankei mandara*). In addition, some particularly precious cult images, such as the calligraphic work "Namu Myōhō rengekyō" by Nichiren, are also called mandala.

The paradigmatic form of mandala in Japanese Esoteric Buddhism is called the Mandala of the Two Realms (*ryōkai mandara*) or Twofold Mandala (*ryōbu mandara*). Esoteric Buddhism, in fact, envisions mandala as a combination of two distinct but inseparable parts. The first mandala of the pair, commonly known as *taizōkai* (Sk. *garbhadhātu*, "womb realm" or "matrix") *mandara*, represents the Dharma as it is revealed to the non-enlightened; it presupposes and stimulates an ascetic process toward enlightenment. The other one, the *kongōkai* (Sk. *vajradhātu*, "*vajra* realm") *mandara* represents the unconditioned reality from the point of view of the realized Buddha; it is the result of the previous ascetic process (see Figure. 2.4).[111] As it is already clear from their name, these two mandalas cannot be taken separately, but the full meaning of each presupposes the other. In this sense we can consider it, with Elizabeth ten Grotenhuis, as "a kind of tally."[112]

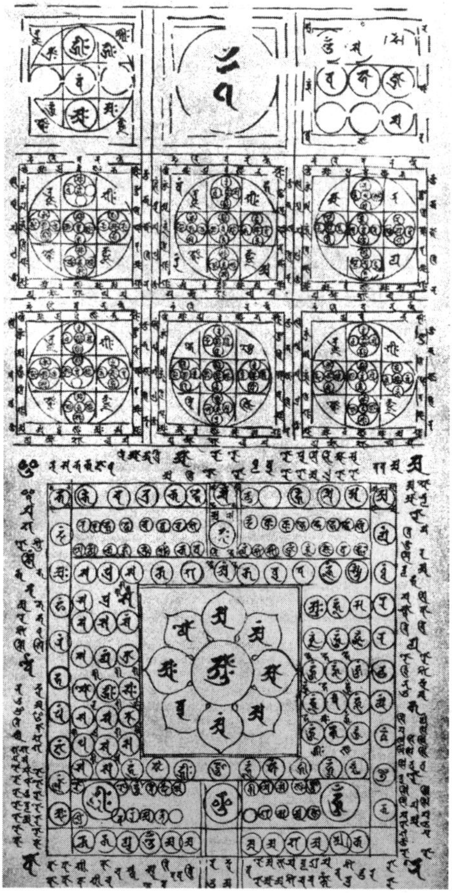

FIGURE 2.4 *Twofold mandala.* Top portion: *Vajra* mandala; bottom portion: Womb mandala. Ryōkai shuji mandara. *In T. vol. 2, insert between pp. 714 and 715. Tokyo: Daizō shuppan.*

According to the *Mahāvairocana Sutra*, all buddhas have a threefold secret body constituted by linguistic signs (Jp. *ji*, Sk. *akṣara*), seals, i.e. ritual gestures (Jp. *in*, Sk. *mudrā*), and visual representations (Jp. *gyōzō*, Sk. *bimba*).[113] Also on the basis of explanations scattered in various texts of the *Jinggang ding jing* lineage,[114] Kūkai interpreted the above doctrine as referring to what he called the four kinds of mandala[115]—the actual forms of the semiotic modality of the cosmos (*sōdai*) discussed previously. For Kūkai the linguistic signs (*ji*), the first "secret body" of the Buddha, refer to the Dharma Mandala, which is constituted by the mantric seeds (*shuji*) of the deities, the texts of the Buddhist scriptures, and also by the *samādhis* of the Dharmakāya. The seals (*in*), the second secret body of the Buddha, refer to the *Samaya* Mandala, which is constituted by ritual tools and symbolic objects held by the deities and their representations, and the deities' *mudrās*. Finally, the third secret body of the Buddha, the images (*gyō*), refers to the Buddha's body endowed with the 32 marks and is expressed by the Great Mandala, the pictorial representation of the forms of buddhas and bodhisattvas, but also the attainment of a deity's *samādhi* through the meditation in five phases (*gosō jōshingan*). The three secret Buddha-bodies, far from being static, are engaged in a continuous activity that is structured according to the patterns of the Karma Mandala, which in fact represents movements and activities of buddhas and bodhisattvas and their sculptural representations. Kūkai also noticed the interpenetration of material entities and animate beings implicit in the above doctrine.

Following these teachings by Kūkai, the Shingon tradition recognizes four different modalities of reproduction of the twofold mandala, known as the "four kinds of mandala" (*shishu mandara*), respectively: Great Mandala, Dharma Mandala, Symbol Mandala, and Action Mandala. The Great Mandala (*dai mandara*) presents the images of the deities depicted in the five colors. The Dharma (*hō*) Mandala contains the written seed letters of the deities. The Symbol (*sanmaya*) Mandala has objects and ritual implements such as sword, thunderbolt (*vajra*), lotus, and wheel (*cakra*) representing the deities. Finally, the Action (*karma*, Jp. *katsuma*) Mandala is a three-dimensional, sculptural (in clay or bronze) representation of the above. There is also another form, in which the contours of the deities are drawn in gold or silver on a blue cloth canvas, as in the case of the Takao mandala dating back to the early ninth century.[116]

This fourfold typology does not provide strictly prescriptive models, but rather loose matrices of mandalic objects. As the *Shishu mandaragi* (ninth century) and its later commentary, the *Shishu mandaragi kuketsu* explain, there are infinite variants of the four kinds of mandala, even though they are all non-separate and interrelated (*furi*),[117] and each of them contains the other three.[118] The four mandalas together constitute a general representation of Esoteric Buddhist world-view. They are not just images of the Buddha, because phenomena are also constituted as integral parts of mandala.[119] As the *Shishu mandaragi* explains, the Great Mandala represents the totality of sentient beings (*ujō*); *Samaya* Mandala represents inanimate objects and the environment in which sentient beings live (*hijō*); Karma Mandala represents the "differentiated activities and the distinct configurations of the Tathāgata" (in other words, it is equivalent to the Dharmakāya's universal salvific activity); and Dharma Mandala represents rules and precepts.[120]

Finally, I would like to draw the attention on yet another category of mandala, which had an enormous influence on Japanese culture, and is usually represented as the previously mentioned five-element *stūpa*. Known as *gorin mandara* (mandala of the five wheels) or *gozō mandara* (mandala of the five internal organs of the human body), it is a simplification of the Mandala of the Two Realms, and was used in visualization rituals but also as a template for the application of correlative cosmology to many aspects of life and culture. In Japan, it is still widely used today in tombstones. The cosmological dimension of mandala began to expand dramatically in the twelfth century, in particular with an important work by Kakuban, the *Gorin kujimyō himitsushaku*, which attempted a systematization of Indian and Chinese correlative thought on the basis of a simple quinary model.[121] With Kakuban, the five-element mandala became a microcosmic model that permitted a continuous circulation between the inside and the outside of one's body from anatomy to a cosmic scale, from body to mind and from matter to spiritual wisdom.

Attempts to show a direct relationship between mandala and various orders of reality were already present in the *Shishu mandaragi* and the *Shishu mandaragi kuketsu*. These two texts describe correspondences between the four kinds of mandala and a number of series of three and four elements. Concerning the former, these mandalas are associated with the Three Jewels (*sanbō*) and the three sections of mandala (*sanbu*: Buddha, Lotus, and *Vajra* sections). In terms of four element series, the mandalas are associated with the material elements, their four fundamental shapes and basic semantic features (earth: square and solidity; water and space: circle/sphere and pervasiveness; fire: triangle and courage/subduing; and wind: crescent and destruction of negative things), and the four principal Esoteric rituals aimed at, respectively, increasing material benefits (*zōyaku*), eliminating calamities (*sokusai*), subjugating evil forces (*chōbuku*), and generating love and respect (*kōchō* or *keiai*).[122] These correlations establish a direct and necessary relation between the four mandalas, their inner parts (the three sections), the Esoteric rites in which they are employed, the goals they aim at, and Buddhism as a whole (the Three Jewels). Their cosmological implications are still rather superficial, limited as they are to a reference to the five cosmic elements and their shapes.

From this account we can extrapolate the main semiotic characteristics of mandala, namely: (i) polymatericity: mandala is a complex device made of many semiotic substances (colors, language, shapes, movements) that appeals to all human senses and faculties; it is thus insufficient to study it only from a pictorial point of view; (ii) plurilinguism: Japanese mandalas are the result of the accretion of and interaction between doctrines and practices from all Asia; mandala itself, as a "text," yields to many "readings" and usages, according to the user's initiation level and ability; (iii) panchrony: even though the mandala may represent an itinerary toward salvation, and therefore temporal succession, in principle it is a synchronous model of the cosmos; (iv) omnicomprehensivity: as articulations of the semiotic modality of the cosmos (*sōdai*), the four mandalas encompass the totality of reality. In detail, the Dharma Mandala contains all doctrines, Buddhist and non-Buddhist, secular and religious; the Great Mandala contains all sentient beings, both lay and religious; the Symbol Mandala contains all inanimate objects, secular and religious; the Karma Mandala contains all events and activities, secular and religious;[123] (v) polysemy: the content of mandala is organized on many levels of sense and semantic fields, as will become clear in the next two sections of this chapter; (vi) semi-symbolism: mandala's symbols are motivated; accordingly, there is a relations of conformity (at least partial) between the various elements of mandalic semiosis (signifiers, signifieds, objects, users, etc.); (vii) "syncretism": mandala is a complex "syncretic" object, in the semiotic sense that it is grounded on a redundancy of the signifier: several "categories can individually or collectively constitute the form of the expression."[124] In other words, a mandala always involves several semiotic systems (painting, sculpture, gestures, sounds, languages, etc.). This is particularly evident in the case of the five-element mandala.

Functions

As is clear from the preceding discussion, mandalas, like all Esoteric semiotic entities, have a complex status and play a number of functions. They can be used as signs and representations, in the sense that they can signify something else, such as the Dharmadhātu, Mahāvairocana's enlightenment, or more generally doctrines or rituals; in this sense, mandala can serve as mnemonic aids. However, representation and memorization are not mandala's primary functions. Rather, mandala is an important liturgical and devotional instrument, a kind of multimedia encyclopedia of esoteric Buddhism, a magical object, and an ideological device. Let us see each of these functions more in detail.

Liturgical and devotional instrument

Mandala is indispensable in all Esoteric rituals from initiation, in which the disciple, his eyes closed, throws a flower on a mandala to determine which deity he is karmically related to,[125] to imperial rites consecrating the monarch as a universal ruler.[126] Mandala is omnipresent in ceremonial halls: hanging on the wall, spread out on the altar, three-dimensionally structuring the space of the temple, mentally in meditation, and also in musical form in the soundscape of Buddhist ritual chant (*shōmyō*). By its nature, mandala is also a liminal space, a mesocosm between the sacred and the profane worlds[127]—the space where the world of the Buddha manifests itself in this world. According to Charles Orzech,

> what occurs [in Esoteric ritual] is the construction of a world—of a *mandala*—in which the adept and the Buddhas, bodhisattvas, or guardian divinities can meet. This fundamental mandalic structure is a simulacra [*sic*] of the cosmos with Mahāvairocana ... at the summit ... The process of construction culminates in the consecration (*abhiṣeka*) of the adept.[128]

In fact, mandala is no mere object but a sacred icon infused the presence of the divine. As Robert Sharf explains,

> Like all Buddhist icons, a Shingon mandala is not so much a representation of the divine as it is the locus of the divine—the ground upon which the principal deity is made manifest [...] To come into the presence of a mandala is to enter the presence of the Tathāgata [...] the mandala ... does not so much serve as an aid for visualizing the deity as it abrogates the need for visualization at all.[129]

In this respect, we should note that mandalas are not unique in being envisioned as objects infused with divine presence. In fact, this is one of the standard features of Buddhist images (sculptures and paintings) throughout Asia; the Shingon tradition developed this understanding in its theory of representation of the sacred.[130] According to the standard Shingon interpretation, mandalas are not mere representations, but the real shape of the Dharmadhātu. Even though they are human-made artifacts, mandala are copies of samples of the absolute reality, and therefore they enjoy an absolute status themselves. For instance, In'yū (1435–1519) proposed an astonishing vision of the Dharmadhātu Palace as a collection of buddha images, which are external projections of Mahāvairocana's enlightenment.[131] The Dharmadhātu Palace in particular contains the originals of the four mandalas, which must therefore appear as painted and sculpted images.[132] The more general issue of the relation between the Buddha and his images is described in the fifth variant of Kūkai's *Sokushin jōbutsugi*,[133] a medieval apocryphal text, through the metaphor of the pearls in Indra's net. According to it, Mahāvairocana's enlightenment is projected outside in the form of sacred images that are copied and transmitted to our world for us to see; however, Buddhist icons already exist innately inside the human mind as part (samples) of Mahāvairocana's universal mind. To the objection that in the metaphor of Indra's Net only the light of the pearls is reflected, but each individual pearl does not merge with all the other pearls, the anonymous author replies that in the case of the Buddha, his images (*ei*) and his bodily substance (*shichi*) are mutually interpenetrated; each icon is thus not essentially different and separated from all other icons and from the real Buddha himself. We have here another case of ostension involving doubles, examples, and samples to give Buddhist icons an unconditioned status.

Esoteric encyclopedia

Because of its status and its role in ritual, mandala is also a multimedia compendium of doctrines and practices and can be used for the transmission and the memorization of the Shingon system of knowledge.[134] Robert Sharf has also described mandala as a "visual commentary" to the scriptures of Esoteric Buddhism: "Looking at a mandala one is able to grasp at a glance not only the color, posture, demeanor, and ritual implements associated with each of hundreds of depicted deities but also the hierarchical and spatial relationships that exist between them."[135] Before him, Ioan Couliano defined mandala as a "mnemotechnical system," meaning by this term a "system of classification" for "the pantheon of the gods and their reciprocal relations, the history of the creation and the destruction of the universe, the anthropology and anthropogony" of Tantric Buddhism.[136] As such, mandala can be interpreted as the totality of knowledge of Esoteric Buddhism—what Umberto Eco calls a "semiotic encyclopedia."[137] As Patrizia Violi explains, the semiotic encyclopedia is "the socially shared inventory of all possible interpretations and the archive of all existing information,"[138] akin to Yuri Lotman's concept of semiosphere.[139]

Magical object

Because it is infused with divine presence and power, mandala can also be used as amulet or talisman to protect its owner or user from illness and misfortune; the practice of mandala is thus a manipulation of signs to affect reality. Giorgio Raimondo Cardona considers mandala a particular type of *pentaculum*. *Pentacula*, magical objects existing in many cultures, "are built on an interplay of correspondences between microcosm and macrocosm: such correspondences allow for the control over otherwise unruly forces that can thus be duly restrained and directed through a model"[140]—this model being the *pentaculum* itself.[141]

Ideological device

This is undoubtedly the least studied aspect of mandala. As a reproduction of reality and epitome of a certain kind of knowledge, mandala presupposes and represents multi-leveled political conceptions and structures of power that have not yet been explored at length in Japan. In India, at least, it would appear that Tantric Buddhism appropriated the image of mandala as a secular model of a polity and its neighboring countries and transformed it into a Buddhist vision of the entire universe.[142] Stanley Tambiah has discussed the political role of mandala in premodern Thailand.[143] In the Japanese case, mandala served as a general vision of the cosmos in which the Japanese emperor played the role of a universal monarch (Sk. *cakravartin*, Jp. *tenrinshōō*), but also as a hierarchical model of the sacredness as related to power relations.[144]

Semiognosis of mandala

We have seen that the *sandai* doctrine lays at the basis of Esoteric semiotics and it also constitutes the general framework of mandalic ideas and practices, to which it offers an ontological ground. Signs (*sōdai*) are not arbitrary, but necessary configurations of the undifferentiated substratum (*taidai*); their manifold operations and transformations (*yūdai*) are the incessant soteriologic activity in which the Dharmakāya is engaged. In this way, Esoteric Buddhism envisions a circuit between ontology (the nature of reality), cosmology (the structure of the universe), knowledge, and soteriology: awakening is explicitly configured as knowing the fundamental structure of reality. Since expressive forms do not exist separately from the cosmic substratum, signs are not different from the reality that generates them. This is how mandala is infused with divine presence and its agency: mandalas are in some sense similar to their substance and embody what they signify. As Patrizia Violi has noted about Esoteric semiotic expressions in general, "they resemble more than anything else that peculiar type of sign described by [Umberto] Eco... as *samples*, signs which are homomaterical, and produced by ostension."[145] In other words, mandala are made of the same substance of what they signify, and signify it by displaying it on the basis of a synecdoche (a part signifying the whole). As microcosms they are related to the underlying macrocosm by a relationship that is not only of analogy and similarity, but also of identity: they are at the same time similar to and parts of the Dharmadhātu they signify through operations of remotivation. These are the main features of the Esoteric Buddhist semiotic field that I have defined "semiognosis."

Remotivation processes of semiognosic nature, in fact, also affected both expression and meaning of mandala. Shingon exegetes remotivated the supports and implements of religious practices so as to turn them into condensations of the universe. Mandala rituals can thus be immersions in the space of enlightenment because of the structure of the mandalic sign itself. A relation of motivation renders expression and meaning, sign and reality, means and ends of the rituals essentially identical; as a consequence, also practitioner, the deity, and its image (*honzon*) become identical. Below I will outline the principal operations carried by the Esoteric tradition in order to change the semiotic structure of mandala.

Manipulating the word: mandala's polysemy

The soteriological value of mandala does not depend just on an act of faith, but it is also grounded on remotivation of language aimed at revealing the non-arbitrariness of signs. The term mandala has a long history in India,[146] and when it arrived to Japan it was already loaded symbolically. The Monier-Williams *Sanskrit English Dictionary* lists the following meanings of the word mandala in its ordinary usage (only entries relevant to the present discussion):

> circular, round; a disk (esp. of the sun or moon); anything round; a circle, globe, orb, ring, circumference, ball, wheel; a district, arrondissement, territory, province, country; a surrounding district or neighbouring state, the circle of a king's near and distant neighbours; a multitude, group, band, collection, whole body, society, company.[147]

In India, moreover, the term mandala also refers to supports for meditation, also called *yantra*; they are often built in religious ritual and ceremonies. The meaning of mandala in religious terminology depends perhaps on the circularity that probably characterized early mandalas as supports of Buddhist meditation.

As a key term of Indian Tantric Buddhism, mandala begins to appear in phonetic transcription in the Chinese translations of Buddhist texts and their commentaries as mantuluo only towards the sixth century. The ninth-century Japanese text *Shishu mandaragi* explains the two main Chinese translations of the term mandala, namely, "altar" and "perfect circle":

> in the past it was called "altar" (*dan*), meaning by it only the sense of "flat, even surface." [This translation] misses other numberless names and meanings... In contrast, people today, by calling mandala "perfect circle" (*rinnen gusoku*), attribute to it all its principles with no exclusion.[148]

Here, "altar" refers to the mandala's primary function as a ritual tool; "perfect circle" to its symbolic meanings. Let us now try to trace the development of this semantic transformation from a square altar to a perfect circle.

The word mandala is normally decomposed into the root *maṇḍa* (the most delicious part of foods and beverages) and the suffix *-la* (completion, possession) and interpreted as "that which possesses [*la*] *maṇḍa*" *Maṇḍa* in turn means: "the scum of boiled rice (or any grain); the thick part of milk, cream; the spirituous part of wine &c; (also 'foam or froth; pith; essence; the head')."[149]

Tantric Buddhism formulates an Esoteric exegesis of the term *maṇḍa*. A secondary ordinary meaning ("essence") is chosen as the main Esoteric sense; then, "essence" is interpreted as "true essence of reality," the ultimate truth of the Dharmakāya's preaching. In short, the original meaning of mandala, "circle," became a semantic marker used to characterize the Esoteric mandala (="that which is endowed with the essence of things [from *maṇḍa* = delicacies]") as "endowed with the perfection of the circle" (*rinnen gusoku*), in the sense that it is as perfect as the circle, and thus perfectly endowed with power and virtue.[150] Thus, the circularity of the object was connected with its "perfection." Why such an emphasis on circularity? It is possible that originally supports for meditation had a circular form. Roderick S. Bucknell and Martin Stuart-Fox argue that both *maṇḍala* and *kasiṇa* (circular objects used in an ancient meditative technique described in the Pāli Buddhist Canon), represent different developments of earlier colored circles used as supports for meditation.[151] The alimentary semantic field, related to the primary and original meaning of *maṇḍa* (which refers, as we have seen, to delicacies and delicious flavors), is reflected in Sino-Japanese translations of mandala as "peerless flavor" (*muhimi*) and "unsurpassable flavor" (*mukajōmi*); here, flavor stands here metaphorically for the sublime qualities of the *bodhi*.[152] The Esoteric mandala also recycles another of the original meanings of the term, that is "a multitude, group, band, collection," and is used to refer to a particular assembly of buddhas, bodhisattvas, and other members of the Tantric pantheon, because mandala gathers in itself (*shūshu*) the powers and virtues of the *siddhi* (spiritual attainments). Importantly, mandala is further attributed a generative power (*hosshō*); it is not a mere "support" for religious practice, instead religious practice *is produced* by mandala. Finally, another ordinary meaning of the Sanskrit term, "a district, arrondissement, territory, province, country," is echoed in Japanese ideas about the sacredness of the country (*shinkoku*), which was sometimes described in mandalic terms.[153]

Manipulating meaning: nondualism and the "perfect circle"

Another example of remotivation is Kakuban's exegesis of the Mandala of the Two Realms aimed at showing their nondual and all-encompassing nature.[154] Here, Kakuban goes through a textual tour de force to show that "dual" (*ryōbu* as in *ryōbu mandara*, "twofold mandala" or "mandala of the two realms") actually means "the nondual one-mind," "countless, numberless," "both one and many," "both non-one and non-many," and, finally, "perfect circle, totality." Let us follow Kakuban's argument at some length.

[The Nondual One-Mind] The character *ryō* [of *ryōbu* and *ryōgai*] means "unit" or "one." As a matter of fact, it is called "pair" [*ryō*] a unit of two elements [or, two ones], and it is called "two" [*ni*] [the combination of two characters] "one" [*ichi*] superimposed. Without the one the two cannot be produced. [...] Now, "twofold world" [of the mandala] [*ryōgai*] has the meaning of "nondual" [*funi*]: this is its true meaning. "Two realms" [*nikai*] is a superficial interpretation, while "nondual" is a deep interpretation. [...] If the term "two worlds" did not exist who could ever express the principle of nondualism? [...]

[Countless, Numberless] "Pair" [*ryō*] is a set of two, and "one" means "numberless." As a well-known verse says, "one is not one, therefore it is called one." The manifold constitutes the one [i.e. the totality]. Even one is numberless; how can a pair of ones be calculable? Moreover, two means "numberless," "infinite," and so forth. If one writes a character twice one expresses the sense of multiplicity; the repetition of the same word twice expresses the sense of numberlessness. For example, when one writes a pair of characters *moku* ["tree"] close to each other the character *rin* ["forest"] is produced, which expresses a luxuriant set of many trees; two characters *seki* ["evening"] superimposed form the character *ta* ["many"], which expresses the non-singularity of all things. There also are several other cases [in which repetition of two characters is used to signify multiplicity]. [...]

[Both One and Many] This is the combination of the two preceding cases. Moreover, "one is not one, therefore it is called one"—thus, "pair" means "many." [In the same way,] the many are not many, therefore they are called many: "pair" thus means "unit."

[Both Non-One and Non-Many] ["Pair"] means "many," "non-one" ["pair"] also means "unit" and thus "non-many." Moreover, the character "two" refers to a number different from one, therefore it is called "non-one"; "pair" is less than three, therefore it is called "non-many." [...] Moreover, the one is the unity of many, not the unity of one, therefore it is called "non-one"; the manifold is constituted by many units, not by many manifolds, therefore it is called "non-many." [...]

[Perfect Circle, Totality] In turn, this means two different things, namely, the character *ryō* [pair] includes at the same time the four cases above; *ryō* means "pair," "to put together," "circle," "to be endowed with" [that is, "that which is endowed with a pair of circles"—the Mandala of the Two Realms]. In other words, *ryō* means "that which possesses principle [*ri*] and wisdom [*chi*], that which is endowed with *samādhi* and *prajñā*, that which integrates abstract principle [*ri*] and its phenomenal manifestations [*ji*], fullness of fortune and wisdom." Thanks to its two wings a bird can fly in the pure circle of the sky, thanks to its two wheels a cart can move on the great square cart of the earth (...).

This document has an incantatory, vertiginous character that contributes to its rhetorical power. Let me try to unpack it. Kakuban envisions nondualism (*funi*, the main feature of enlightenment as opposed to deluded discriminatory knowledge) as a deep correlate (*jigi*) of the superficial meaning (*jisō*) of "two"—in this case expressed by the character *ryō*, "pair, set of two elements." In order to represent a concept resisting formalization such as "non-two," Kakuban first established the semantic axis *one—numberless* and analyzed its two poles. Beginning with this first semantic opposition, reformulated as *one—many*, Kakuban then builds up a semiotic square with the inclusion of a related axis of sub-contrary terms *non-one—non-many*. We have thus four terms (tetralemma) in their three fundamental logic relations: contrary, contradictory, implication. Up to this point, Kakuban follows the classical logic of Nāgārjuna. However, there is an important difference. The Madhyamaka tradition uses the semiotic square in order to negate all its terms one by one; such a strategy aims at showing the causal interrelationship of all things and, at the same time, the impossibility for language and discursive thought to positively represent such interrelationship.[155]

Kakuban departs from the Indian precedent to follow a different procedure. Far from denying the terms of his semiotic square, he ends up affirming all of them. While the first axis is made by the relation *one—many*, the second axis connects the meta-relation *one and many—non-one and non-many* that results from fusing the two relations of contrary terms in the primary tetralemma (i.e. *one—many* and *non-one—non-many*). Then, Kakuban adds another layer of significance by further uniting the two relations of his meta-semiotic square: such fullness of meaning is reached in the fifth section of his text (perfect circle, totality), which is synonymous with mandala (see Figure 2.5). At this stage, the absolute, nondual nature of the term "two" becomes manifest. "Two," as in Mandala of the Two Realms, is not just an attribute of mandala, but one of its constitutive, essential qualities. Mandalas cannot but be twofold, because that word

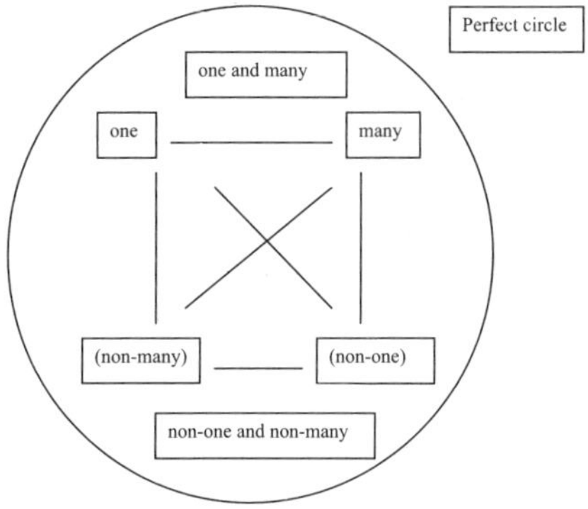

FIGURE 2.5 *Semiotic square of nondualism*

encompasses the totality of meaning. At the same time, "two" cannot but be a mandalic expression. The term *ryō* becomes coextensive with the very semiotic space in which the semiotic square is established—with that particular *topos* where meaning springs forth; as such, "two" is endowed with infinite qualities and powers, perfect as a circle, a mandala in itself. At this point there is nothing more to say, since Kakuban has reached the source of sense itself, the stage of unobtainability (*fukatoku*) of meaning; and yet at the same time everything can be said about mandala as the totality of reality. In this way, Kakuban helps the ascetic to realize through semiotic procedures the absolute value of each phenomenon—and of mandala in particular.

A striking consequence of all this is that we are dealing here with a kind of self-defeating semiotics. If, from the unconditioned point of view, an object does not "stand for something else" but only for itself as a "natural" manifestation of the Dharmakāya, as a microcosm, all categories of the semiotic metalanguage disappear; everything becomes a reflection of everything else. In the realm of *samādhi*, the production of signs and the interpretation of the world are brought to a complete stop. What remains is the ritual reiteration of the (supposedly) original intention of the Dharmakāya. Reflections reflecting reflections, the cosmos is reduced to an infinite and vertiginous play of mirrors, as represented by the well-known metaphor of Indra's Net, in which each pearl reflects all the other pearls. At that point, catroptics takes the place of semiotics for, as suggested by Umberto Eco,

> the catroptic realm is able to reflect (without modifying it) the semiosic realm which exists outside of it, but cannot be 'reflected' by the semiosic (...) These two realms, the former being a threshold to the second, do not have intermediate points, and limit-cases... are points of catastrophe.[156]

In any case, it is important to emphasize that this ultimate dimension of "un-signification" is not necessarily a state in which meaning is centralized, unified, and homogeneous. On the contrary, as Kakuban makes clear, each semiotic unit is an irreducible multiplicity of objects and meanings, and this seems to be the fundamental paradigm of Esoteric Buddhist semiotics and ontology. Such a paradigm also had political effects that can only be sketched in this book.

Why did the Esoteric Buddhist exegetes engage themselves in such a semantic *tour de force*? The restructuring of meaning proved necessary in order to establish mandala as an esoteric object and an esoteric concept as well, as an entity allowing a direct contact with the absolute—just because it shares (it is made to share) the nature of Dharmadhātu and its principles. This is possible only through the establishment of a relation of motivation connecting the expression (mandala) to its meaning (that which possesses the essence), the instrument to its end (*bodhi*, *siddhi*), and the object to its user. Such etymological labor represents a process of remotivation of language aimed at negating the arbitrariness of signs. In early Buddhist usage, mandala referred to a support for meditation; later, with the development of Tantrism, the term came to indicate the platform for initiation and other Esoteric rituals. The need for motivation arose from the fact that efficacy of rituals (and, therefore, their goals) ought to be necessarily related in some way to the supports they used and the spaces where they took place. Only in this way could the result be assured. The need to offer practitioners a strong guarantee to reach their goal (which, according to Esoteric Buddhism is easy, certain, and fast), generated etymological strategies directed at remotivating both the object and its name so as to justify their use by virtue of their consubstantiality with Buddhahood. Mandala thus changed from a mere instrument for meditation or place for initiation, into something fundamentally identical to the end for which it was used. The Esoteric transformation of mandala is thus completed: in a few centuries, it changed from a simple circle used by beginners as a support for meditation, into an extraordinary machine endowed with countless powers, for which nothing is impossible. In the end, mandala itself as a soteriological device takes control of Esoteric practice and produces the attainment of the *bodhi* and all *siddhis*. It is clear that, therefore, Esoteric doctrines are interrelated to semiotic conceptions: they owe their power also to manipulations of signs and meanings. In particular, the concept of "becoming a buddha in the present body" (*sokushin jōbutsu*) reveals a semiotic foundation as based on a ritual logic of samples and doubles.

Transmission of the mandalic episteme

So far I have outlined the semiotic labor necessary for the production of mandala as an esoteric artifact. From an *internal* point of view, however, Esoteric artifacts are not arbitrarily made and handed down on the basis of conventions—including those aimed at remotivation. Transmission of Esoteric artifacts and relative know-how, taking place from master to disciple, is secret and initiatory. The starting point of this initiatory chain is Buddha Mahāvairocana (Dainichi Nyorai): signs and practices related to his teachings are born in the self-presence of the Unconditioned. The myth of the unconditioned appearance of the first copy of the Mandala of the Two Realms is part of this general intellectual framework. In traditional accounts, the Womb mandala appeared in the sky for the first time to the patriarch Śubhakarasiṃha (Shanwuwei) in Gandhara (present-day Pakistan), whereas the *Vajra* mandala was revealed to Nāgārjuna inside the Iron *Stūpa* in South India, where he received the initiation to the *Jinggang ding jing* textual lineage.[157] Both patriarchs supposedly made a faithful copy of each respective apparition; their copies are the prototypes of the most important Shingon sacred image, the Mandala of the Two Realms, commonly known as *genzu mandara*, "picture reproducing the [original] mandala as it manifested itself." According to the tradition, the original set was brought to Japan by Kūkai. In this case, the idea of the perfect reproduction of the Original and unconditioned Mandala superimpose with the idea of the direct, unaltered transmission of the Buddhist Esoteric tradition to Kūkai. Even today, *genzu mandara* are considered to be perfect copies of this original and unconditioned mandala, whose image and meaning are strictly transmitted by means of a causal chain. Mandala is thus a particular case of what Saul Kripke calls "rigid designator,"[158] i.e. an expression that refers to the same object in all possible worlds. In general terms, the transmission of mandala is articulated in three steps. First, there is the occurrence of a primary speech act, in which the Buddha Mahāvairocana, in his original modality of existence and immersed in the supreme *samādhi*, preaches the Dharma (including teachings about mandala); this speech act is reinforced by the appearance of the mandala in the sky (pure space *par excellence*); the picture of mandala is based therefore on a primary, unconditioned display. Next, sacred words and signs, with their meanings and their usages, are kept in a *corpus* of revealed texts and their commentaries, the result of a secret knowledge tracing back directly and without changes to Mahāvairocana himself. Finally, a group of people practice and transmit these teachings. These three steps correspond to the Three Jewels, core of Buddhism and foundation of the supernatural power of its practices and its signs.

The continuous and unbroken nature of the transmission line connecting masters to disciples is also underscored by the root metaphor for Esoteric transmission rituals, namely, decanting (Jp. *shabyō*, lit. "decanting a bottle"), that is, the act of pouring the contents of one bottle into another. Its scriptural source is a passage from the *Nirvana Sutra*: "Ānanda has been with me for more than twenty years. [...] Since he joined me, he has memorized the twelve-division teachings I have taught; once a teaching entered his ear, he did not ask [to be reminded about it] any more. It has been like pouring the content of one bottle into another."[159] Kūkai also used this metaphor in a work on the Shingon lineage: "receiving the transmission is not different from decanting a bottle."[160] This metaphor serves to emphasize continuity going all the way back to the original transmission by the Buddha. In this sense, transmission rituals do more than transmit teachings: they sanction that the transmission is complete and has been unaltered (unadulterated).

These traditions and legends further confirm the idea that mandala (and all other Esoteric expressions as localized fragments of wider mandalas) are unconditioned entities, transcending arbitrariness of signs, cultural codes, and everyday semiotic strategies. Such characterization emphasizes the fidelity and accuracy of initiatory knowledge—and, thus, of everything concerning Esoteric signs and objects. As a consequence, the initiatory signs of the Esoteric episteme cannot in principle be used to lie, because they cannot lie. We find here the paradoxical idea of an absolute sign, directly and ontologically connected to the object or the event for which it should stand. The problematic of the absolute sign is developed on three different levels: the internal structure, as motivated and analogic signs and samples, as we have seen; the power of which these signs are endowed; and their transmission, by way of a rigid causal chain. As we have seen, mandala is the general semiotic representation of Dharmadhātu, and its direct tie with reality is presented as an analytic property. The power of Esoteric signs rests upon this direct connection with the Unconditioned. The "unaware," uninformed usage of mandala as amulet or talisman as in semiopietas—usage that leaves meaning out of consideration, is grounded on the weight of tradition and on an unaltered secret transmission.

Concluding remarks

Mandala is not just a representation of the sacred but a real presence of the invisible world of the Esoteric Buddhist pantheon. The unconditioned Dharmadhātu is itself a mandala, and all phenomena are also structured as a mandala. In other words, while a long Western tradition compares the world with a Book,[161] Esoteric Buddhism understands the universe as an immense Mandala. The universe itself is sometimes presented as a scripture;[162] but as we have seen, words and written characters constitute one of the four fundamental mandalas. Language is subordinate within mandala to a plurality of systems of representation/reproduction of the Dharmakāya's Preaching (*hosshin seppō*). True reality is thus accessible not through a "reading" of phenomena (this metaphor never appears in Esoteric texts), but through manifold semiotic practices of mandala. In fact, mandala presents a stratified knowledge in which language is just one element among many; mandala was thus the primary modeling system of the cosmos for the Esoteric Buddhist episteme in medieval Japan. This hypothesis has been already suggested by Giorgio Raimondo Cardona regarding the Tibetan mandala, an "expressive form" that "is not immediately translatable in the forms of language."[163] In mandala's semiotic system, "the graphic component has the function of modeling contents with vital ideological importance ... the *totality* of what one has to know about the world (hence its secret, initiatory value)."[164]

As a fundamental modeling system, mandala plays descriptive and prescriptive functions: it visually and ritually describes the structure and functioning of absolute reality, while at the same time presenting an ideal vision of order (both cosmic and social) and the ways to attain and preserve it. The "totality of what one has to know about the world," in fact, also includes in particular instructions on how to live according to an ideological imagination of reality and society. In this sense we can understand statements such as the one by Washio previously discussed: by looking at mandala as an embodiment of the "essential value" of life, we are able to "understand the nature of our real existence" and "encounter" our "true being."[165]

By the end of the thirteenth century, everything in Japan had been mandalized in more or less explicitly terms: space, time, salvation, cosmic movements, everyday practices, artistic and intellectual production, birth, death, physiologic activities such as breathing were all described as particular instances of larger cosmic processes.[166] It is not surprising that such a generalized mandalization also played an ideological role for the legitimization of the political and economic role of Shingon and Tendai religious institutions and their attempts to strengthen domination over the lands they managed and the people living there.

In conclusion, we could say that mandala is a diverse and shifting field of "power spots," spaces in the Japanese intellectual arena in which sacredness is ceaselessly converted into knowledge and power—and viceversa. A mandala is a structured and articulated set of various semiotic systems, rooted in an organic correlative principle. It is all-encompassing, self-sufficient, and recursive; nothing exists outside of it. Thus the mandala is able to completely represent the episteme of Esoteric Buddhism in its polymateric semiotic system; as such, mandala presupposes peculiar laws of organization, semiotic concepts and semiotic practices. This unique character makes mandala a representation of the absolute world, of the substratum-space in which semiosis takes place. If meditation on mandala is an immersion into the space of enlightenment, this is made possible not just by belief but, most importantly, also by virtue of the structure of the mandalic sign itself. Special semiotic operations were carried out in order to remotivate the mandala and change it into an icon containing the characteristics of the cosmos. Once expression and meaning, sign and reality, means and ends of meditation were made essentially identical, through a relation of motivation, also the practitioner and the deity (the object of meditation) became identical. Salvation reveals itself as the result of peculiar semiotic conceptions and practices.

CHAPTER THREE

The secrets of languages: Structure of the Esoteric signs

Esoteric Buddhism attributes great importance to the use of language and particular signs; linguistic and semiotic practices are some of the main foci of soteriological activity. In this chapter, after a brief overview of the fundamental Buddhist ideas about language—and in particular, the language of the Buddha, we will explore the Esoteric Buddhist philosophy of language. We will take as our starting point the notion of "secret of language" (*gomitsu*), one of the three foci of salvational activity, and the structure of Esoteric signs. Accordingly, we will discuss the nature and function of mantras (Jp. *shingon*), the phonetic signifier, and of *shittan* (Sk. *siddhaṃ*) graphs, the visual signifier, as well as the universe of meaning with its multiple levels.

Buddhism and language

An important part of the Buddhist teachings is dedicated to issues concerning language; in the following pages I present an overview of the most important among them. According to the Buddhist phenomenologies (Abhidharma and Yogācāra), language is not a dharma (constitutive element of reality) in itself, but is composed of three different dharmas, namely, phonemes (*mon*), words (*myō*), and sentences (*ku*).[1] Signification and communication employ the linguistic dharmas to form words and sentences in accordance with data processed by the consciousness, in parallel with the articulation of reality, from the fundamental distinction subject/object to representations of the "external" world. According to the Yogācāra epistemology, as we have already seen, language creates the world of our ordinary experience through the operations of semiotic "seeds" (Sk. *bīja*, Jp. *shūji*), the basic elements of perception, language, cognition, memory, and self-identity. However, not only do linguistic descriptions of the world have no absolute truth-value, but language is in itself an instrument of fallacious knowledge because, through the categorization and conceptualization of perceptual data and their semantic articulation, it creates the very reality that humans perceive in their state of delusion.[2] The fourth element in the chain of the twelve factors of causation (*pratītya-samutpāda*), namely, *nāma-rūpa* ("names and forms"), expresses the interdependence of cognitive processes and external reality, phenomena and discriminating mind, names and things of the ordinary world of suffering.[3] People consider their own image of the world to be true and corresponding to reality for they attribute to objects the characteristics proper to the linguistic expressions (autonomy, immutability, homogeneity) used to refer to them.[4] This confusion of reality with its linguistic descriptions and mental images is what Buddhism calls "ignorance" (Sk. *avidyā*, Jp. *mumyō*), the first ring the chain of the twelve factors of causation; epistemological ignorance is the first cause of existential suffering. Conversely, enlightenment consists also in understanding the relations between language and reality. Therefore, there is an absolute hiatus separating language from true reality (the world perceived through enlightenment); Mahayana Buddhism, and in particular the Mādhyamika school founded by the Indian philosopher Nāgārjuna (*ca.* CE 150–250), systematically developed this philosophical position.[5]

According to a well-established doctrine, quoted in some Buddhist sutras and widely accepted also by the Esoteric tradition, ordinary discourses and their language (Jp. *gonzetsu*) are: (i) related to superficial aspects of phenomena (*sō gonzetsu*); (ii) uttered in dreams (*mu gonzetsu*); (iii) conditioned by delusions (*mōshū gonzetsu*), and (iv) forever reproducing the seeds of suffering (*mushi gonzetsu*).[6] If the world produced by the discriminating activity of consciousness—that is, the world of our everyday experiences—is illusory, any discourse about such a world (that is, ordinary language) is deluded and ultimately empty; language has no ultimate truth-value, it is like words uttered in a dream. Words only refer to the superficial features of things, not to their essence (which, by definition, is Emptiness—the lack of any positive, linguistically definable quality); words are themselves the product of ignorance, attachment, and suffering, which they contribute in perpetuating. The external world, then, is essentially a linguistic and semiotic construction and thus devoid of ontological reality. This connection between words and things needs to be deconstructed with the help of Buddhism if one is to attain liberation from ignorance, suffering, and the cycle of rebirths. In this sense, at least, language is relevant for Buddhist soteriology in a negative sense, as something to be deconstructed and overcome.

However, language is important to Buddhist soteriology also in another, more direct sense, because speech is, together with the body and the mind, one of three sources of karma (Jp. *sangō*). As we have seen, Buddhism recognizes three main factors of karmic causality, namely, the body, the mouth, and the mind; thus, physical actions, mental activities (thoughts, ideas, desires), and speech determine the karma (in concrete terms, the body, spiritual capacities, and physical and social environment) of one's life. The importance of speech is also obvious from the fact that among the ten evils (Jp. *jūaku*, deeds that result in rebirth into the Buddhist hells), four concern language: respectively, lying (*mōgo*), sowing discord (*ryōzetsu*), slander (*akku*), and ornate language (*kigo*).[7]

Buddhist practice based on ritual manipulation of language is what Esoteric Buddhism calls *gomitsu*, literally, "the secret of speech," one of the three secrets (*sanmitsu*), together with bodily practices (*shinmitsu*, the "secret of the body") and mental practices (*imitsu*, the "secret of the mind"). These three categories encompass all sources of human activities, including those aimed at salvation. Interestingly, the three secrets of Esoteric Buddhism are a transformation of the three karmic activities (*sangō*) which, according to classical Mahayana, constitute the source of karma and, therefore, of suffering. Here, Esoteric Buddhism reverses the traditional Mahayana interpretation and reformulates karmic activities as soteriological practices. Since the three secrets are interrelated, interdependent, and ultimately undifferentiated, Kakuban for example argued that the practice of just one among them is enough to secure liberation:

> it is enough to understand just one aspect of the doctrines, provided that one is moved by the most profound and sincere faith.... One becomes a buddha even by chanting just one syllable of a spell.[8]

This position became the ground for the principle that "the practice of just one 'secret' is enough for becoming a buddha" (*ichimitsu jōbutsu*). According to Kakuban, the religious practice of language can be divided into three forms:[9]

1. "Accurate memorization of formulae (*myō*) without making mistakes on the doctrinal passages." This practice consists in recitation and memorization of the sound of formulae, privileging the vocal aspect of mantras (*shō*); it concerns a theory of mantras and *dhāraṇī*.
2. "Visualization of the shapes of the graphs of the formulae as when, by visualizing on the tip of one's nose the graph *on*, before dawn one attains the *bodhi*": it consists in the contemplation of written graphs, that is, the graphic form of esoteric formulae (*ji*); this aspect concerns a theory of the *siddhaṃ* Indian script known in Japan as *shittan*.
3. "Understanding the true meanings of each syllable": the investigation of the Esoteric meanings and the understanding of the relations between signs and reality (*jissō*); this aspect concerns a semantic theory of Esoteric expressions.

This Esoteric practice of language involves important non-hermeneutical components, as memorization, chanting, and visualization do not necessarily presuppose hermeneutic understanding—an aspects proper to the third and last form.

The word of the Buddha

These ideas about ordinary language forced Buddhists to investigate the status of the words spoken by the Buddha. If language is separate from true reality—that is, if language contributes to human beings' ignorance by creating a false reality, aren't his words also contributing to delusion and suffering? Obviously, the word of the Buddha must have a special status, otherwise his teachings would be useless if not even pernicious. Thus, a distinction was made between the wisdom of the Buddha and the signs conveying it. In fact, Buddhism makes a clear distinction between the Dharma, that is, the wisdom of the Buddha, which is absolute and unconditioned, and the linguistic and semiotic tools (Sk. *upāya*, Jp. *hōben*, "expedient means") employed for its transmission. The choice of the historical Buddha to preach in a dialect of the kingdom of Maghada, and especially the subsequent decision by the Buddhist elders to transcribe the Buddha's teachings in Pāli, a vernacular language, and not in Sanskrit, traditionally the language of the learned and of religion, shows a refusal of older Vedico-Upanishadic beliefs in the existence of an absolute language as the privileged site/vehicle of the Truth. As Frits Staal writes, "in India, once you dispense with Sanskrit, you have abandoned all fixedness of language."[10] (Later, though, Buddhist authors wrote Mahayana texts primarily in Sanskrit, both in order to enhance their status as sacred teachings and to facilitate their diffusion by using a single, primary language.) The choice to privilege contents over expression, doctrines over the language that conveys them, was extremely important for the diffusion of Buddhism, since it allowed the translation of the sacred scriptures—an operation which is impossible when the doctrines are related to a sacred, absolute, and therefore immutable language. Esoteric Buddhism, however, because of its different attitudes toward language, emphasized the importance of original formulae in Sanskrit that were not to be translated.

In any case, non-Esoteric texts such as the *Diamond Sutra* (Ch. *Jingang banruo bolomituo jing*), the *Vimalakirti Sutra* (Ch. *Weimojie suoshuo jing*), and the *Lāṇkāvatāra Sutra* (Ch. *Ru Lengqie jing*), contain paradoxical statements about the impossibility to express the wisdom of the Buddha in ordinary human language. Particularly relevant in this context is a short scripture, the *Buddha Word Sutra* (Ch. *Fo yu jing*), which summarizes the main points of the issue. In this metalinguistic scripture we find that "The discourses of the Buddha are non-discourses," because the Buddha employs words that are radically different from ordinary language: "words of forms [concerning material entities] are not the words of the Buddha"; words concerning the "realms of earth, water, fire, wind, and space [are not] words of the Buddha"; "words of the activity of body, speech, and mind ... cannot be called words of the Buddha." The words of the Buddha, in contrast, are "neither defiled nor undefiled," "neither independent nor dependent," "neither true nor non-true," they are spoken "neither by the common people nor by holy men," they "do not ask for anything," and are "unrelated to any of the factors of ordinary knowledge."[11] The Buddha even says, in the scripture, that in order to attain salvation, one should

> cut off all words, cut off all hindrances, remove all vanity, get rid of all the nets, remove all wrong theories, bring discriminative thinking to a stop. Since there are no words, what is there to say? There is nothing to talk about. In this way, non-words are called words of the Buddha.[12]

The paradoxical status of the words spoken by the Buddha was interpreted in two different ways: either the Buddha did not speak, or he spoke a particular, non-ordinary language. According to the first view, the Buddha conveyed his experience in non-linguistic ways, because his wisdom cannot be communicated through language. This view was developed in particular by the Chan and Zen traditions.[13] A famous example is the so-called "sermon of the flower," in which the Buddha remained silent but held a flower in his hand and showed it to his disciples; only Mahākāśyapa understood, and smiled, without saying one single word. Another example is Vimalakīrti's "thundering silence"—the protagonist of the scripture's refusal to say anything about the nature of the world.[14] In these cases, rejection of language still allows for some form of semiosis.

A second position, in contrast, is grounded in the widely accepted doctrine that the Buddha explained different teachings in accordance to circumstances, contexts, and competence and salvation needs of his audience; this is known as the doctrine of expedient means (Jp. *hōben*). This second position maintains that the Buddha does speak, but uses a peculiar language, which is possible to know and understand. This position in turn opened the way to two different interpretations:

1. The language of the Buddha is a mere "expedient means" devoid of absolute value but necessary in order to help humans to attain a truth transcending every language (Jp. *gongo dōdan*): this is the doctrinal position of most Buddhist schools; some forms of Chan/Zen teachings aimed at the attainment of the Emptiness through the incessant deconstruction of assumptions, concepts, meaningful practices;
2. Absolute truth can be communicated, and the Buddha speaks peculiar words of a non-ordinary language in order to lead sentient

beings to salvation: this is the basic assumption of the teachings of Esoteric Buddhism.

In both cases, a systematic manipulation of linguistic signs was put into practice, in order to bring language beyond its limits, and force it to speak the absolute. Indeed, some authors even tried to reconcile these two positions. Dōhan, for instance, argued that the Zen approach (a transmission outside of scriptures that did not rely on words, Jp. *furyū monji kyōge betsuden*) refers in fact to the fifth kind of language (*nyogigo*), the true one, and therefore to mantras.[15] Often, these words were believed to have power beyond their meanings. The *Fo yu jing* already emphasized the beneficial effect of the words of the Buddha: "These words bestow material happiness upon all sentient beings and open their minds, steering them towards enlightenment."[16]

It is in this context of a special language unique to the Buddha that Mahayana scriptures mention certain words, variously defined as *nyogigo* ("words that are identical to their meaning"),[17] *himitsugo* ("secret words"), and *mitsugō* ("twilight language" or "intentional language," Sk. *saṃdhābhāṣā* or *saṃdhyābhāṣā*),[18] that would express the absolute truth of Buddha's enlightenment and transmit his most profound teachings; these special words came to be treated as Buddhist forms of mantras. It is possible to consider the Buddhist theories on mantras as a special case of the human quest for a perfect language[19]—one that tells the truth about the world but also ensures salvation.

Language, reality, and the structure of signs

One of the central concepts of the Esoteric Buddhist philosophy of language in Japan is *shōji*, literally "voice and words."[20] Kūkai in particular began to examine the nature of language (*shōji*) in its relations with signs in general (*monji*) and with absolute reality (*jissō*). The composite concept of *shōji jissō* lies at the basis of the principal issues of Shingon philosophy of language, such as polysemy and polymatericity of signs, and the relations between ordinary and absolute language and between language and reality.

Shō is the Buddhist pronunciation (*goyomi*) of a Chinese character normally read *sei* (in its Sinitic pronunciation or *on'yomi*) and *koe* (in Japanese, or *kun'yomi*). In modern Japanese it means "voice" as the "sound produced by sound organs of human beings and animals," but also the "sound produced by the vibrations of things, phonic vibration, sound."[21] Like others of Kūkai's metalinguistic terms, *shōji* has a complex meaning, and refers to different phenomena within a broader semiotic field. Kūkai writes:

> The foundations for the attainment of salvation can be laid out only through doctrines based on names,[22] which in turn cannot exist apart from voice and letters [*shōji*]. Since language [*shōji*] is transparent, it manifests the true reality [...] Therefore, the Buddha Dainichi awakens living beings from their long slumber by explaining to them the meaning of voice, letter, and reality. Who, in expounding a doctrine, be it exoteric or Esoteric, Buddhist or non-Buddhist, would not take such approach?[23]

In this passage, Kūkai defines language as "transparent" and capable of "manifesting the true reality" and characterizes the teachings of the cosmic Buddha (Dainichi) as a metalinguistic discourse on the nature of language and signs, and their relations with true reality.

The term *shōji* immediately reminds one of the auditive and visual signifiers of human language (voice and writing). However, as Henmi Sōhan and Tanaka Chiaki suggest, *shōji* refers primarily to the articulations of sonic objects (entities in the external world that are perceived by the ear and processed by the ear-consciousness) and only in a secondary way to verbal language.[24] In this sense, if *monji* indicates, as we have seen, the articulations of the field of visual objects—and, by extension, all signs—*shōji* is the specialized term to indicate signs of the aural field. Kūkai defined *shō* also as "tones and inflections of language"—perhaps with a special reference to the Chinese language: "among *shō* there are long and short, high and low, straight and bent, all of which are called *mon*."[25] Syllables (*ji*) are also complex entities in Kūkai's system. In modern Japanese, *ji* means "written characters"; most premodern commentators, however, agree that this term as used by Kūkai does not refer only to "written characters" or "letters,"[26] but rather to what we would call today linguistic units of both first and second articulation, i.e. nouns and phonemes/syllables. From this fact we can infer an important feature of Esoteric linguistics, namely, the idea that sound (any sound, not only linguistic) is always the signifier of a noun or of a semantic unit. And since every sound signifies something, there is no distinction between levels of articulation.

Even when it refers to verbal language, *shō* has a very general meaning, since it is at the basis of all languages in the universe:[27] "all words in the ten realms are produced by *shō*."[28] Several authors have suggested that *shō* can be understood as a translation of the Sanskrit term *śabda*.[29] *Śabda* refers to certain eternal words, also known as *vāc*, that are supposed to pervade the universe in the ancient Vedic religion.[30] They manifest themselves through the uttering of the letters of the Sanskrit alphabet (*varṇa*), thanks to a specific quality (*nada*) of the air, the physical basis of phonic vibration (*dhvaṇi*). *Śabda* were the subject of philosophical discussions of the Mīmāṃsā and Vaiyākaraṇa schools in India. In a passage of the *Himitsu mandara jūjūshinron*, Kūkai criticizes some Indian theories of language, thus showing that he had at least some knowledge about them,[31] but it is not clear which is the doctrine that he himself supported. Hōjō

Kenzō, for instance, has identified several affinities between the conception of language of the Indian Grammaticians' school (*vaiyākaraṇa*) and that of the *Mahāvairocana Sutra*, in particular as Kūkai developed it.[32] According to Hōjō there are enough reasons to believe that Kūkai supported the doctrine of immutability and eternity of language (*śabda-nityatva*, Jp. *koe jōjūron*). If this is correct, *shō* would thus also refer to phonemes and words understood as abstract types actualized (i.e. made audible) by being uttered.

Voice—or, in any case, the sound of human language—seems to be one of the primary meanings of Kūkai's *shō*, even though it is not clear the relation between the "voice" and the "phonic vibration" (*kyō* or *hibiki*). It is well known that in Indian philosophy of language, very influential in Kūkai's Esoteric Buddhism, voice, in an almost Husserlian sense of *phonè*,[33] "reaches that originary level in which sound is at the limit of sense: the mantra being chanted thus becomes the echo of the whole body,"[34] a part of the cosmic sound pervading the entire universe. Or, as Ryūichi Abé has written, "the materiality of mantra becomes the very somaticity of the practitioners. The letters are now the physical constituents of the practitioners."[35]

Kūkai also gives another definition of *shō*, probably influenced by Indian ideas of a universal, all-pervading sound:

> The term *shō* also refers to the sounds produced by the mutual contact of the four material elements [i.e. earth, water, fire, and air]. The five notes of the musical scale, the eight kinds of sounds, the seven or eight cases [of Sanskrit declensions], are all generated thanks to the *shō*. A *shō* expresses a certain name through *monji* [signs].[36]

This definition has a more general and concrete character. If previously *shō* referred to linguistic expressions as abstract types, endowed with a potential existence but not directly perceivable until uttered, it now becomes the sonic matter in general as a set of expressive possibilities, as the substance of sonic expression, and also as concrete occurrences of sounds articulated by a form (the five notes [*goon*],[37] the eight kinds of sounds [*hachion*], and so forth).[38] Again, as we have seen at the beginning of our discussion, *shō* can be envisioned as the generic term indicating all sound objects (*shōjin* or *shōkyō*), one of the six fields of sensorial objects (*rokujin* or *rokkyō*).

Kūkai's concept of *shōji jissō* seem to describe a locutionary act, that is, a speech act in which an expression is uttered for its meaning and reference.[39] According to John Austin, locution involves three different acts: phonetic, phatic, and rhetic. The phonetic act consists in "uttering certain noises": in our case, in producing the phonic vibration that manifests the *śabda* cosmic words. The phatic act consists in "uttering … noises of certain types belonging *and as* belonging to a certain vocabulary, in a certain construction, i.e. conforming to and as conforming to a certain grammar, with a certain intonation, &c"; in our case, it corresponds to the utterance of *shō* that are also *ji*, elements that are, or concur in generating, words and sentences. The rhetic act is the act of producing the above linguistic sounds "with a certain more or less definite 'sense' and a more or less definite 'reference'";[40] as Kūkai wrote, "*ji*... necessarily explains the name (*myō*) of something. A name always evokes an object (*tai*)." At this point, we can appreciate the complexity of Kūkai's full definition of linguistic phenomena:

> It is called *shō* the phonic vibration (*kyō*) that always arises when breath and air are set in motion even slightly. Sound thus depends necessarily on *shō*; *shō* is therefore the origin of phonic vibrations. *Shō* is never produced in vain; it is called *ji* because it necessarily expresses the name (*myō*) of something. A name always evokes an object (*tai*). Objects are called "the true aspect of reality" (*jissō*).[41]

This is the general definition of language given by Kūkai. *Shō* is defined as the basis of, and therefore distinct from, the phonic vibration (sound) of language; *shō* is also called *ji* (syllable) when it functions as a "name" (*myō*, probably a general term for linguistic units). Names in turn always refer to an object, defined as an external substance (*tai*).

Sign structure

It is possible to interpret the triad *shō-ji-jissō* in semiotic terms on the basis of categories elaborated by Louis Hjelmslev.[42] In this perspective, *shō* would refer to the substance of expression, the totality of expressive possibilities of the linguistic system that are actualized as concrete sounds and phonemes (Kūkai's examples of *shō* are all systematized sounds, such as the five sounds of the musical scale and the eight kinds of sounds); *ji* would refer to the form articulating such possibilities by organizing them into a lexical system; finally, *jissō* would be, depending on the point of view, either the content of an expression or the external referent, or even the thinkable or the expressible. In this context, Umberto Eco's idea of the substantial identity the matter of expression and the matter of content,[43] is a good way to understand Kūkai's identity of *shōji* and *jissō*.

In the semiotic system of Esoteric Buddhism, *shōji* signs are constituted, in Hjelmslevian terms, by two main levels of expression (phonetic and graphologic), each structured in a form and a substance, and by a plane of content, in turn articulated on several levels, and structured in form and substance of content.[44]

At the level of phonetic expression we have a substance of phonic expression (the linguistic sounds constituting the phonic signifier of mantras) organized in:

1 A syntactic form which allows for the generation of sequences of terms of the mantric dictionary; scholars disagree on whether mantras are syntactically organized, but in Japan it is possible to identify at least some simple rules of juxtaposition that control the succession of mantric terms for the creation of a particular linguistic space;

2 A phonological form of a syllabic kind that allows for the generation of the minimal terms of the mantric dictionary (matric seeds or *shuji* and mantras proper or *shingon*).

At the level of graphologic expression, we have a substance of graphologic expression (the total of graphic possibilities of the system, their materials, etc.), and a form that allows for the construction and recognition of *siddhaṃ* characters (the particular writing system of Indian origin used in Japan to graphically represent mantric expressions) on the basis of minimal components (calligraphic strokes).

The plane of content is in turn articulated in substance (the terms of the Esoteric semantic system, but also objects, cosmic series, etc.) and form (the structure that organizes the units of content). For example, in the Shingon lexical system the semantic space occupied by a term such as *kū* (Sk. *śūnyatā*, "emptiness"), is marked off in opposition with the semantic space of the term *u* ("positive presence" "[provisional] existence"), and the semantic space of both is in turn marked off in opposition with that of the term *honpushō* ("originally non-created," that is, unconditioned); in addition, the content of these three terms is determined by the combination of other semantic units (*kū* = "absence of individual substance"; *u* = "conditioned existence"; *honpushō* = absolute nature), that are in turn further decomposable. Incidentally, these three terms constitute the Esoteric meaning of the mantric expression *A* (the first sound of the Sanskrit alphabet). In this way, the presence of a form of the content implies a systematic organization of the Esoteric Buddhist universe.

Mantra: The phonetic signifier

The term *mantra* refers to a wide range of linguistic entities used in various Indian religious contexts. Mantra is essentially a sound or a sequence of sounds, some endowed with grammatical meaning in Sanskrit, functioning as a condensation of sacred power. Perhaps the most comprehensive definition, if not the most useful one, remains the one proposed by Harvey Alper: "a mantra is whatever anyone in a position to know calls a mantra."[45] Mantra seem to share only an Indic origin and the fact that they constitute a non-ordinary use of language. A further common ground might be the Tantric idea according to which the vibrations of the universe sometimes manifest themselves as linguistic sounds, or more precisely as "seed syllables" (*bīja*, Jp. *shuji*), which combine to form mantras.

Mantras spread throughout most of Asia with the propagation of Hinduism and Buddhism; ideas about mantras contributed to developments in semiotics and the philosophy of language in many cultures. Since their power resides in their sound, their pronunciation was transliterated in numerous writing systems "in an effort to duplicate and thereby preserve the sound" of the voice of the buddhas and the deities proclaiming these sacred expressions.[46]

Mantras were brought to Japan by Esoteric Buddhism; their sounds were transcribed in Chinese characters used for their phonetic value (in accordance with a practice that began in China) and are still chanted today in a Japanese vernacularization of their Sanskrit pronunciation. Numerous mantric expressions, based on texts from the Buddhist canon, are still used in Japan in various contexts ranging from meditation and ascetic practices to magic and folk rituals. The most important among them include the mantric seed *A*, representing the Buddha Mahāvairocana in the Womb mandala, also used in a form of meditation (*ajikan*, the "visualization of the letter *A*"); the two seeds *a* and *un*, used in breathing techniques, but also common designations of the wrathful deities protecting Buddhist and Shinto temples; the mantra *a bi ra un ken*, a representation of the Tantric cosmos that is inscribed on many funerary steles at cemeteries throughout Japan; the formula *oṃ maṇi padme hūṃ* (also well known in the West from Tibetan Buddhism); and even "imitation" mantras used in traditional performing arts. We should note that in Japan the original Indian matrix has been modified by the contributions of other East Asian intellectual and religious systems (in particular, Daoist and Confucian semiotic traditions), in turn interacting with Japanese folk ideas and practices.

The Sanskrit term *mantra* is commonly translated into Japanese as *shingon* (lit. "true words," also the name of the Shingon Buddhist sect) and *ju* ("spells," a term from Chinese popular religion, emphasizing mantras' role as magic formulae and amulets and talismans). Other, more specialized translations include *mantora* (a phonetic transliteration from the Sanskrit, also pronounced *mandara*; medieval exegetes elaborated the idea of a deep connection between mantras and mandalas), *shuji* (a translation of the Sanskrit *bīja*, "seed"), *darani* (transliteration of the Sanskrit word *dhāraṇī*, which refers to Buddhist mantric formulae), *myō* (a translation of the Sanskrit *vidyā*, "brightness, intelligence"), and *himitsugo* and *mitsugō* (translations of the Sanskrit *saṃdhābhāṣā*, "words with a dense meaning," and *saṃdhyābhāṣā*, "twilight language," both closely connected to Esoteric Buddhist teachings.[47] In general, mantras are considered the "true words" (the literal meaning of *shingon*), in contrast with ordinary words that are considered "fallacious." Kakuban described the difference between ordinary speech and mantric language by a poetic image: ordinary words are "illusory and without reality" as the image of the moon reflected on a river or on water in a basin, whereas mantras are true, like the "full moon in the arcane sky."[48] Kūkai also emphasized the truthfulness of mantras by defining them as "non-deluded" (*fumō*), "true speech" (*shingo*), and "Suchness words" (*nyogo*, i.e. words in conformity with true reality).[49] The term *shingon* refers to expressions that are relatively short (from a few syllables to a few words) and that are believed to embody the ultimate essence of a sacred being. As such, they are the privileged instruments for the attainment of the soteriological goal of Esoteric Buddhism, "becoming a buddha in the present body" (*sokushin jōbutsu*), but also to secure more material goals, known as "worldly benefits" (*genze riyaku*) such as wealth, health, and success—hence, the magic overtones of terms such as *ju* (spells); the term *darani*, in contrast, refers to longer mantric formulae, typical of Mahayana Buddhism, which seem to have had, in origin, a primarily mnemonic function.

The origin of mantras

The origin of mantras and their constitutive processes is unknown. According to the provocative view proposed by Frits Staal, mantras might be a sort of fossil evidence of the process of development of the human language, fragments of primordial protolinguistic expressions.[50] This view is supported by Indian myths on the mantric origin of language, whose echoes resonate in medieval Japanese texts, as we have seen in Chapter Two. For example, the *Dari jing* defines *shingon* as "spontaneous and unconditioned" (*hōni jinen*) entities, independent even from the Dharmakāya itself;[51] the Dharmakāya merely uses mantras to "express" or "represent" its own enlightenment. In this sense, at least, mantras were the prototype of human language. Kakuban wrote: "When we investigate the origin of names, [we find that] they all come from mantras."[52] Scholars also tend to recognize in mantras the presence of phonosymbolic elements, synesthesies, and association of ideas[53] that might well be "remnants of something that preceded language."[54]

In the Tantric tradition, especially in East Asia, mantras enjoy a peculiar status as the absolute language of the cosmic Buddha Mahāvairocana, as we have seen in Chapters One and Two. Scholars have been debating whether mantras can be considered a language or not. While some deny such a possibility upfront, others have proposed various theories to justify mantras' linguistic nature; in any case, there is a wide agreement on the importance of the context and the actual situation in which mantras are used. Aside from internal, "emic" considerations from indigenous traditions, it is not easy to decide whether mantras are a particular language, a specific linguistic form, or just a particular usage of language; in all these cases, mantras would need to follow clear linguistic rules. According to Frits Staal, the most authoritative critical voice in the field, mantras are mere pieces of texts devoid of meaning that function as ritual objects. Staal follows here a centuries-old Indian tradition. Within Buddhism, Asaṇga was perhaps the most famous representative of this position. According to him, the lack of meaning of mantras constitutes in fact their significance, because only meaningless signs can somehow represent emptiness.[55]

Staal argues that mantras are only endowed with phonological and pragmatic properties and lack syntax and semantics; accordingly, they conform neither to Western nor to (non-Esoteric) Indian theories on language, and therefore cannot be considered linguistic entities, nor even speech acts.[56] According to Staal, mantras are not linguistic entities but ritual elements; as ritual activity is governed by obscure biological constrains, mantric practice does follow rules but lacks meaning and well-defined goals.[57] Staal thinks that meaning is an exclusive property of ordinary language used denotatively; ritual, and mantras as ritual objects, are devoid of it. He explains: "like rocks or trees, ritual act and sound may be provided with meaning, but they do not require meaning and do not exist for meaning's sake."[58] Incidentally, here Staal assimilates mantras to natural objects (rocks, trees), indicating that for him mantras are not human products, but natural, entities—another echo, perhaps, of ancient Indian doctrines on the spontaneous origin of mantras.

However, most scholars do not agree with Staal's provocative thesis, if only because everything that is part of a culture is significant and can therefore be interpreted. In a semiotic perspective, in fact, any entity can become a sign of something else to someone under some respect or capacity, as in Charles S. Peirce's well-known definition; mantras too can be regarded as interpretable cultural units. Users (including many religious specialists) of mantric expressions may not necessarily understand their meaning, but as Wittgenstein has argued, it is not necessary to understand the meaning of an expression in order to use it correctly. As Stanley Tambiah has written in a different context, the structure of the expression of "magic" formulas and their meaning

> must of course be separated from the problem of whether the exorcist actually understands all the words contained in the spell. From his, as well as the audience's, point of view, the spells have power by virtue of their secrecy and their capacity to communicate with demons and thereby influence their actions. However, *mantra* do not fall outside the requirements of language as a system of communication, and their intelligibility to humans is not the critical factor in understanding their logic.[59]

In other words, correct usage and shared assumptions about their validity as communication tools should be enough to consider mantras as endowed with linguistic nature.

The Japanese case is, in a sense, more complex than the Indian one, for the reason that mantras are elements that reached Japan from a foreign culture, with a different phonological system, specific ritual uses, and meanings whose understanding requires special knowledge (for example, even those mantras that in Sanskrit possess an ordinary meaning end up losing it when used in Japan). Instead of arguing whether mantras conform to modern Western linguistic conceptions or not, it is more interesting to focus on the "emic" positions of the actual users and indigenous theorists; in Japanese Esoteric Buddhism, mantras could be used as ritual objects, as Staal rightly argues, precisely because they were given a particular semiotic status.

As we have seen, the general term referring to mantric expressions of the absolute language of the cosmic Buddha in Japan is *shingon* (Ch. *zhenyan*). This term surfaces rather late in the history of East Asian Buddhism, as it appears for the first time in texts translated by Śubhakarasiṃha (Ch. Shanwuwei, Jp. Zenmui; 637–735) toward the end of the seventh century. Indeed, mantras are the product of a peculiar episteme concerning language uses in religious practices (magic, meditation, liturgy, etc.), an episteme that resulted from Buddhist linguistic and semiotic elaborations over several centuries.

The formation of a unified discourse about mantras and *dhāraṇī* in East Asia has been described by Ujike Kakushō.[60] In particular, the identification of mantra (*shingon*) and *dhāraṇī* (*darani*) as synonyms, taken for granted today, presupposes a complex intellectual elaboration. The term *dhāraṇī* was first discussed in Mahayana texts,[61] where it originally referred not to specific linguistic formulae, but to one of the virtues of the bodhisattva, namely, the capacity to remember perfectly all the sayings of the Buddha, in particular the doctrines concerning transcendental wisdom (*prajñā pāramitā*). In this context, memorization presupposes full understanding of and implies the capacity and will to transmit to others the wisdom of the Buddha (internalized through memorization), for the soteriological benefits of both transmitters and receivers.

Among the various forms in which *dhāraṇī* developed, a central role is played by the "*dhāraṇī* of remembering everything one has heard" (Jp. *monji darani*), i.e. the capacity to remember all Buddhist doctrines one has learned; this memory prevents the arising of negative mental states (Sk. *kleśa*, "afflictions"), and thus constitutes one of the virtues acquired through meditation (*samādhi*).[62] Closely related to memory is eloquence, that is, the capacity to transmit the Dharma correctly and effectively. Later, the meaning of *dhāraṇī* was extended to signify tools and methods that were used to enable or facilitate the mastering of the Dharma; it is at this point that the term *dhāraṇī* came to refer to formulae and linguistic expressions used with mnemonic purposes.

Ujike suggests that the conceptual core of *dhāraṇī*, as they came to be understood in East Asia, may have been elaborated in China by itinerant Buddhist preachers, mostly from Central Asia and India, called *dharmakathika* or *dharmabhāṇaka* (Ch. *fashi*, Jp. *hosshi*).[63] In its ideal form, at least, a *fashi* would master several disciplines, memorize abstruse doctrines, and display a stunning eloquence.[64] *Fashi* also used charms and spells to summon deities; indeed, one of the faculties originally included within the *dhāraṇī* was the capacity to understand the languages of the deities. It was easy, thus, to see mantras as expressions of a "foreign language"—the language of the supernatural world; this attitude was later transmitted to Japan with the arrival of Buddhism.[65]

However, *dhāraṇī* were not only envisioned as linguistic tools for the attainment of wisdom and the purification of the mind; they were also believed to generate supernatural powers (*jinzū*) as a side effect of religious practice. These powers can be employed to attain worldly benefits (*genze riyaku*), and dharanic expressions used to this end were called "divine spells" (Jp. *shinju*). These beliefs and practices are common throughout the entire Mahayana; however, the development of Tantric/Esoteric Buddhism indicates a growing importance in Buddhism of linguistic formulae for the attainment of sacred power. Significantly, Ujike argues that the development of Esoteric Buddhism from classical Mahayana can be better understood through the study of the development of ideas concerning these linguistic expressions,[66] and in particular the transformation of *dhāraṇī* into mantras/*shingon*. Whereas *dhāraṇī* are one of the virtues of the bodhisattva, who is engaged in a virtually endless ascetic practice, *shingon* are the primary instruments for becoming a buddha in the present life-time; even though both sets of formulae kept their functions relating to the acquisition of worldly benefits, in this new context the powers of magic spells were justified as produced by linguistic expressions that are the very essence of Mahāvairocana's enlightenment and soteriological power.

The mantric language

In order to overcome the impasse generated by discussions on mantras' linguistic nature, it might be useful to reformulate the entire question in semiotic terms. Semiotics in fact deals with the abstract structures of signification systems, but also with processes in which users actualize these systems in order to communicate, and the ways in which they criticize and modify the structures of signification systems. We could say with Alper that mantras are "machines" producing particular states of consciousness, a transformation of knowledge, and a different image of reality;[67] their use is constrained by epistemic rules and principles.

Phonology

Esoteric Buddhism gives great importance to the study of Sanskrit for the correct pronunciation of mantras; however, as a consequence of the transcriptions of mantras into Chinese characters read in the Japanese fashion, Japanese *shingon* are based on the phonological system of the Japanese language and not on that of Sanskrit. The utterance of *shingon*/mantras follows rules, handed down from master to disciple, governing not only pronunciation, intonation, intensity of voice, rhythm, and melodic structure of each linguistic entity, but also breathing and bodily posture of the performer. Frits Staal argued about "the importance of musical categories for explaining some of the characteristics that distinguish mantras from [ordinary] language," since, according to him, "mantras cannot be understood unless their musical character is taken into account."[68] This is obviously true in the case of that genre of Japanese Buddhist music known as Shōmyō. The term *shōmyō*, a translation of the Sanskrit *śabda-vidyā*, "body of knowledge concerning language," originally referred to grammar, and in particular to the rules for the correct pronunciation of mantras. In Japan, however, it developed into a fully fledged musical genre with its own theory, repertoire, and performance techniques.[69] The approach suggested by Staal is very useful to understand the functioning of *shingon* in complex rituals integrating liturgical, musical, linguistic, and artistic-visual elements. However, it should be emphasized that music explains only some among the many aspects of mantras.

Syntax

It is not clear if mantras follow specific syntactical rules. On one side, Frits Staal denies the existence of a mantric syntax, whereas on the opposite side Donald Lopez and Stanley Tambiah believe there is one. Premodern Japanese Buddhists, faced with mantras they had to interpret without a clear knowledge of Sanskrit, attributed meanings to each sequence of their syllables, usually corresponding to one or two Sanskrit words; these meanings appear to be devoid of clear syntactic connections. However, it is possible to identify syntactic patterns in mantras. The *shingon* linguistic space is generally marked by formulas such as *namu* or *nōmaku* (Sk. *namaḥ*) or *on* (*oṃ*) at the beginning, and *un* (Sk. *hūṃ*) or *sowaka* (*svāhā*) at the end; these sacred linguistic boundaries include "seeds" (Sk. *bīja*, Jp. *shuji*) of deities, invocations, concepts and images—but not at random. The meanings attributed to each single term give a sense of necessity to the succession of syllables. As we will discuss in detail below and in the next chapter, the syllables in a mantra sometimes corresponded to the phases in the salvation process; their ritual meaning gave them a sense of syntactical order. Thus, we could say that the syntax of *shingon* and *darani* consists in a set of rules establishing a sacred linguistic space through the use of particular and fixed expressions, as well as codes associating by analogy a sequence of sounds to phases in a ritual process.

Semantics

In the case of Japanese *shingon*, each expression is clearly endowed with a definite, albeit complex, meaning (not necessarily known by its users). Many mantras show features of what Louis Hjelmslev called as monoplanary or symbolic systems, in which the form of the expression coincides with the form of the content.[70] A good example of such conformity is the well-known mantra that concludes the *Heart Sutra* (Ch. *Banruo bolomituo xin jing*, commonly known in Japan as *Hannya shingyō*). According to Donald López, this is "an encoded summary of the preceding sutra."[71] Lopez calls it "an allegory," since it "simulates the path by providing an encoded narrative."[72] As we will see below, other mantras show similar aspects. In rigorously Hjelmslevian terms, this is enough to deny the mantras' linguistic nature; however, if we follow Umberto Eco,[73] their monoplanary nature does not affect their interpretability and therefore their nature as a semiotic system.

Pragmatics

Mantric expressions are not used in everyday communication; their field of use is ritual, meditation, and magic. Mantras are also tools for the production, conservation, and transmission of the Esoteric knowledge, and for the transformation of that knowledge into power upon reality through illocutionary and performative acts. Stanley Tambiah was perhaps the first to emphasize this important feature in his studies on formulas of potency in Thai Buddhism.[74] Later, Sasaki Kōkan has pointed out that, to the ancient Japanese, ritual recitation of sutras and the exegetical explanation of their contents were ways to transform the fundamental concepts of Buddhism into magical potency.[75] The same is true also for *shingon*, signs that are "receptacles of magic power."[76] Robert Duquenne has also indicated that the power attributed to sutra chanting is the result of a process of "daranization" of texts, that is, the attribution to an entire scripture of the features of the mantras it contains.[77]

The practice of *shingon* does not take place in a spontaneous or random fashion, but is, at least in principle, a rule-governed behavior: it is intentional, endowed with meaning, and the result of learning; it depends on the context and on rules, both tacit and explicit; and it is carried out by performing codified actions aimed at certain results, codified as well. More specifically, in religious rituals in general the role of *shingon* is based primarily on their sound and the contact that through it they establish with the invisible world of the deities, as a sort of lingua franca of the Buddhist cosmos. The concepts and the forces that they evoke and the results they aim at depend both on mantras' direct relation with Mahāvairocana's absolute reality and the fact that they can be understood (and obeyed) by divine beings. In meditation, on the other hand, *shingon* are decomposed in their constitutive entities, each of which is analyzed according to its multiple Esoteric meanings. In other cases, *shingon* can be used as supports for mediation and trance-like states, as talismans (as in the Tibetan *gzuns*), or for apotropaic purposes (protection from diseases and evil spirits). For all these reasons, we can consider *shingon* as components of the language game—or, more precisely, of the "semiotic game" incessantly played on a cosmic level by the Buddha Mahāvairocana in his cosmic preaching (*hosshin seppō*).[78]

Shittan: the graphologic signifier

In origin, mantric expressions were chanted, recited, mumbled (at times in one's mind); their sound had a primary importance. When Buddhist texts containing mantras, *dhāraṇī*, or other spells, where rendered into Chinese, these formulae were left untranslated; their pronunciation was preserved as faithfully as possible through transcription in Chinese characters used phonetically. For several centuries, Chinese translations of Buddhist texts did not include any non-Chinese character. Even the first Chinese-Sanskrit lexicon, *Fan'yu qianzi wen*, compiled by Yijing (635–713) toward the end of the seventh century, does not use Indic letter, and its Sanskrit words (it does not contain sentences) are written in Chinese transliteration. Indian and Central Asian characters were treated, coherently with received Buddhist conceptions of language, as mere tools to transmit the sense of the spoken words of the Buddha.[79]

With the development of Esoteric Buddhism, the transliterated sound of mantras was no longer enough; a higher phonetic accuracy was needed that could only be ensured by the study of original texts—and, therefore, of the Sanskrit writing system. An Indian script known as *siddhaṃ* (Ch. *xitan*, Jp. *shittan*) began to acquire importance in China and especially in Japan. In fact, one of the most striking features of the texts in the Esoteric canon is the presence of several passages written in *siddhaṃ* characters together with their transliterations and explanations in Chinese. Esoteric Buddhism also developed religious practices that integrated mantra chanting with the visualization of *siddhaṃ* characters used to write those mantras. Thus, *siddhaṃ*, which until that moment were known only to a limited circle of experts engaged in translations, became an indispensable subject of study for monks in general (at least, those interested in Esoteric Buddhism).[80]

The *siddhaṃ* script is a Gupta variant of the *brāhmī* writing system that was used in India between the fourth and eighth centuries; long extinct in India, it survives today only in Japan. According to a common etymological explanation, *siddhaṃ* means "that which has been completed," "that which is complete," but also, by extension, "something perfect." Within Esoteric Buddhism "that which is complete, perfect" refers to that which is expressible linguistically through the *siddhaṃ* writing system, as opposed to what is deemed "incomplete" or "imperfect." Another etymology, more prosaic (but perhaps closer to the truth...), is reported by van Gulik. According to it, *siddhaṃ* was originally a popular term used to refer to the alphabet, deriving from the custom of Indian calligraphy teachers to encourage their pupils by inscribing on their writing tablets the augural expressions *siddhaṃ*, "may you be successful!" or *siddhir-astu*, "good luck!"[81]

In China, the *siddhaṃ* script was used predominantly during the Tang period (seventh to tenth centuries); Indic characters used in China after that time had only a limited impact in Japan where Gupta-type *shittan* have always been the most widespread and are still used today.[82] In fact, the oldest texts written in *siddhaṃ* characters existing today in the world are the *Heart Sutra* (Ch. *Banruo bolomituo xin jing*) and the *dhāraṇī* of the Top of Buddha's Head (Sk. *Uṣṇīṣavijayā dhāraṇī*, Jp. *Butchōson darani*), written on palm-tree leaves; they were brought to Japan in 607 and are still preserved at the Hōryūji temple near Nara;[83] the Japanese government has officially designated them as National Treasures (*kokuhō*).

Kūkai is unanimously considered to have been the real founder of the Japanese tradition of *siddhaṃ* studies, a field known today as *shittangaku*. Kūkai explained the importance of *shittan* for a correct pronunciation and a full understanding of mantras;[84] he also wrote an important theoretical text on *shittan*, the *Bonji shittan jimo narabini shakugi*, and manuals on the writing and pronunciation of the Indian characters. All the material on *shittan* present in Japan by the end of the ninth century was collected and systematized in 884 by the Tendai monk Annen (*ca.* 841–915) in an encyclopedic work entitled *Shittanzō*. Subsequently, the increasing importance of Esoteric Buddhism in Japan resulted in the rapid diffusion of *shittan* as an indispensable component of Tendai and Shingon teachings and practices.[85] *Shittan* were used in Esoteric Buddhist texts and ritual manuals until the end of the Edo period (mid-nineteenth century). The most complete collection of *shittan*-related documents, the monumental *Bongaku shinryō* ("Documents on Sanskrit Learning") in one thousand scrolls, was compiled by the Shingon monk Onkō Jiun (1718–1804) at the end of the eighteenth century.[86]

Knowledge and practices concerning *shittan* spread also outside the religious milieu and influenced the philosophical and cultural world of premodern Japan. For example, the phonetic structure of Sanskrit (*varṇapāṭha*) influenced the development of Japanese *kana* phonetic scripts.[87] *Shittan* studies were also directly connected with the philological and philosophical discussions of the Edo period and the birth of the Nativist movement with Keichū (1640–1701).[88] Furthermore, since the Heian period (eleventh century) *shittan* characters began to be written on funerary monuments, pagodas, and amulets; in this way, they also spread outside of monastic and intellectual circles into the general populace. Even today, funerary tablets (*sotoba*) and monuments carry inscribed *shittan* characters as apotropaic formulae to secure that the deceased person will attain ultimate Buddhahood.

An Esoteric grammatology

Originally, the study of *shittan* was simply a component of the study of Sanskrit, but Esoteric Buddhism turned it into a mystical linguistics, separate from the living languages of India and endowed with increasingly important ritual and initiatory features. The *shittan* script was used to write and give a visual, "physical" shape to the absolute language that is the subject of Esoteric Buddhist semiotics.

The limits of ordinary language and the essentially non-linguistic nature of Dharma make it impossible to explain the contents of the Esoteric enlightenment in ordinary words. Esoteric Buddhist thinkers, however, thought that it was possible to give shape to the reality of their universe by employing certain signs and images, in particular the mandala and the representations of the deities it contains. *Shittan*, when treated as iconic signs of Esoteric Buddhist deities and concepts, filled the gap separating the language of the teachings (which explains superficially but does not "represent") from visual signs of mandala (which represent but do not explain). Similarly to spoken language, Esoteric Buddhism has two theories about the origin of *shittan*. One considers them unconditioned, non-created entities, a graphic equivalent of the eternal linguistic sound (*śabda*) of the Indian grammarians. The *Dari jing* states that these letters were not made by the Buddha, but exist spontaneously and unconditioned (*hōni jinen*).[89] As Kūkai explained:

> According to the *Mahāvairocana Sutra*, these characters were not made by the Buddha, Brahmā or other deities, but originated directly from the spontaneous, unconditioned principle … The buddhas contemplate these spontaneous characters through their Buddha-eye.[90]

Other sources describe *shittan* as spontaneous entities that manifested themselves autonomously in the sky.[91] This idea of writing as a spontaneous, unconditioned entity was perhaps also influenced by Daoist elements, such as the "heavenly talismans" (*tianfu*) and the "cloud seals" (*yunzhuan*), symbolic graphs that developed before the flourishing of Esoteric Buddhism.[92] Still another explanation, already mentioned briefly, considers *shittan* graphs the creation of the Buddha, gods, or cultural heroes.

The structure of Shittan graphemes

In their ordinary uses, *shittan* characters were signs (expressions) of their respective linguistic sounds (contents), as in the case of the graph *A* that stands for the sound "a"; *shittan* graphs are not ideographs but "phonographs" (representation of vocal sounds). In Esoteric Buddhism, however, this is but the most superficial use of this script. Within the Chinese cultural sphere the *siddhaṃ* script was treated not as an alphabet, but as another set of ideograms; furthermore, those "ideograms" had a peculiarly mystic nature. As van Gulik explains: "when confronted with the Indian script, the Chinese decided that each Indian syllable was an ideograph in itself, with its own independent meaning," and found a confirmation in the fact that "in Indian mysticism every letter has indeed its own meaning."[93] As a consequence, religious practices developed that were based not only on the chanting of mantras but also on the writing and visualization of *siddhaṃ* characters. Their sounds and meanings were believed to be connected, in a direct, unconditioned way, to the deities of mandala and, by extension, to features of the absolute reality as experienced in religious practices. *Shittan* graphs were considered as the graphological modality of the cosmic Buddha, and as such they were part of mandala; in particular, they constituted the so-called Dharma Mandala (Jp. *hō mandara*), in which written mantric seeds replace the traditional iconographic rendering of the various deities (see Chapter Two). Kakuban expanded this ancient Chinese idea in his mandala of the five-element *stūpa* (*gorin mandara*), in which the five syllables of the mantra *a bi ra un ken* are part of a rhyzomatic network of cosmic codes based on Chinese traditional cosmology and the world view of Esoteric Buddhism (on this subject, see Chapters Two and Four). In this way, *shittan* were definitively consecrated as "multivalued icons" (Luis Gomez), microcosms, absolute entities, in accordance with the traditional view about their origin.

As a consequence, the *shittan* graphs came to be envisioned as visual, graphic signifiers of multimateric signs which, as we have seen, include sounds but also other semiotic substances. In fact, *shittan* have three components, namely, graphic aspect (*gyō*), sound (*on*), and meaning (*gi*). Their graphic aspect, in particular, is further organized in three levels, each in turn articulated in both a substance and a form: a graphologic level (the "calligraphic" aspects of each graph), a combinatorial level (as related to the "syntax," the combinatory possibilities of each graphs), and a grammatological level (pertaining to standard semantic associations of the calligraphic strokes).

The graphologic *substance* includes all the figures and traits (strokes) of which they are composed (calligrams); these are the minimal elements, that is, the basic brush strokes used and combined in various ways when writing the graphs.[94] The graphologic *form* of the *shittan* characters provides a positional and oppositional structure to the elementary graphic figures on the basis of categories such as the main body of the character (*a*, *ka*, *sa*, etc.), additional strokes needed to represent other vowel sounds or compound sounds (*oṃ*, *hṛīḥ*, etc.), but also more abstract elements such as direction (verticality, horizontality, obliquity, circularity, etc.), width, and energy of strokes, and so forth. The combinatorial substance includes all *shittan* graphs, whose total figure varies according to the tradition, ranging from forty-two to fifty-one graphs. The combinatorial form, which gives each actual *shittan* graph a positional and oppositional status, determines the "alphabetical" order in classification systems and provides rules for the combination of individual graphs in larger word units. Finally, the grammatological level controls standard significations commonly associated with calligraphic strokes. A typical example are the so-called "five points" or "five transformations" (*goten*), in which calligrams were added to the basic character *A* in order to represent the altered sounds *ā*, *aṃ*, *aḥ*, *āṃḥ* (see Figure. 3.1). These "five transformations" were normally associated with the five steps in the Esoteric Buddhist process of attaining enlightenment.

Furthermore, all minimal graphologic figures (strokes) were indicated by a Chinese character, to which they were related by formal similarities or other analogical relations. In this way, each stroke was de facto associated to a dictionary and to a semantic system, however simplified and rudimentary.[95] The graphologic substance also included all possible materials used to write *shittan* graphs, such as ink (for manuscripts and prints), stone (for inscriptions on steles and tombs), incense smoke (used in certain forms of visualization), and a more elusive mental matter (as in visualization/meditation).

The universe of meaning of Esoteric signs

So far we have discussed the first two types of the Esoteric practices on signs (*gomitsu*), i.e. the recitation and memorization of mantric formulae and the study and writing of *shittan* graphs. These two kinds of practices,

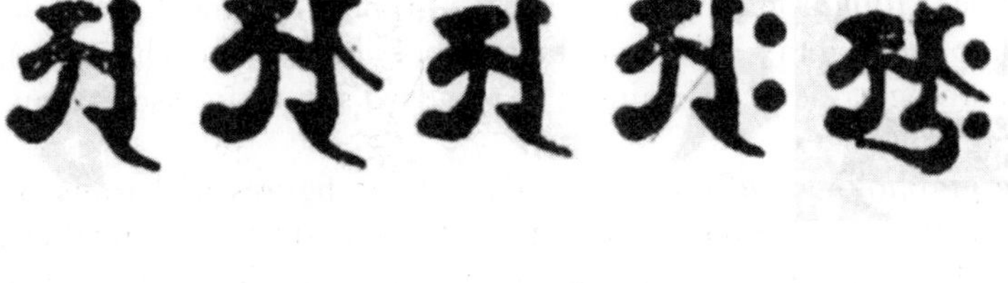

FIGURE 3.1 *The five transformations* (goten) *of the graph* A. *From* Ono rokuchō. *In T. vol. 78, p. 87a. Tokyo: Daizō shuppan.*

based on the manipulation of the phonetic and graphic signifiers of Esoteric signs, are already endowed with salvational power; however, they are preliminary stages to third stage, namely, the "understanding of the true meanings of each graph."[96] Kakuban identifies two levels in this stage, the "general interpretation of the deep meaning of each graph" and the "complete and correct understanding of the Dharma-realm and the Dharma-body."[97] The former refers to the semantic structure of the Esoteric expressions and the related interpretive practices; the latter consists in a sort of "mandalization" of Esoteric signs by exploring their correlative network. This mandalization, which was systematized by Kakuban, operates on two different planes: on the one hand, Esoteric expressions (*shingon* and *shittan*) are treated as minimal mandalas in which the entire Dharma realm is condensed;[98] on the other hand, the mandala of the two realms (*ryōgai mandara*), the fundamental mandala of Shingon Buddhism, is reduced to the two mantric seeds (*shuji*) that generate it, namely, *A* for the Womb (*taizōkai*) mandala and *vaṃ* (Jp. *ban*) for the *Vajra* (*kongōkai*) mandala.[99] In this section I outline the organizing principles of the Esoteric semantic system and its interpretive strategies by following the semiotic and ritual strategies of premodern exegetes. In particular, I focus on the first level of the third stage of the "secret of language" (*gomitsu*), i.e. the "general interpretation of the deep meaning of each Esoteric expression"—the nature of the Esoteric signs, their semantic structure, and the interpretive strategies of Shingon Buddhism. The mastering of this theoretical background lies at the basis of ritual and meditative practices leading to becoming a buddha in this very body (*sokushin jōbutsu*), which corresponds to the second level of the third stage, the "complete and correct understanding of the Dharma-realm and the Dharmakāya," to be addressed in Chapter Four.

The status of the "secret" in Esoteric Buddhism

Esoteric hermeneutics attributes infinite meanings to expressions. Often, this infinity tends to be understood in mystical terms as something incomprehensible to the non-initiated; however, infinite meaning simply refers to ordinary language's impossibility to fully describe any entity in its relations with the entire cosmos—a necessary feature of a conceptual system that emphasizes the essential interrelationship of all phenomena as manifestations of a universal substance (the *dharmadhātu/hokkai*, which is no other than the body of the cosmic Buddha, Mahāvairocana/Dainichi). In other terms, this is a different formulation of the principle of unlimited semiosis, initially theorized by Charles S. Peirce and further developed by Umberto Eco. In it, the endless drift of interpretants is only potential, because in actual interpretive practice the interpreter (or the community of interpreters) tends to bring it to a stop at a certain point of the process;[100] this is indeed what also happens in Shingon exegetical processes.

The existence of a potentially infinite series of meanings can result in positing hidden, secret, initiatory aspects—features of all forms of esoteric knowledge. In his discussion of the "hermetic semiosis" at the basis of Western esotericism, Umberto Eco claims that it is grounded on an empty secret, whose content is forever deferred.[101] Initiation provides instructions on how to get closer to discovering the content of that elusive secret—one that is supposedly related to the fundamental meaning of life and the universe, but can never be revealed.

In the case of Esoteric Buddhism, however, the secret of the initiatory teachings is never empty or absolute; in fact, it is a secret only to the non-initiated. Initiation rituals do not reveal clues for an endless quest for the secret; on the contrary, they explain certain principles for the understanding of reality that are culturally assumed to enable the initiated to attain specific soteriological goals. Thus, the final initiation often reveals not a conceptual content, but practical ways of performing ascetic rituals properly.

As we have already seen, Esoteric Buddhism divides the Buddhist teachings into superficial (*kengyō*) and secret (*mikkyō*). Superficial teachings are the provisional doctrines that were taught by Śākyamuni, or, more generally, by provisional manifestations of the Buddha: the *nirmaṇakāya* (the shape of the Buddha as he appears to ordinary sentient beings) and the *samboghakāya* (the realized Buddha-body of the bodhisattvas). The meaning of these teachings is clear and easy to comprehend. In contrast, secret teachings are "most profound doctrines that are beyond the faculties of sentient beings, dealing with the ultimate secrets of all buddhas' enlightenment."[102] As an unconditioned and multisemiotic discourse performed by the Dharmakāya (Jp. *hosshin*, the absolute and unconditioned modality of existence of the cosmic Buddha) to himself for the pure pleasure of the Dharma, these teachings are envisioned as permanent and immutable.

Since Esoteric Buddhism claims to teach the content of the Buddha's enlightenment (which, according to other Buddhist denominations, is beyond representation and understanding), it would seem to *reveal* secret and hidden things and not to conceal them. This is the first and most obvious problem we face when we translate the Sino-Japanese term *himitsu* ("secret"). A possible clue to solve this paradox is that in the Buddhist tradition, secret is essentially contextual: it refers to something that is unknown to someone but known to someone else. From the perspective of a self-defined "profound" doctrine, its content is "secret" (e.g., unknown) to a more superficial doctrine. Thus, the Buddhist precepts are "secret" for the non-Buddhists, in the same way as the *Lotus Sutra* is "secret" for the followers of non-Mahayana teachings. What is "secret" (unknown) to one tradition is the actual content of the teachings of another tradition. It is the duty of the depositaries of this "secret" knowledge to reveal it to people they consider worthy. We have here two different regimes of secrecy: one that defines Shingon vis-à-vis the outside (what it knows in relation to whom), and one that organizes internal levels of instruction and attainment.

Kūkai defined two fundamental forms of secrecy: the "secret of beings" (*shujō himitsu*) and the "secret of the Tathāgata" (*nyorai himitsu*). Beings are part of the twofold mandala and are innately endowed with its principles (*ri*) and the wisdom (*chi*) to grasp them; however, because of their ignorance, they do not know it. This is the "secret of beings"—or, more accurately, what is "unknown to beings." Mahāvairocana preaches the superficial teachings as expedient means according to the capacities and the situation of the audience, and therefore he does not reveal the most profound doctrines concerning his enlightenment: this is the "secret of the Tathāgata." However, Mahāvairocana does transmit these profound teachings to people with the right capacities to whom such secret teachings are no longer "secret."[103] In Kūkai's treatment, "secret" is the unknown, the unthought-of, that which is ignored—the outside of an intellectual system. The opposite of "secret" is that which is "revealed," "made-known," rather than that which is "evident." Secrecy is organized along a downward vertical axis—or, more precisely, a reversed pyramid. At the wide top are the evident truths, the exoteric teachings; secret teachings are situated deeper and deeper, and access to them is more and more limited. Thus, the secret of the Tathāgata is revealed to some, but kept secret from most; the secret that was withheld from beings has been revealed to all, but is unknown to most.

The Tendai monk Annen (841–915?) developed two more detailed typologies of secrecy, consisting respectively of four and six elements. The *Shingonshū kyōjigi* describes four kinds of secrets:[104] (i) things kept hidden by the buddhas—buddhas preach only doctrines that can be understood by their audience as a strategy to spread Buddhism; this secret corresponds to Kūkai's secret of the Tathāgata; (ii) things secret to beings: for example, ordinary people do not know that all sounds are mantras, but their ignorance is not due to the fact that the Buddha hides this truth from them; their limited capacities prevent them from knowing what is in this case self-evident and this secret corresponds to Kūkai's secret of beings; (iii) linguistic secrets: words spoken by the buddhas have meanings that are deeper than they appear, as Annen writes, "if one interprets them according to their written expression (*mon*), the intention of the Buddha (*butsui*) is lost." This is a reference to linguistic intension, in particular to the connotative aspects of signs, and to the existence of different levels of meaning (isotopies); (iv) the secret of the Dharma-substance (*hottai*): the enlightenment of the buddhas exceeds the capacities of people only exposed to exoteric teachings—even bodhisattvas cannot experience it directly. This is a sort of ontological dimension of secrecy: only those who have undergone a particular training and have achieved the consequent bodily and cognitive transformations can understand this secret.

This typology is a development of Kūkai's ideas. Two elements are relevant here, namely, the recognition of semantic isotopies in language, so that each expression has several meanings that are usually unknown and, thus, "secret"; and the positing of a fundamental "secret" that is related to the ontological nature of the Dharma itself and that can be known only to those who have attained enlightenment.

In the *Taizō kongō bodaishingi ryaku mondōshō*, Annen puts forward a different typology, consisting of six kinds of secrets:[105] (i) the subtle secret of the Dharma-substance (*hottai*), namely, the three secrets (*sanmitsu*, i.e. the operations of body, speech, and mind) of the Tathāgata and those of beings are originally one and the same. This is the basis of the doctrines of original enlightenment (*hongaku*); of course, ordinary people are not aware of their innately enlightened nature and therefore do not know this secret; (ii) the content of the enlightenment of the buddhas: this is at the basis of the distinction between exoteric and Esoteric teachings; while the exoteric Buddha does not explain the content of his enlightenment, which thus remains a secret for his followers, Dainichi (Mahāvairocana) teaches his enlightenment (albeit only to some); (iii) things that cannot be taught to lowly, unworthy people: this kind of secret presupposes a sociology of Esoteric transmission as "underclasses" (*hisen no hito*) may have no access to it; (iv) things that ordinary people cannot comprehend because they lack enlightenment (or awareness): this level posits the existence of epistemological limits; were they ever taught something of this order, they would not understand it; this corresponds to Kūkai's secret of beings; (v) things that cannot be transmitted to those who have not yet practiced meditation (*samādhi*): this category presupposes steps in the education process; at each stage, the following stages are unknown, thus "secret"; and (vi) things that the practitioners keep secret (violations being a very serious sin): these were rules about the management of initiatory knowledge and lineages.

In this second typology, Annen emphasizes rules and presuppositions of initiatory lineages—issues related to the social control of meaning. There are things that cannot be revealed openly, not only because they would not be understood, but also because of the social status or the attainment level of some among the possible recipients; the initiated should internalize this policing attitude toward "secret" meanings.

To summarize, the Esoteric "secret" refers to a particular transmission from the Buddha, namely, teachings revealed by the supreme Buddha, Mahāvairocana, to particularly worthy people. This is related to the definition of the Esoteric Buddhist tradition, but it also implies procedures to establish who can be initiated to these doctrines. Moreover, these teachings are organized on several levels and require procedures to move from one level to the other.

The interpretive apparatus

The nondual cosmology of Esoteric Buddhism stresses that phenomena are identical with the absolute and that the universe is a pansemiotic whole, in which each entity and each event are instances of a communicational activity that the Dharmakāya addresses to itself for pure pleasure and to the beings (*shujō*) for their salvation. Ignorance and karmic conditioning prevent beings from knowing such soteriological nature of phenomena.

In order to understand the Dharmakāya's intention, it is necessary to know its communicational strategies, the structure of its signs and their ritual uses. Esoteric Buddhism developed several interpretive methods to establish the profound, Esoteric meanings of signs (expressions and phenomena). One such method consists in analyzing pairs of originally non-mantric terms based on Sanskrit compound terms (Sk. *sat-samāsa*, Jp. *roku rigasshaku*, "analysis of six combinations"). The six types of compounds are the following: *dvandva* (Jp. *sōishaku*), two nouns connected by the conjunction *ca* ("and") or, less frequently, the disjunction *vā* ("or") and not, as in the other cases, by a grammatical subordination; *tatpuruṣa* (*eshushaku*), the combination of a main noun with a qualifying noun, in which the first member depends on or modifies the second; *karmadhāraya* (*jigasshaku*), a noun or a nominal part preceded by a modifying adjective, both referring to the same object; *dvigu* (*taisū*), in which a numeral is the first member; *avyayībhāva* (*ringonshaku*), a preposition or prefix modifying a noun and functioning as an adverb; and *bahuvrīhi* (*uzaishaku*), descriptive compound of two nouns functioning as an adjective.[106]

Kūkai employs this method to explain the relationship between, respectively, *shō* (voice) and *ji* (words) on the one hand and *shōji* (language) and *jissō* (true reality) on the other hand. Kūkai considers "superficial" the result of the application of *sōishaku* (*dvandva*) mode, according to which "*shōji* are provisional and do not attain the truth, true reality is deep and silent and transcends words; *shō* resonate in vain and do not signify anything, while *ji*, high and low, long and short, form sentences."[107] Kūkai attributes to this compound only a disjunctive value; in his view, syntax reproduces a semantic disjunction, in turn caused by an absolute ontological difference. Kūkai apparently bases his interpretation on the meaning of the Chinese translation of the compound's name, *sōi*, "mutual difference." This interpretation refers to the traditional Mahayana ideas of language outlined previously. In contrast, the application of *jigasshaku* (*karmadhāraya*) produces a profound interpretation: "since there is no *ji* outside of *shō*, *ji* is *shō*; since there is no true reality outside of *shōji*, *shōji* is the true reality; this is explained in detail in the *Commentary to the Mahāvairocana Sutra*, to which I refer."[108] In this case, Kūkai saw the two terms as a single expression related to a unified substance. The *ringonshaku* (*avyayībhāva*) mode also yields a profound interpretation: "*shōji* and true reality are extremely close and inseparable."[109] The results of the remaining two modes, *eshushaku* (*tatpuruṣa*) and *uzaishaku* (*bahuvrīhi*), can be "either superficial or profound" and can be reduced to the previous cases; the *taisū* (*dvigu*) mode does not apply to these cases.

This method for the grammatical analysis of Sanskrit serves to determine the syntactical status, and therefore the sense, of the relevant terms. In Japanese Esoteric Buddhism, however, the six combinations (*rigasshaku*) presuppose conformity between syntax and meaning of the words on the one hand and the structure of the real on the other. The underlying assumption is that a given syntactic structure can explain the meaning of the terms involved and also reveal the true nature of the objects to which those terms refer. In other words, there is an implicit relation between syntactical position, meaning of words, and the deep structure of reality; accordingly, meaning is motivated and isomorphic with reality. Such an essentialized vision of language was certainly not Kūkai's invention, but was widespread in premodern Japan as a fundamental epistemic element.

In addition to the six combinations, the most comprehensive set of esoteric interpretive strategies, however, is the so-called "sixteen gates of obscurity" (*jūroku genmon*).[110] This set appears for the first time in the *Hokkekyōshaku* by Kūkai, in which the author brings together hermeneutic elements from Esoteric texts. It is a heterogeneous set of instructions concerning the knowledge and practices that are necessary to penetrate the "obscurity," i.e. the Shingon semantic system. The sixteen gates of obscurity are:

1. Elimination of delusions (*shajō*)
2. Manifesting the virtues of esoteric Buddhism (*hyōtoku*)
3. Literal meaning of an expression (*jisō*), corresponding to the superficial truth (*sezokutai*) of Mahayana
4. Real meaning of an expression (*jigi*), corresponding to the deep truth (*shintai*) of Mahayana
5. Superficial interpretation (*senryakushaku*), limited to the exoteric level of the teachings
6. Esoteric interpretation (*jinpishaku*), that is, the semantic realm proper of Esoteric Buddhism
7. Polysemy (*ichiji shō ta*), that is, the fact that each Sanskrit syllable contains many meanings
8. Synonymy (*taji ki ichi*): several expressions can be reduced to a single one
9. The interpretation of a single expression can produce many meanings (*ichiji shaku ta*)
10. All expressions refer to a single principle, the same for all of them (*taji shaku ichi*)
11. Proliferation: one syllable can generate many different syllables (*ichiji jō ta*)
12. Reduction: several syllables can be reduced to a single one (*taji jō ichi*)

13 One syllable can destroy numerous deluded ideas (*ichiji ha ta*)
14 Several syllables together can destroy one deluded idea (*taji ha ichi*)
15 Meditation on the meaning of syllables in a sequence in the usual order (from the first one to the last one) (*junkan senten*)
16 Meditation on the meaning of syllables in a sequence in the reverse order (from the last to the first one) (*gyakkan senten*).

These sixteen elements form eight pairs of contrastive items concerning various aspects of meditative practice; the goal of practice, in fact, is precisely that of overcoming these contrasts in the middle path (*chūdō*). In detail, gates 1 and 2 refer to the general Buddhist stances concerning liberation; while Mahayana points to the emptiness of all phenomena by eliminating delusions, Esoteric Buddhism shows the virtues of phenomena and signs. Gates 3 and 4 concern the semantic structure of the Esoteric signs, in particular the combination *shingon-shittan* (especially in the form of mantric seeds, *shuji*); 5 and 6 refer to types of interpretive approach to texts and concepts; 7 and 8 refer to the status of the Esoteric signs; 9 and 10 indicate the results of interpretive activity; 11 and 12 deal with the form of the expression; 13 and 14 refer to the Esoteric syllables' power to destroy the veil of ignorance and dissolve wrong ideas; finally, 15 and 16 indicate how to actually perform meditation on mantric expressions.

The elimination of deluded states of mind (*shajō*) is a sort of *via negativa* that denies ordinary views of reality; in contrast, the active manifestation of the power of Esoteric Buddhism (*hyōtoku*) constitutes Shingon's *via positiva*, through which the salvational power of Esoteric Buddhism can be enacted and displayed. These terms are interpreted in many ways within the various Shingon lineages; some authors associate these two methods with different epistemic attitudes. For instance, Raihō wrote:

> Elimination of delusions [*shajō*] consists in eliminating people's deluded states of mind in order to have them realize the signlessness of the Dharma-essence [*hosshō*]. It consists in not abiding in any single dharma, in not attaching oneself to any single sign; thus, free from attachment, one can practice the Way of the Buddha.
>
> Manifestation of virtues refers to [the method of] not arguing about any dharma's right or wrong, because all dharmas are originally non-created and absolute; all visible objects manifest the Shingon virtues.[111]

As we will see at the end of this chapter, signlessness means for Raihō a particular cognitive dimension in which all signs are interrelated—another way to describe the interconnectedness of the semantic space or, in other words, unlimited semiosis. These two methods combined enable the practitioner to contemplate dharmas as condensations of the semantic universe and, thus, as microcosms condensing all features and powers. In this way, the practitioner literally inhabits a mandalic world in which everything is a manifestation of the absolute Buddha's salvational power and activity. Reliance on either of these two methods also affects one's soteriological path. Again, Raihō wrote:

> According to the superficial interpretation, the elimination of delusions is used in [the process of enlightenment] leading the practitioner from [initial] cause to [final] result [*jūin shika*], while the manifestation of virtues is used by the buddhas [in the process of manifesting themselves in this world] when, from their original condition, they leave their traces [in this world] [*jūhon suijaku*]. According to the profound interpretation, these two methods refer to the two [processes of] upward and downward transformations [*jōge niten*]. [In other words,] according to the superficial interpretation, one first abides in the elimination of delusions and then contemplates the manifestation of virtues. According to the profound interpretation, one first abides in the manifestation of virtues, and then contemplates the elimination of delusions.[112]

The manifestation of virtues, in its deep, true meaning, is the original condition of beings from the perspective of the doctrines of original enlightenment (*hongaku*); once they realize their condition they are also able to eliminate delusions—a process that is the opposite of the received soteriological path. I will return to issues of soteriology in the next chapter.

The meaning of the Esoteric expressions

Let us now turn our attention more in detail to the semantic structure of the Esoteric signs as exemplified by gates three to six. These gates define the structure of the Esoteric semantic system and the fundamental interpretive strategies it involves. *Siddhaṃ* characters, objects, and concept have two basic orders of significance, defined as, respectively, superficial/exoteric and profound/esoteric. The standard, "superficial" meaning (*jisō*, lit. "graph's aspect") corresponds to the superficial truth (*sezokutai*) of Mahayana, whereas the Esoteric aspect (*jigi*, lit. "graph's meaning," i.e. the true meaning) refer to the deep truth (*shintai*) of Mahayana. To these levels of meaning correspond different interpretive attitudes. "Superficial and abbreviated interpretation" (*senryakushaku*) produces the superficial meaning, while the "deep and secret interpretation" (*jinpishaku*) extracts the profound meaning of signs and objects.

The attribution of a complex meaning to Sanskrit sounds and *shittan* graphs is a peculiar development of Buddhist teachings dating in China from at least the third century CE. Originally, Sanskrit syllables had a mnemonic function: each was given a "meaning" constituted by a key term or expression from a sutra or a school. These meanings formed the units of content, a kind of basic vocabulary, of a Buddhist tradition. Examples of these mnemonic repertoires appear in various scriptures translated into Chinese. Meaning was not attributed in a totally arbitrary way, since the sound of each syllable usually formed the initial element of the term to be memorized.[113] As explained by Ujike Kakushō, Mahayana mnemonic techniques were related to the capacity of memorization (*dhāraṇī*), one of the virtues of the bodhisattva.[114] Just to make a few examples, the syllable *A* stands for *ādyanutpāda* (original uncreatedness, unobtainability), *i* for *indriya* (sense organs), *ṛ* for *ṛddhi* (supernatural powers), *kha* for *kha* (the sky, void), *ba* for *bandhana* (bondage, karmic conditioning), *ra* for *rajas* (defilements), *la* for *lakśaṇa* (sign), and *va* for *vāc* (speech, words).[115] Esoteric Buddhism consistently applied the principle of the double truth (*nitai*) to the *siddhaṃ* letters (and no longer just to the phonemes), which thus came to acquire two mutually contradictory levels of sense: for instance *A*, from "origin" (as the first letter of the Sanskrit alphabet) came to mean "lack of origin"; *va* from "speech" turned out to signify "something transcending language." Scriptural commentaries further complicated the situation, because they projected onto the syllables/graphs a three-fold conceptual grid (*santai*: respectively, emptiness, provisional being, and absolute), thus resulting into a complex semantic structure articulated in several levels.

In any case, the two-level semantic structure of Esoteric signs represents the relation between semiosophia and semiognosis. The superficial level is called *jisō*, and the deep, Esoteric level is called *jigi*. *Jisō* refers to a signification based on appearances, the shape of a sign: the primary meaning at this level is usually a term that begins with the same sound as its expression. For example, the *jisō* of the expression *va* is *vāc*, that is, "word, language." In this way, the syllable *va* is treated as the condensation of another sign that it stands for, namely, *vāc*, whose meaning is illustrated according to mainstream exoteric teachings.

The structure of the true meaning, *jigi*, on the deep, Esoteric level, is very complex. As we have seen, *jigi* can be the opposite of the superficial meaning: in the case of the syllable *ha*, whereas the *jisō* is "cause" (from the Sanskrit *hetu*, "cause"), the *jigi* is "no causation" or "uncausedness." *Jigi* can also be—and this is more interesting from a semiotic viewpoint—a meta-term transcending the dichotomy (a dichotomy that is intrinsically fallacious because it results from attachment to false ideas) between *jisō* and its contradictory. This meta-term is defined as "unobtainable" or incomprehensible (*fukatoku*), an expression defining a situation of conceptual nondualism: the real meaning is "not obtainable" (unattainable) within ordinary language (since any concept can be denied by its contradictory), whose dichotomic nature it transcends. Once one reaches the semantic level of "unobtainability," one realizes the real nature of language and therefore reaches enlightenment. In the case of the mantric seed *ha*, the ultimate *jigi* is "cause is unobtainable." One should note that unobtainability is not the result of a process of negation as in the Buddhist traditional strategy established by Nāgārjuna. On the contrary, "unobtainability" presupposes the coexistence of all terms and concepts related to the original expression being analyzed as the ultimate consequence of esoteric polysemy. In other words, "unobtainability" renders the concepts it applies to not "empty" (as in Nāgārjuna's Mādhyamika), but absolute, as elements of the unconditioned Dharma realm.[116] We have already encountered this in Kakuban's interpretation of nondualism discussed in Chapter Two.

Raihō defines in the following way the differences between *jisō* and *jigi*:

> According to our lineage, whenever one uses graphs there is a difference between their aspect and their meaning. As for the graph's aspect [*jisō*]: when one ignores the principles of the graphs, names and meanings are distinct. One pronounces the graphs based on provisional conventions [*konryū*, Sk. *samaropa*]; but this refers only to the [superficial] aspects of the graphs and is not identical [*sōō*] to their meanings [...].
>
> As for graph meaning [*jigi*]: since linguistic expressions [*shōji*] are the true aspect [of reality, *jissō*], each single graph is the [ultimate] essence and substance [*shōtai*] of reality. Both sound [*shō*] and graphic form [*ji*] of every graph have meaning: the graph is the meaning, therefore this is called "graph meaning." Let us make an example.
>
> The graphic form and the sound of [the *siddhaṃ*] graph *ha* (Jp. *ka*) are of themselves not meaningful; intonation and length resonate in vain and have no meaning. On the basis of an ordinary, provisional convention the character *ha* is said to mean "activity": this is a linguistic expression at the level of the graph aspect. Let us now consider the graph meaning. The same syllable *ha* is a word [*shōji*] whose sound [*shō*] is meaningful [*gi*]. It means "activity" because the five senses are the sources of creation. Therefore the graph is action, and apart from it [and the action it produces] there is no meaning of "activity." In other words, the sound in its totality is the meaning of "activity." Since there is no meaning apart from the graph [embodying and performing it], this is called graph meaning.
>
> When one uses the graph aspect, one is using the four kinds of fallacious ordinary speech. When one uses the graph meaning, one is using the speech that conforms itself to meaning as used by transcendent beings [buddhas and bodhisattvas].
>
> Question: it is usually said that "activity" is the graph aspect, while "unobtainable [*fukatoku*]" is the graph meaning. Why is this different from your explanation?
>
> Answer: There are many different interpretations concerning graph aspect and graph meaning. I explained the graph aspect as a graph without meaning [*umon mugi*], and the graph meaning as a graph with meaning [*umon ugi*], as it is stipulated in [Kūkai's] *Shōji [jissō]gi* and the *Unjigi*. Now, concerning the meaning "activity" as graph aspect and "unobtainable" as graph meaning, when people penetrate the Shingon

> teachings and understand the difference between semioticity [*usō*] and signlessness [*musō*], they come to realize that [the realm of] signs is the graph aspect and that signlessness is the graph meaning. Actually, there are four kinds of aspect and meaning of graphs, as explained in the commentaries.[117]

Unobtainability can thus be understood as the ultimate goal of the interpretation process. It is situated outside semiosis, and it corresponds to the point at which a sign ceases to be a sign. An unattainable term transcends the articulations of sense and resists interpretation, situating itself at the level of nondualism (*funi*).

This Esoteric semantic structure was first defined by Kūkai in his *Bonmōkyō kaidai*, in which he associated *jisō* with exoteric Buddhism (*kengyō*) and *jigi* with Esoteric Buddhism (*mikkyō*). However, Kūkai also put forth another interpretation, according to which *jisō* refers to the idea that each graph/sign has only one, specific meaning, whereas *jigi* assumes that each graph/sign has countless meanings. For example, in the case of the syllable *ha*, the *jisō* is "operation" (*sagō*, a synonym here of the previously mentioned "cause"), whereas the *jigi* is the unobtainability of operation (*sagō fukatoku*). *Fukatoku* is here a synonym of the Middle Path (*chūdō*) leading to enlightenment. Kūkai wrote: "When one contemplates unobtainability [one sees that] all written characters have penetrated the profound principle of the Dharma-nature; being all undifferentiated and homogeneous, one does not see individual meanings or features/signs."[118] Whereas the theoretical basis for this doctrine can be found in the *Shōji jissōgi*, similar arguments are made in many other texts, such as the *Unjigi* and the *Bonji shittan jimo narabini shakugi*.

In this way, the pair *jisō/jigi* is almost interchangeable with another pair, *senryakushaku* (superficial meaning) and *jinpishaku* (profound meaning), corresponding to gates of obscurity numbers five and six. Raihō (1279–1330?) gives the following definition of these two levels of meaning:

> Superficial [meaning] is like that of provisional words provisionally uttered by common folks and saintly people [i.e. monks]. When one interprets them, their meaning is shallow; sentences are long but their meaning is simple. [...] Profound [meaning] refers to the external manifestation of profound matters by the mind. Since these matters cannot be transmitted to unworthy people, they are called profound and secret.[119]

This definition presupposes that different cognitive attitudes toward language and signs result in different semiotic practices. Those for whom language is merely a conventional means of communication can only say and understand "shallow things," whereas utterances and semiotic activity of those who understand the ontology of language and its role in the process of salvation in general constitute "the external manifestation of profound matters by the mind." This is a form of unconditioned activity in which the enlightened mind, essentially identical with Mahāvairocana's mind, free of conditionings, puts forth microcosmic semiotic formations that embody the structure and the power of the universe. Levels of sense give a soteriological value to words, concepts and phenomena, and therefore play a fundamental role in Esoteric Buddhism as representations of its soteriologic trajectory.

In terms of the semiotic approach previously outlined, we can reformulate the Esoteric semantic system in the following way. The plane of content is constituted by a form (a structure organizing the units of the content) and by a substance (the total sum of the semantic units contained by the esoteric encyclopedia). Form and substance of the content parallel form and substance of the expression (both verbal and graphic); its units are not just words and sentences, as in ordinary linguistics, but also syllables and phonemes. As such, the totality of the expression is constituted by the Sanskrit phonetic system and the *shittan* graphemic system. The substance of the content, at the *jisō* level, is constituted by a limited, if varying, set of concepts based on the Sanskrit alphabet. Units of content can be further decomposed in smaller units such as semantic markers, but always in a controlled fashion determined by the fundamental Esoteric vocabulary. Thus, units of the content on the *jigi* level are directly connected with the less numerous units at the *jisō* level. Underlying all this is the matter of content, constituted by the totality of the thinkable, speakable, and representable within the Esoteric episteme. From the perspective of its constitutive system, the Esoteric episteme, despite claims of unlimited polysemy, multiplicity of signification, and so forth, appears strikingly structured, limited, and predictable in its conceptual outcomes. Interpretive creativity finds its place in the application of the system to new areas, not yet covered by traditional exegesis and in the usage of alternative ways to define the conceptual units on the various semantic levels.

For example, the syllable/graph *ha* (Jp. *ka*) is, as we have seen, mainly associated on the superficial level (*jisō*) with the concept "cause." "Cause" is distinguished from "action," "soteriological practice," or even "nirvana" (and the structure that organizes the relations between these four terms is precisely the form of the content) by the semantic markers differentiating these terms from each other. Now, *ha* can also be associated, on the deep level (*jigi*), with the unobtainability of causation, but also with the element wind, the geometric form of the half-circle, and so forth: the form of the content is in fact structured along subsets (semantic fields and axes).

Kakuban points out that in the Esoteric episteme *jisō* and *jigi* are used to represent numberless levels of sense related to the inexhaustibility of the meaning of each single expression and to the infinite variety of the psychophysical states of the practitioners interpreting them. These isotopies regulate the homogeneity of interpretation, on both planes of *jisō* and *jigi*;

the ultimate, most profound isotopy is, as we have already seen, the level of "unobtainability" (*fukatoku*). In semiotics, the term "isotopy" refers to a homogeneous level of sense of a term or even of a text, chosen on the basis of pragmatic decisions.[120] For instance, once it has been established that in a certain context the syllable/graph *va* in the sequence *a va ra ha kha* corresponds to the element water, all the other terms in the set should be interpreted according to the series of cosmic elements. The goal of both initiation and meditative practices is that of penetrating deeper and deeper into the meaning of a mantric text from one level of sense to the next until one paradoxically reaches "unobtainability."

A good example of the isotopic structure of the Esoteric sense is provided by the meaning of the three syllables of the name Amida as described in Kakuban's *Amida hishaku*. I have summarized Kakuban's exegesis in the following table (see Table 3.1).[121]

This diagram illustrates the correlation of the three syllables making up the name of the Buddha Amida with concepts and stages of the Shingon soteriological process. The underlying idea is that all the elements in this diagram are always-already present in the name of Amida; uttering it or thinking of it amounts to actualize those features, thus triggering their salvific power. The various three-item series, to which the syllables of the name Amida are associated, constitute successive steps in a process toward liberation and the attainment of Buddhahood. In particular, the third term in each series represent a feature of the final soteriological goal.

We have thus the following interpretive process. First, the name Amida is decomposed in its three constituting syllables, each of which is treated as a full-fledged mantra in its own. Interpretation begins with the signifier and proceeds deeper and deeper, identifying in each syllable the signifier of a conceptual element of increasingly Esoteric and complicated doctrines. In this way, the overall structure of the interpretive process of the name Amida reproduces, almost iconically, the ascetic itinerary toward salvation. One starts with the absolute single mind, the cosmic substratum of original enlightenment and guarantee of secure attainment; it proceeds through the mandala, represented here by its three main sections (*sanbu*), then moves to the three truths of Tendai Buddhism and the three truths of Shingon Buddhism, and finally culminates in the salvation process itself (cause, practice, and ultimate Buddhahood). This interpretive process also simulates the actual education curriculum of learned monks (*gakuryo*), going from the study of classical Mahayana, to that of increasingly complex Esoteric Buddhist teachings, and culminating with ritual practices ensuring the becoming buddha in the present body of the ascetics. (On the education system of Esoteric Buddhism, see Chapter One.)

The isotopies of meaning represent the soteriological trajectory proper to Esoteric Buddhism: salvation is already present in the name of a divine entity, as is the case of Amida in this example, and practices cannot turn out to be vain; I will deal with this subject more in depth in Chapter Four. One

TABLE 3.1 *Esoteric semantic isotopies of the name Amida*

Isotopies	A	MI	DA
The single mind	The undifferentiated single mind is originally uncreated	The undifferentiated single mind is without self (*muga*) and at the same time it is the Great Self (*taiga*)	In the undifferentiated single mind all dharmas are unconditioned, absolute, and quiescent
Three sections of mandala	Buddha Section: nondualism of principle (*ri*) and wisdom (*chi*), of substance and semiotic appearance in the Dharma realm of the undifferentiated single mind	Lotus Section: like a lotus flower, so the emptiness of beings and dharmas according to the wisdom of sublime contemplation (*myōkanzatchi*) is never polluted by the six sense objects	Vajra Section: the wisdom of sublime contemplation (*myōkanzatchi*) of the Tathāgata is strong and absolute, and destroys the enemies (delusions)
Three truths (first set)	Emptiness (*kū*): the Dharma essence of the undifferentiated single mind is forever devoid of unreality and delusion	Conditioned existence (*ke*): the dharmas of the undifferentiated single mind are like mirages and form conditioned existences	Middle path (*chūdō*): the dharmas of the undifferentiated single mind transcend the two previous categories
Three truths (second set)	Being (*u*): substance and semiotic appearance of the single mind are by nature innate and uncreated, and therefore not subject to extinction	Emptiness (*kū*): the Dharma-essence of the single mind is unattainable	Non-emptiness (*fukū*): all dharmas of the single mind constitute the virtues of the Dharmakāya and are infinite
Salvation process	Cause: the realm of the buddhas and the realm of beings depend on the single mind's enlightenment or delusion	Practice: when attachment to the idea of self in beings and dharmas ceases and emptiness is understood, one attains Buddhahood	Buddha: nondualism and the absolute nature of principle (*ri*) and wisdom (*chi*) of the single mind, that is, Buddha-nature

should remember, however, that the process of distinguishing the various isotopies involved in each mantric expression, being a discriminating activity, still belongs to an initial, superficial interpretive level (*jisō*). After his exegesis, Kakuban adds that the meanings of Amida are actually not separate and distinguished, and that the semantic structure of "Amida" in fact reproduces Indra's net (which, as we have already seen, is a Buddhist model to represent unlimited semiosis).

Proliferation and dissolution of sense

Hermeneutic-meditative practices of Esoteric Buddhism, and their textual simulation-inscriptions, constitute a process of gradual proliferation and dissolution of sense. From the starting point, at a relatively superficial level, the practitioner courses through the semantic encyclopedia of Esoteric Buddhism, gradually penetrating more advanced teachings. The final point of this process is, paradoxically, the dissolution of sense in the *samādhi* (deep meditation) and/or the complete relativization of the apparatus that articulates and categorizes signs—as represented by the ultimate stage of unobtainability (*fukatoku*).

The goal of the proliferation of sense is to make the practitioner experience directly the essential identity of all phenomena and of each phenomenon with the Dharma-realm and the Dharmakāya in the name of the undifferentiatedness (*byōdō*) that characterizes them. Each sign, expression, concept, or phenomenon contemplated upon is inflated to make it identical with the absolute. To sum up, we can identify four phases in the process of proliferation and dissolution of sense:

1. Decomposition of a term in its constituting elements (in the case of *hrīḥ*, respectively: *ha, ra, ī, aḥ*; in the case of Amida: *a*, *mi*, *da*)
2. Identification of the superficial meaning (*jisō*)
3. Analysis of esoteric meanings (*jigi*)
4. Since the ultimate esoteric meaning marks the realization of unobtainability (*fukatoku*) of discriminations, every thing is considered nondual (*funi*), absolute and unconditioned, intentional and meaningful manifestation of the Dharmakāya, a kind of indexical expression produced by an original act of ostension.

Here it is important to note that dissolution of sense does not mean the dissolution of all phenomena into emptiness or undifferentiatedness; in fact, these terms never occur in Esoteric Buddhism if not referred to the exoteric teachings (*kengyō*). The goal of meditation and visualization is the interpretive actualization of pre-defined similarities and of the semantic interconnectedness of all phenomena, as a means for the practitioner to embody the cosmos and, at the same time, to identify with it. Such an experience is defined by Shingon exegetes as "becoming a buddha in the present body" (*sokushin jōbutsu*).

Dissolution of sense is the result of the realization of "unobtainability" (*fukatoku*), the attainment of a meta-level no longer linguistic through the meditative experience of the interconnectedness of all things. *Fukatoku* in fact means that a term cannot be interpreted from a partial, discriminating standpoint. When an expression is judged as *fukatoku*, it stops being a sign as it no longer stands for something else under some respect or capacity. Unobtainability can thus be understood as the ultimate goal of the interpretation process. It is situated outside semiosis, and it corresponds to the point in which a sign ceases to be a sign. An unattainable term transcends the articulations of sense and resists interpretation, situating itself at the level of nondualism.

Some medieval authors, most notably Raihō and Gōhō (1306–62), carried out this proliferation of sense by developing a fourfold system of semantic levels known as *shijū hishaku* (lit., "four levels of secret interpretation"). By expanding on the double structure of meaning (superficial/deep) discussed above, these authors envisioned each sign as endowed with four levels of sense: a superficial one (*senryakushaku*) and three secret ones (respectively, *jinpishaku*, *hichū jinpishaku*, and *hihichū jinpishaku*). By following the interpretive process from one level to the other, the practitioner is able to realize the absolute and unconditioned nature of signs and, consequently, their salvific power.[122]

The superficial level (*senryakushaku* or *jisō*) is related to the shape or the sound of a Sanskrit character and is in any case part of the received, non-Esoteric Buddhist conceptual system. The deep, or secret, level (*jinpishaku* or *jigi*) constitutes a radical negation of the previous meaning. As we have already seen, if the superficial meaning of *vāc* is speech, its deep meaning is the unobtainability (*fukatoku*) of speech; if the superficial meaning of the *siddhaṃ* character *ha* is "operation," its deep meaning is the unobtainability of operation. Unobtainability refers here to the fact that at this level signs are beyond dualistic distinctions. The third level is the secret within the secret meanings (*hichū jinpishaku*). The unobtainabililty we reached in the previous level is defined at this level as the superficial meaning (*jisō*), and the deep meaning (*jigi*) here is "perfect and luminous" (*enmyō*). At the previous stage, we learned that the profound meaning of each sign is unobtainable; however, the idea remained that there might be something to obtain (such as the meaning or a referent) that is separate from the means of obtaining it (the sign). Since a distinction remained between signifier (*nōsen*) and signified (*shosen*), this is still a superficial meaning (*jisō*). The profound meaning is attained when one contemplates that there is no signified outside of the signifier and that the sign as it stands is perfect and clear (*kyotai enmyō*); at the third level of sense, the distinction between signifier and signified has been surmounted and we reach a stage in which a sign is a "pure and perfect circle containing all virtues" (*rinnen shutoku*, *shōjō muku*), that is, a kind of mandala. This is the level of emptiness (Sk. *śūnyatā*, Jp. *kūshō*), in which there is nothing to obtain (*mushotoku*).

The fourth and last level is the most secret of the secret meanings (*hihichū no jinpishaku*). The previous meaning, "perfect and clear" (*enmyō*), is the superficial level (*jisō*) of this stage, and a different distinction between signifier and signified is the new and ultimate deep meaning (*jigi*). At the previous level, the distinction between signifier and signified was abolished by a return to the homogeneous perfect purity of the one-mind (*isshin*). The third level corresponds to the stage of eliminating delusions (*shajō*) in order to realize the principle of the singular Dharma realm (*ichi hokkai*). However, graphs are indeed signifiers; the principles they signify constitute the very substance (*tai*) of the universe; within perfect purity there still is another pair of signifier and signified, and the three secrets (*sanmitsu*) are evident. This is the true meaning that expresses the virtues (*hyōtoku*) of the plural Dharma realm (*ta hokkai*). At this ultimate level, the superficial meaning (*jisō*) is the provisional doctrine of the singular Dharma realm (*ichi hokkai*); the deep meaning (*jigi*) is the ultimate doctrine of the multiple Dharma realm (*ta hokkai*).

From this treatment, we learn that, according to some medieval Shingon exegetes, within the four levels of sense, the previous level's deep meaning (*jigi*) becomes the next level's superficial meaning (*jisō*); we are thus dealing here with a connotative semiotics. The categories of *jisō/jigi* and *shajō/hyōtoku* are used together in order to represent the semantic system of Esoteric Buddhism; at the end, we find an ontological and epistemological distinction between singular Dharma realm (*ichi hokkai*) and plural Dharma realm (*ta hokkai*). We also notice that the final, most secret isotopy is virtually identical with the first, superficial level of sense. Distinctions (including that between signifier and signified) are no longer denied, but on the contrary they are rendered absolute as manifestations of the innate multiplicity of the Dharma realm. At this level, thus, we realize that each sign, each entity, is an absolute and unconditioned entity.

We can summarize the fourfold isotopic structure in the following way:

- First level (*senryakushaku*): denotative meaning (common sense, or received Buddhist meaning).
- Second level (*jinpishaku*): beginning of Esoteric connotations: underlying doctrinal principles of a certain sign, concept or object; "unobtainability" (*fukatoku*).
- Third level (*hichū jinpishaku*): beyond the opposition of semioticity and signlessness (*usō* and *musō*), this level indicates a fundamental principle of the Dharma as indicated by a specific sign, concept or object; the sign embodies the singular Dharma realm (*ichi hokkai*).

- Fourth level (*hihichū jinpishaku*): the essence of the Dharma does not exist separately from each concept and object—this is the level at which each sign is realized as being absolute and unconditioned; its distinctiveness is absolute and unconditioned, and it is part of the plural Dharma realm (*ta hokkai*); this is the ultimate meaning of unobtainability.

Two concrete examples from the modern encyclopedia of Shingon teachings, the *Mikkyō daijiten*, namely, the meanings of the offering of flowers and incense to the Buddha, help us clarify this interpretive structure further:[123]

1. Superficial level: offerings are made to please the Buddha.
2. Secret level: flowers represent the sum of all good deeds, and incense represents earnest devotion (*shōjin*).
3. Secret within secrets level: each flower and each incense stick is produced by the combination of the six cosmic elements and are therefore differentiated aspects of Mahāvairocana and the Dharma realm.
4. Most secret level: there is no all-pervasive Dharma realm beyond each individual flower and incense stick; accordingly, offering one to a buddha means to offer it to the entire Dharma realm.

The second example is the status and meaning of the Bodhisattva Maitreya (Jp. Miroku), the future Buddha:

1. Superficial level: he is the lord of Tuṣita Heaven.
2. Secret level: Maitreya connotes a particular form of one aspect of the enlightenment produced by Mahāvairocana's *samādhi* of great compassion.
3. Secret among secrets level: Maitreya is Mahāvairocana in his complete form.
4. Most secret level: Maitreya is one of the innate virtues of the practitioner.

Finally, the Shingon scholar-monk Gōhō (1306–62) applied the four-level semantic system to interpret the status of sacred icons.[124] On a superficial level (*senryakushaku*), images are expedient means (*hōben*) that merely point to the Buddhist Dharma, which is essentially beyond language and representation. On the second level (*jinpishaku*), images are copies of the true Buddha and contribute directly to soteriology. On the third level (*hichū jinpishaku*), images are not different from the true Buddha; in fact, as a result of their empowerment (*kaji*) by the Buddha, images become identical to the real Buddha and acquire real soteriological powers, such as preaching the Dharma and bringing benefits to all beings. On the fourth and last level (*hibichū jinpishaku*), images are the *nirmaṇakāya*, conditioned manifestations of buddhas and bodhisattvas in the human world, exactly like the historical Buddha Śākyamuni himself. Indeed, images are the real Buddhas for us in our age, and have direct salvific efficacy for us just as Śākyamuni had for the beings of his age.[125]

From these examples we see that the Esoteric interpretive practice consists in proliferating sense in order to bring signification to a stop. When a sign is expanded into an embodiment of the entire universe, then there is nothing more to interpret. Semiosis is brought to a final stop; what remains is the ritual contemplation of reality as it is in its absolute and unconditioned essence. The absolute and unconditioned nature of the signs and phenomena was also the subject of numerous speculations within the Tendai tradition as well. An early modern Tendai Esoteric text written by the monk Tenkai (1536–1643) states:

> One must know that all things in this world are generated by the five-syllable mantra *a bi ra un ken*; green willows and red flowers are produced by Mahāvairocana Tathāgata. At this level of understanding, the pine tree as pine tree and the red foliage as red foliage constitute the original material aspect [of reality, *shikisō*]. The mind should not think that a pine tree is just a pine tree.[126]

A pine tree is not just a pine tree, but the "original material aspect of reality"—of course, also endowed with mental functions, since it is impossible to separate Mahāvairocana's body from his mind. Still, it *is* a pine tree.

It is worth noting that the above fourfold structure was mostly employed to interpret concepts and objects, rather than for the contemplative analysis of mantric expressions. Mantras were subject to analogous processes of proliferation and dissolution of meaning that did not necessarily involve a systematic fourfold typology. Rather, the absolute nature of *siddhaṃ* graphs was attained through vertiginous raids across the entire semantic encyclopedia of the Esoteric episteme.

Case study: the mantric seed *vaṃ*

Let us now discuss in detail a concrete example of the way in which the complex semantic network associated with a *shittan* character unfolds in Esoteric interpretive visualizations by analyzing the mantric seed *vaṃ* (Jp. *ban*) as presented by Kakuban (see Figure. 3.2).

The text opens with a statement outlining the general characteristic of this graph, described as the "wondrous substance of Mahāvairocana Dharmakāya, the Esoteric designation of the all-illuminating absolute Buddha, the emperor of secret mantras, the main icon (*honzon*) of the profound principle and of true wisdom."[127] In a dense and complex prose,

FIGURE 3.2 *The* shittan *graph* ban *(Sk.* vaṃ*). From* Kongōkai mandara *(Kanchūnbon). In T. vol. 1, third insert at the end of the volume. Tokyo: Daizō shuppan.*

Kakuban continues by enumerating the characteristics and virtues of the graph *vaṃ* in a list that mobilizes a number of Esoteric teachings such as the ten stages of mind, the mandala of the two realms, and the relation between language (*shōji*) and true reality (*jissō*). These virtues are at source of the seed's incomparable power that enables one to easily attain liberation in the form of either rebirth in a pure land or enlightenment in the present life. Next, Kakuban lists the main meanings (*jigi*) of *vaṃ*:[128]

1. Condition separate from language
2. Element water
3. *Stūpa*
4. Great compassion
5. *Vajra*
6. Wisdom body (of the Dharmakāya)
7. Initiation
8. Most excellent
9. All-pervading
10. Enlightenment

11 Single mind
12 The two mandala realms
13 The three secrets (*sanmitsu*)
14 The four kinds of mandalas
15 The five buddhas
16 The six elements.

As a full analysis of this series would require a lengthy exegesis, I will limit myself to note a few significant points. To begin with, the first meaning, "a condition separate from language" is the negation of the superficial meaning (*jisō*) of the syllable *va* (from *vāc*, "speech"), which constitutes the graphic and phonetic basis of the seed *vaṃ* and the starting point of the Esoteric system of semantic isotopies. In the cosmology of Esoteric Buddhism, *vaṃ* is associated to the element water (second meaning), and is the seed of the five-element mandala in the *Vajra* system, in its shape of a five-element *stūpa* (third meaning). The seed *vaṃ*'s association with the *Vajra* system is reflected by the fifth and sixth meanings (the wisdom body of the Dharma body being the modality of the Buddha in the *Vajra* mandala). The fourth meaning (great compassion) is one of the attributes of Mahāvairocana. Next, meanings seven through eleven represent the soteriological path that takes place when one is initiated to the seed *vaṃ*: it begins with initiation to the most excellent teachings about the all-pervading Buddha (Mahāvairocana), and it ends with enlightenment and the realization of the single mind. Finally, the last five meanings present an overview of the Esoteric universe, from its visual form (the mandala) to its substance (the five buddhas and the six elements). We also notice the deep structure of this semantic series: it ranges from the meaning of one Sanskrit syllable (*vaṃ*, designating a condition beyond language) to increasingly larger conceptual formations such as the salvation process and the structure of the universe. Significantly, the last meaning refers to the substance of the universe—a further indication that Esoteric semantics aims at creating a systematic continuity between a signifier and the cosmic substance, as we have seen in our previous discussion of proliferation and dissolution of sense.

Kakuban next argues that each of the above sixteen "meanings" can be analyzed according to ten categories:[129]

1 Negative method to attain the truth
2 Differences in Esoteric designations
3 True meaning of the negative and the positive paths
4 Visualization of signs
5 Cancellation of sins and cessation of ignorance
6 Rebirth in the Pure Land

7 Becoming a buddha in the present body
8 The all-pervading Dharma-realm
9 Performing practices to bring benefits to other beings
10 Dialogue to dissolve doubts.

Again, a full discussion of this list would take us too far. It suffices to note that these ten categories correspond to stages in the ascetic-meditative process. It begins with the negative method, that is, exposure to the exoteric teachings; it continues with the entrance into the Esoteric path, the practice of meditation on *siddhaṃ* and mantra, and the attainment of salvation (rebirth and becoming a buddha), followed by the performance of the activities of a fully enlightened buddha. The list ends with a clarifying dialogue, as in the Esoteric education process already discussed in Chapter One.

After a dense and meandering treatment of Buddhist doctrines associated with the graph *vaṃ*, Kakuban adds instructions on an "abbreviated" contemplation of the seed, which is based on ten semantic fields:

1 *Stūpa*, matrix of the Dharma realm
2 Dharma body of absolute wisdom
3 Great compassion
4 Uncontaminated
5 Purifying
6 Homogenizing
7 Incessant continuity
8 Harmonizing
9 Revitalizing
10 Indestructible destroyer.

The mantric seed *vaṃ* is to be contemplated on the basis of each of these ten characteristics. Once again, I will not discuss each of them in detail. Suffice it to say that *vaṃ* is the seed of the entire Dharma realm and of the Dharma body as seen from the *Vajra* mandala (this is why the latter is characterized by "absolute wisdom"); as such, *vaṃ* is endowed with the eight features of the element water, to which it is traditionally related (meanings three to ten); these features are semantic markers that the Esoteric Buddhist cultural encyclopedia attributes to water and are also associated with the power that meditation on *vaṃ* bestows upon the practitioner.

Kakuban's text concludes with some considerations on the Esoteric teachings concerning the Dharma body and the indication of some sources on the subject written by Kūkai.[130] In the *Banjigi*, which is representative of Kakuban's production and also of the textual strategies of many Shingon texts, the author starts with the analysis of the superficial meaning of a mantric expression and gradually expands the interpretive scope, turning the mantras into mandalas.

The absolute nature of signs

At this point, we can address the issue of semioticity (*usō*) and signlessness (*musō*) as it is discussed within the Shingon tradition.[131] As we have already seen, classical Mahayana Buddhism tends to be suspicious of signs: as conventional artifacts, they are not the "real thing" but part of the cycle of suffering and rebirth. Shingon, in contrast, reverses this traditional position by attributing to signs a fundamental role in ontology, epistemology, and soteriology. As a consequence, the received relation that opposes semioticity (as the realm of delusion and suffering, a synonym of *saṃsāra*, the cycle of reincarnation) to signlessness (as the realm of emptiness and enlightenment) is dissolved. Raihō wrote:

> There are many kinds of semioticity [*usō*] and signlessness [*musō*]. According to the superficial and abbreviated interpretation, semioticity refers to the apparent, phenomenal aspect of material and mental dharmas as they are understood by common people; signs appear before the mind and are easy to know and understand. Signlessness refers to the fact that substance and essence of the dharmas are illusory, empty, and provisional; individual substance [*jishō*, Sk. *svabhāva*] is empty, without materiality and without shape; no single semiotic aspect exists. According to the deep and secret interpretation, semioticity refers to the fact that each individual sign among all dharmas is clear and abiding. Signlessness means that in each sign ther are all signs, and each sign is not static. Since [each sign] is endowed with the totality of signs, [properly speaking] it is "not one sign [*mu-issō*]," therefore it is called "no-sign" [*musō*]. This does not mean that it is without materiality and without shape. The former meaning is the ordinary interpretation according to the exoteric teachings, the latter refers to the Shingon "positive" interpretation [*hyōtoku*].[132]

For Raihō signs are not just entities in a semiotic simulacrum of the real; rather, each sign is "clear and abiding," that is, absolute and unconditioned, embodying "the totality of signs" yet endowed with materiality and shape. It is their peculiar status that makes Esoteric signs direct and necessary vehicles of salvation, as we will see in the next chapter.

To sum up, dharmas transcend all dichotomic categorizations: they are at the same time endowed with marks (*sō*) (on a superficial level), devoid of marks (*musō*) (on a deep level), neither endowed with marks (*hisō*) nor devoid of marks (*hi-musō*) (on the ultimate level). In this case, Kakuban envisions a semiotic square beginning from the primary semantic axis *endowed with marks (sō) versus devoid of marks (musō)*, and affirms the simultaneous truth of all four components of the tetralemma. This semiotic square can be represented in the following way (see Figure 3.3).

The semiotic square, a general schema representing all possibilities of production of sense, collapses into a non-formalizable point, what Esoteric texts define as "unobtainable" (*fukatoku*). This is the reason why dharmas are said to transcend the way of language. In other words, the contradictoriness of the Esoteric meaning (*jigi*) vis-à-vis the superficial sense (*jisō*) is justified by a sort of implosion of meaning (ultimate "unobtainability").

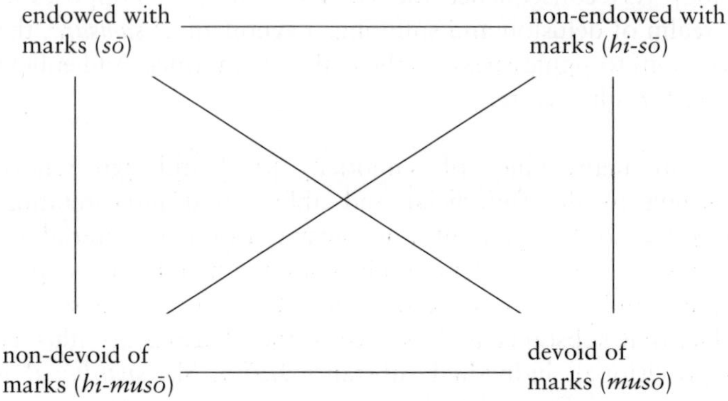

FIGURE 3.3 *Semiotic square of semioticity*

CHAPTER FOUR

Inscribing the diamond path: A semiotic soteriology

One of the most important tasks of premodern Japanese exegetes was that of defining the elusive and radical idea of "becoming a buddha in this very body" (*sokushin jōbutsu*), the ultimate soteriological goal of Esoteric Buddhism. It can be interpreted in at least two different ways: either as the final stage of the liberation process of a bodhisattva, in which case "in the present body" means "in the present life-time" (the present life is seen as the last reincarnation); or as the idea that ultimate attainment is not sanctioned by a visible and dramatic bodily transformation (the acquisition of the 32 signs of a realized Buddha), but by the realization that one's ordinary body is itself the sublime body of the Buddha. Both interpretations were already present in Indian Buddhism, but a slow process of accumulation of merit that would eventually result, after countless rebirths, in becoming a buddha, was the normal understanding of the salvation process in that context. In contrast, East Asian Buddhism in general, not only the Esoteric tradition, began to focus on the final stage of soteriology, the moment in which a being attains enlightenment and becomes a buddha. In Japan Kūkai was the first to discuss the possibility of attaining liberation in a single lifetime, the present one, in a text written in 817 entitled *Sokushin jōbutsugi* (The Meaning of Becoming a Buddha in the Present Body), which subsequently became the subject of many commentaries. Kūkai presents this soteriological goal as a profound awareness, resulting from meditation and other religious practices, of the essential nature of the universe and the place of the practitioner in it; as we have seen in previous chapters, such awareness involved a semiotic outlook as it concerned the nature and mechanisms of signs, language, and representation processes. However, Kūkai's text was only a starting point. For example, it was necessary to clarify the relation of an individual's becoming a buddha with Mahāvairocana's all-pervading Dharma body (the fact that Mahāvairocana was already a buddha). Exegetes also had to define the actual result of becoming a buddha: was it a visible transformation, or a purely mental one? Was such a new buddha endowed with peculiar signs and supernatural powers or not? More radically, was it really a process of "becoming" a buddha, or rather a realization (sudden or gradual) of one's innate "always-already" being a buddha? These are some of the questions medieval commentators tried to answer to.

A doctrine based on an apocryphal variant of Kūkai's *Sokushin jōbutsugi*,[1] presents three modalities of "becoming buddha in this very body," namely, as a consequence of the innate principle of original awakening (*rigu jōbutsu*, lit. "becoming a buddha as an innate principle"), as the result of empowerment and ritual action (*kaji jōbutsu*, lit. "becoming a buddha due to ritual empowerment" [*kaji*]), and as a miraculous phenomenon in which the practitioner displays his Buddha-body to all (*kendoku jōbutsu*, lit. "becoming a buddha [in which its] virtues are manifest").[2]

The first modality is innately shared by all beings of the Dharma realm as their common ontological substratum, even though it is unknown to their deluded minds. In principle (*ri*), at least, all beings are always-already potential buddhas. The third modality, the display of the features (*kendoku*) of a Buddha, is clearly the most problematic one. As a matter of fact, very few narrations of Buddhist miraculous events describe beings actually becoming buddhas. The most famous example is an episode from the hagiography of Kōbō Daishi (Kūkai). The saint was participating in a monastic debate in the presence of the emperor, in which the most talented scholar monks presented the doctrines of their respective traditions. Kūkai explained Shingon's becoming a buddha in present body by entering *samādhi* and displaying the features of a realized Buddha. This story was later taken as an example of *kendoku jōbutsu*. It is not clear, however, whether all practitioners could ever achieve the same effect in their present life.[3]

The second modality of *jōbutsu*, the one achieved through ritual action and empowerment (*kaji*), however, is particularly relevant to this chapter because it involves the manipulation of signs and symbols in a ritual context. The scholar monk Raiyu (1226–1304) wrote:

> *Sokushin jōbutsu* occurs when the icon [*honzon*, i.e. the central deity of a ritual] and the practitioner interpenetrate each other without obstruction. The three secrets (*sanmitsu*) of the deity empower (*kaji*) the three karmic activities (*sangō*) of the practitioner, which then turn into the three secrets of the Tathāgata.[4]

In other words, *sokushin jōbutsu* is the result of the process of ritual interaction of the practitioner with the icon (*honzon*) called *nyūga ganyū* (lit., "[the deity] enters one's self, and one's self enters [the deity]"), in which the icon acts as a mediator between Mahāvairocana and the practitioner.

Eventually, the practitioner becomes not just an "imitation" of Mahāvairocana, but a "sample" of the Dharma body of the Buddha—and therefore, a fully realized buddha him/herself. Becoming a buddha, thus, is the result of the transformation of the semiotic status of the practitioner, from a separate individual to a "double" of the Buddha—a transformation that is supposed to take place in ritual. In Esoteric Buddhism, then, soteriology is also a matter of semiotic operations being carried out on both the practicing subject and the signs and objects employed in the rituals.

In this chapter, I will describe the ways in which such a semiotic soteriology takes place, by analyzing a number of rituals and their underlying conceptual principles. Virtually all Shingon rituals require or presuppose one form or another of visualization, and therefore it is important to understand the latter's epistemic assumptions, its rhetoric, and the ideological effects it may produce.

The Esoteric rhetoric of vision

Esoteric Buddhism is characterized by a strong emphasis on "visual culture," and becoming a buddha is the result of ritual processes (*kaji jōbutsu*) involving vision in a broad sense. In order to *envision* oneself as a buddha, one has to *visualize* representations of the buddha, and the result of such visualizations has to be *displayed* in some way (*kendoku jōbutsu*). Many premodern Shingon texts describe and/or presuppose visionary experiences and the particular knowledge acquired through them. Esoteric practices are usually described as the controlled manipulation of images during meditation and as the gradual transformation of their meaning or status. Esoteric rituals in general presuppose a vision of events occurring in the invisible realm of buddhas and deities. Esoteric Buddhism created a virtual dimension of reality in which religious specialists manipulated symbols as *aliases* of certain entities and actions, in the belief that in this way they were able to affect their "real" equivalents. The ritual/meditative mastering of vision and meaning is equated with mastery upon the self and reality, and the final outcome of these practices is the attainment of putative supernatural powers (*siddhi*) and buddhahood in the present body.

The Shingon "rhetoric of vision" is the idea that visualization (Jp. *kangyō*, *sanmai* or *sanmaji*, the latter two being transliterations of the Sanskrit *samādhi*), an altered, non-ordinary state of body-language-mind, would put the practitioner in contact with the "invisible world" (*myōkai* or *meikai*) of buddhas, bodhisattvas, *vidyārājas*, *kami*, and other kinds of supernatural beings (monsters, ghosts, dragons, and so forth). As explained by Raihō in his *Shingon myōmoku*, Shingon meditation was essentially eidetic and consisted in the visualization of particular images. Even signless or formless meditation (*musōkan*) is a contemplation of the ultimate semiotic nature of the Dharma realm. Whereas meditation based on images (*usō*, in themselves signs of a deeper, hidden reality) focuses on specific features of the Dharma realm as represented by particular, non-ordinary images (buddha images,

Sanskrit graphs, etc.), in formless or signless meditation (*musō*) the practitioner has to see *all* things, thoughts, events, and actions in the ordinary world as aspects/signs of the Dharma realm (each of these signs being a component of Dharmakāya's preaching or *hosshin seppō*). Since "in each sign there are all signs," as Raihō wrote,[5] the highest form of meditation is the one that focuses on aspects of everyday reality.

A few points should be emphasized, however, when dealing with the status of vision and visualization in the Shingon tradition. First, as already pointed out by Robert Sharf, "'visualization' is a dubious choice for an English equivalent of terms such as *kansō* and *kannen*" which are normally used in Shingon ritual manuals to refer to meditation. As Sharf explains, "These technical Sino-Japanese terms refer to procedures whose elements are often more discursive, literary, or tropical than they are visual or graphic." Sharf suggests that more appropriate translations would be terms such as "'think,' 'imagine,' 'contemplate,' 'discern.'"[6] At least in one case studied by Sharf, *kansō* (contemplation) was "treated liturgically," that is, the scriptural passage to be visualized was "intoned quietly or vocalized inwardly," indicating that

> the execution of the *kansō* consists not in 'visualization' or even in 'meditation' so much as in recitation. And even if the practitioner did want to linger over or meditate upon the content of the liturgy he would find himself severely constrained by the need to finish the rite within the time allotted.[7]

Sharf is right in emphasizing the role of discursive thought and rhetorical imagery in meditation practice. However, the etymology of many Western terms referring to mental experiences (such as "imagine" and "contemplate") do point to some visionary experiences, even though they need not be produced in meditation, but could be evoked by reading a scriptural passage, in dreams, or by looking at a sacred image. Therefore, whenever I refer to visualization, I mean it in this broader sense as a vision of the "invisible world" of the Tantric pantheon condensed in the mandala and diffused in countless premodern literary, visual, and ritual texts.

Second, in those cases in which visions were actually involved, Shingon visions and visualization were not forms of self-suggestion, individual fantasies, or reveries as in common understanding. Ioan Couliano, among others, defines "visualization" or "inner perception" of a mandala as "the interiorization of mandalic schemas with the help of dramatic scenarios unfolding in the practitioner's fantasy."[8] On the contrary, Shingon meditation was to a large extent intersubjectively controlled, disciplined, and codified within a certain community (lineage), to the point that its contents (deities, concepts, etc.) often influenced (or determined) the practitioners' dreams.[9]

Third, visualization as a view on the "invisible world" of Mahayana mental states, Shinto lore, and Tantric mythology was not an exclusive characteristic of the Shingon tradition, but was common to many forms of Japanese institutional Buddhism (the so-called *kenmitsu* system discussed in Chapter One); however, the Shingon and Tendai sects grounded visualization in their own semiotics, ideology, and ritual procedures.

Fourth, the conceptual apparatus of visualization was not restricted to religious specialists; the idea of a hidden side of reality—the world of *ura* (what lies behind something) as opposed to the *omote* (the apparent aspects of things)—which manifests itself in dreams and visions, was one of the distinctive features of Japanese medieval mentalities.

Finally, visualization and manipulation of symbols were only part of the activities of Esoteric practitioners. Shingon affiliates built bridges and dams to enhance agriculture, communications, and commerce. Many priests were also experts in medicine and other forms of practical technology; others were involved in more secular activities, such as managing temples and their possessions, serving as warriors, working as merchants, etc.—all activities that, from a Shingon initiatory perspective, were aimed at the construction of a mandala in the profane world.

Visualization was not practiced only in order to become a buddha in this very body or, in different rituals, to be reborn into the Pure Land (a Buddhist paradise). As synthesized by the expression *jiri rita* (benefits for oneself and the others), the soteriological power acquired by an individual through religious practices (including visualization) could be used for the salvation of all beings by virtue of the recursive nature of Shingon soteriology. In fact, it has been pointed out that Esoteric Buddhism considers *samādhi*, a form of deep meditation, as the original condition of the universe.[10] Visualization, in whatever forms it occurred (including their discursive renditions), was a way to retrieve/restore such original state.

Visualization of otherwise invisible levels of reality was not necessarily a static contemplation, as in popular understanding. On the contrary, ritual texts describe it as often taking on a dramatic and theatrical aspect, but always in codified and controlled form. The passage translated at length below is from a ritual text describing visualizations to be performed in order to become a buddha:

> The five syllables *a vaṃ raṃ haṃ khaṃ* are the seeds of the five *cakra* rings [i.e. natural elements]—earth, water, fire, wind, and space. Above the earth ring is the water ring, above the water ring is the fire ring, above the fire ring is the wind ring, and above the wind ring is the space ring. Above the space ring one should visualize the graph *kan* [Sk. *hāṃ*?]. This graph, whose color is that of deep darkness, gradually expands and becomes bigger and bigger. On the wind ring one visualizes the graph *vaṃ*. It turns into the water ring. On top of it one visualizes the graph *hara* [Sk. *pra*?] in golden color. It turns into a golden turtle, on whose back one visualizes the graph *so* [Sk. *su*], which in turn transforms itself into Mount Sumeru,

constituted by the seven precious materials.[11] Then, there is the graph *ken* [Sk. *khaṃ*?], which transforms itself into the seven golden mountains surrounding Mount Sumeru. One then visualizes the body of the Buddha Vairocana in the sky. His pores exude perfumed milk; like rain, it pours between the ranges of the seven golden mountains and becomes the milky sea of the fragrant water of the eight virtues. In correspondence to the heart [of Mahāvairocana?], on Mount Sumeru is the graph *hrīḥ*, which turns into an eight-petal lotus pervading the entire Dharma realm. On the lotus there is the letter *A*. It turns into the precious hall [Mahāvairocana's Palace] with eight flowers and eight pillars, so high and large that it has no limits, and adorned with every kind of treasures of great beauty. A crowd of Tathāgatas amounting to a hundred million times [*koṭi*] the number of grains of sand contained in sixty rivers Ganges, together with eight kinds of supernatural beings,[12] the inner and outer bodhisattvas of offerings—all of them are gathered around the Dharma Realm Palace. Inside the palace there is another graph *hrīḥ*. It turns into a large lotus, upon which is a mandala altar. On the mandala there is the Lion Seat [i.e. the throne of the Buddha], on the Lion Seat there is another lotus, upon which is the pure circle of the full moon. On the moon disk there is another graph *hrīḥ*, which transforms itself into the great lotus of the sublime moon. On top of it is the graph *vaṃ*, which radiates a great light illuminating the entire Dharma realm. When touched and illuminated by this light, all beings subject to the suffering of the three conditioned realms,[13] the six destinations [of rebirth],[14] the four kinds of birth,[15] the eight difficulties [to perform Buddhist practices],[16] attain liberation. The syllable *vaṃ* turns into a *stūpa* constituted by a square, a circle, a triangle, a crescent, and a sphere, because it is made of the five elements—earth, water, fire, wind, and space. This *stūpa* turns into the Tathāgata Mahāvairocana. The color of his body is like that of the moon, on his head is a crown with the five Buddhas,[17] his heavenly robe is made with precious silk, his body is adorned with jewel laces; a light illuminates the ten directions of the Dharma realm. Abiding on the moon disk is Vairocana's retinue constituted by the four buddhas,[18] the eight bodhisattvas of ritual offerings, the four bodhisattvas converting the beings, the thousand buddhas of the present *kalpa* [cosmic cycle], the twenty heavenly deities [located on the margins of the Womb mandala], and countless bodhisattvas.[19]

Here, a simple mantra unfolds into a gigantic cosmic vision. In it, boundaries between images and reality, sounds and graphs, buddhas and things, practicing subjects and the objects of their practice are constantly questioned and redrawn. *Shittan* graphs transform themselves into buddhas and other entities of the Esoteric world; they are at the same time the fundamental semiotic structures of the material world and the elements in the universal mechanism of salvation.

Shittan letters play an important role in the creation of the Esoteric universe, as in the case of the syllable *su* that produces Mount Sumeru, the cosmic mountain; here the initial syllable of the name of the mountain is treated as endowed with the power to literally "re-present," make-appear, give shape to, its own object. Similarly, *hrīḥ* becomes a cosmic lotus, the sublime shape of the Dharma realm; *A* becomes the residence of Mahāvairocana himself; *vaṃ*, another seed syllable of Mahāvairocana, is presented as the all-pervasive soteriological power of the cosmic Buddha. It is probably not necessary to "visualize" them in meditation, as Robert Sharf would suggest, it is enough just to "imagine" or "think" about them in a discursive fashion; this would not diminish the grand scale and the complex set of images that was associated with this ritual.

Visualizations of *siddhaṃ* graphs (*jirinkan*)

We have seen that Esoteric expressions have a semantic core constituted by concepts and interpretations traditionally recognized and accepted (semiosophia). However, this semantic core has almost exclusively preliminary functions as a conceptual introduction to the Esoteric episteme, and remains an abstract, the starting point of rituals and visualization (semiopietas and semiognosis). In this section I will describe the mechanisms that establish a correlation, or more precisely, a relationship of conformity between the structure of a mantric expression, the structure of the salvation process in which it occurs, and the "meaning" of the mantra's elements; this correlation makes it so that Esoteric Buddhist cosmology collapses onto its soteriology.

As we have already seen, Raiyu wrote that "becoming a buddha as the result of ritual empowerment" (*kaji jōbutsu*) occurs when an icon and a practitioner interpenetrate during the performance of a ritual;[20] Esoteric rituals (in particular, visualization) transform the three centers of karmic activity (*sangō*: speech, body, and mind) into the Buddha's three foci of salvation and bliss (*sanmitsu*). But how did this process actually take place?

There are three sets of practices that enable this transformation. First, meditation ensures the physical identification of the practitioner's body (*shingō*, bodily karma) with the body of the sacred being (*shinmitsu*, secret of body) of the icon used in the ritual, in the process known as *nyūga ganyū* (lit. "[the deity] enters me, and I enter [the deity]"); at this point, the practitioner is physically identical to the deity. Second, the practitioner recites the deity's mantra, thus realizing the identity of his/her karmic speech (*gogō*) with the sacred being's secret of speech (*gomitsu*); at this stage, the practitioner becomes a buddha through the secret of speech. Finally, the ascetic visualizes a set of mantric syllables ordered in a circular, mandalic pattern (*jirinkan*); at this stage, the practitioner realizes the original nondualism of his/her own karmic mental activity (*igō*) and the icon's secret of the mind (*imitsu*).

These three phases involve manipulation of semiotic entities (images, sounds, and graphs), but it is the third stage, the visualization of *siddhaṃ* graphs, that is most relevant to our discussion here as the culmination of the entire soteriological process. Each graph is envisioned as the mantric seed of a buddha or of one of its essential features; meditation consists in visualizing the actual transformation of each graph into a buddha and in focusing on the various semantic components of each graph. Next, as examples, I will present four visualization techniques involving *shittan* graphs: a simplified version of the five-element mandala, breathing techniques, incense smoke visualization, and toilet purification.

In the visualization of the simplified mandala, the mantric seeds of the five elements (earth, water, fire, wind, and space) are arranged in a circular, mandalic structure at the center of the moon-disk (*gachirin*) representing the pure, enlightened mind (*bodaishin*). The practitioner contemplates the superficial meaning (*jisō*) and the deep meaning (*jigi*) of each graph in clockwise (*jun*) order and/or in counter clockwise (*gyaku*) order.[21] Ritual manuals present two different positions of the graphs, which are to be read in a prescribed order (usually, clockwise). Visualization is further articulated in several forms and steps.[22] The first example relates the five graphs to the five buddhas of the Womb realm (see Figures. 4.1a and 4.1b), the second to the five buddhas of the *Vajra* realm (see Figures. 4.2a and 4.2b).[23]

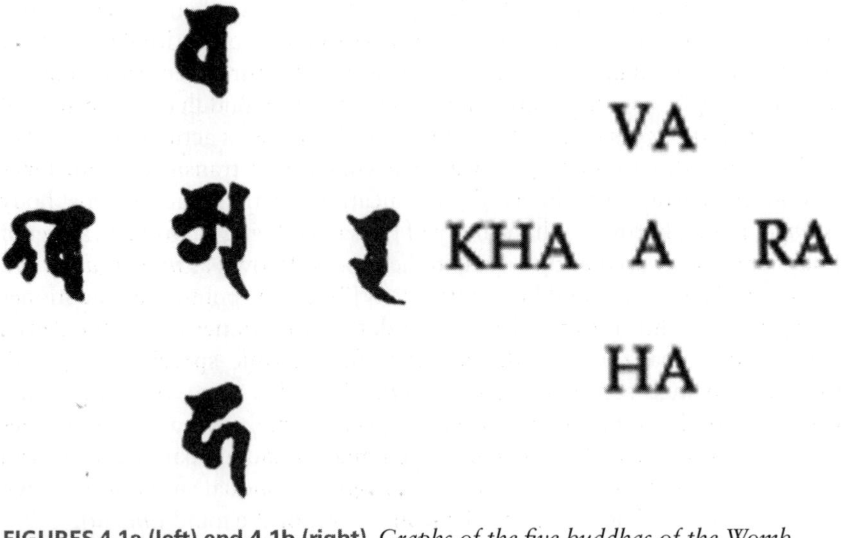

FIGURES 4.1a (left) and 4.1b (right) *Graphs of the five buddhas of the Womb mandala. From* Mikkyō daijiten, *p. 1238c. Kyoto: Hōzōkan, 1983.*

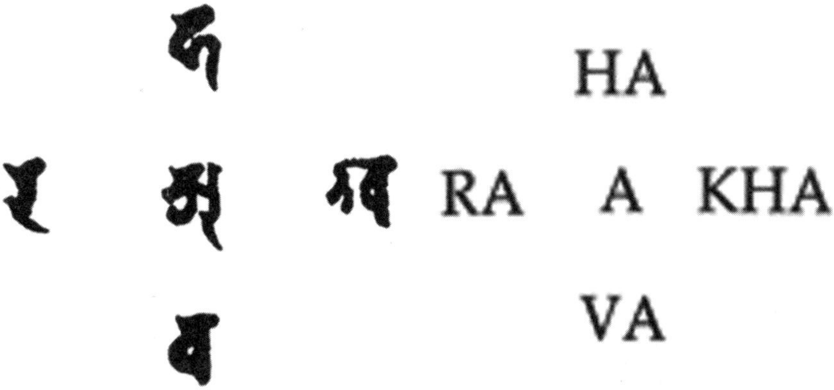

FIGURES 4.2a (left) and 4.2b (right) *Graphs of the five buddhas of the* Vajra *mandala. From* Mikkyō daijiten, *p. 1238c. Kyoto: Hōzōkan, 1983.*

The orientation of the graphs in the diagrams indicated the goal of the ritual, respectively, self-enlightenment (*jishō*), guidance to others (*keta*), and the combination of the two (*jitakenzai*), with the practitioners identifying themselves with the central graph (and thus, with the cosmic Buddha Dainichi). In the first example, we have the following three patterns (see Figures. 4.3a, 4.3b, 4.4a, 4.4b, and 4.5a, 4.5b).

Self-enlightenment is represented by graphs oriented toward the center of the diagram; guidance to others is represented by orienting the graphs toward the outside of the diagram; their combination is represented by graphs written in their usual form. The position and the orientation of the graphs in the diagrams are semiognosic devices, since the textual expression is directly related to its content and its performative effect.

Our second example of visualizations consists in breathing techniques. Breath has always been important in the Tantric tradition, which understood it as the life principle and the subtle substance of the universe. In premodern Japan, the Shingon sect even considered meditation on breathing (*shūsokukan*) as the most direct way to become a Buddha in the present body. *Shūsokukan* consists in a combination of breath control and contemplation of written mantric seeds (*shuji*). Inspiration and expiration were associated, respectively, to the seeds *A* and *un*.[24] Kakuban describes the efficacy of breath meditation in the following way:

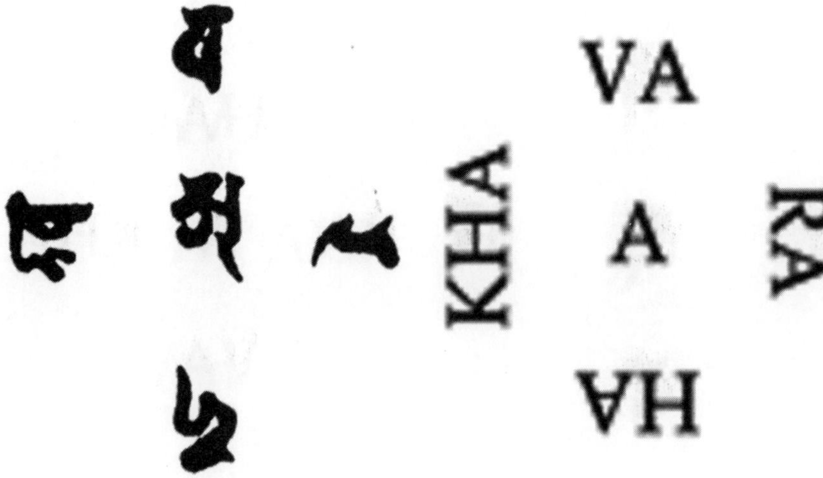

FIGURES 4.3a (left) and 4.3b (right) *Graphs of self-enlightenment. From* Mikkyō daijiten, *p. 1239a. Kyoto: Hōzōkan, 1983.*

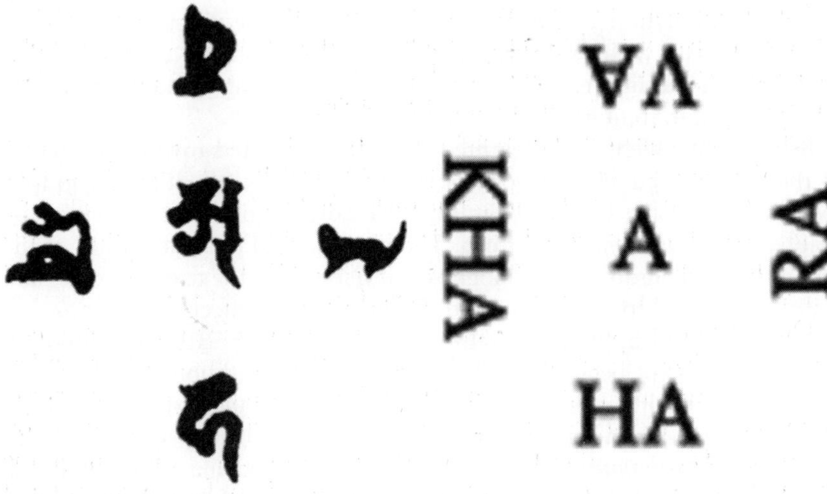

FIGURES 4.4a (left) and 4.4b (right) *Graphs of guidance to others. From* Mikkyō daijiten, *p. 1239a. Kyoto: Hōzōkan, 1983.*

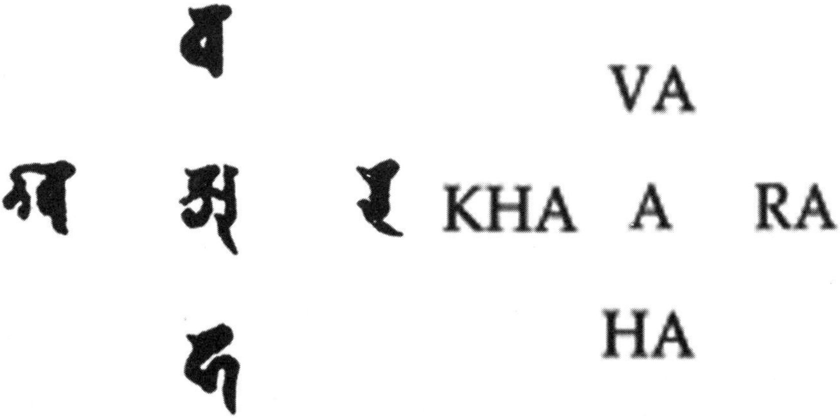

FIGURES 4.5a (left) and 4.5b (right) *Graphs of self-enlightenment and guidance to others combined. From* Mikkyō daijiten, *p. 1239a. Kyoto: Hōzōkan, 1983.*

> When one opens and closes one's mouth, the two letters *A* and *un* are spontaneously generated; when one raises one's hands and moves one's legs, the element wind and the element consciousness are necessarily arisen. It suffices to focus one's mind, control breath, and concentrate oneself on the mantric seed of sacred being. This is the deep meaning of the secret of yoga, the most direct way toward sudden enlightenment in one's present body.[25]

In other words, the secret of yoga is based on two mantric seeds, *A* and *un*, and their incessant, spontaneous production in breathing; these are veritable "natural *dhāraṇī*."[26] Kakuban explains the meaning of breathing in the following way:

> In expiration, the letter *un* comes out from the mind's lotus pedestal and, guided by great compassion, diffuses itself throughout the ten directions and reaches all worlds without exceptions, touches the three karmic activities of all beings and purifies and eliminates all karmic hindrances going back to a beginningless time.[27]

Next, "in inspiration, this letter penetrates the entire body [of the practitioner], eliminates the defilements (Sk. *kleśa*, Jp. *bonnō*) of one's pure substance, establishes itself in the palace of the letter *A*, and abides in enlightenment without thoughts."[28] It is interesting to note that breathing is not only associated with individual salvation (*jiri*, lit. "personal benefits"), but is envisioned as contributing to universal welfare (*rita*, lit. "benefits to others"):

> When breath comes in and goes out [of oneself]
> The letter *A* permeates the inside and the outside
> Going out, it brings benefits to others [*rita*]
> Coming in, it benefits myself [*jiri*].[29]

Breathing techniques are a good example of symbolic practices, as salvation is associated with what is perhaps the most natural, spontaneous activity of beings (breathing).

A curious form of meditation involving *siddhaṃ* characters, described in the ritual text *Guanzizai pusa xin zhenyan yiyin niansong fa*, consists in visualizing the smoke wafting up from incense burners as the graph *hṛīḥ* (see Figure. 4.6), a "miraculous design" called "great compassion that allays suffering"; it is supposed to spread in the air and pervade all aspects of existence (see Figure. 4.7 and 4.8). The ritual text on the subject states: "when incense is burned one venerates the sacred form and the smoke activates the mantra." Also in case, the incense letter will bring soteriological benefits to both the performer of the ritual and all other beings.[30]

FIGURE 4.6 *The* shittan *graph* hṛīḥ *(Jp.* kiriku*). From* Denjushū. *In Takakusu Junjirō and Watanabe Kaigyoku (eds),* Taishō shinshū daizōkyō, *vol. 78, p. 249c.*

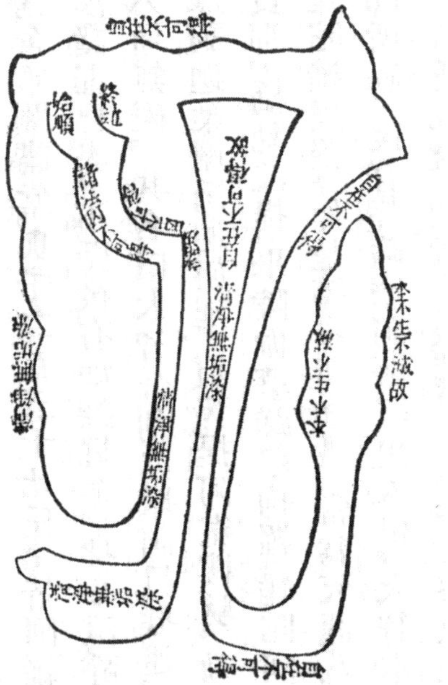

FIGURES 4.7 (left) and 4.8 (right) *Images for incense smoke visualization. In* Guanzizai pusa xin zhenyan yiyin niansong fa. *In Takakusu Junjirō and Watanabe Kaigyoku (eds),* Taishō shinshū daizōkyō, *vol. 20, pp. 32b and 34a.*

Finally, *shittan* graphs and their mantric values can be used also by uninformed users outside of strictly meditative contexts. A stunning example is the graph *un* as the seed of Ususama Myōō (Sk. Ucchuṣma *vidyārāja*) used in Japanese temple toilets to cleanse impurities caused by excrements. The initial letter of the seed is the same as the first letter of Ususama's name, and is thus not arbitrary. In addition, the sound of defecation is normally rendered in the Japanese language as "*nnnn*," which is pronounced in the same way as *un*. In this way, the sound of the polluting act is also the very instrument of its purification; these two acts (polluting and purification) are thus deeply related by virtue of semiotic mechanisms centered on the mantra *hūṃ* (*un*), its sound, and its meanings.

The inscription of the soteriological path

We have seen that the Esoteric episteme and its related practices treated *siddhaṃ* graphs as minimal mandalas and embodiments of entire Dharma realm. Let us now see in more detail the mandalization process of Mahāvairocana's mantra *aḥ vi ra hūṃ khaṃ* (Jp. *a bi ra un ken*) as it occurs in Kakuban's *Gorin kujimyō himitsushaku*. This mantra is not simply chanted, but used in a complex ritual way. Its meanings are first contemplated and then dissolved (in what I have defined, in Chapter Three, proliferation and dissolution of sense) as the practitioner gradually realizes that the graphs are "doubles" or "samples"—ostensive signs—of the Dharma realm in its totality. With the attainment of such knowledge of the nature of signs, practitioners de facto "become buddhas in their present body."

The *Mahāvairocana Sutra* describes the context of the original utterance of this mantra as follows:

> The Dharmakāya in its original and absolute modality of being (*honji hosshin*) entered the "powerful and quick *samādhi* of the mutual interpenetration of all Tathāgatas" and explained the *samādhi* of the substance of the Dharma realm with these words:
> I understand the original uncreatedness of things;
> I have transcended the path of language;
> I have attained liberation from all wrong ideas;
> Causality is now far away from me,
> And I now know that emptiness is like the sky.[31]

Here, Mahāvairocana in his absolute modality of existence as the Dharmakāya in its original condition describes the essence of his wisdom: he understands the fundamental nature of the universe and cannot make mistakes, he is free from all conditionings, including those of karma, and abides in a realm beyond the reaches of ordinary language. Next, Mahāvairocana enters a more "concrete" variant of such absolute state, the "*samādhi* of the adamantine pleasure of subjugating the four demonic entities," and pronounces his principal mantra:

> *Namaḥ samantabuddhānāṃ aḥ vi ra hūṃ khaṃ*
> [Jp. *nōmaku samanda bodanan a bi ra un ken*]

An approximate translation would sound like "Hail to all buddhas, [in particular those represented by the five syllables of the Womb mandala, namely] *aḥ vi ra hūṃ khaṃ*!"

These original (and mythical) utterances by Mahāvairocana to himself while immersed in *samādhi* are the beginning of the Esoteric semiosis. This mantra has a particular status because it was uttered directly by the Dharmakāya on the threshold between signlessness and semioticity. It has the power to eliminate all obstacles to the attainment of salvation, as is clear from the name of the *samādhi* ("of the original undifferentiatedness of all Tathāgatas") in which it was originally uttered. Its power is guaranteed by the fact that the utterer of the mantra has personally succeeded in eliminating all conditionings; the formula is thus a distillate of Mahāvairocana's wisdom. Finally, the mantra is true and efficacious because Mahāvairocana utters it out of compassion for the suffering of sentient beings.

By referring to these utterances, Kakuban's text establishes a "veridiction contract" between author and reader, which offers the proof of the truth and efficacy of the mantra *aḥ vi ra hūṃ khaṃ*. Truth and efficacy are also sanctioned by a citation attributed to Amoghavajra (Ch. Bukong, Jp. Fukū), the most influential patriarch of East Asian Esoteric Buddhism, placed at the end of the discussion of the mantra: "The teachings concerning these five syllables were transmitted to me by [my master] Vajrabodhi (Ch. Jinggang zhi, Jp. Kongōchi) Tripitaka. I believed them and practiced them for a thousand days. In an autumn night of full moon I attained the *samādhi* that wipes away all impediments."[32] With this quotation, Kakuban traces a lineage of this mantra going back to India through China and thus to the mythical origin of Esoteric Buddhism itself. The patriarch of the tradition himself stated that this mantra enabled him to attain a *samādhi* that opened him the gate to liberation.

The meaning of a bi ra un ken

After the description of the original utterance and the efficacy of the mantra, Kakuban begins to analyze it. He divides it in two portions, "*Nōmaku samanda bodanan*" and "*a bi ra un ken.*" *Nōmaku* (Sk. *Namaḥ*) is a common initial marker of the mantric linguistic space (see Chapter Three), and is translatable as "hail" or "praise be to..." *Samanda bodanan* means "all buddhas" but Kakuban translates it as the "three treasures," i.e. the Buddha, the Dharma, and the Samgha. The first segment sanctions the practitioner's trust in the mantra—and ultimately, in Buddhism (therefore, the reference to the three treasures). The second segment constitutes the actual spell, *a bi ra un ken*, described as the "spell appropriate to all buddhas."[33] Kakuban then offers an analysis of the sequence.

> The graph *aḥ* (Jp. *aku*) means "practice" and represents the original uncreatedness. The two dots to the right [in the *siddhaṃ* graph] mean "purification." The graph subjugates the four demonic entities and thus eliminates all suffering... As the earth generates the ten thousand things, so the graph *A*, the element earth, produces infinite practices of the six supreme virtues (*pāramitā*). "Earth" means "solid, homogeneous." The noble *bodhicitta* [the desire for enlightenment] is resistant and indestructible, therefore it produces the fruit of ten thousand virtues. If Shingon practitioners, when throwing of the flower (in the initiation ritual) plant the seed of *bodhicitta* of initial enlightenment [the desire for enlightenment that results from practice as distinct from the innately enlightened mind] on the graph *A*—the innate *bodhicitta* of the pure

> mind, they will be freed forever from all diseases and they will quickly attain the supreme enlightenment... These are the reasons why the graph *A* also means "increase [of benefits]."[34]

This is a typical example of Esoteric semiotic interpretation. The meaning of an expression is the result of the analysis of the shape of the graph (here for example we find the reference to the dots, known in Sanskrit as *visarga*, that transform *A* into *aḥ*), its superficial and deep meanings in their various ramifications—all made into a more or less coherent whole indicating that the principles of salvation are already included in the shape and meaning of the sign employed in the religious practice. Let us try to unpack the above passage by outlining the trajectories followed by Kakuban.

A is the first sound of the Sanskrit alphabet and is present in all *shittan* graphs (in order to eliminate it, one has to add a particular sign called *virama*). This fact is perhaps at the origin of the association of *A* with the element earth. As the earth, characterized by solidity, homogeneity, and indestructibility, is the mother of all things, so the sound/graph *A* is at the source of all Buddhist practices, of *bodhicitta*, and of liberation. The expression "ten thousand things," indicating "all things," is written here with two characters *mangyō*. Now, in Buddhist terminology *gyō* also means "practice," in particular "religious practice." Kakuban uses it here with this meaning, thus drawing a directly linguistic relation between a characteristic of the earth and one of the letter *A*. *A*'s connection with religious practice is also emphasized by its traditional association with the *bodhicitta*, as in the moon-disk visualization (in which one purifies one's mind by associating it with the bright moon disk and other Esoteric symbols). In Mahayana, the arousal of the *bodhicitta* (the desire for enlightenment), is the beginning of a long journey toward liberation extending over countless life-times; Esoteric Buddhism, in contrast, envisions *bodhicitta* as the very substance (as the earth, solid and indestructible) of enlightenment. In the realm of original enlightenment, the itinerary toward enlightenment takes always place in a space that coincides with the substratum of enlightenment itself: in other words, the ascetic process and the ascetics themselves coincide with the final goal. On a deeper level, *A* represents the principle of original uncreatedness of all things, free from conditionings and endowed with the power to eliminate them wherever they are present.

For these reasons Kakuban writes that the ascetic who establishes a special relation with the seed *A* in the initiation ceremony will be set free from all diseases and will attain the supreme *bodhi*. Suffering, diseases, and karmic conditionings in general are represented by the arch-enemy of the Buddha, Māra, and his four retinues of demons—subjugated by the letter *A*. *A*'s beneficial power is indicated by the two dots on its right (Sk. *visarga*) and by the meaning of "increasing benefits." In this way, Kakuban is able to bring together the three levels that, according to Melford Spiro, characterize Buddhism: soteriology aiming at the attainment of ultimate salvation, a series of process aimed at the accumulation of merit, and magical practices of protection.[35]

> The graph *vi* (Jp. *bi*) means "tie" and represents the unobstructed *samādhi*, that is, liberation transcending comprehension. The graph *va* is associated with the element water, therefore it washes away the impurities of afflictions, so that body and mind can devote themselves to the thousand practices of enlightenment without losing concentration. The graph *va* means that the element water enables one not to lose concentration, therefore it represent the vast ocean of all virtues [that can be acquired thanks to it].[36]

On a superficial level, *vi* stands for "tie," "bondage," impediment in general, from the Sanskrit *bandhana*. It is worth noting that here the initial phoneme /b/ of *bandhana* has been transformed into /v/; this is not particularly surprising since in the Japanese phonological system there is no distinction between /v/ and /b/. Here, a phonetic peculiarity generates a semantic short-circuit connecting two semantic fields (impediments and ultimate liberation) that are originally different and unrelated. In fact, on a deeper isotopy, *vi* indicates "liberation transcending comprehension." This latter meaning is based, perhaps, on the main Esoteric meaning of *va* (as we have seen, from *vāc*, "speech"), that is, a condition transcending language and discursive thought and therefore beyond comprehension. Liberation is produced directly by the syllables *va* and *vi* because of *va*'s correspondence with the element water. As water refreshes and washes away all physical impurities, so the graph *va* washes away mental impurities (i.e. afflictions: Sk. *kleśa*, Jp. *bonnō*) and facilitates the practices to attain enlightenment. Here, there is a shift from body (washing the body) and mind (purifying the mind). Furthermore, since *va* enables the practitioner not to lose concentration during meditation, it also indicates/represents/produces the infinite merits resulting from religious practice, traditionally represented by the metaphor of the ocean and strengthened here by its semantic connection with the element water. This correlation is based on the homology associating the five mantric seed to the five elements and the five geometrical forms. It is possible that some of the symbolic powers attributed to esoteric expressions might have had an immediate experiential basis.

> The graph *ra* is the purification of the six sense organs. By burning the wood of the afflictions, it eliminates sins and impediments of the six sense organs and enables one to experience the fruit of enlightenment.[37]

The syllable *ra* is the beginning of the Sanskrit word *rajas* meaning "dirt, dust." On a deep level, it represents the purification of the six sense organs contaminated by the afflictions. On a cosmological level, *ra* corresponds to the element fire that "burns" (destroys) the impediments of the sense organs and enables the practitioner to attain enlightenment. Here the metaphorical associations are clear: physical, material "dirt" (*rajas* —> *ra*) is associated with psychophysical impurity (afflictions); in the mantric system, the initial syllable of the word "dirt" turns into a spell that can destroy mental impurities. This is strengthened by the Esoteric association of *ra* with fire, employed in Tantric rituals (such as the *homa*) to purify but also to sanctify material substances. Once impurities have been transformed into pure substance, one attains enlightenment.

> The graph *hūṃ* (Jp. *un*), as explained in detail in Kūkai's *Unjigi*, contains three elements, respectively *ha*, *ū*, and *ma*. They refer to the three gates of liberation. As the wind sweeps away the dust, so the element wind represented by the syllable *ha* sweeps away all afflictions of the mind and enables one to attain the four kinds of nirvana. When the wind of causes represented by the graph *ha* is extinguished, one attains the great quiescence and bliss of nirvana.[38]

The seed *hūṃ* is one of the most complex *shittan* graph. It is perhaps for this reason that Kakuban does not explain it, but refers instead to Kūkai's *Unjigi*, the classic text on the subject.[39] The three gates of liberation (*san gedatsumon*), that is, the three meditative states that lead one to nirvana (respectively, emptiness, *kū*; signlessness, *musō*; and absence of vows, *mugan*), are represented by the three graphic components of *hūṃ*, namely, *ha*, *ū*, and *ma*. The seed *ha*, the matrix of *hūṃ*, corresponds to the element wind. On the superficial level it means "cause," from the Sanskrit *hetu* (the initial syllable *he* being a graphic derivative of *ha*); on the deep level, it is associated with nirvana (as the extinction of causality). As the wind sweeps away the dust, so the graph *ha* sweeps away the afflictions and opens up the way to nirvana. Interestingly, nirvana is interpreted etymologically as "cessation of the wind"; Kakuban associates the attainment of nirvana ("cessation of wind"), here represented by the Esoteric isotopy of the graph *ha*, to the "cessation of wind" of causality and of afflictions represented by the graph's superficial level. The semiotic operations under Kakuban's interpretation can be identified as follows: the meaning of a complex mantric seed is based on the meanings of its graphic matrix (in this case, *ha*); the two main isotopies, one superficial and one profound, signify opposite principles, namely, "cause" *versus* "nirvana," further strengthened by "wind" *versus* "cessation of wind"; in addition, concrete, material metaphors (water, wind, etc.) indicate abstract doctrinal and soteriological principles.

> The graph *khaṃ* (Jp. *ken*) represents the sky/space, the Dharma realm pervading all things without obstructions just like space. As the element space enables all things to grow without hindrance, so the element space represented by the graph *khaṃ* pervades all lands, pure and impure, and constitutes the karmic environment (*eshō*) of both laity and monks.[40]

The seed *khaṃ* is the fifteenth transformation of the syllable *kha*, which as a noun means in Sanskrit "sky" and "empty space." The sky and the element space are associated with the seed *khaṃ*, referring to the final attainment of wisdom. The last syllable of Mahāvairocana's mantra thus represents the ultimate awareness that emptiness is all-pervading and therefore it is the foundation of everyday reality as well.

Considerations

From our analysis emerges the complexity of the manifold relations between the planes of expression (phonetic and graphic) and the plane of content, as well as between the various "meanings" of the mantric seeds. This complexity is due to processes of remotivation of language and signs that characterize the semiotics of Esoteric Buddhism. Remotivation turns mantric expressions (and Esoteric symbols in general) into inscriptions of the salvation process.

In his discussion of Mahāvairocana's mantra, Kakuban describes the semantic network associated with each of the five syllables, and turns them into representations/actualizations of the standard ascetic path in five steps:

(i) The arousal of the desire for enlightenment (*bodhicitta*), understood here as the innate and undestructible substance of the original enlightenment which ensures the attainment of the soteriological goal (graph *A*);
(ii) Religious practices, in which the ascetic's concentration and resolve are threatened by doubts, afflictions, and karmic obstacles (*bi*);
(iii) Purification produced by meditation, which enables the attainment of the fruit (*ra*);
(iv) Nirvana, envisioned here as a state of absolute calm which constitutes the moment of liberation from afflictions (*un*);
(v) The ensuing transformation of the consciousness apparatus and the related wisdom, which enables the practitioner to view ordinary reality (to the enlightened one, the *only* reality) with different eyes (*ken*).

Thus, the formula *a bi ra un ken* encompasses the journey toward salvation. This mantra is a sort of recording of the original voice of the Buddha Mahāvairocana, as well as a reproduction of the ascetic's itinerary toward buddhahood. The certainty of salvation to be attained through the practice of this mantra is guaranteed, as we have seen, by the initial veridiction contract (the original utterance of the mantra by Mahāvairocana) and by the final sanctioning by Amoghavajra; moreover, the formula contains—not in mystical and ineffable ways, but in theoretically describable terms—the totality of the Esoteric wisdom and the salvation process.

The conformity of expression, meanings, and soteriological function is not purely theoretical. If the very form of the mantra is homologous to the path toward liberation, chanting and visualization of that mantra is in itself walking on that path. Accordingly, mantras are not just supports for practice or "symbols" of enlightenment: they are the very substance of the enlightenment process. An important consequence, from the standpoint of the Shingon teachings, is that all those who chant or visualize a mantra will experience its power and attain its purported goal—in other words, all initiated will become buddhas in their present bodies. In this sense, at least, it is possible to talk about the "symbolic omnipotence"—or, rather, the *semiotic* omnipotence of Tantric Buddhism: symbols are not just indications or representations, but, literally, the very essence of that which they stand for. This is the reason why, as Kakuban writes, meditation of the mantra *a bi ra un ken* is equivalent to the performance of the bodhisattva practices for countless eons. Symbolic practices are efficacious in and of themselves; deep knowledge of the exoteric Dharma and direct practice of the six supreme virtues (*pāramitās*) are not necessary in order to become a buddha in the present body by following Mahāvairocana's teachings.

The journey through the mandala

After explaining the equivalence of the mantra *a bi ra un ken* with the path toward buddhahood, Kakuban addresses the relation between that mantra and the five-element mandala (*gorin mandara*)—a relation based on a complex network of cosmic homologies. In this section of the *Gorin kujimyō himitsushaku*, Kakuban's prose is extremely dense, as he was trying to inscribe directly in the text the interdependence of concepts and the interrelation of phenomena that characterize the Dharma realm. Again, such interdependence and interrelation are not the result of an individual's mystical visions, but are grounded in and sanctioned by the entire Esoteric episteme and world-view.

The five-element mandala is an alloformic representation of Mahāvairocana based on his fundamental mantra *a va ra ha kha*, of which *a bi ra un ken* is a transformation. As such, this mandala originates from the core of the mandalas of the two realms: in the *Vajra* realm the five elements come from the seed *vaṃ*, while in the Womb realm they proceed from the seed *aḥ*. These two graphs are the mantric seeds of Mahāvairocana in each of the two mandalas. The five-element mandala is thus a condensation of the entire Dharma realm and of its two main semiotic manifestations.

The pure *bodhicitta*, i.e. the originally enlightened mind in its innate form, is the seed of the five elements, that is, the material substance of both the Dharma realm as Mahāvairocana's body and the practitioner's body. The main protagonists of this visualization based on the five-element mandala are the five buddhas located on the lotus flower at the center of the Womb mandala and, in various combinations, also in the *Vajra* mandala. Each represents/embodies some characteristics of the soteriological processes, especially the five steps leading to enlightenment and the five types of wisdom acquired through it. Mahāvairocana, the cosmic Buddha, is the most important among the five Buddhas. Situated at the very center of the mandala, he represents the principle of enlightenment and the range of powers associated with it. All around him are four other buddhas: below him, to the east, is Akśobhya, to the south is Ratnasaṃbhava, to the west is Amitābha, and to the north is Amoghasiddhi. Collectively known as the five buddhas (*gobutsu*), they serve as the ground point for a number of five-elements cosmic series that structure the Tantric universe and guide the practitioners in their rituals.

The practice of the five-element mandala consists in visualizing the universe as a five-element *stūpa*, also called *caitya* in the text. In India the *stūpa* is a funerary monument, sometime of large dimensions, that enshrines relics of the Buddha. It symbolizes the formless body of the Buddha and the essential structure of the cosmos. The East Asian equivalents of *stūpas* are tower-like buildings, known in English as pagodas, which enshrine relics or other sacred objects. The *stūpa* described in this ritual is a vertical object in the form of a pagoda composed of five geometrical elements used as supports for meditation. They are, respectively, from bottom to top, a square, a triangle, a circle, a crescent, and a sphere. This kind of *stūpa* is still used in Japanese cemeteries as a memorial monument in tombs. Through the visualizations in this ritual, the ascetic is supposed to reconfigure his/her body as a *stūpa*, envisioned here as the mystical cosmic body of Mahāvairocana, and to become a buddha him/herself.

Kakuban presents several visions/visualizations, which, on the basis of Chinese correlative principles, dissolve the distinctions between the practitioner's inner self and external reality—or, in other words, the distinction between subject and object. In the process, the practitioners, after they have inscribed within their bodies the five-element mandala, are meditatively decomposed into the constitutive elements of reality; thus, they can realize their essential identity with the entire macrocosm. As Kakuban wrote, "since the icon (*honzon*) and the practitioner are originally the same, each of us is always-already enlightened. I am the buddhas of the past."[41]

These visualizations are based on multiple interrelations of several subtle substances (breath, light, sound, writing, etc.), in which the hidden structure of the entire universe is recreated and embodied by the practitioner. As we have already seen, the universe is organized on interconnected series of five elements that form closed causal chains. For example, Kakuban correlates the five Buddhas, the five stages of the enlightenment process, and the five wisdoms thereby attained, with the cosmic elements (earth, water, fire, wind, and space), the five directions (east, south, west, north, and the center), the five seasons (spring, summer, fall, winter, plus an intercalary period in the summer), the five aggregates (Sk. *skandha*, psychophysical constituents of reality), the five viscera of the body (liver, spleen, heart, lungs, and kidneys), the five souls, the five phases (Ch. *wuxing*, the five natural elements according to the Chinese cosmology, namely, earth, fire, water, wood, and metal), fundamental colors, planets, Chinese and Indian deities, and so forth;[42] in this way, the mantra *a va ra ha kha* and its variant *a vi ra hūṃ khaṃ* become condensations of the entire encyclopedia of the Esoteric knowledge. The body is the privileged site for experiencing such a cosmic structure. Once mastered and embodied through initiation, knowledge, and ritual action, cosmology opens up the way to liberation.

The structure of the visualization ritual of the mantra *a bi ra un ken* and the five-element mandala it generates can be described as follows. First, the Tantric-Daoist cosmology of the human body is presented, with all the complex correlations governing it and the practices necessary to maintain balance. Then, three levels of attainment (*siddhi*) and the respective mantras are introduced. Next, the text describes the production of the "living-body relic"—the meditative destruction of the ascetic's ordinary body and the creation of a *stūpa*-like cosmic body.

The visualization process aims at establishing a connection between the graphs of the mantra and their multiple meanings on the one hand, and the parts of the human body and the elements in the external world they correspond to by virtue of the correlative logic of the East Asian Esoteric episteme. According to both Indian Tantrism and traditional Chinese medicine, the human body is a microcosm. The central apparatus of the body, the five organs (liver, lungs, heart, kidneys, and spleen), is directly related to the five phases (the five material elements of Chinese cosmology, i.e. wood, metal, fire, water, earth) on the outside and controls five souls or spiritual functions, corresponding to forms of the *qi* (Jp. *ki*, breath/energy): the celestial soul (Ch. *hun*, Jp. *kon*), the terrestrial soul (*po*, *haku*), the superior soul (*shen*, *shin*), the will (*shi*, *shi*), and the intellect (*yi*, *i*).[43]

Next, the three kinds of attainment (*siddhi*), are: the "intruding *siddhi*," centered in the abdomen; the "protruding *siddhi*," centered in the heart; and the "perfect *siddhi*," centered in the top of the head (*uṣṇiṣa*), the location of supreme wisdom. Each is related to a mantra, respectively *a ra pa ca na*; *a vi ra hūṃ khaṃ*; and *a vaṃ raṃ haṃ khaṃ*.

The sites of the three *siddhis* in the body correspond to the three "cinnabar fields" (Ch. *dantien*) in Daoism. According to Daoist medical soteriology, the control of these three centers of pure energy enables the practitioner to achieve liberation from the coarse body and become an "Immortal" (Ch. *xianren*, Jp. *sennin*). Daoist soteriology and, more generally speaking, Chinese cosmic anthropology, had a clear impact on this ritual. By becoming aware of the profound relation between the individual and the universe, the initiate is able to control the cosmic forces and, as a consequence, to embody the cosmos—which, as we have seen, is actually a *stūpa*, a reliquary body. It should be noted that the soteriological transformation of the practitioner's body into a buddha-body is described in the text as an effect of an "empowerment" (*adhiṣṭhāna*, Jp. *kaji*) resulting from the ascetic's interaction with the Buddha (or an icon thereof).

At this point, Kakuban introduces the visualization on the mandala of the seed *āṃḥ* (Jp. *ānku*), in which the human heart appears as the sublime lotus, the symbol of the Dharma realm and of enlightenment.[44] In this case as well, the relation between support and goal of meditation is not random or arbitrary. The graph *āṃḥ* is the fifth and last of the five transformations (*goten*) of the Sanskrit letter *A*, that is, the total sum of all previous four transformations (*a*, *ā*, *aṃ*, *aḥ*). Esoteric graph *par excellence* (it does not exist in the ordinary Sanskrit graphic system), *āṃḥ* represents both the Dharma realm in its totality and enlightenment in its most complete form. The five transformations of Sanskrit graphs are homologated to the five steps of the enlightenment process and come to coincide with *āṃḥ*, so that the mantric seed is the representation of original enlightenment and of the certainty to attain buddhahood. This is another example of an Esoteric expression being related to its contents and its effects by motivation.

Liberation is envisioned as the dissolution of sense, understood as the realization of the provisional nature of distinctions and articulations produced by the ordinary, deluded mind.[45] Becoming a buddha, then, is the result of the use of motivated signs, essentially identical with both their referents and the ascetics employing them, in which the ascetic itinerary (and the certainty of attainment) is inscribed. As represented also by the graph *āṃḥ*, the practice of esoteric Buddhism is an enormous circuit of sameness; entrance in the circuit always entails salvation. This fundamental circularity is also expressed by the mantra of the Vajra realm *vaṃ hūṃ traḥ hṛīḥ aḥ* [Jp. *ban un taraku kiriku aku*], in which each graph is both the basis of original enlightenment at a given level of attainment and the power that destroys the conditionings still present in the previous graph (and in the practitioner meditating on it). The final graph *aḥ* represents the original enlightenment of Mahāvairocana; as such it coincides with the initial graph *vaṃ*, representing Mahāvairocana's enlightenment as the result of practice. In other words, the ascetic follows a reverse path from that of Mahāvairocana: from the realized buddha to original enlightenment; but once one realizes original enlightenment, one is necessarily already enlightened. At this point, the ascetic identifies him/herself with Mahāvairocana.

Based as it is on the manipulation of images, signs, and ritual objects, this bodily and mental soteriological process described in the text is primarily semiotic, culminating in the production of a perfect body, a "living-body relic" which, as we have seen, is a condensation of the entire universe. This visualization technology implies a semiotics in which there is no distinction between the practitioner, the signs and objects he employs, their meanings, and the external reality (the deities of the mandala and, ultimately, the entire Dharma realm) of which they are part and which they refer to. The characteristic circularity of Esoteric Buddhist soteriology is particularly apparent in the text: the support of meditation (the moon disk mandala) is equivalent to the part of the body it affects (the heart/mind), to the mental functions on which it operates (the apparatus of consciousness), and finally to the results achieved (the three *siddhis* and the three bodies of the Buddha); on the other hand, as a mandala it is coextensive with the entire universe (Dharma realm), with the mind, and with the substance of semiotic activity (the Sanskrit letter *A*). As a result of this circularity, salvation is continuously produced and certainly realized.

Amida's *dhāraṇī*

Becoming a buddha in the present body was not however the only form of salvation for Kakuban, who also valued the perspective of a rebirth into Amida's Pure Land (in accordance with Pure Land Buddhism that became popular in Japan since around the eleventh century). Thus, after discussing Mahāvairocana's mantra, Kakuban presents Amida's *dhāraṇī*, which is supposed to trigger one's deliverance in the Pure Land. The formula is the following:

> *Oṃ amṛta-tese hara hūṃ*
> [Jp. *on amirita teizei kara un*][46]

Kakuban does not refer to the context of the original enunciation of this formula, but begins instead directly with the analysis of this mantra in nine syllables (*kujimyō*).[47]

This mantra is delimited by the two Esoteric indicators *oṃ* and *hūṃ*, signaling respectively the beginning and the end of a mantric linguistic space. Each of the three units included between them, respectively *amṛta*, *tese*, and *hara*, has meaning in Sanskrit ordinary language: *amṛta* means "immortality" and refers metonymically to the *soma*, the divine food of immortality; *tese* means "light" and "high-pitched"; finally, *hara* means "take away."[48] The entire mantra, then, is not a purely Esoteric formula, but is endowed of a superficial meaning that was at least partially comprehensible in Sanskrit ordinary language. A translation sounds as follows:

> Hail (*oṃ*), you who are endowed with the light (*tese*) of immortality (*amṛta*), take me away with you (*hara*)! So be it![49]

These three meaningful units are taken as representing the main features of Amida and his typical way of salvation. Amida is in fact the Japanese rendering of two Sanskrit terms, Amitāyus and Amitābha, referring respectively to "eternal life" and "glorious light"; furthermore, according to standard Pure Land doctrines, Amida will appear to each dying individual and take him/her away with him to his paradise. Accordingly, we could say that also in this case, the mantra presents/embodies the main features of both the agent and the process of salvation it invokes.

In Japan, the communicative value of this mantra is obviously different, since its components are meaningless in ordinary language and their understanding requires a specific competence. However, the interpretation of this mantra is remarkably similar to its Sanskrit original. To the Japanese practitioners, the two Esoteric markers /*on*/ and /*un*/ serve to delimit a mantric utterance; as we have already seen in Chapter Three, /*on*/ signifies a statement of trust or faith, whereas /*un*/ sanctions the completion of the ritual utterance and, as a consequence, the realization of the request accompanying the mantra.

The linguistic space delimited by these two units loses any relation with ordinary language, but acquires, through commentaries, a direct relation of motivation with the entities it signifies/evokes/embodies, much in the same way as in the Sanskrit case. In Japan as well, then, this mantra evokes the main features of Amida and the modalities of salvation Amida ensures. Such transformation of the mantric linguistic space also utilizes modifications in the plane of expression, so as to conform it more closely to the nebula of content that the Sanskrit original aims to convey.[50] Thus, the original word *teje* is turned into *tese*, in order to include in the mantra the concept of "truth" (*satya*) based on its initial syllable *sa*, which resonates in the second syllable /*se*/ of *tese*. In the same way, the Sanskrit *hara* is interpreted in Japan as *kara*, meaning "action," to emphasize Amida's soteriologic action.[51] Kakuban presents the semantic structure of Amida's mantra as follows:

- *On*: the three bodies of the Buddha; faith and devotion; offerings. This indicates devotion to Amida understood not as a distinct buddha, but as a manifestation of the Dharmakāya; chanting this mantra is an offering to the buddha.
- *Amirita*: "sweet dew" (Jp. *kanro*), the supernatural drink of immortality, one of Amida's main features.
- *Teizei*: Amida's all-pervading light, his supernatural power to transform things, his embodying the force of the six elements, his courage in fighting the enemies of Buddhism, his anger that punishes the violators of the Buddhist precepts.
- *Kara*: Amida's salvific action toward the practitioner. It means: becoming a buddha (through one's realization of original enlightenment); action (aimed at salvation); activity (through unlimited supernatural powers); devotional practices, meditation; and the utterance of the forty-eight vows to save all beings.
- *Un*: it guarantees the final result: the destruction of the enemies of Buddhism, establishment of Suchness (*shinnyo*), and fear for demons and non-Buddhists.

This was the syntagmatic analysis (*kugi*), term by term, of Amida's nine-syllable formula. The atomic analysis of its meaning, graph by graph (*jigi*), further elucidates the salvific power of this *dhāraṇī* and emphasizes its structural homology with the soteriological path leading one to rebirth into Amida's Pure Land. Each syllable embodies the entire formula and thus the entire salvific process it entails; but the inscription of soteriology also takes place at the level of single words, sentences, and even of entire texts. In other words, the inscription of soteriology occurs on all levels of the Esoteric signs on the basis of the peculiar recursive structure of the Esoteric universe.

After inscribing the soteriological itinerary (and the certainty of its success) in Amida's *dhāraṇī*, Kakuban turns the formula into a mandala (*kuji mandara*, see Figure. 4.9)—in a process similar to what he had done before to the five-graph mantra, which he related to the five-element mandala.

I will not discuss here the details of the visualization of the mandala of Amida's *dhārāṇī*; I will focus instead on the principles of the *dhārāṇī*'s mandalization. For Kakuban the representation of Amida's mantra in nine graphs as a mandala is the ascetic itinerary that turned the bodhisattva Dharmakāra into the Buddha Amitābha through a purification process that took place over five *kalpas* (aeons), as explained in the scriptures. Kakuban

FIGURE 4.9 *Kakuban's nine-graphs mandala* (kuji mandara). *From* Gorin kujimyō himitsushaku *by Kakuban. In Takakusu Junjirō and Watanabe Kaigyoku (eds),* Taishō shinshū daizōkyō, *vol. 79, p. 19a–b. Tokyo: Daizō shuppan.*

homologates this process to the transformation of the graph *ha*, the seed of Dharmakāra at the beginning of his asceticism, into the graph *hrīḥ*, the symbol of Amitābha as a fully realized Buddha. In turn, *hrīḥ* is the mantric seed of Amitābha's great *dhāraṇī*. The graph *ha* was not chosen at random. As we have seen in Chapter Three, *ha* represents the cessation of karmic conditionings and the attainment of nirvana. This produces a series of implications:

- It is not possible for Dharmakāra not to become Amitābha, as it is not possible for the graph *ha* not to become the graph *hrīḥ*;
- The transformation of one graph into another, carried out by the practitioner in meditation, reproduces and is fully equivalent to all practices performed by the bodhisattva Dharmakāra for five *kalpas*—a good indication of the purported superiority of the Esoteric practices vis-a-vis those of traditional Mahayana;
- This transformation—not just of one graph into another, but more essentially, of a practitioner into a Buddha—is easy and possible for anyone. Thus, those who perform these symbolic practices cannot fail to repeat Dharmakāra's itinerary.

The nine-graph mandala, in turn, produces the Great *dhāraṇī* of sweet dew (*Amirita dai darani*), that is, the extended mantra of Amida.[52] It follows in Kakuban's text the formula we have just discussed and is another example, much more detailed and articulated, of the peculiar nature of the mantric linguistic space, in which the salvation process is inscribed and enacted.

At the end of this process of manipulation of Esoteric signs, Kakuban achieves a surprising result. The practices for rebirth into Amida's Pure Land coincide with the practices that led the bodhisattva Dharmakāra to become the Buddha Amitābha. In other words, successive rebirth into a Pure Land (*junji ōjō*) is identical with becoming a buddha in the present body; visualization based on semiotic manipulations of Esoteric entities allows one to experience two doctrinally different and irreconcilable phenomena as identical. The identity of both soteriologies is also emphasized by another factor. The graph *ha*, the seed of the nine-syllable mandala and symbol of Dharmakāra's transformation into Amitābha, is the last graph of the Sanskrit alphabet. It traditionally represents the outcome of a salvific process that follows a reverse path as to the one originating with the syllable *A*, the first letter of the alphabet and symbol of Mahāvairocana.[53] Kakuban gives a more direct salvific relevance to the meanings traditionally attributed by Esoteric Buddhism to the graphs *A* and *ha*. For Kakuban, the practices centered on Mahāvairocana, based on the five-element mandala (*gorin mandara*), and the practices centered on Amitābha, based on the nine-graph mandala (*kuji mandara*), even though originally heterogeneous and aiming at different forms of salvation, lead the practitioner to the same ultimate goal.

Texts as simulation of practice

So far we have discussed the structure of Esoteric signs and Esoteric semiotic strategies as applied mainly to minimal units such as graphs/syllables, words, and mantras. However, Esoteric semiotic strategies, especially the inscription of the soteriological process, are also deployed at the level of entire written texts. In general, Shingon texts have two main points in common: (i) they claim that the doctrines they present and the practices they describe ensure two salvation goals, namely, the acquisition of worldly benefits (*genze riyaku*), a category that incorporates both apotropaic and merit-making elements, and the attainment of ultimate salvation (either as becoming a buddha in the present body or as rebirth into a pure land); and (ii) they employ a number of semiotic strategies to ensure the achievement of those goals. These semiotic strategies consist in inscribing the soteriological process into the whole text itself by transforming it into a mandala or by giving it Esoteric meanings it did not originally have; these procedures and strategies make the texts representations/embodiments of the macrocosm and of the salvation itinerary. For instance, a text such as Kakuban's *Gorin kujimyō himitsushaku*, which we have extensively quoted, is a description of two mandalas, namely, the five-element mandala (*gorin mandara*) and the nine-syllable mandala (*kuji mandara*). Reading that text in a ritualized setting amounts to practice those mandalas and therefore results in attaining the goals they promise.

Ordinary acts of reading in search for meaning (that is, probing the expression to determine its content) are only one of the ways in which premodern Japanese people engaged with Buddhist texts. In fact, Buddhist texts have an important non-hermeneutic dimension that requires different forms of interaction and use based on an enhanced awareness of the texts' material nature and ritual functions.[54] Accordingly, the most common uses of Buddhist scriptures throughout history are ritual acts such as chanting, copying, decorating, burying; even hermeneutical reading often involves a ritual/soteriological orientation.

Esoteric Buddhism in particular envisions discourse as a "simulation" of religious practice. If language and reality are essentially the same, language mirrors the world and discourse can simulate reality—much as in Pasolini's understanding of film as the "language of reality" (see Chapter Two). In this section I will outline some of the ways in which Shingon authors inscribed within texts the very experience of the soteriological process. Here, salvific experience can only be postulated as based on textual sources, and for our purposes it is not necessary that liberation was actually experienced in that specific way by any particular practitioner; instead, I would like to show that salvation was textually represented in certain ways I hope to clarify.

Most Shingon texts can be defined as instances of an initiatory discourse containing philosophic, religious, and ritual elements; these texts have the explicit goal of leading their readers/users to salvation. For such texts to actually have salvific power, it is necessary to establish a "veridiction contract" between the author and the readers. In it, the enunciator, that is, the author as textual strategy, must believe to be true what he discusses in the text and must make the reader believe it to be true too. The reader, as another textual strategy, must have the desire to be saved and must believe that what the enunciator says is true. The enunciator, on his part, must possess (and must be believed to possess) a particular competence that enables him to write the text in the first place: in our case, he must be, if not a fully enlightened ascetic, at least, the depositary of a special knowledge about salvation that has been faithfully handed down to him and that goes back to a publicly recognized enlightened master; as the depositary of such a knowledge, he is capable to lead deluded beings to salvation. The truth of the veridiction contract is supposed to be objective and absolute, not just textual and fictional. The veridiction contract and the goal of the text that comes with it are stated in various places of that text. In the case of Mahāvairocana's mantra included in the text by Kakuban previously discussed, we find both veridiction contract and the goal of the mantra at the very beginning, in the description of the original enunciation, and towards the end, in Amoghavajra's citation (see pp. 138–39).

The truth-effect of the text is further enhanced by dialogues and citations. Dialogues reproduce in a textual dimension the master-disciple relationship that characterizes the transmission of Esoteric Buddhism; they also emphasize the original contract between a wise and enlightened enunciator and his readers. Citations, on the other hand, are used to inscribe in the text words by other enunciators, as additional authorities corroborating the author's claims to truth. However, the ultimate guarantor of the truth of the enunciation is, according to the Shingon teachings, the cosmic Buddha Mahāvairocana. As the totality of the universe and both enunciator and recipient of his Dharma preaching (*hosshin seppō*), Mahāvairocana is also the true self of the author of the text and its readers, as in Pasolini's pantheistic "B." (Brāhma), speaking to himself through the signs of reality. Citations can also produce a de-personalizing effect; if enlightenment is the dissolution of subjectivity, the truly enlightened enunciator does not emphasize his own subjective and idiosyncratic experiences, but reinforces his claims by quoting other authoritative sources. Through this anonymous discursivity, the text testifies to the successful identification of an individual author with the universal principle, much in the same way as a single expression is found to embody the totality of the universe (as we have explained it in this book). For example, Kūkai's *Shōji jissōgi* states in the introduction that "words are transparent and manifest the true reality" as "emanations" of the absolute Buddha who, through his own teachings shows sentient beings the way to find back their original essence and become buddhas themselves.[55] In this case, the author's discourse is based on the teachings of his master Huiguo, an enlightened master himself, and ultimately, on the original enlightenment of Mahāvairocana. In this way, the enunciator's (Kūkai's) competence is guaranteed by an indisputable authority and his discourse can presents itself as a reproduction of the supreme truth.

The veridiction contract alone, however, is not enough. The Esoteric discourse can be considered true and effective especially because it simulates the soteriological process in which author and reader are engaged (or, perhaps, are supposed to be engaged) through the reading of the text; as we have seen, Esoteric discourse is not just a representation but a veritable reproduction of the salvation process. Typically, Esoteric Buddhist texts are structured in different stages. First, texts often begin with the analysis of their title, character by character. Then, we find a detailed analysis of doctrinal subjects and of ritual matters. Gradually, the language of the text becomes more complex, as it attempts to represent insights about the ultimate nature of reality—which, as we have seen, presupposes complex signification processes. Finally, the text presents a condition of nondualism, as the proof that the reader/practitioner has attained insight. This discursive simulation occurs in several steps that can be associated with different levels of consciousness.

The *Shōji jissōgi*, Kūkai's most explicit treatise on semiotic matters, is a good example of how a doctrinal text maps and simulates the soteriological process. It opens with a word-by-word analysis of its title, as if it were a mantra.[56] Next, the text discusses at length conceptual issues such as particularities of phenomena and the ideative and discriminative process producing ordinary, deluded reality, in a detailed analysis of the six object fields and in particular the signs of the visual field.[57] In this phase, corresponding to an ordinary state of consciousness in which all information comes from the senses and are elaborated by the intellect and categorized; events occur in space and time and are the products of causes; objects and events are distinct and can be treated separately. Gradually, however, the distinctions between an object and its image, between a thing and its name are questioned, an operation that corresponds to a different level of consciousness.

Then, the text introduces the concept of interdependence:[58] we are now on another level of consciousness, in which distinctions are no longer absolute and self-evident, and even though objects and events still have a distinct identity, there is no clear-cut line separating them from the totality that grounds their existence. Finally, this transition phase is over and we arrive at a stage of deep meditation (*samādhi*).[59] Predictably, this stage is described not on the basis of the individual experience of the author, but through a citation from the *Mahāvairocana Sutra* describing Mahāvairocana's own *samādhi*. This citation is not a rhetorical strategy; since for Kūkai absolute wisdom (awakening) configures itself as the fusion of the subject with the Buddha (*nyūga ganyū*), the practitioner's enlightenment is nothing other than Mahāvairocana's enlightenment. In this phase, corresponding to yet another level of consciousness, one realizes the original, undifferentiated state of the universe: objects and events are parts of a single reality and are all interpenetrated. At this point, the structure of knowledge is also transformed—this is the primary goal of the text, and the presence of this different dimension of reality (understood by Buddhism as the absolute and unconditioned aspect of reality) is recognized also within the everyday, ordinary world.[60]

What we have described so far is homologous to the meditative process of the Esoteric practitioner. S/he begins by concentrating on a specific object (often, a linguistic entity), analyses it (in what we have called proliferation of sense) to find that particularities are parts of the absolute, then s/he dissolves particularities in the totality (Dharma realm), and finally is able to see everyday reality as the true and highest form of the absolute. Significantly, this process also parallels the four isotopies of Esoteric semantics. What is important to emphasize, though, is that enlightenment is not presented as a vague mystical and ineffable state, but as the result of ritual action based on discursive practices consisting in semiotic manipulations. In other words, the process described in Esoteric texts is a mediation between the structure of the cosmos and the soteriological itinerary to understand it on the one hand, and the interpretation process of Esoteric signs on the other.

Pragmatic aspects of Esoteric signs

The manipulation of meaning proper to semiognosis, however, was not the only path to salvation; semiopietas, the non-initiatory and uninformed use of esoteric semiotic expressions, was also a very important component of the Esoteric Buddhist system. Most mantras and *shittan* graphs discussed in this chapter were believed to produce their effects also when chanted and visualized by non-experts; the most striking example is perhaps that of the syllable *un* chanted in temple toilets discussed on p. 137. However, a question remains: on the basis of what principles, were the esoteric signs believed to produce their effects?

The use of magic and ritual languages such as *shingon* and *darani* is often still explained today by recourse to the concept of "sympathetic magic" as defined by Frazer in the nineteenth century. This concept presupposes a systematic confusion, on the part of the performers of magical utterances, of words and things and the superstitious belief in the action of ineffable and mysterious powers. Stanley Tambiah has convincingly criticized the presuppositions behind Frazer's idea of sympathetic magic, and has shown that a magic language, or a language used for magical purposes, is not "mumbo-jumbo shot through with mystical ideas resistant to rational examination."[61] On the contrary, the magic use of language reveals the working of metaphoric thought and a complex association between the semantic properties of the objects evoked in magic and the participants to those rituals. Tambiahs's suggestion is heuristically useful also to understand the functioning of mantras/*siddhaṃ* in Japanese Buddhism.

As we have seen, the first *gomitsu* (secret of language) practice described by Kakuban, the simplest, consists in chanting and memorizing *shingon*. Let us investigate the conceptual presuppositions of this kind of "easy practices." We should begin by noting that mantras serve to create a sacred communicational situation, a ritual interaction in which divine beings (buddhas, bodhisattvas, etc.) are addressed by asking questions, making statements, praising, ordering, promising, thanking—in other words, by borrowing a well-known terminology from Austin's speech-acts theory, mantras essentially serve an illocutionary purpose. The use of *shingon* generates (or is believed to generate—which, for our purposes here, amounts to the same thing) effects that are more or less well defined and known in advance, such as meditation (entering *samādhi*), receiving worldly benefits, rebirth into a Buddhist paradise (Pure Land), or becoming a buddha. These effects can be attributed to mantras' perlocutionary force. In this sense, the chanting (voiced or silent) of *shingon* and *darani* is not just an utterance or an act of thought, but an activity producing effects on reality.

This particular power of mantras is based on Indian traditional linguistic doctrines. As Frits Staal writes, "in India language is not something with which you *name* something. It is something with which you *do* something"; also for this reason, in India "language was generally approached within a ritual perspective."[62] We cannot understand *shingon*'s illocutionary power without reference to the Buddhist concept of karma and, in particular, the Esoteric doctrine of the three secrets (*sanmitsu*). The fact that language is envisioned as one of the factors producing both suffering and liberation points to an underlying theory of language as activity; in Esoteric Buddhism, speech is one of the universal activities of the Dharmakāya (the Buddha in its absolute modality). Thus, the illocutionary use of *shingon* is not a form of "superstition," but is solidly grounded in the episteme of Esoteric Buddhism.

Various scholars, such as Wade Wheelock, Donald Lopez, and Stanley Tambiah, have attempted to apply to mantric phenomena in South and South-East Asia the speech acts theory developed by philosophers of language such as John Austin and John Searle:[63] this approach has yet to be employed extensively in the East Asian context. When one tries to apply the speech acts theory to mantric rituals, however, one should not lose sight of the fact that, as is the case with most Western philosophy of language, this theory has been developed in order to study ordinary language in its communicative function, whereas Esoteric Buddhist thought and practices do not share this concern. In our case, we should focus on the "emic" perspective, internal to the tradition, according to which mantras address deities in a performative way in order to produce linguistic effects upon, and transformations of, reality. These effects are not incorporeal, but dramatically bodily and material (healing diseases, acquisition of worldly benefits, rebirth in paradise or fall into hell, and becoming a buddha). Kakuban, for example, wrote:

> This five-syllable mantra [*a bi ra un ken*] is the general spell of all buddhas of the ten directions... By chanting it one can be reborn in the Pure Lands of the ten directions, in the realm of Maitreya [the future Buddha] or in the cave of the Asura, according to one's desire.[64]

According to Austin, to be effective, the performatives of ordinary language must be uttered according to certain rules, which he calls "conditions of felicity."[65] Specifically, there should exist a conventional procedure that is considered able to produce a determined effect and which implies the utterance of certain words by certain people in certain circumstances; people involved and the circumstances of the utterance should be the appropriate ones; the procedure should be carried out correctly and completely; and if the procedure requires that the participants have certain thoughts and states of mind, the participants should have those thoughts and states of mind and should behave accordingly.

Let us now examine, point by point, to what extent Austin's rules can be applied to a description of the performative effect of mantras as they are defined and used by the Shingon tradition. The conventional procedure controls Esoteric rituals and practices and determines their effects (altered states of consciousness, different relation with reality, transformation of knowledge, magical effects, etc.). However, it is not necessary to *utter* certain mantric words, because *shingon* are considered even more effective when mentally visualized. Mantric expressions used in a ritual are not chosen at random, and each ritual has its own specific mantras. The persons involved are practitioners and performers of the rituals (including meditation); the circumstances are primarily ritual; many premodern exegetes also extended these categories to non-specialists and to everyday situations (outside of strictly defined ritual contexts). The Shingon teachings presuppose the correct and integral performance of the procedure in the scrupulous respect of all its rules as the essential condition for triggering the power of mantras; however, simplified uses of mantras were also recognized and, indeed, encouraged. The Buddhist tradition describes the practitioner's psychophysical state in a ritual; ignoring these norms makes the performance useless or, in certain cases, even dangerous.

The conditions of felicity discussed above are valid in two different situations: (i) the use of mantric expressions by those who know their grammar and syntax and understand their meaning; (ii) talismanic uses by people who know practically nothing about them. Stanley Tambiah has studied and discussed a similar context of use in northern Thailand.[66] The second case is not particularly problematic: anyone can chant or listen to a mantra even without a previous knowledge of its theoretical presuppositions; all is needed is for that person to believe, up to a certain point, in the power of that mantra and to know that in a certain context a certain formula produces a certain effect. We should note that a more effective application of speech acts theory to ritual uses of language within the Buddhist tradition (and, presumably, also within other traditions as well), should take into account other phenomena outside of Austin's original formulation. Particularly important in Buddhist practice are what we could define as "transitive speech acts," in which the effects of mantric utterances are transferred to a different person than the utterer, as when monks perform a ritual for others (this is related to the Budhdist idea of *ekō*, Sk. *pariṇāma*, i.e. the transfer of merit to others); and also linguistic acts that do not involve *speech* but are centered instead on writing, as in the case of illocutionary (performative) transcription of written formulas done in order to modify reality (as in the case of amulets and talismans). In other words, we should consider the performative aspects of both speech (the phonetic signifier) and writing (the grammatological signifier) of mantric signs.

Shittan, either individually or in sequences, are also used as talismans and amulets, and as powerful salvific devices in cemeteries, where they are inscribed on funerary steles called *sotoba* and in tablets known as *ihai*. Kakuban in fact includes the "visualization of graphs" among the practices of the "secret of language" (*gomitsu*). This practice does not necessarily require the understanding of the deep meaning of the graphs, but nevertheless results in great salvific power. Similarly, numerous and widespread practices based on the manipulation (copy, burial, illustration, ingestion, etc.) of Buddhist scriptures can be treated as performative acts centered on visual and material signs and objects.[67] A useful starting point for such a study is Giorgio Raimondo Cardona's treatment of the performative power attributed to amulets, in which "the inscription acts on its own... and brings benefits to those who carry it with them but without their participation except than their mere carrying it":

> The magical illocutionary act, if it is possible to establish such a level, has writing itself as a propositional content. A magical goal is achieved not by speaking and uttering formulas with one's voice, but by performing operations that have as their content writing as a whole. Since this is not a linguistic circuit, such writing can be showed, displayed, applied [onto surfaces], touched, worn...[68]

Of course, this "circuit," this process going from the performance of a magical act to its effects, is at the basis of the practices related to the *shittan* we have described above. What is essential, but Cardona does not indicate, is an act of faith, or at least, an investment of value by the participants, who agree to immerse themselves in this magical-communicative space where the forces triggered by writing operate by virtue of its (writing's) own special relations with the structure of the Esoteric cosmos. It is at this point that *shittan* acquire the value of *pentacula*—in Cardona's words,

> magical objects built upon a play of correspondences between microcosm and macrocosm. These correspondences ensure the control over forces that cannot be governed otherwise, but that can be appropriately bridled and directed by a model.[69]

As in the case of *shittan*, a *pentaculum* can be used as an amulet, as a support for meditation, or as a talisman marking a sacred space such as a temple or any place where religious practices are performed. Here lies perhaps the key to understand the power of writing. Writing is a microcosm in which the structure of the world is inscribed; it is a model that "reproduces force lines, condenses events, makes everything smaller and ciphered—but does not hide [that which it stands for]."[70]

Visualization and the transformation of the body-mind

The soteriology of Esoteric Buddhism can be defined as a set of semiotic practices aiming at the transformation of the ordinary body-language-mind complex into forms of altered states that are defined as "becoming a buddha." The privileged locus of Shingon practices is the mind, or more precisely, the heart/mind complex. First of all, we should mention that Buddhism traditionally associates the mind (Sk. *citta*) and mental states (*caitta*) with the heart (*hṛdaya*); the mind was located not in the brain, as in contemporary understanding, but in the heart. The Sino-Japanese word *shin* (read *kokoro* in *kun'yomi* standard Japanese) means both heart and mind, but Esoteric Buddhist texts distinguish between the heart, variously called *karidaya*, *kiridaya*, *karida*, *karidashin* from the Sanskrit *hṛdaya*, and from the *shittashin* (Sk. *citta*), the mental functions which are rooted in that bodily organ. Symbolic practices (mantras, visualization) transform the heart that awakens one's *bodhicitta*, thus resulting in enlightenment; the transformation of the mind (from nine consciousnesses to five wisdoms) also affects the body (attainment of whole-body relic, becoming a buddha in the present body).

Indian and Chinese physicians noted a morphological resemblance between the lotus flower and the human heart. The lotus is a very important metaphor in Buddhism; as is well known, the fact that the lotus has its roots in the mud of putrid ponds but develops into a beautiful and pure white flower was often used to represent the process of enlightenment. The lotus was later associated with the human heart (*hṛdaya*), the bodily location of the mind (*citta*) and the physical site where enlightenment takes place. According to a theory that can be traced back to the *Commentary to the Mahāvairocana Sutra*, the heart of human beings has the shape of an eight-petal lotus;[71] a man's heart is turned upwards, while that of a woman is turned downwards. Kakuban for example wrote:

> The heart is the *puṇḍarīka* [lotus flower] inside the human body, a relic of the Dharmakāya. It contains Mahāvairocana's four bodies and is identical to all buddhas' supreme wisdoms in their originally pure substance.[72]

Gōhō also wrote that in the human chest there is a lump of flesh in eight parts; in men it is vertical, in women horizontal;[73] one should visualize it opening up to form a white, eight petal lotus. Let us see this type of visualization more in detail. A ritual text states:[74]

> The shape of the *hṛdaya*-heart of ordinary people is like a closed lotus. Its muscles form eight sections. In men it is turned upward, in women it is turned downward. In visualization one should open one's heart to form a white lotus with eight petals. Upon it as a platform one should see the letter *A* in golden color. The letter *A* is like a square yellow altar, and the practitioner sees oneself on it. From the letter *A* comes out the syllable *ra*, which burns one's body and reduces it to ashes. From the ashes the syllable *va* is generated, of a pure white color. From it, *a vaṃ raṃ haṃ khaṃ*, the mantra of the five elements [of the cosmic *stūpa*], is produced. This mantra takes its place on the five parts of the body, from the waist to the top of the head. This is the pure *bodhicitta*. These five syllables concur in the creation of the roots of great compassion.

Kakuban also addressed the subject:

> The *hṛdaya*, the heart of human beings, has the shape of an eight-petal lotus flower. [...] In meditation one has to transform the heart-lotus into an eight-petal white lotus in full blossom. You should then visualize on it the character *āṃḥ* in the color of a *vajra*. This corresponds to the ultimate perfection of skilful means, to Mahāvairocana Tathāgata, to the wisdom of Dharmadhātus's essence, to the original state of the Dharmakāya in its aspect of quiet extinction [...] Only buddhas can understand this.[75]

As mentioned before, the five Buddhas are located on the eight-petal lotus at the center of the Womb mandala. Enlightenment results from opening up one's heart in visualization so as to reveal inside oneself the same eight-petal lotus we find at the center of mandala. As a support for meditation, the practitioner used a white disk representing both the moon as an image of the eight-petal lotus (which is painted in an almost circular way) and the heart of the practitioner himself, as well as the pure enlightened mind achieved through this practice. More precisely, in the Womb mandala (*taizōkai*) the human heart is visualized as an eight-petal lotus; closed, it symbolizes "the cause containing the principle," open, it reveals the attainment of buddhahood. On the other hand, in the *Vajra* mandala (*kongōkai*) the heart is contemplated as the lunar disk expressing the substance, circular and luminous, of the enlightened mind (*bodhicitta*). Together, they correspond to two fundamental practices of Esoteric Buddhism, namely, the visualization of the *shittan* graph *A* (*ajikan*) and that of the moon disk (*gachirinkan*).[76] In this practice, soteriology merges with physiology as the practitioners modify their body/mind in visualization to embody enlightenment.

In East Asia, the Esoteric Buddhist identification of the mind with the heart assumes even stronger materialistic orientations because of the role played in it by Chinese cosmology. A ritual text in Chinese, the *Sanzhong xidi po diyu zhuan yezhang chu sanjie mimi tuoluoni fa*, extensively quoted by Kakuban in his *Gorin kujimyō himitsushaku*, proposes a set of correlations associating among others the five internal organs of the human body, the five agents of Chinese cosmology, the five seeds of Mahāvairocana's mantra and, significantly, the five souls of the Chinese psychology. Here is an excerpt from relevant passages in that text:

> The letter *A* ... controls the liver. [...] The liver controls the celestial soul (*kon*). The breath/energy (*ki*) of the *kon* becomes the east and wood. [...] Wood controls the spring, and its color is green/blue. [...] The liver protrudes outside and becomes the eyes; it also controls the muscles. The muscles stretch out and become the nails. [...]
>
> The syllable *vaṃ*... controls the lungs. [...] The lungs control the terrestrial soul (*haku*)... It controls the nose and corresponds to the west and to metal. Metal controls autumn, and its color is white. [...]
>
> The syllable *raṃ*... controls the heart. The heart controls the superior soul (*shin*)... South is fire, and fire controls the summer. Its color is read. [...] The heart protrudes outside and becomes the tongue; the heart further controls the blood; the blood stretches outside and becomes milk. It also controls the ear, and turn into the nostrils, the septum of the nose, the jaws, and the chin. [...]
>
> The syllable *haṃ* ... controls the kidneys. [...] When they stretch out they become sperm. The kidneys control the will (*shi*), and correspond to the north and water. Water controls winter, and its color is black. [...] [The kidneys] control the ear. They protrude outside and become the bones, which control the marrow. The marrow stretches out and becomes the ear holes. The bones in turn stretch out and become the teeth. [...]
>
> The syllable *khaṃ*... controls the spleen. [...] The spleen controls the intellect (*i*), and becomes the center and earth. Earth controls the summer and its color is yellow. [...] The spleen... controls the mouth.[77]

We can see here the recursive cosmology of the East Asian Esoteric universe, with its ceaseless circulation between inside and outside, mind and body, and the body and the world. Such a recursive cosmology is directly reflected in soteriology: the main tool of meditation (the moon disk mandala) is equivalent to the part of the body it affects (the heart/mind), the mental functions on which it operates (consciousness), and ultimately to the results achieved (*siddhi* and the Buddha-body). On the other hand, as a mandala the moon disk is coextensive with the entire universe (the Dharma realm), with the substance of mental activity (*amala vijñāna*), and the substance of semiotic activity (the *shittan* graph *A*). As a result of this circularity, salvation is continuously produced and certainly achieved. The heart/lotus/moon disk complex is another Esoteric macrosign deriving, like the five-element mandala (*gorin mandara*), from the central part of the mandala of the two realms (*ryōbu mandara*)—the lotus where Mahāvairocana, the other four buddhas, and their four attendant bodhisattvas reside. The Dharma realm, first condensed in the five-element mandala, is then embodied by the practitioner; the transformation of one's mind that signals the attainment of enlightenment takes place only when the heart/lotus opens up, and salvation is attained when one visualizes the shape of one's heart change. From a closed lotus, the heart becomes an open lotus like the center of mandala, and practitioners see themselves at its center. In this form of visualization, all boundaries are dissolved: the practitioner's body becomes his/her heart (the outside merges with the inside), the heart is a lotus, the lotus is a mandala (e.g., the entire universe), and the practitioner is Mahāvairocana (the inside merges with the outside).

To summarize, Shingon soteriology is the result of a number of operations on the body (heart)-language (mantra)-mind (mandala) complex of the practitioner. To attain enlightenment one has to transform one's mind. To transform one's mind, one has to act upon one's heart, the material basis of the mind. The easiest way to do that is to visualize representations of the enlightened heart/mind such as the lotus and the moon. These images are considered representations of the *bodhicitta*; in visualization, the mind becomes the visualized image—the *bodhicitta*, Dainichi, the entire Dharma realm.

Kōshū, a Tendai scholar monk of the early fourteenth century, developed an even more concrete, and very surprising understanding of the transformation of the mind leading to enlightenment. He wrote:[78]

> in the water section inside the human body there are the lungs; in them there is golden water; in it there is a three-inch snake: that is our sixth consciousness. The lungs correspond to the west and are the location of the wisdom contemplating the sublime aspect of things (*myōkanzatchi*). This wisdom is [the transformation of] the sixth consciousness, the one that discriminates between right and wrong; it is our thinking mind. Its mantra is *hūṃ*, the seed of Benzaiten [the Japanese version of the Indian goddess Sarasvatī].

Let us try to unpack this dense passage. Kōshū refers to the Esoteric physiology based on a five-element correlative system ultimately derived from the Chinese cosmology—the same system employed by Kakuban and other before him. As a microcosm, the human body is a replica of the mandalized universe of Esoteric Buddhism. The five elements are embodied in the five organs, and in particular the lungs are the sites of water. In the Buddhist tradition, water is a rich symbolic element, associated with serpents but at the same time representing purification and wisdom. Kōshū assumes that, as there are the *nāgas* serpents at the bottom of the macrocosmic sea, so there should be a miniature *nāga*—a small snake—in the microcosmic sea of the human body (the lungs). As *nāgas* are the keepers of the Dharma and therefore are in control of ignorance and awakening (it is up to them to reveal or not to reveal certain Buddhist teachings in the human world), so the little snake in the body controls the sixth consciousness (*ishiki*), the mental center in which perceptual data are organized and cognitive judgments are formulated (see Chapter One). Normally, the sixth consciousness is the origin of dualistic, deluded knowledge. The ordinary cognitive mechanism can be transformed into a contemplative device of awakening (*myōkanzatchi*), but it can also turn into something darker and dangerous: a practitioner who is unable to control the sixth consciousness will turn into the demon Māra, the arch-enemy of Buddhism, or into a disbeliever (*gedō*). The fourteenth century *Heike monogatari*, an important and influential work in medieval Japanese literature, states: "one becomes Māra after a transformation of the sixth consciousness, and therefore also the appearance of Māra resembles that of every sentient being."[79] Kōshū's main concern is how to turn the sixth consciousness into one of the five Esoteric wisdoms (*gochi*), namely, the "wisdom to observe the sublime aspect of things" (*myōkanzatchi*)—in a process we described in Chapter One. This is associated with the Buddha Amida, the west, water, the lungs, and the seed *hūṃ*. Among others, *hūṃ*, a multivalent mantra, is the seed of the goddess Benzaiten, who is a serpent-like female deity. The visualization of correlations resulting in the practitioner's identification with Benzaiten also brings about the transformation into the awakening of the little snake in the body. This association between a female deity, a snake, and the transformation of the mind into awakening is probably a distant echo of Indian Yoga theories about the serpent Kundalini located in the spine (not too far from the lungs), re-elaborated in light of East Asian medicine and correlative systems. Kōshū further explains:[80]

> the unconditioned (*musa*) and innate (*honnu*) form of sentient beings is that of a snake. This unconditioned body (*tai*), without going through any changes, reveals the innate Dharma body. In the beings' sea of the principle [*rishō*] there is a snake of about three inches.

The implications of this statement are manifold: the serpent, symbol of darkness and ignorance, is defined as the material out of which all sentient beings are made; the very "stuff" of ignorance is the instrument of awakening; awakening is the result of ritual interaction with the goddess Benzaiten, one which is characterized by heavy sexual features. Obviously such a ritual interaction with the sensual goddess Benzaiten, was meant for men. Two body organs are particularly relevant to it: the heart and the female sexual organ, both associated with the serpent and both represented by another multi-faceted symbol, the lotus flower. In this way, a religious practice that began with the Yogācāra tradition as focusing on the mind through a sustained meditation on the consciousness apparatus and its functioning, was developed by Esoteric Buddhism in very allegorical and bodily terms. On the one hand, it became a manipulation of expressions and representations (mantras, images); on the other hand, the focus on the mind gradually shifted to the lotus and to its sexual symbolism. In fact, it is not unusual to find sexual references in texts describing the attainment of enlightenment. Esoteric Buddhism brought together in one, unified field two discourses that were originally quite distinct, sex and mind.

The most striking example of the unification of mind and body, visualization and sex, is represented by a medieval Shingon heretical movement known as Tachikawaryū ("Tachikawa lineage"). Extant sources report that the founder of this heretical movement was the monk Ninkan (active 1101). When he was exiled to Izu, not far from present-day Tokyo, for *lèse majesté*, he changed his name into Rennen and began to practice heretical teachings, especially after his encounter with an *onmyōji* (a ritual specialist of yin-yang doctrines) from Tachikawa (near Tokyo), who became his disciple with the name Kenren.

The teachings of the Tachikawaryū are characterized by a radically materialistic cosmology: texts present the universe as a transformation of a golden turtle, drifting in the ocean, that became the two fundamental fluids (blood/female and semen/male), the lotus and the *vajra*, and the other elements of Esoteric cosmology.[81] Tachikawaryū also attempted to make salvation natural, necessary, and automatic,[82] and carried to the extremes the Shingon teaching that to the initiate each word spoken is a mantra and each gesture is a *mudrā*.[83] They explained everything in sexual terms. As Yūkai critically argued in his *Hōkyōshō*, an anti-Tachikawaryū tract, adepts of this lineage "consider the path of yin and yang, of man and woman, the secret technique to become a buddha in the present body, and [think that] there is no other doctrine to attain salvation."[84] An example of this attitude is offered by one of the few extant Tachikawa texts, the *Aun jigi*, which reduces complex Shingon doctrines to breathing and sexual intercourse with soteriological value.[85]

Similar ideas were also presented in texts belonging in other lineages. For example, the *Hachimanchō no nukigaki: Ajikan no honmi*, an apocryphal attributed to Shinran,[86] presents a sexual interpretation of the formula "Namu Amidabutsu," the standard devotional formula (*nenbutsu*) of Pure Land Buddhism offered to the Buddha Amida. In it, Amida, the Buddha of eternal life, is connected to the principle of life (breath) and the production of life (heterosexual intercourse). The Dharmakāya of expedient means generates the two graphs *A* and *un*, representing the two phases of breathing (respectively, inspiration and expiration) and the two fundamental cosmic principles (yang and yin); *A* and *un* together give birth to the name Amida, which is in turn interpreted as referring to heterosexual sex. The text also says that the place where a man and a woman have a sexual intercourse is the threefold Buddha body. Next, the initial term of the formula, *namu*, is explained according to the same sexual logic: *na* is the father and *mu* the mother.[87] This word is an unconditioned (*jinen*) entity. And the term *jinen* (natural, unconditioned) is interpreted according the two series:[88]

> *Ji* = water = moon = night = yin = menstruation = mother
> *Nen* = fire = sun = day = [yang] = sperm = father

The *Nukigaki* engages in semiotic plays to show the unconditioned nature of *nenbutsu* and the necessity of salvation: the formula "Namu Amidabutsu" contains all the principles of life and the order of the cosmos; birth is equal to rebirth into Amida's Pure Land; sexual intercourse is equal to the recitation of the *nenbutsu*. Accordingly, there is no need for specific religious practices, and salvation can be achieved in this very body, here and now, without efforts (actually, in a rather pleasurable way):[89]

> Man and woman are originally nondual; therefore, the cycle of rebirths (*saṃsāra*) is pure and there are no defilements to purify; there are no passions to despise; there is no Buddha to pray to for his advent. Therefore, the enlightenment of the Buddha and the rebirth [in the Pure Land] of sentient beings are nondual, both in name and in substance.

The collection *Misōde no shita* ("Under the Sleeves") has a similar content.[90] It delves into Shingon semiotics to expose the deep, hidden principles and the fundamental nondualism of names and things. In particular, a section explains the substance of Amida and the *nenbutsu* as located in the five organs, at the very center of the human flesh-body.[91]

In these cases, salvation is no longer a matter of the transformation of the mind, but is produced by bodily practices centered on actual or imagined sexual intercourse. This radical shift was made possible by the general nondualistic outlook of the Esoteric episteme (mind and body are nondual, therefore they can replace each other in soteriology), but also by the fact that the mind had a physical ground (the heart as one of the five organs); the symbolism of the lotus also played an important role.

Buddhist subjectivities

An important aspect of the scholar monks' activities was the creation of discourses on subjectivity based on their world-view. Esoteric Buddhism, in particular, presents a two-tiered subjectivity. From a superficial, exoteric point of view, subjects are ongoing stages in an endless process of reincarnation, in what we could call "karmic subjectivity." On a deeper, Esoteric level, however, individuals are essential parts (samples) of Mahāvairocana; this is their "adamantine subjectivity." The five-element mandala was an important semiotic shifter between these two models and was used to explain in a nondual fashion the complex Esoteric vision on subjectivity. Exposure to the five-element mandala determines a restructuring of the practitioner's self into a microcosm of the absolute: only then is complete self-identification with Mahāvairocana in its material form as an icon (*honzon*) possible (see Figure. 4.10). Kakuban wrote: "If one considers the six elements as an icon to worship (*honzon*), beings themselves become that icon. Since the image and the practitioner are originally the same, each of us has always been enlightened. I am the buddhas of the past."[92]

Practices consist mainly in visualizing the universe as a five-element *stūpa*, which comes to coincide with the ascetic himself. In this way, by becoming a *stūpa*, that is, the mystic and cosmic body of the Buddha, the

FIGURE 4.10 *Five-element mandala embodied. From* Gorin kujimyō himitsushaku, *by Kakuban. In Takakusu Junjirō and Watanabe Kaigyoku (eds),* Taishō shinshū daizōkyō, *vol. 79, p. 13a. Tokyo: Daizō shuppan.*

practitioner is able to become a buddha himself. Such a goal is achieved through visualizations (in the general sense discussed in this chapter), in which the hidden structure of the entire universe, based on multiple interrelations of several subtle substances (breath, light, sound, writing, etc.) is recreated and embodied by the ascetic. This bodily and mental soteriological process is primarily semiotic, based as it is on the manipulation of images, signs, ritual objects, and is achieved by the production of a perfect body, a "whole-body relic" (*zenshin shari*), which is a condensation of the entire Dharmadhātu—a *stūpa*-like cosmic body which is the result of a meditative destruction of the ascetic's ordinary body.

The ritual universe of Shingon's subjectivity, as we have seen, is organized on the basis of interconnected five-element series (cosmic elements = seasons = directions = colors = viscera = stages in the process of enlightenment = buddhas = wisdoms = mantric seeds = planets = cereals = souls, and so forth), in a systematic correlative cosmology. Kakuban explains: "He who understands the true nature of the five elements and constructs the four kinds of mandala reproducing them (...), experiences nirvana."[93]

Kitabatake Chikafusa (1293–1354) described in the following way the transformative experience into an adamantine subjectivity caused by Shingon practice:

> Material entities will be forgotten, the mind itself will be forgotten, and only the original essence will be there to permeate the Dharmadhātu spherical [all-encompassing] as the moon in the sky ... [W]hen I contemplate upon myself, I see that I abide in the original form of the Tathāgata, that I am enjoying the Dharma-pleasure of the three secrets, and that all my movements are the secret of the body of the Tathāgata, all my words are the secret of the language of the Tathāgata, and the same is true for all my countless thoughts [as the secret of the mind of the Tathāgata]: they are interpenetrated like [the reflections in] Indra's Net.[94]

Final considerations: the logic of semiotic soteriology

In this chapter we have seen that Esoteric Buddhism envisions soteriology as the ritual result of the semiotic manipulation of mantras and *siddhaṃ* graphs (as well as other objects such as icons and texts) structured as mandalas. In visualization (which, as we have seen, does not need to be a meditation, but can simply constitute a form of reflection or thinking) these entities are examined from a point of view that closely resembles semiotic analysis: their signifier(s), their signified(s) (levels of meaning), and their performative effect upon reality in general. Esoteric Buddhism emphasizes that the entities it employs in its soteriological project are not just "indices" (such as the famous "finger pointing at the moon") or "symbols," but rather "icons," full-fledged embodiments of the principles they signify. It is possible to envision at the basis of such semiotic attitude a particular logic of identity ensuring that "signs" are "identical" to their meanings and "referents." Tsuda Shin'ichi has already pointed to the existence of such logic, which he calls "logic of yoga," based on a verse from a central esoteric scripture, the *Sarvatathāgatatattvasaṃgraha* (Ch. *Jingangding jing*), namely, *yathā sarvatathāgatās tathā haṃ* ("as all the Tathāgatas, so am I," i.e. "I am identical to all Tathāgatas"). According to Tsuda, adepts of Tantrism interpreted this verse in two ways, respectively, "if the individual existence and the ultimate reality are homologous, then they are identical," and "if the individual existence successfully reorganizes itself to be homologous with the ultimate reality, then the former can unite itself with the latter."[95] Tsuda attempted to express in various ways the principle of yoga identity that underlies the Tantric system.[96] In my view, the fundamental logic postulate of the Shingon epistemic field can be formulated as:

> For any entity A and B, if A is similar to (i.e. possesses at least one quality of) B, then A is identical to (i.e. possesses all qualities of) B.

This principle is particularly significant when applied to explain the relationship between a specific phenomenon and the Dharma realm or the Dharma body:

> For any phenomenon A, if A is similar to (i.e. possesses at least one quality of) the Dharma realm (or the Dharma body), then A is identical to (i.e. possesses all qualities of) the Dharma realm (or the Dharma body).

Such logic of undifferentiatedness, albeit domesticated and neutralized in order to dilute its antinomian potential, also lies at the basis of Shingon ritual practices, often ignored or despised by some scholars as a degeneration of "true" Esoteric Buddhism—thus forgetting that ritual aimed at cosmic integration and political and ideological legitimization displayed and enacted the fundamental principles underlying the Esoteric episteme. Ritual is not a degeneration of so-called "pure" Esoteric Buddhism or a remnant of earlier impure forms, but on the contrary it is directly related to the postulates of the Esoteric episteme itself. The *Shingon naishōgi* (1345) by Kitabatake Chikafusa describes the practices leading to salvation in the following way:[97]

> The fundamental principle of the [Shingon] teachings is that one can become a buddha in this very body. All sentient beings... have a body, language, and a mind—the three centers of karmic activity [*sangō*]. When these are not active [producing karma], they become the three

> secrets [*sanmitsu*] of the Tathāgata. When one composes a *mudrā* with one's hands, one's body becomes identical [*sōō*, Sk. *yukta* or *yoga*] with the icon of the [corresponding] divine being [*honzon*]: this is the secret of the body [*shinmitsu*]. When one chants a mantra with one's mouth, that mantra comes to coincide with the speech of the [corresponding] divinity: this is the secret of language [*gomitsu*]. When the mind abides in *samādhi* and I visualize the deity undisturbed by random thoughts, my mind coincides with the mind of the divinity: this is the secret of mind [*imitsu*].

This passage describes the process to become a buddha in the present body. The practitioner must perform a set of expressions that are conventionally considered to be equivalent, on the basis of the logic indicated above, to the buddha or bodhisattva they stand for. However, as we have seen in the last two chapters, visualization of mantras presuppose (at least, in theory) a complex semiotic labor aimed at the identification and dissolution of their various levels of meaning. At that point, the ascetic is virtually identical with the icon used in ritual. As Kakuban wrote:

> Since ignorance and enlightenment are [originally] within myself, there is no buddha-body outside of [my own] three centers of karmic activity [i.e. body, speech, and mind]; since truth and delusion are identical and undifferentiated, one can attain [rebirth into] the Pure Land within the five destinations.[98]

Put in different terms, salvation is not the attainment of a state different from, and outside of, one's own present condition. Becoming a buddha does not mean abandoning the human condition to turn into a buddha; rebirth into the Pure Land does not mean to abandon one's present condition for a distant paradise. One's body, speech and mind are already the hardware necessary for salvation. Through the identity of the three secrets (*sanmitsu*), the ascetics restructure themselves as embodiments of their icons' deities on the basis of the logic of *yoga*.[99]

As Tsuda Shin'ichi has explained, meditation on mandala and other semiotic practices translate the bodhisattva's career into mental states and kinds of visualizations. Whereas in the "classical" Mahayana traditions the bodhisattva practices, that is, the perfection of the six supreme virtues (*pāramitās*), are direct, concrete, and virtually endless efforts aimed at the actual salvation of actual beings, in Esoteric Buddhism practices are essentially symbolic, such as chanting *shingon*, visualization of images, and performance of rites, as discussed in this chapter. Raihō explained the particular status of Esoteric practices as different from their "classical" counterparts.[100] In particular, he reinterpreted the time frame traditionally deemed necessary to attain enlightenment, i.e. the three uncountable *kalpas* (Jp. *san daiasogi kō*), as a form of awareness. He does so by opposing a "vertical" interpretation, based on differences, to a "horizontal" view, formulated from the standpoint of the undifferentiated cosmic substance:

> *Kalpa* is a Sanskrit word. The exoteric teachings interpret it as a span of time and accordingly [conceive of liberation as a] progress over time from a stage to another; after three great *asaṃskhyeya* [countless] *kalpas* have elapsed, one attains the true awakening. The Shingon [tradition,] [in contrast,] interprets *kalpa* as "false views" [*mōju*, Sk. *vikalpa*] and overcomes them. The three delusions are transcended in the moment of a single thought.
>
> When *kalpa* is understood "vertically" as discrimination between before and after, it is called "time," but "horizontally" it refers to coarse and fine discriminations, so that an entire uncountable [*asaṃskhyeya*] *kalpa* unfolds in the moment of a single thought. As the result of "vertical" discrimination, the three times [*sanze*, i.e. past, present, and future] amount to an infinite time span. According to the Shingon "horizontal" sense, however, one should know that in the mind there is no discrimination, and therefore the divinities of the mandala manifest themselves in the instant of a single thought. Exoteric Buddhism [in contrast] understands the Dharma-nature [*hosshō*, Sk. *dharmatā*] in a "vertical," differentiated way. Therefore, the thousand buddhas appear in the three times, and many *kalpas* are needed in order to attain the enlightenment.[101]

In this passage, Raihō displays once more the logic underlying the Esoteric episteme. A slight shift in the signifier produces a great difference in the signified with an enormous impact on salvation. *Kalpa* ("cosmic cycle") is interpreted as *vikalpa* ("discrimination"); time is reduced to a mental operation. Accordingly, whereas the exoteric teachings take a literalist approach and state that the attainment of liberation requires the performance of religious practices extending over numberless *kalpas*, for Esoteric Buddhism salvation only requires a correct (i.e. non-discriminating) thought process—literally, it takes place in the "instant of a single thought."

It is possible that the paradigmatic example of such symbolic practices is the *gosō jōshingan* (five-phase visualization of the bodily transformation into a buddha) described in the *Jingangding jing*.[102] As pointed by Tsuda Shin'ichi, this sutra explains: (i) the method to attain a certain level of enlightenment, (ii) the mantra (*shingon*) that can replace such direct method; and (iii) the resulting experience—a state of awareness and the concrete image representing and replacing it, such as the moon-disk (*gachirin*) or other forms (*sanmayagyō*).[103] In this manner, visualization of a certain Esoteric symbol directly results, on the basis of initiatory conventions, in the attainment of *siddhi*. However, Tsuda's reference to the "symbolic" nature of the Esoteric practices remains rather vague and even suggests that they are not "real" Buddhist practices but mere simulations or counterfeits. In my discussion, on the contrary, I showed that Esoteric practices are based on the use of particular semiotic expressions based on a coherent epistemic system, which is in turn related to the cosmology and soteriology of Esoteric Buddhism. Salvation is not something to be achieved in mystical, ineffable experiences transcending the ordinary world, but through manipulation of semiotic entities envisioned as *doubles* of their referents. Since these practices were believed to bestow numberless powers upon the ascetic practicing them, we can call their result with Tsuda Shin'ichi a case of "symbolic omnipotence."[104]

Esoteric texts aim at the elimination of all forms of dualism opposing words and things, study and practice, practice and its description—ultimately, signifier and signified, sign and reality. Ritual texts present themselves as isomorphic with the cosmos and as simulations of religious practice; they are thus representations of the ultimate nondualism envisioned by the Esoteric world-view. Paradoxically, this inscription within language and texts of the Buddhist Esoteric cosmology and soteriology takes place while the authors emphasize the impossibility for ordinary language to tell the truth about the world. The linear surface of the text denies what is nevertheless achieved at the level of the structure of the text and of the semantic system it mobilizes. We could say that texts of Esoteric Buddhism are somehow similar to René Magritte's "logograms," such as the famous drawing representing a pipe in which the contour of the subject was marked by the sentence *ceci n'est pas une pipe* ("this is not a pipe").[105] Douglas Hofstadter developed a similar paradox in his own "ambigrams."[106] In both cases we have a text in which a massage contradicts the translinguistic form in which that message is constructed. In other words, language denies something that actually takes place at the level of the semiotic structuring of the text.

CHAPTER FIVE

The empire and the signs: Buddhism, semiotics, and cultural identity in Japanese history

Thus far, we have explored the episteme of premodern Japanese Esoteric Buddhism in its main components (ontology, semiotics and epistemology, and soteriology) from a synchronic perspective. A history of semiotic ideas in Japanese Buddhism, with their continuities, ruptures, and transformations is well beyond the scope of this book. I would like to mention, though, that the establishment of Zen Buddhism as a separate institutional organization with a distinctive discourse after the fourteenth century brought about significant changes to Buddhist semiotics. Moreover, the development of Neo-Confucianism since the seventeenth century, together with the impact of Western civilization after the sixteenth century, also affected the ways in which the Japanese conceived of and used their signs. The most dramatic and radical epistemic rupture, however, happened with the Meiji Restoration (1868), in which Japan embarked in a process of systematic modernization and westernization—the seeds of Japan as it is today. The form of modernization chosen by the government at that time involved persecution of Buddhism, the dismantling of centuries-old systems of knowledge, and the eradication of traditional religious practices the systematic abandonment. As a consequence, the premodern Buddhist semiotics outlined in this book, rather than forming the basis for a new, modern Japanese semiotic discourse, was largely ignored and deleted from cultural memory. Cultural forgetting and lack of studies make it difficult, then, to indicate what remains of it today, and in which forms it influenced the development of semiotic ideas and practices in Japan outside of Buddhism in the past.

In this final chapter, I attempt to outline one possible intellectual genealogy connecting Esoteric Buddhist semiotics as we outlined it in this book to contemporary Japanese discourses of cultural identity. For this endeavor, Roland Barthes offers us an unexpected but important clue. *The Empire of Signs*, from its very title, suggests a connection between signs and the *imperium*—a connection between the ways in which Japanese culture is conceptualized as centered on the imperial institutions and the peculiarities of Japan's own semiotic episteme. In other words, we can detect a possible continuity between semiotic ideas and practices and a certain vision of the Japanese imperial system and of Japanese culture in general. This chapter expands on Barthes's intuition by attempting a genealogy of this connection. I will show that throughout Japanese history, several semiotic notions were harnessed to describe Japanese identity; often, these semiotic notions were directly related to a definition of the role of the emperor. It appears that modern ideas about Japanese uniqueness are transformations of Edo period (1600–1868) Nativist notions, which in turn are transformations of earlier, medieval Buddhist doctrines I have discussed so far in this book.

Japan as the "divine country" (*shinkoku*) and its wondrous semiotics

Several medieval texts dating back to the thirteenth and fourteenth centuries report that when the two archaic gods Izanagi and Izanami churned the primordial ocean to generate the islands of Japan, the most sacred and powerful spell of Buddhism appeared.[1] It is the five-syllable mantra *a bi ra un ken*, known in this case as the "formula of Buddha Dainichi" (*Dainichi no inmon*), representing, as we have seen, the enlightenment of Mahāvairocana, the cosmic Buddha of Esoteric Buddhism and, at the same time, the semiotic structure of the universe. Another textual tradition interprets that formula as one representing the Womb mandala. This numinous event meant that, as Yamamoto Hiroko puts it, "primordial Japan was created out of the principles of Esoteric Buddhism."[2] Thus, medieval scholars envisioned Japan as the original land of the cosmic Buddha, and the four Chinese characters in the official name of the country, the "Country of Great Japan" (Dainipponkoku), were reinterpreted as the "original land of Dainichi" (Dainichi no honkoku). Buddhist exegesis further developed the idea that Japan was a "sacred realm" (*shinkoku*)—the land of the Shinto gods (*kami*) and, at the same time, of the Buddha. Japan's sacred nature manifests itself in the very shape of the country: medieval Buddhist documents represent Japan as a one-pronged *vajra*,[3] the main ritual implement of Esoteric Buddhism symbolizing the cosmic substance, its power and essence, and enlightenment. In other words, medieval Buddhist exegetes constructed the land of Japan as a motivated sign—a symbol encompassing the entire Esoteric Buddhist episteme. Semiotics operations (manipulations of language, signs, meanings) played a key role in this. Through them, Japan became the semiotic synthesis of the universe—a geopolitical mandala, the most sacred country on earth. However, it is clear that, despite some obvious chauvinistic and isolationistic implications (which became prominent only toward the end of sixteenth century), the notion of *shinkoku* was essentially used by Buddhist institutions to assert their ideological, political, and economic role.[4] Not only was it not meant to define an exclusivistic cultural attitude; on the contrary, it presupposed the entire Buddhist transnational world-view, in which Japan, far from being a central entity, was explicitly defined as "marginal."

Now if Japan was a mandala, everything in it was sacred, as a direct manifestation of the Buddhist truth. The Japanese language was one of the privileged objects of this kind of Esoteric exegesis. Toward the second half of the twelfth century Buddhist intellectuals begin to develop the idea that Japanese language was essentially identical with the absolute language spoken by the Buddha. However, scholars focused in particular on the lofty language of classical *waka* poetry, which was compared with Esoteric Buddhist formulae in Sanskrit such as mantra and *dhāraṇī*. The poet Saigyō (1118–90) was among the first intellectuals to develop such conceptions. To him is attributed the following statement:

> *waka* poems are the true body of the Buddha. Therefore, to recite a poem is like vowing to make a statue of the Buddha; to remember a stanza is like chanting a secret mantra. Through poetry I have achieved the Buddhist Dharma [i.e. attained enlightenment].[5]

Another Buddhist intellectual, the Zen monk Mujū Ichien (1226–1312), was both more explicit and comprehensive in his treatment of language:

> Although *dhāraṇī* employ the ordinary language of India, when the words are maintained as *dhāraṇī*, they have the capacity to destroy wickedness and remove suffering. Japanese poetry also uses the ordinary words of the country; and when we use *waka* to convey religious intent, there will necessarily be a favorable response [from the deities]. When *waka* embody the spirit of Buddhism, there can be no doubt that they are *dhāraṇī*.[6]

This identity of *waka* poetry with *dhāraṇī* spells became a standard and accepted idea in medieval literary theory. But we have to wait until the Edo period before the absolute value of the Japanese language was explicitly and forcefully theorized in the work of the Shingon monk and philologist Keichū (1640–1701). Known as the first exponent of the Nativist school (*kokugaku*), Keichū was the link connecting medieval doctrines on language with a rediscovery of Japanese classics and a valorization of the spiritual importance of the Japanese language—the first step in the development of the Nativist semiotic ideology.[7] Later Nativist authors, such as Kamo no Mabuchi, Motoori Norinaga, and Hirata Atsutane, further developed Keichū's theory to make Japanese language one of the most evident features of the uniqueness and superiority of Japanese culture. Keichū wrote that each of the forty-seven syllables of the Japanese language is to be considered a *dhāraṇī*, and as such it is endowed with profound meaning and supernatural power. Keichū is also to be credited for introducing into the intellectual debate the concept of *kotodama*, which he defined as an "invisible divine spirit," the "result of the spiritual power present in the spoken words."[8] He focused his attention on the phonetic aspects of language, traditionally downplayed in favor of writing. Human voice, the sound of language, is the result of the vibration produced by wind that enters the body and resonates in the organs. Linguistic sounds are not peculiar to humans: all orders of being, from buddhas and *kami* down to demons and animals and nature, produce meaningful sounds.[9] Keichū's panlinguistic universe is based on the philosophy of language of Kūkai (774–835), as systematized in the *Shōji jissōgi*. Before Kūkai, our attempt to trace a genealogy of Japanese semiotic ideology would take us too far: perhaps, to Chinese Daoist ideas and practices of language on the one hand, and to Indian philosophy of language on the other. In any case, it is possible to see that Edo period Nativist scholars developed a semiotics that attributed a sacred nature to Japan and its language, but the roots of their ideology are to be found in preexisting cultural formations, and in particular in the medieval Buddhist episteme.

A Nativism (*kokugaku*) and the spirit of the Japanese language (*kotodama*)

During the Edo period (1600–1868), language became an important field of inquiry. A new intellectual tradition in particular, known as *kokugaku*, "national learning" or, in the rendering of H. D. Harootunian (1986), Nativism, developed an intellectual discourse on Japanese authenticity based on a careful study of ancient and classical texts, such as the *Kojiki*, the *Man'yōshū*, and the *Genji monogatari*. The main exponents of this traditions were Keichū, Kada no Azumamaro (1669–1736), Kamo no Mabuchi (1697–1769), Motoori Norinaga (1730–1801), Fujitani Mitsue (1768–1823), and Hirata Atsutane (1776–1843). The peculiar semiotics that grounds modern discourses of Japanese identity arose from within this cultural context. These authors envisioned the peculiarity of the Japanese experience of the world as poetic and irrational. It was based on a unique language whose sounds were considered directly in contact with the reality they signify without the mediation of writing—a language whose signs are incapable of lying, and whose magical qualities are called *kotodama* (the "spirit of the words").[10]

Kamo no Mabuchi began to associate a sense of Japanese moral and cultural superiority with the qualities of their language. He wrote:

> the fifty sounds [of the Japanese phonological system] are the sounds of Heaven and Earth, and words conceived from them are naturally different from the Chinese characters... ever since Chinese writing was introduced we have mistakenly become enmeshed in it... but the fifty sounds suffice to express all words without the nuisance of the characters.[11]

In Mabuchi's view, foreign ideas (mainly, Chinese Confucianism and Indian Buddhism) are abstruse and complex, and can be expressed only through the unnatural mediation of writing; they were distortions of the simple, perfect, and natural ways of ancient Japan, and ended up by corrupting the Japanese:

> Japan has always been a country where the people are honest. As long as a few teachings were carefully observed and we worked in accordance with the Will of Heaven [represented by the emperor] and Earth, the country would be well off without any special instruction. Nevertheless, Chinese doctrines were introduced and corrupted men's hearts.[12]

Later, Motoori Norinaga further developed Mabuchi's themes by attributing to the ancient Japanese a strong sense of irrational wonder for the deeds of the Japanese deities (*kami*) and poetic sentiment toward nature and humans. Motoori was a strenuous opponent of the rationalistic tendencies of Neo-Confucian philosophy and the complexities of the Buddhist cosmology, which he criticized in the following way: "in the foreign countries... men have tried to explain the principle of Heaven and Earth and all phenomena by... fallacious theories stemming from the assumptions of the human intellect and they in no wise represent the true principle."[13] In contrast, Motoori stressed that "the acts of the gods cannot be measured by ordinary human reasoning";[14] "one must acknowledge that human intelligence is limited and puny while the acts of the gods are illimitable and wondrous."[15] Only the Japanese are innately equipped to realize and accept this: "The True Way is one and the same, in every country and throughout heaven and earth. This Way, however, has been correctly transmitted only in our Imperial Land."[16] As a consequence, "our country is the source and fountainhead of all other countries, and in all matters it excels all the others. It would be impossible to list all the products in which our country excels, but foremost among them is rice."[17] Motoori further expands on the reasons of Japanese superiority:

> Our country's Imperial Line, which casts its light over this world, represents the descendants of the Sky-Shining Goddess [sun goddess Amaterasu]... the Imperial Line is destined to rule the nation for eons until the end of time and as long as the universe exists. That is the very basis of our way. That our history has not deviated from the instructions of the divine mandate bears testimony to the infallibility of our ancient traditions. It can also be seen why foreign countries cannot match ours... their dynastic lines, basic to their existence, do not continue; they change frequently and are quite corrupt. Thus one can surmise that in everything they say there are falsehoods and that there is no basis in fact for them.[18]

We see here outlined the usual connection between the superiority of Japan, centered on the emperor, and the allegedly particular epistemological attitudes of the Japanese. In other words, the Japanese are able to experience the absolute principle of things by virtue of their kinship to the gods through the centralizing mediation of the emperor. Subsequently, Hirata Atsutane further increased the dose of chauvinism in Nativist thought:

> People all over the world refer to Japan as the Land of the Gods, and call us the descendants of the gods. Indeed, it is exactly as they say... Ours is a splendid and blessed country, the Land of the Gods beyond any doubt, and we, down to the most humble man and woman, are the descendants of the gods... Japanese differ completely from and are superior to the peoples of China, India, Russia, Holland, Siam, Cambodia, and all other countries in the world.[19]

One of the themes that run through the entire Nativist discourse concerns the nature and function of language—and Japanese language in particular. All the authors emphasize sound rather than written characters, in an open polemics against Confucian "grammatology" that takes the Nativists to identify speech with authenticity. For Kamo no Mabuchi the phonological system of the Japanese language embodies the "Yamato spirit," the fundamental principle of the entire Japanese culture, because those sounds are a symbolic representation of the cosmic order sustaining Japan as the "land of the gods."[20] Mabuchi and other Nativists posited at the basis of the Japanese language a spiritual essence they called *kotodama*, after a rare and archaic word appearing in the *Man'yōshū* and the *Kojiki*.[21] As Keichū wrote: "since in words there is a spirit, if one speaks words of blessing happiness comes, if one speaks words of cursing distress is the result."[22] According to the linguist Tokieda Motoki, *kotodama* refers to the primitive belief according to which in words there is a spirit that makes happen the things one says. For example, if one says "it's going to rain," then it will rain.[23] This belief, explained Toyoda Kunio, is based on the synonymy in ancient Japanese of the two terms "word" and "fact," both pronounced *koto*—even though they are written with different Chinese characters.

For the Nativists, the connection between language and signs in general, cultural identity, and imperial ideology was clear and explicit. They considered the language of the Japanese empire, and in particular its phonological system, the only perfect one; foreign languages were imperfect and wrong, similar to cries of "beasts and birds."[24] The perfection of the Japanese language was due to the sacredness of the language itself, the country, and its ruler, the emperor. Among the most important Nativist thinkers, Hirata Atsutane was the most fanatical supporter of the theory of *kotodama*, to the point that he found the ground of his imperial ideology in the Japanese phonetics, which he envisioned as a sublime, divine, and spiritual entity.[25] Atsutane also developed a form of Cratylism (the philosophical challenge to the idea of the arbitrariness of language), in which each sound of the Japanese phonological system corresponded to an element of his theology and cosmology (deities' names, orders of reality, etc.).[26] In his view, the combination of such sounds would disclose and enact the cosmic operations of the Japanese *kami*.

Contemporary authors generally believe that a well-defined notion of *kotodama*, which supposedly arose during the Nara period (710–784), runs through the entire history of Japanese thought until today. In reality, there are several problems with this view: (i) there is no theory or explanation of the term *kotodama* and the conception of language it implies dating back to the Nara period; the term itself was very rare in ancient texts; (ii) as far as it can be ascertained, the term *kotodama* never appears in medieval texts establishing connections between Japanese poetry and Indian theories of mantric language; (iii) *kotodama* becomes an important philosophical term only with the development of Nativism, in which it is used as one of the crucial marks of Japanese cultural identity and superiority. In particular, the Shingon monk Keichū, as we have seen, was the first to discuss *kotodama* in connection with Tantric philosophy of language. It is likely, then, that *kotodama* was a very successful philosophical anachronism—a rare, archaic word appropriated by the Nativists in order to carry out their intellectual and ideological agenda by projecting back onto a mythological past contemporary Buddhist ideas about language and culture. In any case, it is clear that the role of the term *kotodama* in Japanese intellectual history cannot be taken for granted.

Zen modernism

We find some of the themes addressed by Edo-period Nativist authors in several threads of early twentieth century Japanese intellectual discourse, in particular in attempts to define the essence of Japanese culture at the interface of the "West" and the "Orient." A modernist interpretation of Buddhism played a central role in this discourse.[27] Two authors are particularly important for our discussion: the philosopher Nishida Kitarō (1870–1945) and the Buddhist scholar and cultural activist Suzuki Daisetz Teitaro (1870–1966). Nishida is perhaps the most influential modern Japanese philosopher, the founder of the so-called Kyoto School. D. T. Suzuki is well known for his tireless effort to spread a certain vision of Zen Buddhism and Japanese culture to the West. Especially influential was also the ideological manifesto of wartime Japanese government, entitled *Kokutai no hongi* ("Fundamentals of Our National Polity"), written by several of the leading intellectuals of the time and edited by government officers. This text, published in 1937 by the Japanese Ministry of Education, was distributed to all households of the country in order to indoctrinate all citizens to the militaristic and quasi-fascist ideology of the time. In this section I shall address the semiotic assumptions of Japanese Buddhist modernism, as they are related to wartime *kokutai* ideology.

Nishida Kitarō addressed what he envisioned as the basic features of Japanese culture:

> Japan's historical world, being an identity between subject and environment, and between man and nature, may also be said to have developed self-identically [...]. A Japanese spirit which goes to the truth of things as an identity between actuality and reality, must be one which is based on this. Although I say "goes to things," that is not to say to go to matter. And although I say "nature," that is not to say objective or environmental nature. To go to things means starting from the subject, going beyond the subject, and going to the bottom of the subject. What I call the identity between actuality and reality is the realization of this absolute at the bottom of our selves, instead of considering the absolute to be in an infinite exterior.[28]

The "self-identical development" of Japanese culture is a transposition of the *wakon yōsai* paradigm that guided modernization in the late nineteenth century. Foreign cultural elements (*yōsai*, lit. "Western technologies") adopted by the Japanese do not modify the core of Japanese civilization, the "Yamato spirit" (*wakon* or *Yamato-damashii*), which remains identical to itself even through the transformations of its external appearances. Nishida identifies the basic feature of the Japanese spirit with the gist of his own philosophical enterprise—the attainment of the essential and immediate "nature": "the absolute at the bottom of ourselves." In this way, all true Japanese are wise, enlightened beings. Nishida further explains:

> As for the characteristics of Japanese culture, it seems to me to lie in moving from subject to object, ever thoroughly negating the self and becoming the thing itself; becoming the thing itself to see; becoming the thing itself to act. To empty the self and see things, for the self to be immersed in things, "no-mindedness" [in Zen Buddhism] or effortless

> acceptance of the grace of Amida (*jinen hōni*) [in True Pure Land teaching]—these, I believe, are the states we Japanese strongly yearn for [...]. The essence of the Japanese spirit must be to become one in things and in events. It is to become one at that primal point in which there is neither self nor others.[29]

In other words, what Nishida considers the highest forms of Japanese philosophy, Zen and Jōdo Shinshū traditions of Buddhism, guide the Japanese to immerse themselves in things, to become "acting things." This is not a hermeneutics, for meaning is irrelevant here: what matters is the fusion of subject and object in a pure act. This semiotics of objectual immediacy is centered on the emperor. As Bernard Faure notes, "Interestingly, the translator of the excerpt, Masao Abe, the best known representative of the Kyoto School in the West, has omitted the following sentence [at the end of the excerpt quoted above]: 'This [process leading the "Japanese spirit to become one in things and events"] seems to have as its center this contradictory autoidentity that is the Imperial Household.'"[30] Leaving aside the complex issue of the meaning of "contradictory autoidentity,"[31] what matters here is the central role of the emperor in the achievement of the Japanese spirit through the enactment of its peculiar semiosis that dissolves the subject in the act. Nishida's semiotics, which involves the "unity of subject and object" (*shukaku gōitsu*) or "the state of undifferentiation of subject and object" (*shukaku mibun no jōtai*), is based on an epistemology of direct, unmediated experience—"pure experience" (*junsui keiken*)—which Nishida identifies to the Buddhist experience of enlightenment and defines as to "know reality exactly as it is (*jijitsu sono mama*). It is to know by entirely abandoning the artifices of the self and by following reality... 'pure' means precisely the condition of experience in itself, without the admixture of any thinking or discrimination."[32]

D. T. Suzuki shared a similar vision. For him,

> The basic idea of Zen is to come in touch inner workings of our being, and to do this in the most direct way possible, without resorting to anything external or superadded. When Zen is thoroughly understood, absolute peace of mind is attained, and a man lives as he ought to live.[33]

We find here once again the idea of achieving the absolute within oneself, an absolute that is at the same time the true principle of reality. As Robert Sharf explains, "Suzuki began to render any and all Zen cultural artifacts—from *kōan* exchanges to dry-landscape gardens—as 'expressions of' or 'pointed toward' a pure, unmediated, and non-dual experience, known in Zen as *satori*."[34] However, as both Faure and Sharf have shown, Suzuki's interpretation of Zen, as based on Nishida's philosophy, is totally unwarranted by the history of the Zen tradition in East Asia. The concept of "experience" as used by these authors is especially problematic in its anachronism.[35]

Despite the efforts of apologetes to present Zen as "an uncompromisingly empirical, rational, and scientific mode of inquiry into the nature of things," Zen modernism was

> predicated upon, and inexorably enmeshed in, the Nativist and imperialist ideology of late nineteenth- and early twentieth-century Japan. Zen is touted as the very heart of Asian spirituality, the essence of Japanese culture, and the key to the unique qualities of the Japanese race.[36]

There are historical reasons for that. Japanese modernization during the Meiji era (1868–1912) started with a violent persecution of Buddhism.[37] As a consequence, Sharf explains,

> Buddhist leaders actively appropriated the ideological agenda of government propagandists... They became willing accomplices in the promulgation of *kokutai* (national polity) ideology—the attempt to render Japan a culturally homogeneous and spiritually evolved nation politically unified under the civil rule of the emperor.[38]

In order to show their nationalistic zeal, Zen, and Japanese Buddhism in general, also became an active accomplice of the militaristic and authoritarian policy implemented by the Japanese government between 1868 and 1945.[39]

The conceptual schema underlying Nishida's and Suzuki's highly ideological semiotics is strikingly similar to the ideas expressed in the *Kokutai no hongi*.[40] One of the key concepts in the text is "sincerity" (*makoto*), praised as the highest virtue of the Japanese. Sincerity is related to the nature of Japanese language, in particular its special power called *kotodama* (the "spirit of words"). Let us follow here the argument of the *Kokutai no hongi*:

> *Kotodama* means language that is filled with sincerity, and such language possesses limitless power and is comprehensible everywhere without limitation [...] the word that possesses sincerity, by reason of *kotodama*, must inevitably be carried out. Thus, sincerity is found in the fundamental principle of the word able to become the deed. There is no room for self in sincerity. All of oneself must be cast aside in speech, for it is in the deed and in the deed alone that sincerity is to be found.[41]

According to the text, the Japanese language is only used to tell the truth, and to say things that can be carried out; it cannot be used to lie. Individuality (or, as Barthes would put it, subjectivity, centeredness, meaning) is separate from language, which by speaking the truth solely refers to and produces disinterested action. In a different section, the text emphasizes the idea of self-effacement that results from this vision of language: "In the inherent character of our people there is strongly manifested alongside this spirit of self-effacement and disinterestedness [...] The spirit of self-effacement is not a mere denial of oneself, but means living to the great, true self by denying one's small self."[42] The meaning of "living to the great, true self" is further explained in the text:

> Our country is established with the emperor, who is a descendant of Amaterasu Ōmikami [the Shinto sun goddess], as her center, and our ancestors as well as we ourselves constantly have beheld in the emperor the fountainhead of her life and activities. For this reason, to serve the emperor and to receive the emperor's great august Will as one's own is the rational of making our historical "life" live in the present; and on this is based the morality of the people. [...] By implicit obedience is meant casting ourselves aside and serving the emperor intently. To walk this Way of loyalty is the sole Way in which we subjects may "live". Hence, offering our lives for the sake of the emperor does not mean so-called self-sacrifice, but the casting aside of our little selves to live under his august grace.[43]

In other words, there is no space for autonomous, subjective activity: the meaning of one's life is to be found in the imperial will. The text explains: "in our country, differences of opinion or of interests that result from one's position easily [merge] into one through our unique great harmony which springs from the same source."[44] That "same source" is obviously the emperor: "In our country, Sovereign and subjects have from of old been spoken of as being one, and the entire nation, united in mind and acting in full coöperation, have shown forth the beauties of this oneness with the Emperor at the centre."[45] There is a strong emphasis on "oneness," on the identity of opposites (possibly an and echo of Nishida's "contradictory self-identity"), on harmony as a natural, ontological condition of the Japanese: "This mind of fellowship and union which makes possible the singleness of this national foundation constantly runs through national life."[46] The *Kokutai no Hongi* leaves no space for interpretation and free production of meaning: "There must be no self in truth. When one speaks and acts, utterly casting oneself aside, there indeed is truth, and there indeed shines truth."[47]

The *Kokutai no Hongi* mobilizes an archaic word such as *kotodama*—which, as we have seen, was first discussed by Edo period Nativists—in order to define the nature of Japanese language, the inherent character of the people, and the central role of the emperor in all this. In particular, Japanese language is used not to convey meaning and personal interpretations (an aberration which results from Western individualism), but to enact, perform, carry out deeds. In proposing a theory of a language of events rather than of meaning, the *Kokutai no Hongi* sounds similar to Roland Barthes's semiotic fantasy in the *Empire of Signs*. The important difference between the two, however, is that the former grounds its vision of language and truth in theology and the divine nature of the emperor and its subjects. In other words, speaking the truth is a divine commandment that preserves the sacred ordering of the Japanese military state. Roy Andrew Miller has pointed out how the ideas of sincerity, action, and utmost respect for the imperial orders in the *Kokutai no Hongi* were used to enforce mindless and uncritical obedience to the authoritarian regime:[48] here we see the most dangerous effect of the connection between semiotics and ideology in the formation of cultural identity.

All the afore-mentioned texts and authors, despite their different genres, vocabularies, and audiences, share a number of fundamental assumptions: Japanese culture (and the life of the Japanese) is centered on the figure of the emperor; the Japanese people, whose paramount virtue is sincerity (*makoto*), have the ability to attain the true essence of things; the Japanese language is unique in that it possesses a "spirit" (*kotodama*) which enables it to tell the truth and to make things happen—what is said must be converted into deeds. Once again, signs cannot be used to lie (at least not by the Japanese), signs are directly related to the truth, the essence of reality without the mediation of interpretation and meaning, and language is perfectly transparent to reality. All this is predicated upon the figure of the emperor—the "empty center" of Japan.

The discourse of Japanese uniqueness

The modernist semio-ideological edifice did not collapse after the end of World War II, but some of its components were further developed in a popular and influential genre of pseudo-academic works known today as *nihonjinron* (discourses on the Japanese) or *Nihon bunkaron* (discourses on Japanese culture), a flourishing editorial industry addressing issues and features of Japanese culture and of the Japanese people from the perspective of cultural essentialism. Peter Dale summarizes the three major assumptions of *nihonjinron* in the following way:

> Firstly, they assume that the Japanese constitute a culturally and socially homogeneous racial entity, whose essence is virtually unchanged from prehistoric times down to the present day. Secondly, they presuppose that the Japanese differ radically from all other known peoples. Thirdly, they are consciously nationalistic, displaying a conceptual and procedural hostility to any mode of analysis which might be seen to derive from external, non-Japanese sources.[49]

Nihonjinron rhetoric and ideology constitute, in a more or less conscious fashion, a large part of the conceptual and emotional tools employed by many Japanese today to define their ideas of cultural identity. The first thing that strikes the interpreter is the entanglement of ideological and semiotic issues. Japan is defined as a static, ahistorical geopolitical entity, whose boundaries are the frontiers of today's Japanese state, and whose center is an equally ahistorical imperial system; the Japanese are envisioned as a homogeneous people sharing a culture whose basic determinations, which are immutable, can be described as a specific episteme—a distinct way to manipulate signs and relate to reality.

Masao Miyoshi and H. D. Harootunian argue that *nihonjinron* "produced… a conception of Japan as a signified, whose uniqueness was fixed in an irreducible essence that was unchanging and unaffected by history, rather than as a signifier capable of attaching itself to a plurality of possible meanings."[50] This emphasis on the signified seems very different from Barthes's endeavor, for which Japan was pure, meaningless signifier; the results, however, are surprisingly similar. In such essentialistic treatments of cultural specificities, signifier and signified are almost interchangeable. What the authors have in mind is, in fact, not either one of the two components of a sign, as in traditional semiotics, but rather some vaguely defined symbols in which the form is not separate from its content—an essentialized and condensed image of Japanese culture. Interestingly enough, these symbols of Japanese culture are extremely close to the most trivial Japonesque stereotypes (group orientation, women as the embodiment of culture, art as the expression of *satori*, technology as art, etc.)

Here I shall restrict myself to discuss only some of the most important features of the *nihonjinron* epistemic field, namely, naturalization, binarism, immediacy, and linguistic uniqueness. By "naturalization" I mean the reduction of culture to nature: cultural traits are ultimately reduced to natural characteristics, namely, environment, climate, or even the peculiar functioning of the Japanese brain. In this way, nationalistic authors operate an essentialization of culture in order to set Japanese culture apart and make it illegible from the outside. As Tetsuo Najita writes, in Japan "culture has been thought to be perfectly knowable, understandable from within, not requiring translation—not even the mediations of 'language' and other 'signs' as 'a matter of the human spirit—*kokoro*.'"[51] *Nihonjinron* authors "proceed from the presumption that the Japanese are "unknowable" except to Japanese, and that the role of social science is to mediate and define their self-knowledge in terms accessible to the world of others."[52]

This move presupposes a strong sense of dichotomy between "us" and "them"; it is not by chance if "binarism" is one of the main features of *nihonjinron*. Everything in *nihonjinron* is described in terms of binary oppositions in which one pole represents the Japanese side (which, as an essence, is therefore closer to nature), and the other pole stands for the rest of the world. The most common binaries are: nature/culture; East (specifically Japan)/West (sometimes used to refer to the rest of the world, more often designating the US); front (*omote*)/back (*ura*); surface (*tatemae*)/

hidden intention (*honne*); inside (*uchi*)/outside (*soto*). These binaries are not necessarily homologous, although some authors envision a series

nature—East—Japan—inside—back—hidden intention,

as opposed to its opposite

culture—West—US—outside—front—surface.

Once Japanese culture has been structured in this way, the Japanese supposedly become able to connect directly with the essence of nature and things without useless "rationalizations"—mediations such as meaning or interpretation.

One of the most important conceptual nuclei of the entire *nihonjinron* edifice is the polarity of "Japanese spirit" (*wakon* or *Yamato-damashii*) and "Western technology" (*yōsai*). Popular since the Meiji period, when it substituted a previous Confucian slogan (*wakon kansai*, "Japanese spirit and Chinese technology"), it presupposes an idea of Japanese culture as the combination of an organizing essence of a more or less spiritual nature (the Japanese spirit) and of foreign additions (western technologies). Foreign additions remain on the surface and never affect the underlying spirit (although it is always possible to envision a potential, corrupting threat—when the spirit is hidden under too many layers of foreign stuff, people might lose sight of it...). The spirit configures itself as a structuring principle which is not structured: in this way, the Orientalistic dichotomy between a rational West opposed to a spiritual East is maintained and affirmed: only rationality can be structured; spirituality, because of its intrinsic vagueness (emptiness?) operates on the level of structuring. David Pollack summarizes decades of Japanese nationalistic semiotics, centered on the use of the dichotomy opposing Japanese spirit and foreign cultures, when he writes that the Japanese language is "almost entirely antithetical" from the Chinese,[53] thus reiterating a rhetoric of uniqueness. Essential to the Japanese language, according to Pollack, is the separation of the spoken word from its written form—a separation which was painfully aware to the Japanese since their first written text, the *Kojiki*: the "content, felt to be quintessentially Japanese, was unformed and ineffable, while that which gave form—the informing or formal aspects of meaning—remained in some sense 'alien,' at once powerfully attractive and fundamentally disquieting."[54] More generally, argues Pollack, "for the Japanese, what was 'Japanese' had always to be considered in relation to what was thought to be 'Chinese' [...] the notion of Japaneseness was meaningful only as it was considered against the background of the otherness of China."[55] Since Naoki Sakai has already produced a convincing critique of Pollack's position,[56] I shall limit myself to underline some of the classic topoi of Japanese cultural nationalism in Pollack's argument: the ahistorical and essentializing treatment (Japan and China are assumed to be unchanging and homogenous essences); dichotomic oversimplification (the opposition Japan/China ignores the important roles played by India and the Korean states in the definition of premodern "Japanese" culture); the centrality of language, which becomes a sort of cultural "prison-house"; the ignorance of multilinguism, a common practice throughout Japanese history (literate people used to write in Chinese and in more or less standard written Japanese, while speaking—and sometime also writing in—their local dialect; in addition, it was not unusual for intellectuals to also have a basic knowledge of the *shittan* script); the ineffability of Japaneseness; and the dramatic separation between form (structured and rational but essentially alien—i.e. previously Chinese and now Western) and content (ineffable and understandable only to the Japanese themselves).

The term *wakon yōsai* lends itself to political and ideological uses,[57] and appears to be at the basis of most discourses on Japanese cultural identity. The expression *wakon*, which I translated above as "Japanese spirit," actually means "Yamato spirit." Yamato is the ancient name of the central part of the Japanese archipelago, and was used throughout premodern Japanese history as a mystified and heavily ideological kernel of power and cultural identity. The focus on Yamato hides the cultural diversity of the Japanese archipelago by positing an ideal and unifying center (both ideological and cultural); it also hides the complex historical processes that determined the formation of the modern Japanese nation-state and present-day Japanese culture as natural transformations of an ahistorical center.[58]

Nihonjinron gives particular importance to the Japanese language as one of the privileged loci of Japanese cultural essence.[59] Authors in general distinguish between supposedly purely indigenous words (*Yamato kotoba*) and foreign words (*gairaigo*, words of Sanskrit, Chinese, and Western origin). *Yamato kotoba* are the main concern of *nihonjinron* authors; as Tanizaki Jun'ichirō put it, "Our nation's language (*kokugo*) bears an unalienable relationship with our national character (*kokuminsei*)";[60] or, in the words of Watanabe Shōichi, "*Yamato kotoba*... have their roots... in the wellsprings of the soul of our race."[61] Miller and Dale have already pointed to the racial overtones in *nihonjinron* treatment of the Japanese language. What is particularly interesting for us here is the fact that the indigenous words are considered to be endowed with an ineffable content; untranslatable, they are supposedly understandable only to the native Japanese.[62] Foreign loan words, in contrast, are the carriers of concepts and rational notions, described as essentially aliens to the Japanese mentality—an application of the *wakon yōsai* model to linguistic phenomena. The authors don't seem to pay much attention to the fact that many Yamato words were of foreign origin, or that they are now used mostly in archaic forms of poetry, or even to the fact that the Japanese language is a complex linguistic system in continuous transformation.

Nihonjinron is aware of the "limitations of language"—the fact that language in general cannot reach the essence of things and the deepest recess of the human heart. However, they maintain that Japanese language—and, specifically, the semiotics of silence that accompanies Japanese language—is free from such limitations and enable the Japanese to reach through language the essence of things: "such devices [typical of the Japanese language] as allusion, ambiguity and lingering resonance... serve as effective ways to both transcend the essential limitations of language, and to bear down to objects."[63] We have seen throughout this book that in Japan the idea of a direct connection between language and reality—a connection that bypasses signification and ordinary semiotic practice—described by Roland Barthes, actually enjoys a long pedigree in Japanese intellectual history. Authors have tried to explain this supposed peculiarity of the Japanese language in "scientific" terms and in the "hard facts" of nature. Particularly famous is the theory, now completely discredited, formulated by Tsunoda Tadanobu, according to whom the brain of the Japanese lateralizes language differently from that of members of other cultures. Tsunoda writes:

> My tests show that the left cerebral hemisphere of the Japanese receives a wide range of sounds: not just the linguistic sounds (consonant and vowel sounds) but also such non-linguistic sounds as the utterance of human emotions, animal cries, Japanese musical instruments, the sounds of a running brook, wind, waves, and certain famous temples bells.[64]

We are clearly dealing here with an attempt to show a continuity uniting the Japanese language, traditional sounds of Japanese culture (such as musical instruments and temple bells) and natural sounds. Tsunoda tried to give a "scientific" foundation to the claim that Japanese language can convey the essence of things, also because it is not essentially different from the sounds that produced by the things themselves.[65]

Nihonjinron authors also emphasize the silent capacity of the Japanese language to transmit the deepest emotions of its native speakers. Countless pages have been written on secret and intuitive techniques of silent communication, known as *haragei* ("belly technique") or with the Buddhist term *ishin denshin* ("mind to mind transmission").[66] Kishimoto Hideo wrote: "One of the characteristics of the Japanese language is to be able to project man's experience in its immediate and unanalysed form."[67] As Dale sarcastically puts it, "Given the unheralded 'homogeneity of (Japanese) existence' (*dōshitsuteki sonzai*, the postwar euphemism for racial purity), the Japanese have developed an innate capacity over millennia for intuiting exactly what all other Japanese are thinking."[68] In this, *nihonjinron* is employing the rhetoric of pure experience deriving from Zen modernism and the philosophy of the Kyoto School.

Semiotics has also been put at the service of Japanese cultural essentialism, as in an essay by Ikegami Yoshihiko on the semiotics of Japanese culture from the perspective of Barthes's idea of the "empty center."[69] In this essay, Ikegami reformulates the standard repertoire of *nihonjinron* binary oppositions in terms of the semiotics of the empty center from the standpoint of cultural typology:

> A culture with an empty center would thus tend to work centripetally—it is somewhat like the astronomer's 'black hole,' which draws and absorbs everything into itself—without suffering any change at all. A culture with an empty center can accommodate and keep in it apparently diverse elements, not in a state of conflict, but in a state of harmony with each other.[70]

And also:

> Thus the function of the empty center can now be redefined as homologization. The philosophy of homologization says that anything and everything deserves to be given its own proper place within the whole cultural scheme. The empty center homologizes ... It seems that the country [Japan] can better be characterized as "the Empire of homologization" with its strong empty center.[71]

Next, Ikegami proceeds to define another "deep-seated current or 'drift' in Japanese culture, namely, a marked tendency toward semiotically blurred articulation, or in other words, a tendency not to clearly mark off one cultural unit semiotically from others."[72] A set of usual stereotypes follows: in Japanese culture, man is incorporated within culture; there are no significant distinction between the terms 'man' and 'god,' 'man' and 'animal,' 'man' and 'tool'; the group is more important than the individual;[73] the context is more important than the text ("the text of the Japanese language tends to merge very much with the context in which it is used; the 'text' is not clearly articulated in contrast to the 'context'").[74] The entire discussion is concluded by a reference to Zen's *kōan*.[75] In other words, Japanese culture is presented as a-systematic in its refusal to uphold "standard" binary oppositions; as a consequence, it appears "irrational" (Zen's influence)—always in comparison to a mystified "West." One would assume that the distinctions between sign, meaning, and referent is blurred as well—so that the signifier can re-present the things as they are without individual interpretive mediation. In addition, the unfortunate expression "the Empire of homologization" has frightful totalitarian overtones: Japanese culture is presented as an inexorable mechanism that reduces all individual differences to sameness, with a disturbing implicit reference to the pre-war ideology of national polity (*kokutai*). This approach to the semiotics of culture is dramatically different from the one proposed by Yuri Lotman, Boris Uspenky, and the other semioticians of the so-called Tartu School. The latter employs broad binary categories to identify dominant ideological tendencies in specific historical periods and in locales. Japanese semiotics, in contrast, employs largely ahistorical categories to show continuity in Japanese culture since the remotest antiquity.

Japan as a semiotic paradise

When Roland Barthes described in his *L'empire des signes* a fantasy realm, a "fictive nation" he called "Japan,"[76] characterized by "an unheard-of symbolic system, one altogether detached from our own,"[77] he was in fact rehearsing deeply-rooted and century-old images.[78] His "Japan," the elsewhere, is the secret site of the semiotician's desire, where there is the "possibility of difference… of a revolution in the propriety of symbolic systems."[79] In spite of his critical disclaimers, Barthes appears to be prisoner of an Orientalistic discourse, as is clear from the subjects discussed in the book and the overall treatment. "Japan" is presented as the opposite of the "United States"[80] and, more generally, of the "West." Furthermore, Barthes's emphasis on Zen as the paradigm of the entire Japanese culture from food to *pachinko* slot machines is taken directly from D.T. Suzuki, who wrote: "Zen typifies Japanese spirituality. This does not mean that Zen has deep roots within the life of the Japanese people, rather that Japanese life itself is 'Zen-like.'"[81] Barthes's book is thus a vaguely poststructuralist rendition of the more traditional Japonaiseries offered by tourist guidebooks: Japanese food (*bentō* lunch box, *sukiyaki* stew, and upscale tempura restaurants),[82] the puzzling urban structure of Tokyo (without street names and numbers and supposedly without a center),[83] with its crowds and its numerous train stations and *pachinko* parlors,[84] people bowing instead of shaking hands, the beauty of souvenir packages[85]—all these are described together with Bunraku theater, *haiku* poems, calligraphy, and the exotic faces of people.[86] Furthermore, Barthes's attention is caught by "traditional" elements, and he is very careful not to describe/analyze anything belonging to contemporary Japan and its rapid industrialization: he explicitly "leav[es] aside" what he calls "vast regions of darkness (capitalist Japan, American acculturation, technological developments)," and the "constipated parsimony of salaries, the constriction of capitalist wealth," the mass of "vulgar 'souvenir[s]' (as Japan is unfortunately so expert at producing)"—some of the most visible and striking features of Japan at that time.[87] Even when Barthes addresses student protest, he describes it as essentially different from its Western counterpart.[88]

What does Barthes see in these features he isolates to form his Japan? In other words, what are the features of Japan that make it a perfectly post-structuralist (postmodern) place? In brief, Barthes's Japan is devoid of interiority and center: everything is pure surface (there is no depth), mere distinctive feature, combinatorial entity which does not stand for a meaning, also because the central Meaning of Western metaphysics, God, is absent—a land without meaning, paradoxical paradise of the semiotician. The food, for example, is "entirely visual," "not deep ... without a precious heart, without a buried power, without a vital secret: no Japanese dish is endowed with a center."[89] Furthermore, food is a combination of "purely interstitial object[s], all the more provocative in that all this emptiness is produced in order to provide nourishment"[90]—in short, food is an "empty sign."[91] Empty signs, interstitial signifiers, can be found everywhere in Barthes's "Japan," from cities to short poems. For example, whereas in the "West" "all" cities are "concentric" and, "in accord with the very movement of Western metaphysics... [their] center... is always full: a marked site [where] the values of civilization are gathered and condensed," Tokyo "does possess a center, but this center is empty"[92]—the "visible form of invisibility [that] hides the sacred 'nothing.'"[93]

Analogously, Bunraku theater challenges Western notions of the body and interiority centered on sin and, ultimately, God. Even more explicitly, the *haiku* poetic form, in Barthes's treatment, gives a final blow to Western metaphysics and its obsession with presence, depth, and meaning: "the haiku means nothing," it "never describes,"[94] it has no symbolic value; *haiku* "constitute a space of pure fragments... without there ever being a center to grasp, a primary core of irradiation."[95] In other words, "neither describing nor defining, [...] the haiku diminishes to the point of pure and sole designation. *It's that, it's thus*, says the haiku, *it's so*. Or better still: *so!*"[96] Here we have a clear reference to "the spirit of Zen,"[97] as that peculiar Japanese intellectual system "which causes knowledge, or the subject, to vacillate: it creates an emptiness of language", it produces "the exemption from all meaning."[98] Barthes gives a semiotic explanation of D. T. Suzuki's Zen modernism, in which we find the interpretive key of Barthes's whole system. Here I would like to stress that Barthes's account of the Japanese mentality gives intellectual reputation and authority to all those who say that the Japanese mind is "unfit for abstract thinking."[99] "Abstract thinking," which in this case refers to traditional philosophical reflection, seems to presuppose, in the mind of these authors, a central, fundamental signified, a transcendental meaning that gives sense to thought.

Barthes's "Japan" is a veritable "empire of signs"—a fragmented set of pure signifiers pointing to reality without any interference from meaning (metaphysical Meaning). Japanese culture is an immense play of surfaces and fragments producing a "vision without commentary," the "designating gesture of the child pointing at whatever it is"[100]—no meaning, no interpretation, no agency, no ideology, no subject. In Barthes's book the Japanese appear capable to refer to reality as it is, directly, without mediation or intentionality, in a pure catroptic gesture: "So!"—whatever that may be.

Japanese signs, the signs of that empire, cannot lie. Why should they? Fragments refracting other fragments, they are not manipulated by subjects displaying their conscious (or unconscious) agency. We can understand why Edmund White, in his blurb on the back cover of the book, calls Barthes's Japan "a test, a challenge to think the unthinkable, a place where meaning is finally banished. Paradise, indeed"—a paradise in which the semiotic dream of a perfect sign becomes real. In this paradise, signs cease to be signifiers, since they are forever detached from any signified: here semiotics undoes itself. Signs cannot be used to lie; the distinction between words, meanings and objects is obliterated; signs do not refer to other signs within a semiotic universe, they are Reality. In this system the world is made of countless epiphanies in which experience, language, and thought coincide with their objects.

Barthes's book became very influential in Japanese semiotic circles and contributed to the consolidation of Orientalistic stereotypes in semiotics. The idea of Japanese signs as epiphanies of direct experience of reality, which extended to Japanese language itself, has been used to represent the semiotics of Japanese culture attitude, and has become an important factor in the definition of Japanese cultural identity. In addition, the idea of an empty center was decidedly appealing to intellectuals who were striving to develop new models more suitable to the new international visibility of Japan. In this respect, it is particularly interesting that Barthes decided to call his semi-fictitious semiotic realm an "empire." This is not a mere Orientalist exoticism: this appellation has a deeper, and more disquieting meaning. In fact, the "empty center" of Japan is the imperial palace in Tokyo and, more precisely, the emperor himself—the "sacred 'nothing,'" the center of the circular system of the Japanese imaginary.[101] Japanese intellectuals were quick to associate Barthes's idea of the empty center with the figure of the emperor and its "symbolic" but fundamental and essentially ineffable role to define Japan. Whereas this move served to relativize and diminish the importance of the center, as advocated by authors such as Yamaguchi Masao and Ōe Kenzaburō,[102] it could also be used to "re-enchant" it by lending it an aura of necessity and a-historicity.

Conclusion: mastering the signs

In this chapter I have attempted to trace a genealogy of Japanese semiotic ideas in connection to visions of cultural specificity and imperial ideology; Roland Barthes's poststructuralist interpretation of Japan can, in a sense, be traced back to medieval Buddhist doctrines.

Among the common themes running through the history of Japanese semiotic ideology, the most important are: (i) the sacred nature of language:

language is an autonomous entity, directly related to the source of the sacred, and endowed with power upon reality; (ii) language determines (in a very strong sense) the cultural and psychological identity of its speakers; (iii) the connections between language and subjectification: its speakers are made to conform themselves to the moral principles and customs enforced by the language itself; (iv) language, when properly employed, cannot be used to lie; (vi) free interpretation is not allowed; the meaning of language must be retrieved to realize the cosmic order to which the users of the language must conform themselves; (vii) language is connected to the center of Japanese edifice of power, the emperor.

For example, in the medieval Buddhist speculations on the sacredness of language, meaning plays an important part. The goal of the Esoteric Buddhist semiotics is that of eliminating the boundaries between language and reality, mind and matter, thought and action, to dissolve the human subject into a microcosm of the universe. The absolute language cannot be used to lie—it is a replica of the inner structure and functioning of the cosmos. In this respect, we can see important lines of continuity connecting this vision with later ideological formations: the Japanese language is directly in contact with the essence of reality; it is true; it induces action (actually, linguistic utterances are the noblest actions as soteriological practices: speaking is a mantra; writing poetry is praising the buddha, etc.); language not only does not challenge authority, but reinforces it by showing the subtle order of the cosmos which is reflected in society; finally, language and signs are centered on the ultimate source of "meaning" and authority, the cosmic Buddha Dainichi, whose emissary on earth is the Japanese emperor.[103] Similarly, Edo period Nativism maintains that it is in ancient Japanese language that one can find the essence of Japanese culture and therefore the correct principles of behavior that follow the Way of the Gods (Shinto) as represented by the figure of the emperor. This constituted the springboard for the authoritarian ideology of the modern Japanese nation-state, according to which its citizen were almost ontologically bound to "naturally" follow the Will of the emperor: no meaning here, no interpretation, no subject—only a powerful "So!" (to borrow once again Barthes's words).

However, such a representation of continuities and similarities downplays important and significant differences. The Esoteric Buddhist discourse on language was connected to doctrines on the sacredness of Japan and was used to give legitimacy, symbolic capital, and ideological stability to the religious institutions at a time of important social changes. It developed within the transnational framework of Buddhist culture, and did not stress a sense of Japanese cultural supremacy. In contrast, chauvinistic nationalism was the primary effect of the Edo period Nativist semiotic interventions, which initially aimed to retrieve the archaic, "original" Japanese identity against Tokugawa Neo-Confucian orthodoxy. During the Meiji period and modernization, Nativist ideas on language became one of the tools for the construction of a sense of national identity. With the formation of an authoritarian, quasi-fascist regime in the Thirties, the concept of *kotodama* was used as an ideological justification of obedience and submission to the government acting in the name of the emperor. After World War II, scattered ideas on the uniqueness of Japanese language, the remnants of previous discourses, were adopted by *nihonjinron* to reconstruct a sense of Japanese cultural identity in a global reality.

As we can see, the permanence of certain conceptual interests and structural similarities in the treatment of language and signs hide very different ideological agendas. However, something troubling remains constant: the "empire of signs" presupposes an "emperor of signs," an ultimate master of signification—a master signifier that sutures the various antagonisms (between inside and outside, among the various local traditions, within history, etc.) at the basis of Japanese society. This "ideological fantasy," as Slavoj Žižek would call it, is the bottom line of nationalistic culturology. The advanced processes of globalization of Japanese culture show that the dream of Japanese uniqueness based on a peculiar rapport with the signs is now mainly a delusion, rather than a powerful and mobilizing ideological tool. It may still have a nostalgic appeal among certain strata of the Japanese populace, and it could still play a dangerous xenophobic role.[104] It must be strongly emphasized, though, that this "emperor of signs" was almost never identified in Japan with a specific ruler, and the emperor had only rarely the power and authority to control the production of signs in Japan. It is now time to develop different discourses on Japanese culture, by relying on different historical accounts and traditions of the archipelago based on diversity, openness, and multiplicity.[105]

Practices and ideas concerning various spheres (social, legal, economic, interpretive, ascetic, sexual, etc.) of everyday life—with the result that they (episteme and technologies of domination) supported and strengthened each other, thus imposing a lifestyle that was generally "Buddhist." Esoteric Buddhism developed its own epistemology, cosmology, and soteriology, diffused through control over what we could consider the mass media of the time (instruction, preaching, book production and circulation, performances, festivals, and so on), and the political support of state institutions. The creation of new social organizations such as professional guilds (*za*), confraternities (*kō*), and new professional figures and groups (such as *jinin* and *yoriudo*, professionals at the interface of religious institutions and common people in charge of tax collecting, trading, ritual activities, and policing) affiliated with religious institutions, contributed to the consolidation of such system of "Buddhist" domination, which gradually extended its influence over the interpretation of everyday activities.

Japanese Buddhist lifestyle was the result of neither an intellectual and emotional acceptance of Buddhism, understood as a voluntary and conscious act (conversion and faith), nor a transformation of a "foreign" Buddhism to adapt itself to pre-existing conditions (the so-called "Japanization of

Buddhism"). On the contrary, discursive regimes, institutions, practices and ideologies all together contributed to transform "Buddhistically" the everyday life (in general, not just cults and beliefs) of the Japanese. "Becoming a Buddhist" was a "natural" consequence of the imposition and diffusion of certain social and individual practices in the spheres of production and exchange, semiotics, power, and subjectivity—of Foucault's technologies of domination. From this perspective, Buddhism loses its modern value as an essentialized entity whose autonomous agency changes individuals and society (or, in other accounts, it is society or the individual as reified agents of change in Buddhism); Buddhism, individuals, and society are the result of the operations of technologies of domination, institutions, and apparatuses of various kind. In this respect, Buddhism is not an autonomous and ahistorical essence, but a "sense effect," the result of social and discursive practices related to the definition of a Buddhist "field," the performance of practices homologated as Buddhist, and coercion to preserve this newly established formation. Social practices related to the academic study of all this are also involved in the production and maintenance of a Buddhist field and a Buddhist ordering of reality.[106]

The invisible world evoked through visualization (in the sense proposed in Chapter Four, that is, a set of strategies to make the invisible visible) lay at the core of medieval Japanese world-view, power relations, and social practices. It is by making the "invisible world" visible that religious institutions were able to influence power relations and formulate ideological positions. Bruce Lincoln has written:

> unlike secular ideologies... religious ideologies regularly offer analyses of the fundamental nature of humanity and of the cosmos itself. But like other modes of ideology, religious ideologies also devote careful attention to the nature and proper order of a third entity intermediate to the microcosm of the individual and the macrocosm of the universe: that is, the meso-cosm of human society.[107]

The Shingon correlative system was very powerful, and its echo can be found in most cultural forms of premodern Japan. As Bruce Lincoln suggests,

> within a totalistic and totalizing system of thought... —a system which centered upon the homology of microcosm and macrocosm... —all pieces of the system were mutually reinforcing. The system thus possessed enormous persuasive power, by virtue of the vast scope and variety of phenomena which could be explained within it.[108]

This exegetical work was obviously related to issues of legitimacy and orthodoxy. The scholar monks, in particular, envisioned themselves as the guardians of tradition, correct transmission, and therefore, as the controllers of semiotic production concerning the Buddhist teachings. In a way, they were "masters of signs." I would like to suggest that Shingon exegetes were examples of what Jean Baudrillard calls "semiurges," creators of pervasive systems of signs that succeeded in producing a "reality effect."[109] Esoteric Buddhist semiurgy aimed at creating a systematic and consistent vision of reality—or, in other words, a hegemonic intellectual formation. To borrow from Slavoj Žižek's theory of ideological effects, Shingon semiurges used a vast range of representations connected to the cosmos, the state, the monarch, the individual body, language, signification, and so forth, to create an imaginary dimension (a fantastic ideological scenario), in order to conceal and/or control the antagonisms at the source of the real—of their society.[110] This imaginary dimension was not just an empty set of images, but acquired a strong sense of reality.

In other words, the semiotic labor of the Shingon scholar monks, these medieval Japanese semiurges, consisted in an attempt at "suturing" or quilting together the various contradictory, irreconcilable elements of Japanese culture and society through the study and the transmission of texts to create a sense of order, stasis, and control. "Tradition" and self-identity were the result of their efforts. However, without the support of centers of power, the mobilization of systems of coercion, and the control over premodern mass media, it could not survive; after the general restructurings of the Japanese religious field that followed the Meiji Restoration with the anti-Buddhist persecutions of 1868–71, and the defeat of Japan in World War II, Buddhism gradually lost its symbolic authority as the main institution for the production of meaning in Japan. Yet, the Esoteric Buddhist episteme is not completely extinct. We can still find fragments of it in Buddhist religious practices involving manipulation of mantric formulae and *shittan* graphs, in rituals that are inscriptions of a soteriological program, and in more general (and often, vaguely expressed) ideas about language and signs. However, the most striking and unexpected manifestation of the Esoteric Buddhist episteme today can be found in popular texts of Japanese mass culture (*anime*, *manga*, video games), many of which present invisible entities that are evoked and made visible (visualized?) through the performance of gestures, rituals, and particular words of power.

NOTES

Preface

1 Barthes, 1982, p. 3.

2 Ibid., p. 83.

3 Ibid., p. 4.

4 See Sharf, 1995b.

5 See Suzuki, 1972, 1996.

6 On Schopenhauer's interest in Buddhism, see Schopenhauer, 2007.

7 Several authors since the 1970s have begun to employ conceptual tools mediated from Buddhist thought in order to develop research relevant to semiotics. The pathfinders in these attempt include: Hofstadter, 1979; Matte Blanco, 1975; Maturana and Varela, 1987; Merrell, 1991; Morin, 1986; Varela, Thompson, and Rosch, 1991.

8 Suzuki, 1927–34; Watts, 1936.

9 Quoted in Sharf, 1995a, pp. 127–8.

10 Sharf, 1995b, p. 248.

11 See also Faure, 1991, 1993.

12 Faure, 1991.

13 On semiotic ideas based on the *Lotus Sutra*, see Stone, 2006a.

14 See Klein, 2002.

15 Rambelli, 2007, esp. pp. 88–128.

16 Especially significant have been the contributions by Stanley Tambiah (1968, 1970), Bernard Faure (1991), Allan Grapard (1987), David Eckel (1992), Donald Swearer (2004), Alexander Piatigorsky (1976, 1984), Youxuan Wang (2001), Mario D'Amato (2003, 2008), José Cabezon (1994), Charles Orzech (2002–2003), Richard Payne (1998), Varela, Thompson, and Rosch (1991), Ryūichi Abé (1999), and Steven Heine (2000, 2004); works on Buddhist textuality include Susan Klein on allegorical interpretations (2002) and Charlotte Eubanks on the status and functions of Buddhist texts (2011). On Buddhist semiotics, see also Fabio Rambelli (1989, 1994, 1999, 1999–2003, 2006, 2007, 2008).

17 Boon, 1982, p. 116.

18 On the origins and consequences of this misunderstanding, see Urban, 2003; White, 2006.

19 Abé, 1999.

20 Faure, 1991.

21 See Faure, 1998, Sharf, 1999.

22 Pasolini, 1988, esp. pp. 204–78.

23 Below it there is the Realm of Desire (Sk. *kāmadhātu*, Jp. *yokkai)*, where human beings and other forms of existence live; above it, there is the Realm of Formlessness (Sk. *arūpadhātu*, Jp. *mushikikai*) of pure meditation.

24 See Droit, 1989, 1997.

Chapter 1

1 Spiro, 1982, pp. 11–14 and *passim*.

2 Greimas and Courtés, 1986a, p. 129.

3 See Komatsu, 1988.

4 There is a vast scholarly literature on Tantrism. Among the classical studies, see Tajima, 1959; Bharati, 1965; Rambach, 1979. Recent excellent scholarship includes White (ed.), 2000; Davidson, 2002, on Indian Tantrism; Davidson, 2005, on Tibetan Buddhism; Orzech, Sørensen, and Payne (eds), 2011, and Strickmann, 1996, 2002, and 2005 on East Asia; Kushida, 1964, 1979, Yamasaki, 1988, and Abé, 1999, on Japan.

5 Boon, 1990, p. 159.

6 Ibid., p. 165.

7 Ibid.

8 Certeau, 1990, p. 53.

9 Dumont, 1979, pp. 342–3.

10 Strickmann, 2002, p. 201.

11 Ibid., p. 198.

12 Kuroda, 1975.

13 Ibid., p. 537.

14 Ibid., p. 434.

15 Ibid., pp. 445–6.

16 Ibid., p. 537.

17 For balanced critical assessments of Kuroda's scholarships, see for instance Sueki, 1996; Taira, 1996; and Sasaki, 1988, pp. 29–52.

18 Among examples of Kuroda-related scholarship, see Satō, 1989, Sasaki, 1988, and Taira, 1991.

19 On the term exo-esoteric episteme (or "*kenmitsu taisei* episteme"), see also Iyanaga, 2002, p. 146.

20 See Kūkai, *Ben kenmitsu nikyōron* (trans. in Hakeda, 1972, pp. 156–7). On the main criteria of Buddhist hermeneutics, see Lopez (ed.), 1988.

21 Komatsu and Naitō, 1985.

22 The other repositories (sections) are, respectively, the sutras, the precepts, the canonical commentaries, and the transcendent wisdom (*prajñā pāramitā*) texts. See *Dasheng liqu liuboluomituo jing*, p. 868b; see also Kūkai's treatment of the subject in his *Ben kenmitsu nikyōron*.

23 For a list of Mahayana texts that include chapters with *dhāraṇī*, see for example Ujike, 1984; Misaki, 1988, pp. 18–25.

24 Ujike, 1984.

25 The most influential Tantric masters in China during this time were Śubhakarasiṃha (Ch. Shanwuwei, Jp. Zenmui; 637–735), Vajrabodhi (Ch. Jinggangzhi, Jp. Kongōchi; 671–741), and Amoghavajra (Ch. Bukong, Jp. Fukū; 705–74).

26 Ujike, 1984.

27 See Certeau, 1982.

28 Lamotte, 1988, p. 15.

29 Kūkai, *Sokushin jōbutsugi*, p. 402a.

30 The texts are, respectively: *Ben kenmitsu nikyōron*, by Kūkai; *Kenmitsu fudōju* and *Gorin kujimyō himitsushaku* by Kakuban; and *Shingon myōmoku* by Raihō. Each author stresses different aspects of the *kenmitsu* paradigm in accordance with the main trends of debate in his time. Kūkai is especially concerned with the uniqueness of Esoteric Buddhism in relation to the other schools; Kakuban underlines the absolute character of the Esoteric teachings and shows how they overcome the idea, very popular at the time, that the efficacy of Buddhism was close to an end (what is known as the End of Dharma, *mappō*); and Raihō emphasizes the essentially enlightened nature of all things.

31 The *nirmaṇakāya* (Jp. *ōkejin*) is the conditioned, physical body of a Buddha as it appears for the benefits of human beings; the *sambhogakāya* ("body of enjoyment," Jp. *hōjin*, "reward body") is the body acquired by a bodhisattva upon completion of his practices when he becomes a Buddha.

32 Raihō, *Shingon myōmoku*, pp. 734c–5a.

33 The concept of *mappō*, though not referred to in Kūkai's texts, came to play a major role in Japanese culture after the eleventh century. Esoteric Buddhism tended to deny that the Dharma was going to extinguish itself, opposing to the concept of *mappō* the unconditioned nature and Esoteric power of the Dharmakāya's teachings.

34 This idea probably resulted from the identification of the linguistic thought of the *Shi moheyan lun* (p. 605b) with dharanic conceptions and practices; see Chapter Three.

35 The different conceptions of *ri* and *ji* are the main theme of Raiyu's *Shoshū kyōri dōi shaku*, a contrastive analysis of Shingon and other Mahayana schools.

36 Esoteric Buddhism posits the nondualism (non-differentiation) of buddhas and ordinary unenlightened beings.

37 See for instance Kakuban's *Kenmitsu fudōju*, in particular the following verses: "*Ken* teachings explain the initial stage [of practice leading to Buddhahood (*inbun*)], *mitsu* teachings explain the final stage [of attainment of Buddhahood (*kabun*)]"; "*Ken* principle (*ri*) has no relationship with the sense organs (*rokkon*), *mitsu* sees them as the four [Buddha-]bodies (*shishin*); *ken* principle has no relationship with objects (*rokkyō*), *mitsu* sees them as the three adamantine mysteries (*san*[*mitsu*]*kon*[*gō*]); *ken* principle has no relationship to the mind apparatus (*rokushiki*), *mitsu* knows that the mind apparatus is the universal wisdom of the Dharma-body"; "*ken* principle has neither signs (*sō*) nor activities (*yū*), *mitsu* Suchness ([*shin*]*nyo*, Sk. *tathatā*) is endowed with substance-signs-dynamic manifestations (*sandai*)." On the *sandai* doctrine, see Chapter Two.

38 The idea of so-called "iconography without icons," as a supposedly fundamental attitude of Brāhmanism that was adopted by Buddhism as well, was introduced by Ananda Coomaraswamy (1927). For a critical review of the discussion on Buddhist aniconism, see Swearer, 2004, pp. 25–30.

39 Seckel, 2007, p. 7.

40 See Rambelli, 2008.

41 Quoted in Seckel, 2007, p. 47.

42 The Three Jewels represent the three fundamental components of Buddhism, i.e. the Buddha, his teachings (Dharma), and the clergy (Samgha).

43 In Eco, 1976, pp. 151–313.

44 Ibid., pp. 224–6.

45 On the importance of re-creating the original context of mantras, see Lopez, 1990, pp. 369–72.

46 Kūkai, *Shōrai mokuroku*, trans. in Hakeda, 1972, p. 144.

47 Kūkai, *Bonji shittan jimo narabini shakugi*, p. 361.

48 Lincoln, 1991, p. 168.

49 The stages in the soteriological path are: arousal of the desire for enlightenment (Sk. *bodhicitta*, Jp. *bodaishin*), experience of enlightenment (Sk. *bodhi*, Jp. *bodai*), performance of salvific practices for others, entrance into nirvana, and perfection of expedient means.

50 For this terminology, I am indebted to Allan Grapard's (1993) threefold catagorization of the orders of significance in Japanese representations of sacred space, namely, geosophia, geognosis, and geopiety.

51 It is very difficult to evaluate the role of common sense in ideas and practices relating to signs in the Esoteric episteme, especially in light of the almost total lack of research on this subject. Buddhist collections of stories (*setsuwa*), for instance, suggest that signs are clues to a hidden reality and at the same time instruments for action upon it: they not only foretell and express events but also give rise to them (see Rambelli, 1990). It is not clear, however, whether these texts reflected widespread popular ideas on signs and semiosis or were vehicles for the diffusion of a new, Buddhist-continental semiotic mentality.

52 Without the superficial interpretation of signs (*jisō*), the deeper truth (*jigi*) cannot be conveyed, but the Esoteric truth cannot be taught to people lacking the status or the capacity to receive it—this is why it is called "secret" (*himitsu*). On these subjects, see Chapter Three.

53 Grapard, 1993, pp. 374–5; the original uses "geosophia" and "geognosis" instead of "semiosophia" and "semiognosis."

54 Ibid., p. 375. The original has "earth itself" instead of my "signs themselves."

55 Kūkai, *Shōji jissōgi*, p. 401c; see also Chapter Three.

56 On mantric expressions as inscriptions of soteriology, see Lopez, 1990. For an analysis of Shingon inscription strategies, see Chapter Four.

57 See also Kuroda, 1989.

58 Grapard, 1993.

59 See, respectively, Sanford, 1994, and Unno, 1998.

60 On a number of issues related to Buddhist visions of the mind and their complexity, see for example Piatigorsky, 1984.

61 *Dari jing*, p. 1c.

62 An abbreviated version is the *Hizō hōyaku*, partially translated in Hakeda, 1972, pp. 157–224.

63 See Cabezón, 1994.

64 On the Yogācāra tradition of though, see for example Yokoyama, 1986, 1996; Takemura, 1985, 2001; Hirakawa *et al.* (eds), 1982; Matsukubo, 2001; in English, see Lusthaus, 2002.

65 Ryōhen, *Hossō daijōshū nikanshō*, p. 127.

66 These seeds include the seeds to become a Buddha; lack or destruction of these Buddha-seeds prevents one from attaining Buddhahood and keep one forever prisoner of the cycle of rebirths.

67 Sources define a great *kalpa* as the time necessary for a heavenly being to reduce to dust a stone block of 800 leagues by touching it slightly with its clothes once in three years: Ryōhen, *Hossō nikanshō*, p. 152–3.

68 Raihō, *Shingon myōmoku*, pp. 731–2.

69 On the Shingon doctrines concerning *bodhicitta*, see *Mikkyō daijiten*, p. 2051.

70 See for example, *Dari jing shu*, p. 580a; Kūkai, *Himitsu mandara jūjūshinron*, pp. 284–5; see also *Mikkyō daijiten*, p. 1243a–b.

71 Particularly important for this doctrinal development concerning the status of *amala vijñāna* in East Asia was the apocryphal *Shi moheyan lun* attributed to Nāgārjuna; see *Mikkyō daijiten*, p. 52a–b.

72 Shōgei, *Reikiki shishō*, pp. 30–2; see also Ogawa, 1997, p. 154. On this ritual, see Rambelli, 2002a.

73 For a general study of the role of monastic communities in medieval Japan, see Kuroda, 1980. See also Adolphson, 2000; Hirase, 1988. On the life and activities of learned monks in the Shingon tradition during the medieval period, see for example Hashimoto, 1988; Tomita, 1988.

74 On monastic education in Japan, see Hori, 1978; Toganoo, 1982b. On the

ancient and medieval Shingon education curriculum, see Saitō, 1978, esp. pp. 44–74; the curriculum during the Kamakura and Muromachi periods is discussed in detail on pp. 64–73.

75 Ishikawa, 1977, pp. 86–9; Ogata, 1980, p. 83.

76 Saitō, 1978, p. 87.

77 Ibid., pp. 64–7; see also *Mikkyō daijiten*, pp. 290b–291a.

78 Ibid., 1978, p. 68; see also Tanaka, 1999, pp. 78–83.

79 Hirota, 2000, p. 69.

80 On the monastic curriculum in Nara, see Yamazaki, 1993.

81 Nagamura, 1988, p. 47; Abé, 1999, pp. 372–6.

82 On *rongi*, see Chisan kangakukai (eds), 2000. On Tendai *jikidan* (*dangi*), see Hirota, 1993; Tanaka, 1999, especially pp. 78–114.

83 Kōshū, *Keiran shūyōshū*, p. 609b.

84 On initiation rituals for professions, see Rambelli, 2007, pp. 187–97. On *kuden* in general, see Stone, 1999.

85 Raiyu, *Shinzoku zakki mondōshō*, p. 425.

86 See Kushida, 1979, p. 176.

87 On the style and functions of medieval commentaries, see Kikuchi, 1997.

88 Itō, 2000, esp. pp. 36–42.

89 Besides, on what basis can we claim to be more enlightened and less prone to "sophistries" than the medieval Japanese people?

90 See Orzech, 1989.

91 Grapard, 1989, p. 182.

92 Ibid., p. 161.

93 Grapard, 1988, pp. 264–5.

94 See Grapard, 1987.

95 Ibid.

96 The absolute value of phenomena and particularities—i.e. of *difference*—is one of the major themes of most Esoteric and *hongaku* ("original enlightenment") texts from the mid-Kamakura period. On the plural nature of Tantric symbols and entities, see Boon, 1990, pp. 79–83; on the Buddhist discourse on original enlightenment, see Stone, 1999.

97 Tsuda, 1978, 1981. I should emphasize, however, that my treatment of these subjects is different from Tsuda's, which lacks explicit semiotic concerns. For a more thorough discussion of the logic of yoga, see Chapter Four below.

98 Raihō, *Shingon myōmoku*, p. 731a.

99 Grapard, 1992, p. 174.

Chapter 2

1 Kūkai, *Shōji jissōgi*, p. 402b; from Hakeda, 1972, p. 240, slightly modified.

2 Kūkai, *Kongōchōgyō kaidai*, p. 91. On the materialistic ontology and the role of material objects in Esoteric Buddhism, see Rambelli, 2007.

3 The operations of atoms, especially in connection with semiotics, are described by Kūkai in his *Shōji jissōgi*, pp. 403a–4a.

4 This idea is expressed in more systematic terms by Kakuban in his doctrine of the five Buddha bodies, the so-called *goshinsetsu*. According to this doctrine, a fifth and more fundamental modality of existence and manifestation of the Buddha exists, variously called *musō hosshin* (signless *dharmakāya*), *rokudai hosshin* (six-element *dharmakāya*), and *hokkaishin* (Dharmadhātu-body). See also Kamei, 1942; Katō, 1978; Matsuzaki, 1962.

5 The *sandai* doctrine *sub specie semiotica* was propounded for the first time by Kūkai in his *Sokushin jōbutsugi* (pp. 381b–84a; partial trans. in Hakeda, 1972, pp. 227–8) as a development of some concepts in the *Dasheng qixin lun* and the *Shi moheyan lun*, and became one of Shingon's central tenets.

6 Raihō, *Shingon myōmoku*, pp. 730a–b.

7 See Ui, 1919, pp. 801–2.

8 *Shoke kyōsō dōishū*, p. 570.

9 See Eco, 1975.

10 See for instance Raiyu, *Sokushingi gūsō*, pp. 224–9; Ui, 1919, p. 808.

11 Pasolini, 1988, p. 204.

12 Ibid. Italics in the original.

13 Ibid., p. 205. Italics in the original.

14 Ibid., p. 230.

15 Ibid., p. 255.

16 Ibid., p. 261.

17 Ibid., p. 262.

18 Ibid., p. 247.

19 Ibid., p. 262. Italics in the original.

20 Eco, 1967, p. 152; Eco, 1980, pp. 95–6.

21 Pasolini, 1988, p. 278. Italics in the original.

22 Ibid., pp. 278–9.

23 Eco, 1980, p. 95.

24 Ibid., p. 96.

25 Ibid., p. 261.

26 See *Mikkyō daijiten*, pp. 92a–c, 95a–b.

27 *Shingon honmoshū*, pp. 174–8.

28 Ibid., pp. 781–3.

29 See also Nakamura, 1973.

30 On this issue, see for instance Nakamura, 1967, and Rambelli, 1990. On *ryōi* as marvelous signs that reveal the law of Karma and the action of the Buddha, see LaFleur, 1983, pp. 26–59.

31 Most scholars agree in attributing to Huiguo (CE 746–805), Kūkai's Chinese master, the identification of the Buddha Mahāvairocana with the Dharmakāya and the idea that the Esoteric teachings are the teachings of the Dharmakāya himself.

32 Hakeda, 1972, pp. 78–9.

33 According to the sutras, the preaching of the Dharma by other buddhas was also done by the use of many different—and, for humans, difficult to understand—semiotic substances. An interesting case is the *Vimalakīrti Sutra* (*Weimojie suoshuo jing*; Watson (trans.), 1997). In the translation of the *Laṇkāvatāra Sūtra* by Bodhiruci (*Ru Lengqie jing*; Suzuki (trans.), 1932), besides a description of polymateric sermons, there is also a controversial statement (also referred to by Kūkai) concerning the preaching by the Dharmakāya.

34 Serres 1977, pp. 257–72.

35 *Dari jing*, p. 1.

36 *Dari jing shu*, p. 580a.

37 Ibid., pp. 579a, 579b.

38 *Dainichikyōsho shishin shō*, p. 594b.

39 Ibid., p. 635b.

40 Ibid., p. 594b.

41 See Gómez, 1995; see also Tamaki, 1983, pp. 170–2.

42 See Kūkai, *Kyōōkyō kaidai* and *Rishukyō kaidai.*

43 Kūkai, *Dainichikyō kaidai (hokkai joshin)*, p. 4.

44 See Orzech (trans.), 1995.

45 Abé, 1999, p. 276.

46 Ibid.

47 *Dari jing*, p. 31a; translation based on Abé, 1999, p. 301, slightly modified.

48 Abé, 1999, p. 301.

49 *Dari jing*, p. 31a; translated in Abé 1999, p. 301.

50 Abé, 1999, p. 290.

51 *Dari jing*, p. 10a.

52 *Shōji jissōgi*, p. 402c.

53 *Kenmitsu fudōshō*, p. 5.

54 *Shittanzō*, p. 365a.

55 Translation based on Iyanaga, 1983, p. 122.

56 Ryōchū, *Kangyō gengi bun denzūki*, fasc. 3. See Iyanaga, 1983, pp. 124–5.

57 Another medieval text attributes the invention of the Chinese language to

the Yellow Emperor himself who took inspiration from the trails of wild geese flying in the sky: *Yōtenki*, p. 58. The same text, however, also says that Cangjie was a manifestation of the Buddha Śākyamuni and invented writing upon the order of the Yellow Emperor: ibid. p. 66.

58 Kūkai, *Bunkyō hifuron*, p. 1.

59 Bodman, 1978, p. 162; *Bunkyō hifuron*, p. 1.

60 *Bunkyō hifuron*, p. 1.

61 As in *Li qu jing*, p. 789c.

62 *Dari jing*, p. 10a.

63 *Shōji jissōgi*, p. 401c.

64 Ibid., 403a.

65 Kūkai, *Hannya shingyō hiken*, pp. 555–6.

66 See for instance Onozuka, 1967; Morimoto, 1976; Kamata, 1989; Yamazaki, 1977, pp. 123–52; Miyasaka and Umehara, 1968, p. 137 *et passim*.

67 See also Henmi 1957; for a discussion of *shōji*, see Chapter Three.

68 Ibid.

69 Kūkai, *Shōji jissōgi*, p. 403a; Abé, 1999, p. 279.

70 *Shōji jissōgi*, p. 403c.

71 The same interpretive direction is expressed also by both Yoshito Hakeda, who translates *monji* as "expressive symbols," (Hakeda, 1972, p. 234 and *passim*) and Miyasaka Yūshō, according to whom *monji* are not only written letters, but all systems of signs and thus can be defined as "signs that convey meaning" (Miyasaka, 1976, p. 26). Other scholars have introduced concepts such as *aya* and *iroai* (decorative patterns); indeed, the examples of *monji* proposed by Kūkai are typical decorative patterns, also called *moyō*, a synonym of *aya*, in modern Japanese.

72 *Shōji jissōgi*, p. 402c–3a.

73 Dōhan, *Shōji jissōgishō*, pp. 10–11.

74 Raiyu, *Shōji jissōgi kaihishō*, pp. 80–2.

75 *Shōji jissōgi*, pp. 402c–3c.

76 Kūkai, *Issaikyō kaidai*, p. 271.

77 *Ha jigoku giki*, p. 912a; Rambelli 2000, p. 379 with slight modifications.

78 Tsuda, 1977, 1978, 1981, 1985.

79 See Graham, 1986.

80 Vandermeersch, 1982, p. 27.

81 Lincoln, 1991, p. 168.

82 Boon, 1990.

83 Gernet, 1982, p. 62.

84 See Rambelli, 2004.

85 On five-element correlations in Esoteric Buddhist texts from China and Tibet, see Toganoo, 1982a, pp. 411–20.

86 For a description of Mount Sumeru and the Buddhist cosmology, see Sadakata, 1997.

87 Kakuban, *Gorin kujimyō himitsushaku*, p. 15a. On the four kinds of mandala see below. The four Buddha bodies are *hosshin* (*dharmakāya*), *hōjin* (*samboghakāya*), *ōjin* (*nirmaṇakāya*), and *tōrushin* (the body of equal outflow represented by objects in the everyday reality). The three secrets (*sanmitsu*) are the three human activities (bodily movements, speech, and thought) resulting in becoming buddha in this very body. The four saintly beings are buddhas, bodhisattvas, self-enlightened buddhas (*pratyeka-buddhas*), and disciples of Śākyamuni (*śrāvaka*). The six destinations or forms of existence are gods, humans, demi-gods (*asura*), animals, hungry ghosts, and denizens of hell. The five paths are the four lower levels of the six destinations. The four kinds of birth are from one's mother's womb, from eggs, from humidity, and from transformation of another entity. The four kinds of demons are Māra and his retinue, heretics, evil spirits, evil deities.

88 Yōsai (Eisai), *Shutten daikō narabini jo*.

89 Such texts include the *Gozō mandara waeshaku*, a commentary to Kakuban's work composed in the Kamakura period (late thirteenth to early fourteenth centuries); it expands all aspects of the correlative systems by including agriculture (labor cycle in the fields, cereals, etc.), parts and aspects of the body (fingers, etc.), Chinese divination systems, sounds, music, and even Chinese and Japanese poems. Next, the *Gochi gozōtō himitsushō*, written by Dōhan (1178–1252) in 1236, develops the issue of the nondualism of matter and mind and adds further lists of deities from the Indian and Chinese pantheon. (I am grateful to professor Manabe Shunshō for making these texts available to me, and to professor Kawakami Toshiaki for his help in decyphering them.) Additional references to correlation systems can be found in the *Kangen ongi*, a tract on musical theory, and the *Ryōjin hishō kudenshū*, a section on poetics included in the collection *Ryōjin hishō*.

90 Pasolini, 1988, p. 262. Italics in the original.

91 Eco, 1990b, p. 25.

92 Yōsai, *Shutten daikō narabini jo*, pp. 651b–2a.

93 Raihō, *Shohō funbetsushō*, p. 715b.

94 Ibid., p. 715c.

95 Ibid., p. 726bc.

96 On the symbolism of the *stūpa*, the classic study is Snodgrass, 1985.

97 *Keiran shūyōshū*, 664c.

98 See Orzech (trans.), 1995.

99 *Miaofa lianhua jing*, pp. 32b–4b.

100 *Nihon shoki*, 1, pp. 111–18; Aston (trans.), 1956, pp. 40–50.

101 See Breen and Teeuwen, 2011, pp. 129–67.

102 Kōshū, *Keiran shūyōshū*, p. 609b.

103 See Abé, 1999, pp. 220–35.

104 Among the numerous books on mandala, see for example Tajima, 1959; Toganoo, 1982a; Rambach, 1979; Yamasaki, 1988; Grotenhuis, 1999.

105 Neven, 1984–1985, p. 11.

106 Grotenhuis, 1999, p. 2.

107 Tucci, 2001, p. 25.

108 Yamasaki, 1988, p. 126.

109 Tōji hōmotsukan (ed.), 1990, no page indication.

110 Kūkai, *Shōrai mokuroku*, p. 25a–b; translation based on Hakeda, 1972, pp. 145–6 with minor changes.

111 Grotenhuis, 1999, pp. 33–95.

112 Ibid., pp. 74–6.

113 *Dari jing*, p. 44a.

114 For details, see Rambelli, 2007, p. 19 n. 38.

115 Kūkai, *Sokushin jōbutsugi*, pp. 282c–3a.

116 Grotenhuis, 1999, pp. 80–4.

117 *Shishu mandaragi kuketsu*, p. 283a.

118 *Shishu mandaragi*, pp. 252–3.

119 Ibid., p. 252.

120 Ibid.

121 Kakuban's work is based on a text, commonly known as *Ha jigoku giki* (full title *Sanzhong xidi po diyu zhuan yezhang chu sanjie mimi tuoluoni fa*, English translation in Rambelli, 2000), and its variant (*Foding zunshengxin po diyu zhuan yezhang chu sanjie mimi sanshen foguo sanzhong xidi shenyan yigui*). On these texts, see Matsunaga, 1929; Kanbayashi, 1931; Nasu, 1954; Osabe, 1971; Misaki, 1988, pp. 499–508; Matsunaga, 1978; Rambelli, 2000.

122 *Shishu mandaragi*, pp. 252–5, 257–8; *Shishu mandaragi kuketsu*, pp. 260, 268–9.

123 *Shishu mandaragi*, pp. 256–7.

124 Greimas and Courtés (eds), 1986b, p. 204.

125 Abé, 1999, pp. 134–6.

126 Rambelli, 2002–3.

127 See Mus, 1935, p. 100.

128 Orzech, 1998, p. 5.

129 Sharf, 2001, pp. 189–92.

130 See Swearer, 2004; Davis, 1997; Rambelli, 2007, pp. 75–81; Rambelli and Reinders, 2012, esp. Chapter One.

131 In'yū, *Kohitsu shūshūshō*, pp. 361–2; *Senpo intonshō*, pp. 244–7.

132 *Senpo intonshō*, p. 246.

133 *Sokushin jōbutsugi, ihon* 5.

134 Such mnemonic function is a result of the process of mandalization of

dhāraṇī mantric formulae, which, according to Ujike Kakushō (1984, 1987), characterizes East Asian Esoteric Buddhism.

135 Sharf, 2001, p. 188.

136 Couliano, 1984–85, p. 54.

137 Eco, 1984, pp. 109–10.

138 Violi, 1992, p. 100.

139 Lotman, 1990.

140 Cardona, 1987, p. 181.

141 Elizabeth ten Grotenhuis reports that when a plague struck a village in Fukushima prefecture in the 1870s, "The priest of the temple in which the Taima mandara was enshrined urged the villagers to come and pluck bits of the painting off its two vertical sides and to eat the sacred icon as medicine" (1999, p. 13).

142 Davidson, 2002.

143 Tambiah, 1976.

144 Satō, 2003. For some preliminary considerations concerning the ideology of Esoteric Buddhism in premodern Japan, see Iyanaga, 2002–3.

145 Violi, 1999, p. 269; she refers to Eco, 1976, p. 226.

146 See Toganoo, 1982a, pp. 1–6.

147 Monier-Williams, 1986, p. 775.

148 *Shishu mandaragi*, pp. 250–1.

149 Monier-Williams, 1986, p. 775.

150 Actually, the situation is more complicated, because East Asian mandalas are not just squares; but since it is "perfect," a mandala must contain all geometrical forms.

151 Bucknell and Stuart-Fox, 1986.

152 *Dari jing shu*, p. 625c.

153 Rambelli, 1996; Satō, 2006.

154 Kakuban, *Himitsu shōgon funigishō*, pp. 51–3.

155 On Buddhist uses of the tetralemma, see Hebert, 2012.

156 Eco, 1985, p. 36.

157 The legend of the appearance in the sky of the Womb mandala to Shanwuwei is reported for the first time in Japan between the end of the tenth and the beginning of the eleventh century (see, among others, Ryōken, *Taizōkai mandara son'i genzu shōshi*, pp. 1029b, 1040a-b). The origin of the *Vajra* mandala appears already in Chinese documents of the Tang era (see Orzech (trans.), 1995). On the origin of these legends and on the meaning of the term "image of the original appearance" (*genzu*), see Toganoo, 1982a, pp. 99–104.

158 Kripke, 1980.

159 *Dabanniepan jing*, p. 601b–c.

160 Kūkai, *Himitsu mandarakyō fuhōden*, p. 112.

161 Blumenberg, 1981.

162 Gómez (trans.),1995; Rambelli, 2007, pp. 112–20.

163 Cardona, 1988, pp. 9–10.

164 Ibid., 1987, p. 51.

165 Ryuki Washio, in Tōji hōbutsukan (ed.), 1990, no page indication.

166 For a general summary see Kuriyama, 1973.

Chapter 3

1 These three linguistic elements belong to the Incorporeal Dharmas (*fusōō gyōhō*); these dharmas are different from material entities (*shikihō*), the objects of the sense organs and forms of articulation of reality; from mind (*shinpō*), which is pure consciousness; and from mental factors (*shin shouhō*), affective and intentional states. On Buddhist phenomenology, see Takakusu, 1975.

2 Kajiyama, 1983.

3 The twelve factors of conditioned causation are: (i) ignorance; (ii) potential action; (iii) discrimination; (iv) names and forms; (v) sense organs; (vi) contact; (vii) perception; (viii) desire; (ix) attachment; (x) existence; (xi) birth; (xii) death.

4 Ibid., p. 32.

5 Murti, 1987.

6 See *Shi moheyan lun*, pp. 605c–6a. For similar ideas, see for instance *Ru Lengqie jing*, p. 544c–5a, 546c–7a, and *passim*; *Jingang sanmei jing*, p. 371a.

7 The other ten evil deeds are: murder of sentient beings, theft, lasciviousness, greed, anger, and stupidity. The first three are related to the body, whereas the latter three are related to the mind. On the soteriologic power of words, see Rambelli, 1990.

8 *Gorin kujimyō himitsushaku* by Kakuban, p. 21b.

9 Ibid., p. 12a.

10 Staal, 1979b, p. 9.

11 *Fo yu jing*, pp. 878b–c.

12 Ibid., p. 879a.

13 Faure, 1991.

14 *Weimojie suoshuo jing*, p. 551c; Watson (ed.), 1997, p. 110.

15 Dōhan, *Shōji jissōgishō*, p. 12.

16 Fo yu jing, p. 879a.

17 *Shi moheyan lun*, p. 605b.

18 See Bharati, 1965; Bucknell and Stuart-Fox, 1986.

19 As discussed in Eco, 1995.

20 This term is used in the *Commentary to the Mahāvairocana Sutra* (*Darijing shu*) to discuss the nature of language and its relation to reality. However, that text employs more frequently other terms to refer to language, such as *yuyan* (Jp. *gogon*), *yinsheng* (*onsei*), *yingxiang* (*onkyō*), *wenzi* (*monji*).

21 Shinmura (ed.), 1983, p. 829.

22 Another possible meaning is "doctrines concerning names," related to the Confucian philosophical theme of the "rectification of names" (*sheng ming*) to make things adequate to their definitions.

23 Kūkai, *Shōji jissōgi*, p. 401c.

24 Tanaka, 1964, p. 101.

25 *Shōji jissōgi*, p. 402b.

26 Henmi, 1957.

27 On the languages of the various kinds of beings in the Buddhist universe, see for example *Da fangguang fo huayan jing*, p. 80a.

28 *Shōji jissōgi*, p. 402b.

29 According to Yamazaki Seiichi, this interpretation was first formulated by Ui Hakuju (Yamazaki, 1977, p. 126), and is widely accepted today: see for example Ōyama, 1920; Yamazaki, 1977; Miyasaka, 1976; Hōjō, 1976, 1982, 1984; Tokunaga, 1984.

30 See Padoux, 1990.

31 *Kūkai, Himitsu mandara jūjshinron*, pp. 296–9.

32 Hōjō, 1976, 1982, 1984. Yamazaki Seiichi believes in a possible influence of the Mimāmsā school (Yamazaki, 1977).

33 As discussed in Derrida, 1967.

34 Gil, 1978, p. 1142.

35 Abé, 1999, p. 303.

36 *Shōji jissōgi*, p. 401c.

37 According to the traditional Chinese musical theory, the five notes correspond approximately to the first, second, third, fifth, and sixth degrees of the Western major scale.

38 The eight kinds of sounds (metal, stone, silk, bamboo, gourd, earth, leather, and wood) are classified according to the material of the musical instruments producing them. The same term refers also to the eight modes of court music and to the eight virtues of Buddha's voice. Both the five notes and the eight kinds of sounds constitute structures articulating the phono-musical matter.

39 Austin, 1975, pp. 92–3.

40 Ibid.

41 *Shōji jissōgi*, p. 402b.

42 See Hjelmslev, 1961.

43 Eco, 1984, pp. 52–3.

44 The form of expression is "a system of empty positions, a structure, through which the expressive occurrences ... [of the substance of expression] acquire

their positional and oppositional character" (Eco, 1975, p. 76). The substance of expression is a *set* of "concrete occurrences of expressive artifacts ... representing elements selected from an original amorphous material," that is, the matter of expression. The matter of expression is a "continuum of physical possibilities that is used as amorphous material ... for pertinent and discreet elements to be used as expressive artifacts" (ibid.).

45 Alper, 1989a, p. 4. For a history of mantric doctrines and practices in India, as they related to the subjects discussed in this chapter, see Toganoo, 1982b, pp. 429–69; Bharati, 1965; Padoux, 1990; Miyasaka, 1979, pp. 97–113; Alper (ed.), 1989; Yelle, 2003.

46 Lopez, 1990, p. 359.

47 See Bucknell and Stuart-Fox, 1986.

48 Kakuban, *Shingachirin hishaku*, p. 250.

49 Kūkai, *Dainichikyō kaidai*, p. 672.

50 Staal, 1989.

51 *Dari jing*, p. 10a.

52 Kakuban, *Kenmitsu fudōshō*, p. 5.

53 See for example Bharati, 1965.

54 Staal, 1985a, p. 550.

55 Quoted in Ujike, 1984, p. 135.

56 On this, see Alper, 1989a.

57 Staal 1985a, 1986.

58 Staal, 1986, p. 218.

59 Tambiah, 1985, p. 21; see also Tambiah, 1970, pp. 195–222.

60 Ujike, 1984, 1987.

61 The *Dazhidu lun*, with its typology of five hundred major kinds of *dhāraṇī*, is perhaps the most exhaustive text on the subject. *Dhāraṇī* are also addressed in the *Large Wisdom Sutra* (*Da banruo boluomituo jing*).

62 Ujike, 1984, p. 38.

63 Ibid., p. 80.

64 Ibid., pp. 77–81.

65 Ujike, 1984, p. 86.

66 Ibid., p. 31.

67 Alper, 1989b, p. 258.

68 Staal, 1989, p. 65.

69 On Shōmyō, see Harich-Schneider, 1973; Kushida, 1964, pp. 409–80.

70 Hjelmslev, 1961.

71 Lopez, 1990, p. 367.

72 Ibid., p. 368. For a detailed analysis of this sutra based on Tibetan commentaries, see also Lopez, 1997.

73 Eco, 1975, pp. 128–9.

74 Tambiah 1985, 1970.

75 Sasaki, 1987, p. 54.

76 Ibid., p. 62.

77 Robert Duquenne, lecture given in Samsø, Denmark, August 1989.

78 Harvey Alper (1989b) was perhaps the first to apply to mantric phenomena Wittgenstein's concept of language game.

79 For a list of early Buddhist texts translated into Chinese dealing with Indian linguistic issues, see Takubo and Kanayama, 1981, pp. 61–6.

80 On the history and characteristics of *siddhaṃ* characters in East Asia, and Japan in particular, see Gulik, 1980; Chaudhuri, 1998.

81 Gulik, 1980, pp. 54–5.

82 On the history of the developments of Buddhist Esoteric scripts in China, see Takubo and Kanayama, 1981.

83 For a reproduction of these texts, see Takubo and Kanayama, 1981, pp. 55–7.

84 *Shōrai mokuroku*, p. 31c; Hakeda, 1972, p. 144.

85 See Gulik, 1980, and Iyanaga, 1983. A general cultural trend considered *shittan* characters as microcosms, condensations of the Esoteric universe; a good example of this intellectual attitude is the Kamakura texts entitled *Shittanrin ryakuzu shō* by Ryōson.

86 On Jiun, see Watt, 1984.

87 Mabuchi, 1993. Scholars stress that *shittangaku* is useful to learn ancient and medieval Indian and Chinese glottology (see for example Bodman, 1978)

88 See Murphy, 2009.

89 *Dari jing*, p. 10a.

90 Kūkai, *Bonji shittan jimo narabini shakugi*, p. 361a.

91 Kūkai, *Bunkyō hifuron*; see also *Li qu jing*, p. 789c.

92 Strickmann, 2002, 2005.

93 Gulik, 1980, p. 39.

94 These elementary calligraphic figures are reproduced and discussed in Gulik, 1980, pp. 66–71.

95 See Gulik, 1980, pp. 67–71.

96 Kakuban, *Gorin kujimyō himitsushaku*, p. 12a.

97 Ibid., p. 12a–b.

98 The most obvious cases are the two main mantras (and their variants) discussed in Kakuban's *Gorin kujimyō himitsushaku*, namely the five-syllable mantra (*a bi ra un ken*) and Amida's *dhāraṇī* (*oṃ amṛta teje hara hūṃ*) discussed in Chapter Four. Countless other texts, however, also carry out similar procedures of mandalization of single mantras or mantric seeds, especially *A*, *vaṃ*, *hūṃ*.

99 A good example of such reduction of mandala is in Kakuban, *Abankai mandara ryakushaku*, pp. 61–9.

100 Eco, 1990.

101 Ibid.

102 Raihō, *Shingon myōmoku*, pp. 734c–5a.

103 Kūkai, *Ben kenmitsu nikyōron*, p. 381c; Hakeda, 1972, pp. 156–7.

104 Annen, *Shingonshū kyōjigi*, p. 449b.

105 Ibid., *Taizō kongō bodaishingi ryaku mondōshō*, p. 492b.

106 On the six kinds of compounds (*sat-samāsa*) that constitute the Sanskrit analysis system (*vigraha*), see Goldman and Sutherland, 1987, pp. 198–229; *Mikkyō daijiten*, p. 2330a. For Kūkai's usage, see Hare, 1990, esp. pp. 256–68.

107 Kūkai, *Shōji jissōgi*, p. 402a.

108 Ibid. Kūkai refers to the *Dari jing shu*, pp. 650c, 657a, 658a.

109 Kūkai, *Shōji jissōgi*, p. 402a. As Hare notes concerning the usage of the *ringonshaku* in Kūkai's *Kongō hannyakyō kaidai*, which apply to this case as well, "Kūkai stresses inseparability, thus confusing the Sanskrit indeclinable compound with a subtype of the copulative compound known as the elliptical dual (*ekasesa*)" (Hare, 1990, p. 268); *ekasesa* is a compound of two nouns closely associated as a natural pair.

110 Kakuban, *Hannya shingyō hiken ryakuchū*, p. 215.

111 Raihō, *Shingon myōmoku*, p. 730.

112 Ibid.

113 The most influential Buddhist mnemonic lists are the ones included in *Dabanniepan jing* and *Da fangguang fo huayan jing*: see Takubo and Kanayama, 1981, pp. 167–72. In Esoteric Buddhism, particularly important were the lists in the *Dari jing* (p. 30b-c) and in the *Yuqie jingang ding jing shi zimupin*; see ibid., pp. 172–6.

114 Ujike, 1984, 1987.

115 Based on *Yuqie jingang ding jing shi zimupin*, pp. 338b–9a.

116 Interpretive procedures involving several levels of meaning, more or less directly derived from Esoteric Buddhist hermeneutics, for the understanding of literary texts in medieval Japan have been studied in Klein, 2002.

117 Raihō, *Shingon myōmoku*, p. 730.

118 Quoted in *Mikkyō daijiten*, p. 959a.

119 *Shingon myōmoku*, p. 734b.

120 Greimas and Courtés (eds), 1986a, pp. 187–9; Greimas and Courtés (eds), 1986b, pp. 127–8. See also Eco, 1979; Eco, 1990.

121 Based on *Amida hishaku*, pp. 151–2; see also Inagaki, 1994.

122 These four levels of meaning have some doctrinal basis; they are discussed at length by the Tōji school of medieval Shingon centered on the scholar monks Raihō and Gōhō; the Mount Kōya's lineage of Yūkai only distinguishes between a first, superficial level, identified with exoteric teachings, and a second, profound level, identified with the Esoteric doctrines of the Shingon tradition. For details, see *Mikkyō daijiten*, p. 931b–c.

123 *Mikkyō daijiten*, pp. 931c.

124 Gōhō, *Gōhō shishō*, pp. 102–5.

125 For further details, see also Rambelli, 2007, esp. pp. 75–81.

126 Tenkai, *Ichijitsu shintō sōjō kuketsu*, p. 245; see also Misaki, 1999, p. 396. On the significance of the expression "green willows and red flowers" in the East Asian Buddhist tradition, see Misaki, 1999, pp. 586–644.

127 Kakuban, *Banjigi*, p. 98.

128 Ibid., p. 99; see also Kakuban, *Rishukyō shuji shaku*, pp. 97–101.

129 *Banjigi*, p. 99.

130 Ibid., pp. 102–3.

131 For an overview, see *Mikkyō daijiten*, pp. 121b–2a.

132 Raihō, *Shingon myōmoku*, p. 734b.

Chapter 4

1 The text, known as *Ihon Sokushin jōbutsugi*, is attributed to Kūkai but was probably written in the middle ages; see Sanford, 1997, pp. 11–12.

2 See also Raihō, *Shingon myōmoku*, p. 731a.

3 Another popular tale, the *Tsukumogami ki*, described inanimate objects that became buddhas; see Rambelli, 2007, pp. 237–50; Reider, 2009a, 2009b.

4 Raiyu, *Sokushingi gūsō*, p. 145.

5 Ibid., *Shingon myōmoku*, p. 734b.

6 Sharf, 2001, p. 163.

7 Ibid., p. 166. On these issues, see also ibid., pp. 185–7.

8 Couliano, 1984–1985, p. 58.

9 On the role and contents of dreams in the esoteric tradition in Japan, see for example Faure, 1996; Tanabe, 1992; Saigō, 1993.

10 Tamaki, 1982; Yamaori, 1983. As we have seen in Chapter Two, Esoteric Buddhist scriptures describe the original condition of the universe, before the production of conscious languages and sign systems, as the Dharmakāya Mahāvairocana immersed in deep *samādhi* meditation.

11 The seven precious materials (Jp. *shichihō* or *shippō*, Sk. *sapta-ratna*) are gold, silver, glass, crystal, mother of pearl, coral, and agate.

12 The eight kinds of supernatural beings (*tenryū hachibushū*) are gods (*deva*), *nāga* (serpents or dragons), *yakṣa* (demons), *gandharva* (heavenly musicians similar to angels), *asura* (anti-gods, fighting spirits), *garuḍa* (supernatural birds), *kiṃnara* (heavenly singers), and *mahoraga* (giant snakes).

13 Threefold conditioned world: the realm of desire, the realm of pure forms, and the formless realm.

14 The six destinations (Jp. *rokushu*, *rokudō*) are deities, humans, anti-gods (*asura*), animals, hungry ghosts, and denizens of hell.

15 The four kinds of birth (Jp. *shishō*) are in the womb, through an egg, out of humidity, and by metamorphosis.

16 The eight difficulties (Jp. *hachinan*) refer to eight existential situations that hinder the performance of Buddhist practices and therefore the attainment of salvation. They are: being a denizen of hell, an animal, a hungry ghost (these are the three lowest levels of being characterized by extreme suffering and ignorance); living in the heaven of long life (a very pleasurable place that is not conducive to asceticism) or in a marginal land not exposed to Buddhism, having one's sense organs impaired, a tendency to fall prey to wrong opinions, and living at a time when a Buddha is not in this world.

17 The five buddhas, located at the center of the mandala, are: Akśobhya, Ratnasaṃbhava, Amitābha, Śākyamuni, and Mahāvairocana himself.

18 The four buddhas are: Akśobhya, Ratnasaṃbhava, Amitābha, and Śākyamuni.

19 *Foding zunshengxin po diyu zhuan yezhang chu sanjie mimi sanshen foguo sanzhong xidi shenyan yigui*, pp. 912c–13a.

20 Raiyu, *Sokushingi gūsō*, p. 731a.

21 Scriptural bases for this ritual are the *Achu rulai niansong gongyang fa*, esp. p. 19c; and the *Jingangding lianhuabu xin niansong yigui*, pp. 299–310.

22 See *Mikkyō daijiten*, pp. 1238b–9b and p. 938.

23 Ibid., p. 1238c.

24 Kushida, 1964, pp. 201–7.

25 Kakuban, *Aizen'ō kōshiki*, p. 13.

26 Kitao, 1991, p. 76.

27 Kakuban, *Aizen'ō kōshiki*, p. 13.

28 Ibid., p. 14.

29 Kakuban, *Ajikan ju*, p. 233.

30 See also Stevens, 1990.

31 *Dari jing*, p. 9b; Kakuban, *Gorin kujimyō himitsushaku*, p. 12b.

32 Kakuban, Ibid., p. 14a.

33 Ibid., p. 15a.

34 Ibid., p. 12b.

35 Spiro, 1982.

36 Kakuban, *Gorin kujimyō himitsushaku*, p. 12b.

37 Ibid.

38 Ibid. The four kinds of nirvana are: (i) the original condition of purity of all beings; (ii) a condition in which the effects of the afflictions (*kleśa*) have been neutralized, but still one's physical body (an impure entity) is still present; (iii) stage in which beings, now without body, transcend the suffering caused by the cycle of rebirth; and (iv) level in which even mental obstacles are finally overcome and one attains the supreme enlightenment.

39 See Hakeda, 1972, pp. 246–62.

40 Kakuban, *Gorin kujimyō himitsushaku*, p. 12b–c.

41 Ibid., p. 15b.

42 Ibid., pp. 12c–15a.

43 Another important network of organs in the body, mentioned only in passing in the text, is constituted by the six receptacles (Ch. *liufu*, Jp. *rikufu*). While the five viscera are basically depots of breath/energy, the six receptacles function as centers of consumption.

44 Ibid., p. 15b.

45 Ibid., p. 15b–c.

46 As Nasu Seiryū points out, the Sanskrit original is different: it is not *tese* but *teje* (Nasu 1970, p. 193).

47 Kakuban, *Gorin kujimyō himitsushaku*, pp. 17a–19b.

48 See Nasu, 1970, pp. 193–4.

49 See Takubo-Kanayama, 1981, p. 219.

50 According to Umberto Eco's theory of the modes of semiotic production, such transformation of the mantric linguistic space constitutes an instance of *ratio difficilis* (1975, esp. pp. 183–4).

51 See also Nasu, 1970, pp. 193–4.

52 Kakuban, *Gorin kujimyō himitsushaku*, p. 19c.

53 This treatment of the two extremes of the Sanskrit alphabet appears already in Kūkai's *Unjigi*. The esoteric meaning of *A* is centered on the concept of "original non-creation" (*honpushō*), thus on the undoing of causality. In contrast, the deep meaning of *ha* concerns the "unobtainability of cause," that is, on the absolute and unconditioned of causality. In this way, the semantic fields of these two terms appear irreconcilable. However, meditation on the letter *A* reveals that all things come out of the originally uncreated, whereas meditation on the syllable *ha* results in the idea that "the uncaused cause is the first cause of all things" (Kūkai, *Unjigi*, in turn based on *Dari jing shu*, p. 656a). Esoteric meditative practices serve to overcome differences in meaning as a method to represent the unconditioned reality.

54 Rambelli, 2007, pp. 88–128.

55 Kūkai, *Shōji jissōgi*, p. 401a.

56 Ibid., pp. 401c–2c.

57 Ibid., pp. 402c–3c.

58 Ibid., pp. 403c–4a.

59 Ibid., p. 404a–b.

60 Ibid.

61 Tambiah, 1968, p. 188.

62 Staal, 1979b, pp. 9, 10.

63 Austin, 1975; Searle, 1969.

64 Kakuban, *Gorin kujimyō himitsushaku*, p. 22b.

65 Austin, 1975, pp. 14–15.

66 Tambiah, 1970.

67 See Rambelli, 2007.

68 Cardona, 1987, pp. 176–8.

69 Ibid., p. 181.

70 Ibid., p. 188.

71 *Dari jing shu*, p. 579.

72 Kakuban, *Gorin kujimyō himitsushaku*, 15b.

73 Gōhō, *Hizō shiki honshō*, p. 309.

74 *Sanzhong xidi po diyu zhuan yezhang chu sanjie mimi tuoluoni fa*, p. 911b; see Rambelli, 2000, p. 377.

75 Kakuban, *Gorin kujimyō himitsushaku*, 15b.

76 See Yamasaki, 1988.

77 *Sanzhong xidi po diyu zhuan yezhang chu sanjie mimi tuoluoni fa*, pp. 909c–10b; Rambelli, 2000, pp. 371–3. See also Kakuban, *Gorin kujimyō himitsushaku*, pp. 14a–15a.

78 Kōshū, *Keiran shūyōshū*, p. 623b.

79 *Heike monogatari*, quoted in Yamamoto, 1993, p. 240.

80 *Keiran shūyōshū*, p. 517c.

81 See the text quoted in Mizuhara, 1981, p. 122.

82 Ibid., p. 128.

83 Ibid., p. 96.

84 *Hōkyōshō*, p. 848c; Mizuhara, 1981, p. 95.

85 Mizuhara, 1981, p. 95.

86 See also Sanford, 2009.

87 *Hachimanchō no nukigaki*, p. 213.

88 Ibid., p. 214.

89 Ibid., p. 215.

90 *Misōde no shita*, pp. 364–7.

91 Ibid., pp. 369–72.

92 Kakuban, *Gorin kujimyō himitsushaku*, 15b.

93 Ibid.

94 Kitabatake Chikafusa, *Shingon naishōgi*, pp. 234–5.

95 Tsuda, 1978, p. 171.

96 Ibid., pp. 198, 203.

97 Kitabatake Chikafusa, *Shingon naishōgi*, pp. 229–30.

98 Kakuban, *Amida hishaku*, p. 149.

99 Tsuda, 1981, p. 124.

100 Raihō, *Shingon myōmoku*, pp. 731–2.

101 Ibid., p. 731b–c.

102 The five phases of the ritual are the attainment of the *bodhicitta* (the desire for enlightenment), the practice of the *bodhicitta*, the production of the adamantine mind, the experience of the adamantine body, and the all-pervasiveness of the Buddha body.

103 Tsuda, 1977, pp. 134–5.

104 Ibid., 1981.

105 Foucault, 1973.

106 Hofstadter, 1986.

Chapter 5

1 On the myth of creation of the Japanese archipelago, see *Kojiki*, pp. 21–7 (Chamberlain (trans.), 1981, pp. 19–29); *Nihonshoki*, 1, pp. 79–87 (Aston (trans.), pp. 10–18); on the medieval interpretations of this myth in light of Buddhist doctrines, see Yamamoto, 1998, pp. 84–94.

2 Ibid., p. 87.

3 Kōshū, *Keiran shūyōshū*, p. 626b; see also Grapard, 1998.

4 On the notion of Japan as a "sacred land" (*shinkoku*), see Kuroda, 1996; Rambelli, 1996; Rambelli, 2003.

5 Quoted in Hagiwara, 1986, pp. 164–5.

6 In Morrell (trans.), 1985, p. 164.

7 On Keichū, see Nosco, 1990, esp. pp. 49–67.

8 Quoted in Toyoda, 1986, pp. 184–5.

9 Keichū, *Waji shōranshō*, p. 110.

10 On Nativist discourse, see in particular Harootunian, 1986; on language studies in the Edo period, see Naoki, 1991.

11 In Tsunoda, de Bary, and Keene (eds), 1958, vol. 2, p. 519.

12 Ibid., p. 520.

13 Ibid., p. 521.

14 Ibid., p. 524.

15 Ibid., p. 527.

16 Ibid., p. 520.

17 Ibid., p. 523. On the role of rice in the construction of Japanese cultural identity, see Ohnuki-Tierney, 1993.

18 In Tsunoda, de Bary, and Keene (eds), 1958, vol. 2, p. 523.

19 Ibid., p. 544.

20 Kawamura, 1990, p. 15.

21 As Kawamura Minato as shown, the concept of *kotodama* permeates early modern and modern Japanese philosophy of language (Kawamura, 1990); even though different theories and explanations were proposed, they all

assume a peculiar status of the Japanese language. Furthermore, *kotodama* is always associated to a certain cosmology, and a vision of the other world in particular.

22 Quoted in Ibid., p. 76.

23 Ibid., p. 77.

24 Ibid., pp. 16–17.

25 Ibid., p. 40.

26 On cratylism, see Genette, 1995.

27 It is impossible to trace here the complex philosophical and intellectual debates of Japanese modernism. See for example Yamaguchi, 1995a, 1995b; Heisig and Maraldo, (eds), 1995. On Buddhist modernism, see Sharf, 1995a, 1995b.

28 In Tsunoda, de Bary, and Keene (eds), 1958, p. 871.

29 Ibid., p. 869.

30 Faure, 1995, p. 254.

31 See for instance Dilworth, 1969; Carter, 1989.

32 Dilworth, 1969, pp. 95–6.

33 Cited in Sharf, 1995a, pp. 127–8.

34 Sharf, 1995b, p. 248.

35 Sharf, 1995a, 1995b; Faure, 1991.

36 Sharf, 1995a, p. 111.

37 Ketelaar, 1990.

38 Sharf, 1995a, p. 110.

39 Victoria, 1997. Buddhist war ideology was supported by a disingenuous interpretation of epistemological and hermeneutical concepts, such as nondualism (*funi*) and the direct contact with truth and reality.

40 For a selection of excerpts, see Tsunoda, de Bary, and Keene (eds), 1958, vol. 2, pp. 784–95; the complete translation is in Hall (ed.), 1949.

41 Quoted in Miller, 1982, pp. 133–4.

42 Quoted in Tsunoda, de Bary, and Keene (eds), 1958, vol. 2, p. 791.

43 Ibid., p. 787.

44 Hall (ed.), 1949, p. 98.

45 Ibid., p. 99.

46 Ibid., p. 126.

47 Ibid., p. 102. The section on "Truth" (ibid., pp. 100–2) refers explicitly to Nativist scholars Kamo no Mabuchi and Fujitani Mitsue.

48 Miller, 1977.

49 Dale, 1986, p. i.

50 Miyoshi and Harootunian, 1989, p. xvi.

51 Najita, 1989, p. 5.

52 Ibid., p. 14.

53 Pollack, 1986, pp. 4–5.

54 Ibid., p. 7.

55 Ibid., p. 3.

56 Naoki, 1989.

57 See Taki, 1988, pp. 62–3.

58 For an alternative interpretation of "Yamato spirit," see Ōe, 1995, pp. 17–18.

59 See Dale, 1986; Miller, 1982.

60 Quoted in Dale, 1986, p. 79.

61 Ibid., p. 84.

62 See Dale, 1986, pp. 56–73.

63 Suzuki Takeo, quoted in Dale, 1986, p. 89.

64 Quoted in Miller, 1982, p. 71.

65 See also Tsunoda, 1985. For a critique of Tsunoda's research, see Miller, 1982, pp. 64–85, 293.

66 See Dale, 1986, pp. 100–15.

67 In Ibid., p. 219.

68 Ibid., p. 92.

69 Ikegami, 1991.

70 Ibid., p. 15.

71 Ibid., pp. 15–16.

72 Ibid., p. 16.

73 Ibid.

74 Ibid., pp. 16–18.

75 Ibid., pp. 19–21.

76 Barthes, 1982, p. 3.

77 Ibid.

78 Barthes made it clear that he was not analyzing "reality itself"—the "real Japan"; still, the cultural elements he isolated in his book are unmistakably "Japanese."

79 Ibid., pp. 3–4.

80 Ibid., pp. 4, 29.

81 Suzuki, 1972, p. 18.

82 Respectively, ibid., pp. 11–18, pp. 19–22, 24–6.

83 Ibid., pp. 30–6.

84 Respectively, ibid., pp. 95–8, 38–42, 27–9.

85 Ibid., pp. 63–8, 43–7.

86 Ibid., pp. 48–62, 69–84, 85–7, 88–94, 99–102.

87 Ibid., pp. 4, 29, 46.

88 Ibid., pp. 103–6.

89 Ibid., p. 22.

90 Ibid., p. 24.

91 Ibid., p. 26.

92 Ibid., p. 30.

93 Ibid., p. 32.

94 Ibid., pp. 69, 77.

95 Ibid., p. 78.

96 Ibid., p. 83.

97 Ibid.

98 Ibid., p. 4.

99 Yukawa, 1967.

100 Barthes, 1982, pp. 82, 83.

101 Ibid., p. 32.

102 See Ōe, Nakamura, and Yamaguchi, (eds), 1980–82.

103 On the relations between the imperial ideology and esoteric Buddhism see Iyanaga, 1999.

104 Several books by conservative authors published during the last two decades address the theme of the "end of Japan," attribute the causes of the Japanese crisis (first economic, now compounded by the Fukushima nuclear disaster) to Western democracy, internationalization, and individualism.

105 A growing number of authors are working in this fascinating and exciting direction, in particular, Yamaguchi Masao with its archaeology of Japanese modernity (Yamaguchi 1995a, 1995b), and Amino Yoshihiko, with his studies on local diversity, cultural interactions, and international relations in the medieval Japanese archipelago (see, for instance, Amino, 1990, 2012).

106 On this last point see also Lopez, 1995.

107 Lincoln, 1991, p. 173.

108 Ibid., p. 172.

109 Baudrillard, 1981, p. 185 and *passim*.

110 See in particular Žižek, 1989, 1991, 1997. On the concepts of "antagonism" and "suture," see Laclau and Mouffe, 1985.

REFERENCES

Collections and reference works

Dai Nihon bukkyō zensho. 100 vols. Suzuki Gakujutsu Zaidan (eds). Tokyo: Suzuki Gakujutsu Zaidan, 1972 (original edition 1912–22).

Gunsho ruijū. 29 vols. Hanawa Hokiichi, compiler (1746–1821) (rev. edn by Ōta Tōshirō). Tōkyō: Zoku Gunsho ruijū kanseikai, 1959–1960.

Kōbō Daishi zenshū. Kōyasan Daigaku Mikkyō Bunka Kenkyūjo (eds). 8 vols. Tokyo: Yoshikawa Kōbunkan, 1965–68.

Keichū zenshū. 16 vols. Tokyo: Iwanami shoten, 1973–6.

Kōgyō Daishi senjutsu shū. Miyasaka Yūshō (ed.). Tokyo: Sankibō busshorin, 1989 (revised and expanded edition).

Koji ruien. 51 vols. Jingū Shichō (eds). Tokyo: Yoshikawa Kōbunkan, 1967 (orig. edition 1896).

Mikkyō daijiten. Chishakuin Daigaku Mikkyō Gakkainai Mikkyō daijiten saihan iinkai (eds). Kyoto: Hōzōkan, 1970 (rev. edn). Reduced size reprint 1983 (orig. edition 1931).

Muromachi jidai monogatari taisei. 15 vols. Yokoyama Shigeru and Matsumoto Takanobu (eds). Tokyo: Kadokawa shoten, 1973–88.

Nihon Daizōkyō. 100 vols. Suzuki Gakujutsu Zaidan (eds). Tokyo: Suzuki Gakujutsu Zaidan, 1973–1978 (orig. edition 1914–22).

Shingonshū zensho. 44 vols. Shingonshū zensho kankōkai (eds). Kōyasan, Wakayama Prefecture: Shingonshū zensho kankōkai, 1933–39.

Shinshū taikei. 37 vols. Shinshū tenseki kankōkai (eds). Tokyo: Kokusho kankōkai, 1974 (orig. edition 1917–25).

Taishō shinshū Daizōkyō. 85 vols. Takakusu Junjirō and Watanabe Kaigyoku (eds). Tokyo: Issaikyō kankōkai, 1924–32. Also, *Taishō shinshū Daizōkyō bekkan: Shōwa hōbō sōmokuroku*. 3 vols. Tokyo: Taishō Issaikyō kankōkai and Daizō shuppan, 1929–34.

Taishō shinshū Daizōkyō zuzōbu. 12 vols. Takakusu Junjirō and Watanabe Kaigyoku (eds). Tokyo: Taishō issaikyō kankōkai and Daizō shuppan, 1924–35.

Teihon Kōbō Daishi zenshū. 11 vols. Mikkyō bunka kenkyūjo Kōbō Daishi chosaku kenkyūkai (eds). Kōyasan, Wakayama Prefecture: Kōyasan Daigaku Mikkyō bunka kenkyūjo, 1991–7.

Tendaishū zensho. 26 vols. Tendaishūten kankōkai (eds). Tokyo: Daiichi shobō, 1973–4 (original edition 1935–7).

Zoku Shingonshū zensho. 100 vols. Zoku Shingonshū zensho kankōkai (eds). Kōyasan, Wakayama Prefecture: Zoku Shingonshū zensho kankōkai, 1975–1988.

Primary sources

Abankai mandara ryakushaku, by Kakuban, in *Kōgyō Daishi senjutsushū*, part 1, pp. 61–9.
Achu rulai niansong gongyang fa (Jp. *Ashuku nyorai nenju kuyō hō*), in T. 19, n. 921.
Amida hishaku, in *Kōgyō Daishi senjutsushū*, part 1, pp. 151–2. See Inagaki, 1994.
Banjigi, by Kakuban, in *Kōgyō Daishi senjutsushū*, part 1, pp. 98–103.
Banruo boluomituo xin jing (*Heart Sutra*, *Prajñā pāramitā hṛdāya sūtra*, Jp. *Hannya haramitta shingyō* or *Hannya shingyō*,), in T. 8, n. 251.
Ben kenmitsu nikyōron, by Kūkai, in KDZ, 1.
Bonji shittan jimo narabini shakugi, by Kūkai, in T. 84, n. 2701.
Bonmōkyō kaidai, by Kūkai, in KDZ, 1.
Bunkyō hifuron, by Kūkai, in KDZ, 3.
Da banniepan jing (*Great Nirvana Sutra*, *Mahā parinirvāṇa Sūtra*, Jp. *Daihatsu Nehangyō* or *Nehangyō*), in T. 12, n. 374.
Da banruo boluomituo jing (*Large Wisdom Sutra*, *Mahā prajñā pāramitā sūtra*, Jp. *Daihannya haramitsu kyō* or *Daihannyakyō*), in T. 5–7, n. 220.
Da fangguang fo huayan jing (*Buddhāvataṃsaka Sūtra*, Jp. *Kegonkyō*), T. 10, n. 293.
Dainichikyō kaidai, by Kūkai, in KDZ, 1.
Dainichikyo kaidai (hokkai joshin), by Kūkai, in *Teihon Kōbō Daishi zenshū*, 4.
Dainichikyōsho shishin shō, by Raiyu, in T. 59, n. 2217.
Darijing (*Mahāvairocana Sutra*, Jp. *Dainichikyō*, original title *Da Pilushena chengfo shenbian jiachi jing*), T. 18, n. 848.
Dari jing shu, by Śubhakarasiṃha and Yijing (*Commentary to the Mahāvairocana Sutra*, (Jp. *Dainichikyōsho*, original title *Da Piluzhena chengfo jing shu*), T. 39, n. 1796.
Dasheng liqu liuboluomituo jing (Jp. *Daijō rishu rokuharamittakyō* or *Rishukyō*), T. 8, n. 261.
Dasheng qixin lun (Jp. *Daijō kishinron*). T. 32, n. 1666. See Hakeda, 1967.
Dazhidu lun (*Mahā prajñā pāramitā upadeśa*, Jp. *Daichidoron*), in T. 25, 1509. See Lamotte, 1944–80.
Fan'yu qianzi wen (Jp. *Bongo senjimon*), by Yijing, in T. 54, ns. 2133A and 2133B.
Foding zunshengxin po diyu zhuan yezhang chu sanjie mimi sanshen foguo sanzhong xidi shenyan yigui (Jp. *Butchō sonshō shin ha jigoku ten gōshō shutsu sangai himitsu sanjin bukka sanshu shichiji shingon giki*), T. 18, n. 906.
Fo yu jing (Jp. *Butsugokyō*), in T. 17, n. 832.
Genji monogatari (*The Tale of Genji*), by Murasaki Shikibu, in Yamagishi Tokuhei (ed.), *Genji monogatari*, 5 vols. (Nihon koten bungaku taikei vols. 14–18). Tokyo: Iwanami shoten, 1958–63. See Waley (trans.), 1970.

Gochi gozōtō himitsushō, by Dōhan, manuscript preserved at Kanazawa Bunko library.
Gorin kujimyō himitsushaku, by Kakuban, in T. 79, n. 2514.
Gozō mandara waeshaku, manuscript preserved at the Kanazawa Bunko library.
Guanzizai pusa xin zhenyan yiyin niansong fa (Jp. *Kanjizai bosatsu shin shingon ichiin nenjū hō*), in T. 20, n. 1041. See Stevens, 1990.
Hachimanchō no nukigaki: Ajikan no honmi, in *Shinshū taikei* 36 (Igishū).
Hannya shingyō hiken, by Kūkai, in KDZ, 1.
Hannya shingyō hiken ryakuchū, by Kakuban, in *Kōgyō Daishi senjutsushū*, part 2, pp. 197–217.
Hasshū kōyō, by Gyōnen, in DNBZ, 29.
Himitsu mandarakyō fuhōden, by Kūkai, in KDZ, 1.
Himitsu mandara jūjūshinron, by Kūkai, in Kawasaki Tsuneyuki (ed.), *Kūkai* (Nihon shisō taikei, vol. 5). Tokyo: Iwanami, 1975.
Himitsu shōgon funigi shō, by Kakuban, in *Kōgyō Daishi senjutsushū*, part 1, pp. 46–53.
Hokkekyō shaku, by Kūkai, in KDZ, 1.
Hōkyōshō, by Yūkai, in T. 77, n. 2456.
Hossō daijōshū nikanshō, by Ryōhen, in Kamata Shigeo (ed.), *Kamakura kyūbukkyō* (Nihon shisō taikei, vol. 15). Tokyo: Iwanami shoten, 1971, pp. 125–58.
Ichigo taiyō himitsushū, by Kakuban, in *Kōgyō Daishi senjutsushū,* part 1, pp. 157–76.
Ichijitsu shintō sōjō kuketsu, by Tenkai, in *Tendaishū zensho,* 12.
Ihon Sokushin jōbutsugi, attributed to Kūkai, in T. 77, n. 2428.
Issaikyō kaidai, by Kūkai, in *Teihon Kōbō Daishi zenshū,* 4.
Jingang banruo boluomituo jing (*Diamond Sutra*, *Vajracchedikā Prajñāpāramitā Sūtra*, Jp. *Kongō hannya kyō*), in T. 8, n. 235; see Conze (trans.), 1988.
Jingangding jing (*Sarvatathāgata tattvasaṃgraha*, Jp. *Kongōchōgyō*, original title *Jinggangding yiqie rulai zhenshi shedashen xianzheng dajiaowang jing*), T. 18, n. 865.
Jingangding lianhuabu xin niansong yigui (Jp. *Kongōchō rengebu shin nenju giki*), in T. 18, n. 873.
Jingang sanmei jing (Jp. *Kongō sanmaikyō*), T. 9, n. 273.
Kangen ongi, in *Gunsho ruijū*, 19.
Keiran shūyōshū, by Kōshū, T. 76, n. 2410.
Kenmitsu fudōju, by Kakuban, in T. 79, n. 2510.
Kenmitsu fudōshō, by Kakuban, in *Kōgyō Daishi senjutsushū*, part 1, pp. 3–6.
Kissa yōjōki, by Yōsai, in DNBZ, 48.
Kohitsu shūshūshō, by In'yū, in *Shingonshū zensho*, 18.
Kojiki, by Ō no Yasumaru (ed.), in Kurano Kenji and Takeda Yūkichi (eds), *Kojiki, Norito* (Nihon koten bungaku taikei, 1). Tokyo: Iwanami shoten, 1958. See Chamberlain (trans.), 1981.
Kyōōkyō kaidai, by Kūkai, in *Teihon Kōbō Daishi zenshū,* 4.
Man'yōshū, in Takagi Ichinosuke, Gomi Tomoe, and Ōno Susumu (eds), *Man'yōshū*. 4 vols. (Nihon koten bungaku taikei, vols. 4–7). See Nippon Gakujutsu Shinkokai (eds), 1965.
Miaofa lianhua jing (*Lotus Sutra*, *Saddharma puṇḍarīka sūtra*, Jp. *Myōhō renge kyō* or *Hokkekyō*), in T. 9, n. 262.
Misōde no shita, in *Shinshū taikei,* 36 (Igishū).

Nihon ryōiki (*Nihon genpō zen'aku ryōiki*), in Endō Yoshimoto and Kasuga Kazuo (eds), *Nihon ryōiki* (Nihon koten bungaku taikei, vol. 70). Tōkyō: Iwanami, 1967.

Nihon shoki, in Sakamoto Tarō *et al.* (eds), *Nihonshoki*, 2 vols. (Nihon koten bungaku taikei, vols. 67–68). Tōkyō: Iwanami, 1965–67. See Aston (trans.), 1956.

Reikiki shishō, by Shōgei, in Takase Shōgen (ed.), *Reikiki shishō, Reikiki shūishō*. Tokyo: Morie shoten, 1933, pp. 1–38.

Rishukyō kaidai, by Kūkai, in *Teihon Kōbō Daishi zenshū*, 4.

Rishukyō shuji shaku, by Kakuban, in *Kōgyō Daishi senjutsushū*, part 2, pp. 97–101.

Ru Lengqie jing (*Laṇkāvatāra Sūtra*, Jp. *Nyū Ryōgakyō*), T. 16, n. 671. See Suzuki (trans.), 1932.

Ryōjin hishō kudenshū, by Emperor Go-Shirakawa, in Kobayashi Yoshinori *et al.* (eds), *Ryōjin hishō sōsakuin*. Tokyo: Musashino shoin, 1971, pp. 5–112.

Sanzhong xidi po diyu zhuan yezhang chu sanjie mimi tuoluoni fa (Jp. *Sanshu shichiji ha jigoku ten gōshō shutsu sangai himitsu darani hō*), in T. 18, n. 905.

Senpo intonshō, by In'yū, in *Shingonshū zensho*, 20.

Shi moheyan lun (Jp. *Shaku makaenron*), in T. 32, n. 1668.

Shingon honmoshū, by Raihō, in *Zoku Shingonshū zensho*, 21.

Shingon myōmoku, by Raihō, in T. 77, n. 2449.

Shingon naishōgi, by Kitabatake Chikafusa, in Miyasaka Yūshō (ed.), *Kana hōgoshū* (Nihon koten bungaku taikei, vol. 83). Tōkyō: Iwanami, 1964, pp. 226–40.

Shingonshū kyōjigi, by Annen, in T. 75, n. 2396.

Shinzoku zakki mondōshō, by Raiyu, in *Shingonshū zensho*, 37.

Shishu mandaragi, attributed to Kūkai, in KDZ, 4.

Shishu mandaragi kuketsu, attributed to Kūkai, in KDZ 4.

Shittanrin ryakuzushō, by Ryōson, in T. 84, n. 2709.

Shohō funbetsushō, by Raihō, in T. 77, n. 2448.

Shōji jissōgi, by Kūkai, in T. 77, n. 2429.

Shōji jissōgi kaihishō, by Raiyu, in *Shingonshū zensho*, 14.

Shōji jissōgishō, by Dōhan, in *Shingonshū zensho*, 14.

Shoke kyōsō dōishū, "Taimitsu yōshū 4", in *Koji ruien*, Shūkyōbu, vol. 1, "Shūkyōbu 8, Bukkyō 8: Shingonshū," p. 570.

Shōrai mokuroku, by Kūkai, in DNBZ, 96.

Shoshū kyōri dōi shaku, by Raiyu, in DNBZ, 29.

Shutten daikō narabini jo, by Yōsai, in *Nihon daizōkyō* (Tendaishū mikkyō).

Sokushin jōbutsugi, by Kūkai, in T. 77, n. 2428.

Sokushingi gūsō, by Raiyu. Kyoto: Shingonshū Chisan-ha shūmuchō, 1994.

Taizōkai mandara son'i genzu shōshi, by Ryōken, in T zuzō, 2.

Taizō kongō bodaishingi ryaku mondō shō, by Annen, T. 75, n. 2397.

Tsukumogami ki, in *Muromachi jidai monogatari taisei* 9. See Reider (trans.), 2009b.

Unjigi, by Kūkai, in T. 77, n. 2430; partial English translation in Hakeda, 1972, pp. 246–62.

Waji shōranshō, by Keichū, in *Keichū zenshū*, 10.

Weimojie suoshuo jing (*The Sutra of Vimalakirti, Vimalakīrti nirdeśa sūtra*, Jp. *Yuimakitsu shosetsukyō* or *Yuimagyō*), in T. 14, n. 475. See Watson (trans.), 1997.

Yōtenki, in Ishida Ichirō (ed), *Shintō shisōshū* (Nihon no shisō 14) Tokyo: Chikuma shobō, 1970, pp. 39–105.
Yuqie jingang ding jing shi zimupin, in T. 18, n. 880.

Secondary sources

Abé, Ryūichi. 1999. *The Weaving of Mantra*. New York: Columbia University Press.
Adolphson, Mikael S. 2000. *The Gates of Power: Monks, Courtiers, and Warriors in Premodern Japan*. Honolulu: University of Hawai'i Press.
Alper, Harvey P. 1989a. "Introduction," in Alper (ed.). *Mantra*. Albany, NY: State University of New York Press, pp. 1–14.
—1989b. "The cosmos as Siva's language-game," in Harvey Alper (ed). *Mantra*. Albany, NY: State University of New York Press, pp. 249–94.
Alper, Harvey P. (ed) 1989. *Mantra*. Albany, NY: State University of New York Press.
Amino Yoshihiko. 1990. *Nihonron no shiza*. Tokyo: Shōgakukan.
—2012. *Rethinking Japanese History*. Ann Arbor, MI.: Center for Japanese Studies, University of Michigan.
Aston, W. G. (trans.) 1956 [1896]. *Nihongi: Chronicles of Japan from the Earliest Times to a.d. 697*. London: Allen and Unwin.
Austin, John L. 1975 [1962]. *How to do Things with Words*. London and Oxford: Oxford University Press.
Barthes, Roland. 1982 [1970]. *Empire of Signs*. New York: Hill and Wang.
Baudrillard, Jean. 1981. *For a Critique of the Political Economy of the Sign*. St. Louis: Telos.
Bharati, A. 1965. *The Tantric Tradition*. London: Rider.
Blumenberg, Hans. 1981. *Die Lesbarkeit der Welt*. Frankfurt am Main: Suhrkamp Verlag.
Bocking, Brian, and Youxuan Wang. 2006. "Signs of liberation? A semiotic approach to wisdom in Chinese Madhyamika Buddhism," *Journal of Chinese Philosophy*, 33/3, pp. 375–92.
Bodman, Richard W. 1978. "Poetics and prosody in early medieval China: A study and translation of Kukai's *Bunkyō hifuron*." Ph.D. Thesis. Ithaca, NY: Cornell University.
Boon, James A. 1982.*Other Tribes, Other Scribes*. Cambridge: Cambridge University Press.
—1990. *Affinities and Extremes*. Chicago and London: University of Chicago Press.
Breen, John, and Mark Teeuwen. 2011. *A New History of Shinto*. Chichester, West Sussex: Wiley-Blackwell.
Broucke, Pol van den. 2002. "Dōhan shōsoku: Dōhan's letter on the visualization of the syllable A," in Sanpa gōdō kinen ronshū henshū iinkai (eds), *Shingi Shingon kyōgaku no kenkyū: Raiyu Sōjō nanahyakunen goenki kinen ronshū*. Tokyo: Daizō shuppan, pp. 1184–1206.
Bucknell, Roderick S. and Martin Stuart-Fox. 1986. *The Twilight Language: Explorations in Buddhist Meditation and Symbolism*. London: Curzon Press and New York: St. Martin's Press.

Buswell, Robert, (ed). 1988. *Buddhist Hermeneutics*. Honolulu: University of Hawai'i Press.
Cabezon, José. 1994. *Buddhism and Language*. Albany, NY: State University of New York Press.
Cardona, Giorgio Raimondo. 1985. *I sei lati del mondo*. Rome and Bari: Laterza.
—1987. *Antropologia della scrittura* (revised edition). Turin: Loescher.
Carter, Robert E. 1989. *The Nothingness Beyond God: An Introduction to the Philosophy of Nishida Kitaro*. New York: Paragon House.
Certeau, Michel de. 1982. *La fable mystique, XVIe-XVIIe siècle*. Paris: Gallimard.
—1986. *Heterologies: Discourse on the Other*. Minneapolis: University of Minnesota Press.
—1990. *L'invention du quotidien. 1. Arts de faire* (rev. edn.). Paris: Gallimard.
Chamberlain, Basil Hall (trans.). 1981 [1882]. *Ko-ji-ki: Records of Ancient Matters*. Tokyo and Rutland, VT: Tuttle.
Chaudhuri, Saroj Kumar. 1998. "Siddham in China and Japan," *Sino-Platonic Papers*, n. 88 (December), pp. 1–124 (monographic issue).
Chisan kangakukai (eds). 2000. *Rongi no kenkyū*. Tokyo: Seishi shuppan.
Conze, Edward (ed.) 1988. *Buddhist Wisdom Books: The Diamond and the Heart Sutra* (revised edition). London: Unwin.
—(ed.) 1987 [1959]. *Buddhist Scriptures*. London: Penguin Books.
Coomaraswamy, Ananda. 1927. "Origin of the Buddha image," *The Art Bulletin*, 11/4, pp. 1–43.
Couliano, Ioan. 1984–1985. "Le Mandala et l'histoire des religions," *Cahiers internationaux de symbolisme*, 48–49–50, pp. 53–62.
Dale, Peter N. 1986. *The Myth of Japanese Uniqueness*. New York: St. Martin's Press.
D'Amato, Mario. 2003. "The semiotics of the signless: The Buddhist doctrine of the signs," *Semiotica*, 147, pp. 185–207.
—2008. "Buddhism, apophasis, truth," *Journal for Cultural and Religious Theory* 9/2, pp. 17–29.
Davidson, Ronald M. 2002. *Indian Esoteric Buddhism: A Social History of the Tantric Movement*. New York: Columbia University Press.
—2005. *Tibetan Renaissance: Tantric Buddhism in the Rebirth of Tibetan Culture*. New York: Columbia University Press.
Davis, Richard H. 1997. *Lives of Indian Images*. Princeton: Princeton University Press.
Derrida, Jacques. 1967. *La voix et le phénomene*. Paris: Presses Universitaires de France.
Dilworth, David. 1969. "The initial formations of 'pure experience' in Nishida Kitarō and William James," *Monumenta Nipponica*, 24/1–2, pp. 93–111.
Droit, Roger-Pol. 1989. *L'oubli de l'Inde: une amnésie philosophique*. Paris: Presses universitaires de France.
—1997. *Le culte du néant: les philosophes et le Bouddha*. Paris: Editions du Seuil.
Dumont, Louis. 1979. *Homo hierarchicus. Le système des castes et ses implications* (revised edition). Paris: Gallimard.
Eckel, Malcolm David. 1992. *To See the Buddha: A Philosopher's Quest for the Meaning of Emptiness*. Princeton: Princeton University Press.

Eco, Umberto. 1967. *La struttura assente*. Milan: Bompiani.
—1976. *A Theory of Semiotics*. Bloomington: Indian University Press.
—1979. *Lector in fabula: La cooperazione interpretativa nei testi narrativi*. Milan: Bompiani.
—1980. [1973]. *Segno*. Milan: Mondadori.
—1984. *Semiotica e filosofia del linguaggio*. Turin: Einaudi.
—1985. *Sugli specchi e altri saggi*. Milan: Bompiani.
—1990a. *I limiti dell'interpretazione*. Milan: Bompiani.
—1990b. *The Limits of Interpretation*. Bloomington: Indiana University Press.
—1995. *The Search for the Perfect Language*. Oxford and Cambridge, MA., USA: Blackwell.
Eubanks, Charlotte D. 2011. *Miracles of Book and Body: Buddhist Textual Culture and Medieval Japan*. Berkeley: University of California Press.
Faure, Bernard. 1991. *The Rhetoric of Immediacy*. Princeton: Princeton University Press.
—1993. *Chan Insights and Oversights: An Epistemological Critique of the Chan Tradition*. Princeton: Princeton University Press.
—1995. "The Kyoto School and reverse Orientalism," in Charles Wei-hsun Fu and Steven Heine (eds), *Japan in Traditional and Postmodern Perspectives*. Albany, NY: State University of New York Press, pp. 245–81.
—1996. *Visions of Power: Imagining Medieval Japanese Buddhism*. Princeton: Princeton University Press.
—1998. "The Buddhist icon and the modern gaze," *Critical Inquiry*, 24, pp. 768–81.
Foucault, Michel. 1973. *The Order of Things*. New York: Vintage Books.
—1973. *Ceci n'est pas une pipe*. Paris: Fata Morgana.
Genette, Gérard. 1995. *Mimologics*. Lincoln, NE: University of Nebraska Press.
Gernet, Jacques. 1982 [1974]. "Piccole variazioni e grandi variazioni (Cina)," in Jean-Pierre Vernant (ed.), *Divinazione e razionalità*. Turin: Einaudi.
Gil, José. 1978. "Corpo," in *Enciclopedia*, vol. 3. Turin: Einaudi, pp. 1096–1160.
Goldman, Robert P. and Sally J. Sutherland. 1987. *Devavāṇīpraveśikā: An Introduction to the Sanskrit Language*. Berkeley: University of California, Center for South and South-East Asian Studies.
Gómez, Luis O. 1987. "Buddhist views of language," in Mircea Eliade (ed.), *Encyclopedia of Religion*. New York: MacMillan, vol. 8, pp. 446–51.
—1995. "The whole universe as a sūtra," in Donald S. Lopez, Jr. (ed.), Buddhism in Practice. Princeton: Princeton University Press, pp. 107–112.
—1996. *The Land of Bliss: The Paradise of the Buddha of Measureless Light: Sanskrit and Chinese Versions of the Sukhavativyuha Sutras*. Honolulu: University of Hawai'i Press.
Graham, A. C. 1986. *Yin-Yang and the Nature of Correlative Thinking*. Singapore: Institute of East Asian Philosophies (National University of Singapore).
Grapard, Allan G. 1982. "Flying mountains and walkers of emptiness: Toward a definition of sacred space in Japanese religions," *History of Religions*, 21/3, pp. 195–221.
—1987. "Linguistic cubism: A singularity of pluralism in the Sannō cult," *Japanese Journal of Religious Studies*, 14/2–3, pp. 211–34.

—1988. "Institution, ritual, and ideology: The twenty-two shrine-temple multiplexes of Heian Japan," *History of Religions*, 27/3, pp. 246–69.

—1989. "Textualized mountain—Enmountained text: The Lotus Sutra in Kunisaki," in George J. Tanabe, Jr., and Willa Jane Tanabe (eds), *The Lotus Sutra in Japanese Culture*. Honolulu: University of Hawai'i Press, pp. 159–89.

—1992. *The Protocol of the Gods: A Study of the Kasuga Cult in Japanese History*. Berkeley: University of California Press.

—1993. "Geosophia, geognosis, and geopiety: Orders of significance in Japanese representations of space," in Deirdre Boden and Roger Friedland (eds), *Now-here. Space and Social Theory*. Berkeley: University of California Press.

—1998. "*Keiranshūyōshū*: A different perspective on Mt. Hiei in the medieval period," In Richard K. Payne, (ed.), *Re-Visioning "Kamakura' Buddhism*, Honolulu: University of Hawai'i Press, pp. 55–69.

Greimas, J.A., and Courtés, J. (eds). 1986a [1979]. *Semiotica. Dizionario ragionato della teoria del linguaggio*. Florence: La Casa Usher.

—(eds). 1986b. *Sémiotique. Dictionnaire raisonné de la théorie du langage 2*. Paris: Hachette.

Grotenhuis, Elizabeth ten. 1999. *Japanese Mandalas: Representations of Sacred Geography*. Honolulu: University of Hawai'i Press.

Gulik, Robert H. van. 1980 [1956]. *Siddham: An Essay on the History of Sanskrit Studies in China and Japan*. (Sata-pitaka Series, vol. 247). New Delhi: Mrs. Sharada Rani.

Hagiwara Masayoshi. 1986. "'Uta' to butsudō," in Mezaki Tokue (ed.), *Mujō to bi* (Bukkyō to nihonjin, vol. 5). Tokyo: Shunjūsha, pp. 135–71.

Hakeda, Yoshito S. 1967. *The Awakening of Faith in the Mahayana*. New York: Columbia University Press.

—1972. *Kūkai. Major Works*. New York: Columbia University Press.

Hall, Robert King (ed.), 1949 [1937]. *Kokutai No Hongi: Cardinal Principles of the National Entity of Japan*. Cambridge, Mass.: Harvard University Press.

Hare, Thomas Blenman. 1990. "Reading writing and cooking: Kūkai's interpretive strategies," *Journal of Asian Studies*, 49/2, pp. 253–73.

Harich-Schneider, Eta. 1973. *A History of Japanese Music*. London: Oxford University Press.

Harootunian, H. D. 1986. *Things Seen and Unseen*. Chicago and London: University of Chicago Press.

Hashimoto Hatsuko. 1988. "Gōhō to Kenbō: Chūsei jiin ni okeru shitei kankei no ichikōsatsu," in Jiinshi kenkyūkai (eds), *Jiinshi no kenkyū*, vol. 2. Kyoto: Hōzōkan, pp. 257–304.

Hayami Tasuku. 1975. *Heian kizoku shakai to bukkyō*. Tokyo: Yoshikawa Kōbunkan.

Hébert, Louis. 2012. "Sémiotique et bouddhisme. Carré sémiotique et tétralemme (catuskoti)," in L. Hébert et L. Guillemette (eds), *Performances et objets culturels*. Québec: Presses de l'Université Laval.

Heine, Steven. 2000. *Shifting Shape, Shaping Text: Philosophy and Folklore in the Fox Koan*. Honolulu: University of Hawai'i Press.

—2004. *Opening a Mountain: Koans of the Zen Masters*. Oxford: Oxford University Press.

—2006. "Empty-handed, but not empty-headed: Dōgen's *kōan* strategies," in Richard K. Payne and Taigen Dan Leighton (eds), *Discourse and Ideology in*

Medieval Japanese Buddhism. London and New York: Routledge, 2006, pp. 218–39.

Heine, Steven and Dale S. Wright (eds). 2000. *The Koan: Texts and Contexts in Zen Buddhism*. Oxford: Oxford University Press.

Heisig, James W. and John C. Maraldo (eds). 1995. *Rude Awakenings: Zen, the Kyoto School, and the Question of Nationalism*. Honolulu: University of Hawai'i Press.

Henmi Sōhan. 1957. "*Shōji jissōgi* ni okeru shōji no gainen ni tsuite," *Mikkyō bunka*, pp. 62–74.

Hirakawa Akira, Kajiyama Yūichi, Takasaki Jikidō (eds). 1982. *Yuishiki shisō* (Kōza Daijō bukkyō 8). Tokyo: Shunjūsha.

Hirase Naoki. 1988. "Chūsei jiin no mibun to shūdan," in Jiinshi kenkyūkai (eds), *Jiinshi no kenkyū*, vol. 2. Kyoto: Hōzōkan, pp. 108–33.

Hirota Tetsumichi. 1993. *Chūsei* Hokkekyō *chūshakusho no kenkyū*. Tokyo: Kasama shoin.

—2000. *Chūsei bukkyō bungaku no kenkyū*. Osaka: Izumi shoin.

Hjelmslev, Louis. 1961 [1943]. *Prolegomena to a Theory of Language*. Madison: University of Wisconsin Press.

Hofstadter, Douglas R. 1979. *Gödel, Escher, Bach: An Eternal Golden Braid*. New York: Basic Books.

—1986. *Ambigrammi: Un microcosmo ideale per lo studio della creatività*. Florence: Hopeful Monster.

Hōjō Kenzō. 1976. "*Shōji jissōgi* wo meguru ichi-ni no mondai," *Buzan kyōgaku taikai kiyō*, 4, pp. 107–22.

—1982. "Kūkai no gengo riron," *Risō*, 594, pp. 39–50.

—1984a. "Mantora wo megutte: Indo dentōteki gengo shisō to Kūkai," *Hikaku shisō kenkyū*, 10, pp. 63–71.

—1984b. "Gomitsu to sono tenkan genri wo megutte," *Buzan gakuhō*, 28–29, pp. 19–45.

—1984c. "*Sokushin jōbutsugi* ni mirareru gengokan no shiza," *Mikkyo bunka*, 150, pp. 74–93.

Hori Ichirō. 1978. "Wagakuni gakusō kyōiku seido," in Hori Ichirō, *Gakusō to gakusō kyōiku* (Hori Ichirō chosakushū, vol. 3). Tokyo: Miraisha, 1978, pp. 547–691.

Ikegami Yoshihiko. 1991. "Introduction: semiotics and culture," in Yoshihiko Ikegami (ed.), *The Empire of Signs: Semiotics Essays on Japanese Culture*. Amsterdam and Philadelphia: John Benjamins, 1991, pp. 1–24.

Inagaki, Hisao. 1994. "The esoteric meaning of 'Amida' by Kakuban: An annotated translation with introduction," *Pacific World*. New Series, Nr. 10, pp. 102–15.

Ishikawa Ken. 1977. *Nihon gakkōshi no kenkyū*. Tokyo: Nihon tosho sentā.

Itō Masatoshi. 2000. *Nihon no chūsei jiin: Wasurerareta jiyū toshi*. Tokyo: Yoshikawa Kōbunkan.

Iyanaga Nobumi. 1981. "Harukanaru shittan moji," *Gendai shiso*, 11/ 9, pp. 121–31.

—1999. "Ḍākiṇī et l'Empereur. Mystique bouddique de la royauté dans le Japon médiéval," *Versus: Quaderni di studi semiotici*, 83/84, pp. 41–111.

—2002. "*Honji suijaku* and the logic of combinatory deities," in Mark Teeuwen and Fabio Rambelli (eds), *Buddhas and Kami in Japan*. London and New York: Routledge Curzon, pp. 145–76.

—2002, 2003. "Tantrism and reactionary ideologies in Eastern Asia: Some hypothesis and questions," *Cahiers d'Extrême-Asie*, 13, pp. 1–33.
Kajiyama Yūichi. 1983. *Kū no shisō: Bukkyō ni okeru kotoba to chinmoku*. Kyoto: Jinbun Shoin.
Kamata Tōji. 1989. "Shinpi taiken to gengo. Yakōbu Bēme [Jokob Boehme] to Kūkai no hikaku shisōronteki kōsatsu", *Kokugakuin Daigaku yōji senmon gakkō kiyō*, 3, pp. 117–71.
Kamei Sōchū. 1942. "Kōgyō Daishi no kyōshugi," *Mikkyō ronsō*, 22/23, pp. 27–59.
Kanbayashi Ryūjō. 1931. "Hajigoku sanshu shichiji-hō kaidai," in *Kokuyaku issaikyō: Mikkyōbu*, vol. 3. Tōkyō: Daitō shuppansha, pp. 80–94.
Katō Seiichi. 1978. "Kōbō Daishi to Kōgyō Daishi no busshinkan," *Buzan kyōgaku taikai kiyō*, 6, pp. 41–7.
Kawamura Minato. 1990. *Kotodama to takai*. Tokyo: Kōdansha.
Ketelaar, James. 1990. *Of Heretics and Martyrs in Meiji Japan*. Princeton: Princeton University Press.
Kikuchi Hitoshi. 1997. "Kuden, hiden, kikigaki: chūshaku to iu media," in Mitani Kuniaki and Komine Kazuaki (eds), *Chūsei no chi to gaku: Chūshaku wo yomu*. Tokyo: Shinwasha, 1997, pp. 271–95.
Klein, Susan Blakeley. 2002. *Allegories of Desire: Esoteric Literary Commentaries of Medieval Japan*. Cambridge, MA.: Harvard University Asia Center.
Komatsu Kazuhiko. 1988. *Nihon no noroi*. Tokyo: Kōbunsha.
Komatsu Kazuhiko and Naitō Masatoshi. 1985. *Oni ga tsukutta kuni—Nihon*. Tokyo: Kōbunsha.
Konishi Jin'ichi. 1986. *A History of Japanese Literature*. Volume Two: The Early Middle Ages. Princeton: Princeton University Press.
Kripke, Saul. 1980 [1971]. *Naming and Necessity*. Oxford: Blackwell.
Kunjunni Raja. 1963. *Indian Theories of Meaning*. Madras: Adyar Library and Research Centre.
Kuriyama Shūjun. 1973. "Kōgyō Daishi no *Gorin kujimyō himitsushaku* to chūsei Nihon bunka ni okeru gozōkan shisō: *Ryōjin hishō no kudenshū* to *Kissa yōjōki* wo chūshin to shite," in Kushida Ryōkō hakushi shōju kinenkai (eds), *Kōsōden no kenkyū*. Tōkyō: Sankibō busshorin, 1973, pp. 241–52.
Kuroda Toshio. 1975. *Nihon chūsei no kokka to shukyō*. Tokyo: Iwanami shoten.
—1980. *Jisha seiryoku: Mō hitotsu no chūsei shakai*. Tokyo: Iwanami shoten.
—1989. "Historical consciousness and hon-jaku philosophy in the medieval period on Mount Hiei," in George J. Tanabe, Jr., and Willa Jane Tanabe (eds), *The Lotus Sutra in Japanese Culture*. Honolulu: University of Hawai'i Press, pp. 143–58.
—1996. "The discourse on the 'Land of Kami' (*shinkoku*) in medieval Japan," *Japanese Journal of Religious Studies*, 23/3–4, pp. 353–85.
Kushida Ryōkō. 1964. *Shingon mikkyō seiritsu katei no kenkyū*. Tokyo: Sankibō busshorin.
—1979. *Zoku Shingon mikkyō seiritsu kaitei no kenkyū*. Tokyo: Sankibō busshorin.
Laclau, Ernesto and Chantal Mouffe. 1985. *Hegemony and Socialist Strategy*. London and New York: Verso.
LaFleur, William R. 1983. *The Karma of Words: Buddhism and Literary Arts in Medieval Japan*. Berkeley: University of California Press.

Lamotte, Etienne. 1988. "The assessment of textual interpretation in Buddhism," in Donald Lopez, Jr. (ed.), *Buddhist Hermeneutics*. Honolulu: University of Hawai'i Press, pp. 11–27.

Lincoln, Bruce. 1991. *Death, War, and Sacrifice*. Chicago and London: University of Chicago Press.

Lopez, Donald S., Jr. 1990. "Inscribing the bodhisattva's speech: On the *Heart Sūtra*'s mantra," *History of Religions*, 29/4, pp. 351–72.

—1995. "Introduction," in Donald Lopez, Jr. (ed.), *Curators of the Buddha: Buddhism in the Age of Colonialism*. Chicago and London: Chicago University Press, pp. 1–29.

—1996. *Elaborations on Emptiness: Uses of the Heart Sūtra*. Princeton: Princeton University Press.

Lotman, Yuri. 1990. *Universe of Mind: A Semiotic Theory of Culture*. Bloomington: Indiana University Press.

Lotman, Jurij [Yuri] M. and Boris A. Uspenskij. 1995 [1973]. *Tipologia della cultura*. Milan: Bompiani.

Lusthaus, Dan. 2002. *Buddhist Phenomenology: A Philosophical Investigation of Yogācāra Buddhism and the Ch'eng Wei-shih Lun*. London and New York: RoutledgeCurzon.

Mabuchi Kazuo. 1993. *Gojūonzu no hanashi*. Tokyo: Daishūkan.

Magliola, Robert. 1984. *Derrida on the Mend*. West Lafayette, IN: Purdue University Press.

Matsukubo Shūin. 2001. *Yuishiki shohō*. Tokyo: Suzuki shuppan.

Matsunaga Yūkei. 1978. "Sanshu shichiji to hajigoku," *Mikkyō bunka*, 121, pp. 1–13.

Matsunaga Yūken. 1929. "Sanshu shichiji hajigiku giki no kenkyū," *Mikkyō kenkyū*, 35, pp. 1–18.

Matsuzaki Keisui. 1962. "Kōgyō Daishi no busshinkan," *Indogaku bukkyōgaku kenkyū*, 10/2, pp. 637–9.

—1986. "*Shishu mandaragi* ni tuite," *Taishō Daigaku kenkyū kiyō* (Bukkyōgakubu bungakubu), 72, pp. 82–3 (79–90).

Matte Blanco, Ignacio. 1975. *The Unconscious as Infinite Sets*. London: Duckworth.

Maturana, Humberto and Francisco J. Varela. 1987. *The Tree of Knowledge*. Boston: Shambhala.

Merrell, Floyd. 1991. *Signs Becoming Signs: Our Perfusive, Pervasive Universe*. Bloomington: Indiana University Press.

Miller, Roy A. 1977. "The 'spirit' of Japanese language," *Journal of Japanese Studies*, 3/2, pp. 251–98.

—1982. *Japan's Modern Myth. The Language and Beyond*. New York and Tokyo: Weatherhill.

Misaki Gisen. 1999. *Shikanteki biishiki no tenkai: Chūsei geidō to hongaku shisō to no kanren*. Tokyo: Perikansha.

Misaki Ryōshū. 1988. *Taimitsu no kenkyū*. Tokyo: Sōbunsha.

Miyasaka Yūshō. 1976. "Kūkai no gengo tetsugaku," *Episutēmē*, n. 2.

—1979. *Mikkyō shisō no shinri*. Kyoto: Jinbun shoin.

Miyasaka Yūshō and Umehara Takeshi. 1968. *Seimei no umi: Kūkai* (Bukkyō no shisō 9). Tokyo: Kadokawa shoten.

Miyoshi, Masao and H. D. Harootunian. 1989. "Introduction," in Masao Miyoshi and H. D. Harootunian (eds), *Postmodernism and Japan*. Durham and London: Duke University Press, pp. vii–xix.

Miyoshi, Masao and H. D. Harootunian (eds). 1989. *Postmodernism and Japan.* Durham and London: Duke University Press.

Mizuhara Gyōei. 1981 [1923]. *Jakyō Tachikawaryū no kenkyū.* In *Mizuhara Gyōei zenshū,* vol. 1. Kyōto: Dōhōsha.

Monier-Williams, Monier. 1986. *Sanskrit English Dictionary.* New Delhi: Marwah Publ. (new edition).

Morimoto Kazuo. 1976. "Kūkai to Derida [Derrida] no gengo shisō," *Episutēmē,* n. 2, pp. 126–45.

Morin, Edgar. 1986. *La methode 3: La connaissance de la connaissance 1.* Paris: Seuil.

Murakami Yasutoshi. 2003. *Kūkai no "kotoba" no sekai.* Osaka: Tōhō shuppan.

Murasaki Shikibu. 1978. *The Tale of Genji.* New York: Knopf.

Murphy, Regan E. 2009. "Esoteric Buddhist theories of language in early Kokugaku," *Japanese Journal of Religious Studies,* 36/1, pp. 65–91.

Murti, T. R. V. 1987 [1955]. *The Central Philosophy of Buddhism.* London: Unwin.

Mus, Paul. 1935]. *Barabuḍur: Esquisse d'une histoire du bouddhisme fondée sure la critique archéologique des textes.* 2 vols. Hanoi: Imprimerie d'Extrême Orient.

Nagamura Makoto. 1988. "'Shingonshū' to Tōdaiji: Kamakura kōki no honmatsu sōron wo tōshite," in Jiinshi kenkyūkai (eds), *Jiinshi no kenkyū,* vol. 2. Kyoto: Hōzōkan, 1988.

Najita Tetsuo. 1989. "On culture and technology in postmodern Japan," in Masao Miyoshi and H. D. Harootunian (eds), *Postmodernism and Japan.* Durham and London: Duke University Press, pp. 3–20.

Nakamura Kyōko. 1967. *Ryōi no sekai: Nihon ryōiki* (Nihon no bukkyō 2). Tōkyō: Chikuma shobō.

Nakamura Kyōko Motomachi. 1973. *Miraculous Stories from the Buddhist Tradition: The Nihon Ryōiki of the Monk Kyōkai.* Cambridge, MA.: Harvard University Press.

Naoki Sakai. 1989. "Modernity and its critique: The problem of universalism and particularism," in Masao Miyoshi and H. D. Harootunian (eds), *Postmodernism and Japan.* Durham and London: Duke University Press, pp. 93–122.

—1991. *Voices of the Past: The Status of Language in Eighteenth-Century Japanese Discourse.* Ithaca and London: Cornell University Press.

Nasu Seiryū. 1954. "Sanshu shichiji hajigoku giki no kenkyū," in Hanayama Shinshō *et al.* (eds), *Indogaku bukkyōgaku ronshū: Miyamoto Shōson kyōju henreki kinen ronbunshū.* Tōkyō: Sanseidō.

—1970 [1936]. *Gorin kuji hishaku no kenkyū.* Tokyo: Rokuyaon.

Neven, Armand. 1984–85. "Le mandala dans le domaine hindou," *Cahiers internationaux de symbolisme,* 48–49–50, pp. 9–15.

Nippon Gakujutsu Shinkokai (eds), 1965. *Manyoshu: The Nippon Gakujutsu Shinkokai Translation of One Thousand Poems, with the texts in Romaji.* New York: Columbia University Press.

Nosco, Peter. 1990. *Remembering Paradise: Nativism and Nostalgia in Eighteenth-Century Japan.* Cambridge, MA.: Council on East Asian Studies, Harvard University.

Ōe Kenzaburō. 1995. *Japan, the Ambiguous, and Myself. The Nobel Prize Speech and Other Lectures.* Tokyo, New York and London: Kodansha International.

Ōe Kenzaburō, Nakamura Yūjirō, and Yamaguchi Masao (eds). 1980–2. *Bunka no genzai*. 8 vols. Tokyo: Iwanami shoten.

Ogata Hiroyasu. 1980. *Nihon kyōiku tsūshi kenkyū*. Tokyo: Waseda Daigaku shuppanbu.

Ogawa Toyoo. 1997. "Chūsei shinwa no mechie: hensei suru Nihongi to *Reikiki* 'Amefuda no maki,'" in Mitani Kuniaki and Komine Kazuaki (eds), *Chūsei no chi to gaku: Chūshaku wo yomu*. Tokyo: Shinwasha, pp. 143–78.

Ohnuki-Tierney, Emiko. 1993. *Rice as Self: Japanese Identities through Time*. Princeton: Princeton University Press.

Onozuka Kichō. 1967. "*Shōji jissōgi* ni mirareru Kūkai no shūkyō: hosshin seppō ni tsuite," *Taishō Daigaku kenkyū kiyō*, 52, pp. 85–90.

Orzech, Charles D. 1989. "Seeing Chen-Yen Buddhism: Traditional scholarship and the Vajrayāna in China," *History of Religions*, 29/2, pp. 87–114.

—(trans.). 1995. "The legend of the Iron Stūpa," in Donal S. Lopez, Jr. (ed.), *Buddhism in Practice*. Princeton: Princeton University Press, pp. 314–17.

—2002–3. "Metaphor, translation, and the construction of kingship in the *Sūtra for Humane Kings* and the *Mahāmāyūrīvidyārājñī Sūtra*," *Cahiers d'Extrême-Asie*, 13, pp. 101–29.

Orzech, Charles D., Henrik H. Sørensen, and Richard K. Payne (eds) 2011. *Esoteric Buddhism and the Tantras in East Asia*. Leiden and Boston: Brill.

Osabe Kazuo. 1971. *Tōdai mikkyōshi zakkō*. Kōbe: Kōbe Shōka Daigaku gakujutsu kenkyūkai.

Ōyama Kōjun. 1920. "Kōso no shōji jissōron," *Misshū gakuhō*, 81, pp. 130–40.

Padoux, André. 1990.*Vāc. The Concept of the Word In Selected Hindu Tantras*. Albany, NY: State University of New York Press.

Pasolini, Pier Paolo. 1988 [1974]. *Heretical Empiricism*. Bloomington and Indianapolis: Indiana University Press.

Payne, Richard. 1998a. *Language Conducive to Awakening: Categories of Language Used in East Asian Buddhism*. Munich: Iudicium.

—1998b. "*Ajikan*: Ritual and Meditation in the Dhingon Tradition," in Richard K. Payne (ed.), *Re-Visioning "Kamakura" Buddhism*. Honolulu: University of Hawai'i Press, pp. 219–48.

—2006. "Awakening and language: Indic theory of language in the background of Japanese Esoteric Buddhism," in Richard K. Payne and Taigen Dan Leighton (eds), *Discourse and Ideology in Medieval Japanese Buddhism*. London and New York: Routledge, pp. 79–96.

Piatigorsky, Alexander. 1984. *The Buddhist Philosophy of Thought: Essays in Interpretation*. London: Curzon Press.

Piatigorsky, Alexander and D. B. Zilberman. 1976. "The emergence of semiotics in India," *Semiotica*, 17/3, pp. 255–65.

Plutschow, H. E. 1990. *Chaos and Cosmos: Ritual in Early and Medieval Japanese Literature*. Leiden: Brill.

Pollack, David. 1986. *The Fracture of Meaning: Japan's Synthesis of China from the Eighth through the Eighteenth Centuries*. Princeton: Princeton University Press.

Rambach, Pierre. 1979. *The Secret Message of Tantric Buddhism*. Geneva: Skira and New York: Rizzoli International.

Rambelli, Fabio. 1989. "Il gioco linguistico esoterico. Per una teoria del linguaggio del buddhismo giapponese Shingon," *Versus. Quaderni di studi semiotici*, 54, pp. 69–96.

—1990."Il potere karmico della parola. Elementi per lo studio della concezione del linguaggio nel *Nihon ryōiki*," *Annali di Ca' Foscari*, 29/3, pp. 271–89.
—1991."Re-inscribing *maṇḍala*: Semiotic operations on a word and its object," *Studies in Central and East Asian Religions*, 4, pp. 1–24.
—1992."Segni di diamante. Aspetti semiotici del buddhismo esoterico giapponese di Kakuban," 2 vols. Ph.D. diss., University of Venice.
—1993. "'Piante e alberi diventano buddha.' La natura nel paradigma tendai," in Fosco Maraini (ed.), *I giapponesi e la natura. Atti del XVI convegno di studi dell'Associazione italiana per gli studi giapponesi*. Florence: Associazione italiana per gli studi giapponesi, pp. 191–209.
—1994a. "The semiotic articulation of *hosshin seppō*," in Ian Astley (ed.), *Esoteric Buddhism in Japan*. Copenhagen: Seminar for Buddhist Studies, pp. 17–36.
—1994b. "True words, silence, and the adamantine dance," *Japanese Journal of Religious Studies*, 21/4, pp. 373–405.
—1996. "Religion, ideology of domination, and nationalism," *Japanese Journal of Religious Studies*, 23/3–4, pp. 387–426.
—1999. "The empire and the signs: Semiotics, ideology, and cultural identity in Japanese history," *Versus. Quaderni di studi semiotici*, 83/84, pp. 15–40.
—1999–2003. "Buddhist Semiotics" (http://projects.chass.utoronto.ca/semiotics/cyber/cyber.html). Last accessed on October 22, 2012.
—2000. "Tantric Buddhism and Chinese thought in East Asia," in David Gordon White (ed.), *Tantra in Practice*. Princeton: Princeton University Press, 2000, pp. 361–80.
—2002a. "The ritual world of Buddhist 'Shintō': The *Reikiki* and initiations on kami-related matters (*jingi kanjō*) in late medieval and early-modern Japan," *Japanese Journal of Religious Studies*, 29/3–4, pp. 265–97.
—2002b. "In search of the Buddha's intention: Raiyu and the world of medieval Shingon learned monks," in Sanpa gōdō kinen ronshū henshū iinkai (eds), *Shingi Shingon kyōgaku no kenkyū: Raiyu Sōjō nanahyakunen goenki kinen ronshū*. Tokyo: Daizō shuppan, 2002, pp. 1208–36.
—2002–2003. "The emperor's new robes: Processes of resignification in Shingon imperial rituals," *Cahiers d'Extrême-Asie*, n. 13, pp. 427–453.
—2003. "The discourse on Japan's sacredness (*shinkoku shisō*) as religious marketing," *Rikkyo Institute of Japanese Studies Annual Report*, 2, pp. 28–55.
—2004. "'Just behave as you like; prohibitions and impurities are not a problem': Radical Amida cults and popular religiosity in premodern Japan," in Richard K. Payne and Kenneth K. Tanaka (eds), *Approaching the Land of Bliss: Religious Praxis in the Cult of Amitābha*. Honolulu: University of Hawai'i Press, pp. 169–201.
—2006. "Secrecy in Japanese Esoteric Buddhism," in Bernhard Scheid and Mark Teeuwen (eds), *The Culture of Secrecy in Japanese Religion*. New York and London: Routledge, pp. 107–29.
—2007. *Buddhist Materiality: A Cultural History of Objects in Japanese Buddhism*. Stanford: Stanford University Press.
—2008. "I segni del sacro nel buddhismo," in Nicola Dusi e Gianfranco Marrone (eds), *Destini del sacro: discorso religioso e semiotica della cultura*. Roma: Meltemi, 2008, pp. 323–33.
Rambelli, Fabio and Eric Reinders. 2012. *Buddhism and Iconoclasm in East Asia: A History*. London and New York: Bloomsbury.

Reider, Noriko T. 2009a. "Animating objects: *Tsukumogami ki* and the medieval illustration of Shingon truth," *Japanese Journal of Religious Studies*, 36/2, pp. 231–57.
—(trans.) 2009b. "*Tsukumogami ki* (The Record of Tool Specters)," *Japanese Journal of Religious Studies* [Online-only supplement, pp. 1–19], nirc.nanzan-u.ac.jp/publications/jjrs/pdf/819a.pdf. Last accessed on October 22, 2012.
Sadakata Akira. 1997. *Buddhist Cosmology: Philosophy and Origins*. Tokyo: Kosei Publishing Company.
Saigō Nobutsuna. 1993 [1972]. *Kodaijin to yume*. Tokyo: Heibonsha.
Saitō Akitoshi. 1978. *Nihon bukkyō kyōikushi kenkyū*. Tokyo: Kokusho kankōkai.
Sanford, James H. 1994. "Breath of life: The Esoteric Nenbutsu," in Ian Astley (ed.), *Esoteric Buddhism in Japan*. Copenhagen and Aarhus: Seminar for Buddhist Studies, pp. 65–98.
—1997. "Wind, Waters, Stupas, Mandalas. Fetal Buddhahood in Shingon," *Japanese Journal of Religious Studies*, 24/1–2, pp. 1–38.
—2009. "Shinran's secret transmission to Nyoshin: The *Hōri Hachiman chō*," in Richard K. Payne and Roger Corless (eds), *Path of No Path: Contemporary Studies on Pure Land Buddhism Honoring Roger Corless*. Berkeley: Numata Center for Buddhist Translation and Research, pp. 57–76.
Sasaki Kaoru. 1988. *Chūsei kokka no shūkyō kōzō: Taisei bukkyō to taiseigai bukkyō no sōkoku*. Tokyo: Yoshikawa Kōbunkan.
Sasaki Kōkan. 1987. "Sō no jushika to ō no saishika: Bukkyō to ōsei to no musubitsuki ni kansuru ichi-shiron," in Kuroda Toshio (ed.), *Kokka to tennō: Tennōsei ideorogī to shite no bukkyō* (Series Bukkyō to nihonjin 2). Tokyo: Shunjūsha, pp. 49–91.
Satō Hiroo. 1987. *Nihon chūsei no kokka to bukkyō*. Tokyo: Yoshikawa Kōbunkan.
—2003. "Wrathful deities and saving deities," in Mark Teeuwen and Fabio Rambelli (eds), *Buddha and Kami in Japan*. London and New York: Routledge Curzon, pp. 95–114.
—2006. *Shinkoku Nihon*. Tokyo: Chikuma shobō.
Satō Ryūken. 1981. "Shingon ni tsuite," in Katsumata Shunkyō hakase koki kinen ronshū henshū iinkai (eds), *Daijō bukkyō kara mikkyō e*. Tokyo: Shunjūsha, pp. 899–911.
Schopenhauer, Arthur. 2007. *Il mio oriente*. Milan: Adelphi.
Searle, John S. 1969. *Speech Acts*. Cambridge: Cambridge University Press.
Seckel, Dietrich. 2007. *Before and Beyond the Image: Aniconic Symbolism in Buddhist Art* (Artibus Asiae Supplementum 45). Zurich: Rietberg Museum.
Serres, Michel. 1977. *Hermès IV. La distribution*. Paris: Minuit.
Sharf, Robert H. 1995a. "The Zen of Japanese nationalism," in Donald S. Lopez, Jr. (ed.), *Curators of the Buddha: The Study of Buddhism under Colonialism*. Chicago and London: University of Chicago Press, pp. 107–60.
—1995b. "Buddhist modernism and the rhetoric of meditative experience," *Numen*, 42, pp. 228–83.
—1999. "On the allure of Buddhist relics," *Representations*, 66, pp. 75–99.
—2001. "Visualization and mandala in Shingon Buddhism," in Robert H. Sharf and Elizabeth Horton Sharf (eds), *Living Images: Japanese Buddhist Icons in Context*. Stanford: Stanford University Press, pp. 151–97.

Shinmura Izuru, ed., *Kōjien*. Tōkyō: Iwanami, 1983 (3rd edition).
Snodgrass, Adrian. 1985. *The Symbolism of the Stupa*. Ithaca, NY: Southeast Asia Program, Cornell University.
Spiro, Melford E. 1982. *Buddhism and Society: A Great Tradition and Its Burmese Vicissitudes*. Berkeley: University of California Press.
Staal, Frits. 1979a. "The meaninglessness of ritual," *Numen*, 26/1, pp. 2–22.
—1979b. "Oriental ideas on the origin of language," *Journal of the American Oriental Society*, 99/1, pp. 1–14.
—1985. "Mantras and bird songs," *Journal of the American Oriental Society*, 105/3, pp. 549–58.
—1986. "The sound of religion (2)," *Numen*, 33/2, pp. 185–224.
—1988. *Rules without Meaning: Essays on Ritual, Mantras and the Science of Man*. New York: Peter Lang.
—1989. "Vedic Mantras," In Harvey Alper (ed.), *Mantra*. Albany, NY: State University of New York Press, pp. 48–95.
Stevens, John. 1990. "Holy smoke: Siddham inscriptions on incense burners," *Studies in Central and East Asian Religions*, 3, pp. 95–100.
Stone, Jacqueline. 1999. *Original Enlightenment and the Transformation of Medieval Japanese Buddhism*. Honolulu: University of Hawai'i Press.
—2006a. "'Not mere written words': Perspectives on the language of the *Lotus Sūtra* in medieval Japan," in Richard K. Payne and Taigen Dan Leighton (eds), *Discourse and Ideology in Medieval Japanese Buddhism*. London and New York: Routledge, pp. 160–94.
—2006b. "Just open your mouth and say 'A': A-syllable practice for the time of death in early medieval Japan," *Pacific World Journal*, Third Series, N. 8, pp. 167–89.
Strickmann, Michel. 1996. *Mantras et mandarins: Le bouddhisme tantrique en Chine*. Paris: Gallimard.
—2002. *Chinese Magical Medicine*. Stanford: Stanford University Press.
—2005. *Chinese Poetry and Prophecy: The Written Oracle in East Asia*. Stanford: Stanford University Press.
Sueki Fumihiko. 1996. "A reexamination of the *kenmitsu taisei* theory," *Japanese Journal of Religious Studies*, 23/3–4, pp. 449–66.
Suzuki, D.T. (Daisetz Teitarō), (ed.) 1932. *The Lankavatara Sutra*. London: Routledge.
—1927–1934. *Essays in Zen Buddhism*. 3 vols. London: Luzac.
—1972 [1944]. *Japanese Spirituality*. Tokyo: Japan Society for the Promotion of Science and Japanese Ministry of Education.
—1996 [1956]. *Zen Buddhism: Selected Writings of D.T. Suzuki*. New York: Doubleday.
Swearer, Donald K. 2004. *Becoming the Buddha*. Princeton: Princeton University Press.
Taira Masayuki. 1991. *Nihon chūsei no shakai to bukkyō*. Tokyo: Hanawa shobō.
—1996. "Kuroda Toshio and the kenmitsu taisei theory," *Japanese Journal of Religious Studies*, 23/3–4, pp. 427–48.
Tajima Ryūjun. 1959. *Les deux grands mandalas et la doctrine de l'ésotérisme shingon*. Tokyo: Maison Franco-Japonaise; Paris: Presses Universitaires de France.
Takakusu Junjirō. 1975 [1947]. *The Essentials of Buddhist Philosophy*. New Delhi: Oriental Books Reprint Corp.

Takemura Makio. 1985. *Yuishiki no kōzō*.Tokyo: Shunjūsha.
—2001. *Yuishiki no kokoro*. Tokyo: Shunjūsha.
Taki Kōji. 1988. *Tennō no shōzō*. Tokyo: Iwanami shoten.
Takubo Shūyo. 1944. *Hihan shittangaku*. 2 vols. Tokyo: Shingonshū Tōkyō Senju Gakuin.
Takubo Shūyo and Kanayama Shōkō. 1981. *Bonji shittan*. Tokyo: Hirakawa shuppansha.
Tamaki Kōshirō. 1982. "Kūkai no shisō no kadai," *Risō*, 11, pp. 2–24.
—1983. "Kegonkyō ni okeru butsudakan," in Hirakawa Akira and Kajiyama Yūichi Takasaki Jikidō (eds), *Kegon shisō* (Kōza Daijō bukkyō, vol. 3). Tokyo: Shunjūsha, pp. 170–2.
Tambiah, Stanley J. 1968. "The Magical Power of Words," *Man*, New Series, 3/2, pp. 175–208.
—1970. *Buddhism and the Spirit Cults in North-East Thailand*. Cambridge: Cambridge University Press.
—1976. *World Conqueror and World Renouncer: A Study of Buddhism and Polity in Thailand Against a Historical Background*. Cambridge and New York: Cambridge University Press.
Tanabe, George J., Jr. 1992. *Myōe the Dreamkeeper*. Cambridge, MA.: Harvard University Press.
Tanaka Chiaki. 1964. "*Shōjigi* no yōshi," *Mikkyō bunka*, 69–70, pp. 98–103.
—1967. "*Shōji jissōgi* kōwa," *Mikkyō bunka*, 81, p. 1–8.
Tanaka Takako. 1999. *Muromachi obōsan monogatari*. Tokyo: Kōdansha.
Toganoo Shōun. 1982a [1927]. *Mandara no kenkyū* (Toganoo Shōun zenshū, vol. 4). Kyoto: Rinsen shoten.
—1982b [1942]. *Nihon mikkyō gakudōshi* (Toganoo Shōun zenshū, vol. 6). Kyoto: Rinsen shoten.
Tōji hōmotsukan, (ed.) 1990. *Mandala. Mihotoketachi no gunzō: Tōji no mandara-zu. (The Universe of Mandala: Buddhist Divinities in Shingon Esoteric Buddhism)*. Kyoto: Tōji hōmotsukan.
Tokunaga Muneo. 1984. "Koe to moji matawa ekurichūru," *Hikaku bunka zasshi*, 2, pp. 36–51.
Tomita Masahiro. 1988. "Kanchiin Shūhō no shōgai ni miru kyōgaku to jiyaku: Chūsei Tōji ni okeru inke to jike," in Jiinshi kenkyūkai (eds), *Jiinshi no kenkyū*, vol. 2. Kyoto: Hōzōkan, pp. 305–92.
Toyoda Kunio. 1980. *Nihonjin no kotodama shisō*. Tokyo: Kōdansha.
Tsuda Shin'ichi. 1977. "Tantora bukkyō ni okeru yōga no ronri," *Risō*, 535, pp. 123–43.
—1978. "A critical Tantrism," *The Memoirs of the Toyo Bunko*, 36, pp. 167–231.
—1981."Mikkyō kenkyū no hōkō: Mikkyō shisō no hihanteki rikai wo mezashite, *Tōyō gakujutsu kenkyū*, 20/1, pp. 117–36.
—1982. "Nihon ni okeru mikkyō no kikiteki tenkai: Kūkai kara Kakuban e," in Tamura Yoshirō Hakase henreki kinenkai (eds), *Bukkyō kyōri no kenkyū*. Tokyo: Shunjūsha, pp. 387–408.
—1985."The hermeneutics of Kūkai," *Acta Asiatica*, 47, pp. 82–108.
Tsunoda Ryūsaku, W. Theodore de Bary, Donal Keene (eds). 1958. *Sources of Japanese Tradition*. 2 vols. New York: Columbia University Press.
Tsunoda Tadanobu. 1985. *The Japanese Brain: Uniqueness and Universality*. Tokyo: Taishukan.

Tucci, Giuseppe. 2001 [1949]. *Theory and Practice of Mandala*. Mineola, NY: Dover Publications.
Ui Hakuju. 1919. *Bukkyō hanron*. Tokyo: Iwanami shoten.
Ujike Kakushō. 1984. *Darani no sekai*. Osaka: Tōhō shuppan.
—1987. *Darani shisō no kenkyū*. Osaka: Tōhō shuppan.
Unno, Mark T. 1998. "Recommending faith in the sand of the mantra of light," in Richard K. Payne (ed.), *Re-Visioning "Kamakura" Buddhism*. Honolulu: University of Hawai'i Press, pp. 167–218.
Urban, Hugh B. 2003. *Tantra: Sex, Secrecy, Politics, and Power in the Study of Religion*. Berkeley: University of California Press.
Vandermeersch, Léon. 1982 [1974]. "Dalla tartaruga all'achillea (Cina)," in Jean-Pierre Vernant (ed.), *Divinazione e razionalità*. Turin, Einaudi.
Varela, Francisco J., Evan Thompson, and Eleanor Rosch. *The Embodied Mind: Cognitive Science and Human Experience*. Cambridge, MA: MIT Press, 1991.
Violi, Patrizia. 1992. "Le molte enciclopedie," in Patrizia Magli *et al.* (eds), *Semiotica: storia, teoria, interpretazione. Saggi intorno a Umberto Eco*. Milano: Bompiani, pp. 99–113.
—1999. "A semiotics of non-ordinary experience: The case of Japanese culture," *Versus: Quaderni di studi semiotici*, 83/84, 1999, pp. 243–80.
Waley, Arthur (trans.). 1970. *The Tale of Genji*. 2 vols. Tokyo: Tuttle.
Wang Youxuan. 2001. *Buddhism and Deconstruction: Toward a Comparative Semiotics*. New York: Routledge.
Watson, Burton. 1997. *The Sutra of Vimalakirti*. New York: Columbia University Press.
Watt, Paul B. 1984. "Jiun Sonja (1718–1804): A response to Confucianism within the context of Buddhist reform," in Peter Nosco (ed.), *Confucianism in Tokugawa Culture*. Princeton: Princeton University Press, pp. 188–214.
Watts, Alan. 1936. *The Spirit of Zen: A Way of Life, Work, and Art in the Far East*. London: J. Murray.
Wheelock, Wade T. 1989. "The mantra in Vedic and Tantric ritual," in Harvey Alper (ed.), *Mantra*. Albany, NY: State University of New York Press, pp. 96–122.
White, David Gordon (ed.) 2000. *Tantra in Practice*. Princeton: Princeton University Press.
—2006. *Kiss of the Yogini: "Tantric Sex" in Its South Asian Context*. Chicago and London: University of Chicago Press.
Yamamoto Hiroko. 1993. *Henjōfu*. Tokyo: Shunjūsha.
—1998. *Chūsei shinwa*. Tokyo: Iwanami shoten.
Yamaori Tetsuo. 1983. "Mikkyō ni okeru naizō ninshiki: Indo to Nihon no aida," *Gendai shisō*, 11/9, pp. 114–20.
Yamasaki Taikō. 1988. *Shingon: Japanese Esoteric Buddhism*. Boston: Shambhala.
Yamazaki Makoto. 1993. "Gakuryo to gakumon," in Honda Yoshinori et al. (eds), *Setsuwa no ba: dōshō, chūshaku* (Setsuwa no Kōza 3). Tokyo: Benseisha, pp. 85–111.
Yamazaki Seiichi. 1977. *Gengo to satori. Shutaisei no tetsugaku no hakai to saiken*. Tokyo: Asahi shuppansha.
Yelle, Robert A. 2003. *Explaining Mantras*. New York and London: Routledge.
Yokoyama Kōichi. 1986. *Yuishiki to wa nani ka*. Tokyo: Shunjūsha.

—1996. *Yuishiki: Wagagokoro no kōzō*. Tokyo: Shunjūsha.
Yukawa Hideki. 1967. "Modern trend of Western civilisation and cultural peculiarities of Japan," in CA. Moore (ed.), *The Japanese Mind: Essentials of Japanese Philosophy and Culture*. Honolulu: University of Hawai'i Press, pp. 52–65.
Žižek, Slavoj. 1989. *The Sublime Object of Ideology*. London and New York: Verso.
—1991. *For They Know not What They Do*. London and New York: Verso.
—1997. *The Plague of Fantasies*. London and New York: Verso.

INDEX

A (Jp. *aji*, first Sanskrit letter and mantric seed) 14, 46–7, 49–50, 88, 89, 101, 109, 133, 139–40, 160
A letter visualization (Jp. *ajikan*) 89, 161
Abankai mandara ryakushaku 212
Abe Masao 181
Abé Ryūichi xvi, 47, 86
Abhidharma xiii, 15, 79
a bi ra un ken see five-syllable mantra
absolute knowledge (Sk. *prajñā*) 18 *see also Bodhi*
Achu rulai niansong gongyang fa 215
afflictions (or defilements, Sk. *kleśa*, Jp. *bonnō*) 20, 23, 92, 135, 141
Aizen'ō kōshiki 215
Ajikan ju 215
Akaniṣṭha Heaven *see* Dharma Realm Palace
ālaya-vijñāna, (Jp. *arayashiki*) *see* store consciousness
alloforms 12, 14–15, 54–5, 144
Alper, Harvey 88, 93
amala-vijñāna (Jp. *amarashiki*) *see* pure consciousness
Amida, Buddha 17, 148–51, 165, 181
Amida hishaku 113–15, 213, 217
Amino Yoshihiko 221
Amoghavajra (Ch. Bukong, Jp. Fukū; 705–74), Tantric master 13, 139
amulets 17, 89, 158, 208
ancestor tablets 58
aniconism 11, 200
Annen (841–895? or 915?) 48, 97, 103
Asaṇga (fourth century CE) 19, 91
atoms (Jp. *mijin*) xvii, 38
A un 89, 133–6
Austin, John 86–7, 156–8
"B." ("Brahma"), pantheistic entity 41, 153 *see also* pansemioticism; Pasolini
Banjigi 122, 214
Barthes, Roland x, xi, 174, 182, 183, 185, 188, 189, 190–2
Baudrillard, Jean 196
Beatniks x
Ben kenmitsu nikyōron 43, 199, 213
Benzaiten (Sk. Sarasvatī) 162–3
bodhi (enlightenment) 74
bodhi tree 10, 11, 12
bodhicitta (Jp. *bodaishin*, "thought of enlightnment" or "enlightened mind") 26, 139–40, 159, 160, 162
Bodhiruci (d. 527) 49
body 58, 146–8, 161–5, 166–7
and mind 159–65
Bongaku shinryō 97
Bonji (Indic characters) *see Shittan*
Bonji shittan jimo narabini shakugi 97, 111, 200, 212
Bonkan taieishū 48–9
Bonmōkyō kaidai 111
bonnō soku bodai ("afflictions are the enlightenment") xviii, 26, 59
Boon, James xv, 3–4, 55
Brāhma 48
breathing techniques (Jp. *shūsokukan*) 89, 133–6, 165
Bucknell, Roderick 71
Buddha's intention (Jp. *butsui*) 31–3, 103
Buddha Word Sutra (Ch. *Fo yu jing*) 82–3, 84, 209
Buddha's secret body (made of semiotic systems) 64
Buddhism as cultural system 1–2

and semiotics xi, 197
systems of domination 194–5
Buddhist philosophy of language 8
Bunkyō hifuron 205, 212
Butsuda hō ("Buddha's law," i.e. the principle of inviolability of temple donations) 34
byōdōshōchi ("Wisdom of the undifferentiated nature of all things") *see* five wisdoms

Cangjie 49, 205
Cardona, Giorgio Raimondo 68, 77, 158–9
catroptics (mirror-like consciousness) 25, 74
Certeau, Michel de 4, 7
Chinese language 48–9, 177 *see also* Sanskrit
chingo kokka (rituals for the protection of the state) 5
clues (types of signs) 12
Commentary to the Mahāvairocana Sutra (Ch. *Dari jing shu*, Jp. *Dainichikyōsho*) 44, 105, 160, 201, 204, 208, 210, 216, 217
Confucianism, semiotics and philosophy of language 49
consciousness (Sk. *vijñāna*, Jp. *shiki*) *see* eight consciousnesses
consciousness of original enlightenment (Jp. *hongakushiki*) 27 *see also* eight consciousnesses; original enlightenment
consciousness-only (Sk. *vijñaptimātratā*, Jp. *yuishiki*) *see* Yogācāra
contemplation *see* visualization
correlative systems xvii–xviii, 14–15, 27, 51, 53–9, 65, 99, 121, 141, 145–6, 161–2, 163, 167
Coulianu, Ioan 68, 128
Cratylism 179
cultural identity, Japan 174, 180, 184–90
cultural semiotics xxi, 189–90

Dabanniepan jing see Nirvana Sutra
daienkyōchi ("Wisdom of the great, perfect mirror") *see* five consciousnesses
Dainichi *see* Mahāvairocana
Dainichi no inmon (Mahāvairocana's formula) 174
Dainichikyō kaidai 204, 211
Dainichikyōsho shishin shō 204
Dale, Peter 184, 187, 188
Daoism 56, 98, 146, 176
Dari jing see Mahāvairocana Sutra
Dari jing shu see Commentary to the Mahāvairocana Sutra
Dasheng qixin lun 203
Dazhidu lun 211
Denjushū 136
dhāraṇī (Jp. *darani*) 6, 16, 17, 28, 81, 89, 92–3, 109, 135, 155, 175 *see also* mantra; *Shingon*
dharanic thought 7
repository (Jp. *darani-zō*) 7
Dharma essence (Sk. *dharmatā*, Jp. *hosshō*) 10, 39
Dharma realm *see dharmadhātu*
dharmabhāṇaka see fashi
dharmacakra (Wheel of Dharma) 10, 11, 12
Dharmadhātu (Jp. *hokkai*, universe of the cosmic Buddha Mahāvairocana) xvii, xviii, 3, 13, 25, 27, 33, 37, 39, 53, 55, 58, 67, 101, 122, 162
Dharmadhātu Palace (Dharma Realm Palace, Jp. Hokkaigū) xvii, 57, 67, 130
multiple Dharmadhātu (Jp. *ta hokkai*) 42, 117, 118
singular Dharmadhātu (Jp. *ichi hokkai*) 42, 117
dharmakathika see fashi
dharmakāya (Jp. *hosshin*, absolute and unconditioned body of the Buddha) xvii, xviii, 3, 8, 10, 13–14, 33, 37, 38, 42–6, 50, 69, 90, 101, 105, 138, 163, 203
as *rihosshin* (Dharmakāya as principle) 43
as the source of signs 37
Diamond Sutra (Ch. *Jinggang banruo boluomituo jing*, Jp. *Kongō hannya haramita kyō*) 82

discrimination (dichotomic thinking) (Sk. *vikalpa*, Jp. *funbetsu*) xviii, 19, 25–6, 80
doctrinal dialogues (Jp. *dangi* or *rongi*) 29, 31
Dōhan (1184–1252) 52, 84
Dragon Palace (Jp. *ryūgū*) 49
Duquenne, Robert 95

Eco, Umberto xvi, 12, 41, 57, 68, 69, 74, 87, 95, 101–2
education 28–31, 113
eight consciousnesses (Jp. *hasshiki*) 20, 21–2, 52, 163 *see also* epistemology; mind; Yogācāra
eight kinds of sounds (Jp. *hachion*) 86
Eisai *see* Yōsai
Emperor of Japan 181, 183, 193
Empire of Signs x, 174, 183, 190–2
empowerment (Jp. *kaji*) 44, 45, 118, 126, 131, 147
"empowerment body" (Jp. *kajishin*) 44–45, 47 *see also* dharmakāya, *hosshin seppō*
emptiness (Sk. *śūnyatā*, Jp. *kū*) xiii, 11, 19, 25, 39, 80, 88, 117, 191
engimono (origin narratives) 17
enlightenment (*kakugo*, *bodai*, *tōshōgaku*, *satori*) xi, xii, xviii, xx, 18, 60, 181 *see also* semiotic strategies; soteriology
episteme xxi, 2, 5–6, 32, 75–7, 185
  of identity 35, 54, 55
  of plural identities 35, 55
epistemology 10, 17–27
Esoteric Buddhism (Japanese) or *mikkyō* xv, xvi–xviii, 4–10, 26, 62, 83–4, 102
  as a discursive formation or episteme 2, 5, 31–4, 35, 58, 60, 64, 69, 74, 77, 119, 121, 154, 165, 167–71, 193, 196
  and esotericization of Japan 6, 35–6, 56, 65
  meaning of "Esoteric" xv–xvi, 3
esotericism (Western) xvi, 4, 102
essence or nature (Jp. *shō*) 21
"essential body" (Jp. *honjishin*) 45 *see also* dharmakāya; "empowerment body"
exegesis *see* interpretation
exo-esotericism (*kenmitsu taisei*, *kenmitsushugi*) 5–10, 15, 198
exoteric Buddhism (*kengyō*) 5
expedient means *see* *Upāya*
experience xi, xii
external appearance (Jp. *gyō*) 21

Fan'yu qianzi wen 96
fashi (Buddhist preachers) 92–3
Faure, Bernard xii, 181
five agents (Ch. *wuxing*, Jp. *gogyō*; five material components in Chinese cosmology) 14, 54–5, 58
five aggregates (Sk. *pañca-skandha*, Jp. *goun*) 18
five Buddha bodies (*goshin*) 203
five Buddhas (Jp. *gobutsu*: Sk. Mahāvairocana, Jp. Dainichi; Akśobhya, Ashuku; Ratnasaṃbhava, Hōshō; Amitābha, Amida; Amoghasiddhi, Fukūjōju) 27, 144–5
five directions 27
five musical notes (Jp. *goon*) 86
five elements (constituting the universe) (Jp. *godai*) 14, 37 *see also* six elements
five-syllable mantra: *a va ra ha kha*; *a vaṃ raṃ haṃ khaṃ*; *a vi rah ūṃ khaṃ* (Jp. *a bi ra un ken*) 99, 119, 129, 137–48, 157, 160, 161, 174
five shapes 56
five transformations (lit. "five points" or *goten*, of the letter *A*) 100, 147
five wisdoms (*gochi*) 24–5, 26–7, 162, 163
five-element mandala (Jp. *gorin mandara*) 57, 65, 99, 144–8, 151, 152, 162, 166–7 *see also* five-element *stūpa*; mandala
five-element *stūpa* (Jp. *gorintō*) 57–9, 65, 99, 121, 145, 166–7 *see also* *stūpa*

five-element series 56
Flower Garland Sutra (Sk. *Buddhāvataṃsaka Sūtra*, Ch. *Da fangguang fo huayan jing*, Jp. *Daihōkō butsu kegonkyō*) xiii, 45, 210, 213 *see also* Kegon
Foding zunshengxin po diyu zhuan yezhang chu sanjie mimi sanshen foguo sanzhong xidi shenyan yigui 207, 215
Foucault, Michel 35, 195
four Buddha bodies 56
four kinds of births 56
four saintly beings 56
fourfold mandala (Jp. *shishu mandara*) 32, 45, 56, 64, 99 *see also* mandala; *sōdai*
Fo yu jing see Buddha Word Sutra
Frazer, James George (1854–1941) 155
Fujitani Mitsue (1768–1823) 176
funerary monuments 58, 65, 89, 97
Funjin (splintered or alternative bodies, Sk. *vigraha*) 12 *see* alloforms

Genji monogatari 176
genze riyaku (worldly benefits) 9, 30, 90, 93, 152
genzu mandara 75–6, 208
Genette, Gérard 219
gestures, ritual (Sk. *mudrā*, Jp. *in*) 64
gochi (five kinds of wisdom) 10
gochi gozōtō himitsushō 206
Gōhō (1306–62) 28, 116, 118–19, 160
Gōhō shishō 214
Gómez, Luis 99
gomitsu (secret of speech) 81, 101, 131, 156 *see also sanmitsu*
Go-Uda, retired emperor 28
Gorin kujimyō himitsushaku 56, 57, 59, 65, 138, 139–51, 152, 161, 199, 206, 209, 212, 215, 216, 217
gosō jōshingan 170
Gozō mandara waeshaku 206
Grapard, Allan 35, 36, 54, 55, 200, 201
Grotenhuis, Elizabeth ten 60, 63
Guanzizai pusa xin zhenyan yiyin niansong fa 136–7
Gulik, Robert van (1910–67) 97, 99

ha 109, 110, 111, 112, 116, 142
Hachimanchō no nukigaki: Ajikan no honmi 164–5, 217
haiku (poetry) 190, 191
Ha jigoku giki see Sanzhong xidi po diyu zhuan yezhang chu sanjie mimi tuoluoni fa
Hakeda, Yoshito 43
Hannya shingyō hiken 205
Hannya shingyō hiken ryakuchū 213
Harootunian, H. D. 176, 185
heart 159–61
Heart Sutra (Ch. *Banruo bolomituo xin jing*, Jp. *Hannya shingyō*) 28, 95, 97
Heike monogatari 163, 217
Henmi Sōhan 85
himitsugo ("secret words") 84, 89
Himitsu mandara jūjūshinron 18, 85, 201, 210
Himitsu mandarakyō fuhōden 208
himitsu nenbutsu (Esoteric worship of the Buddha Amida) 17, 164–5
Himitsu shōgon funigishō 208
Hirata Atsutane (1776–1843) 176, 178, 179
Hizō hōyaku 201
Hizō shiki honshō 217
Hjelmslev, Louis 87–8, 95
Hofstadter, Douglas 171
Hōjō Kenzō 85–86
hokkai taishōchi ("Wisdom of the substance-nature of the Dharma realm") *see* five wisdoms
hokkaigū see Dharma Realm Palace
Hokkekyōshaku 106
Hōkyōshō 164, 217
hō mandara (Dharma mandala) *see* fourfold mandala
hōni (also *jinen hōni*, *hōni jinen*: absolute entities; unconditioned; spontaneous) 17, 47, 50, 90, 98, 181
Hōryūji temple 97
hosshi 92 *see fashi*
hosshin seppō (the Dharmakāya [i.e. Mahāvairocana] preaches the

Dharma) xviii, 8, 9, 14, 16, 37, 40, 42–6, 50, 77, 96, 128, 153 *see also* pansemioticism
Hossō daijōshū nikanshō 201
hrīḥ 100, 130, 131, 136–7
Huangdi nei jing su wen 56
Huiguo (746–805) 204
Hūṃ (Jp. *un*) 94, 142, 162–3 *see also* *Un*
hyōtoku ("manifestation of virtues") 107–8, 117, 123

Ichijitsu shintō sōjō kuketsu 214
ichimitsu jōbutsu (becoming a buddha through the practice of one single secret [among the *sanmitsu*]) 81
Ichinengi 56
ideological fantasy 194
idō ("easy path" to salvation) 17
ignorance (Sk. *avidyā*, Jp. *mumyō*) 19, 80
Ikegami Yoshihiko 189
illusion (*māyā*) xii
images (of the Buddha, Sk. *bimba*, Jp. *gyōzō*; also, Jp. *honzon*, image of the central deity of a ritual) 11, 12, 64, 67–8, 70, 118–19, 126, 127, 145, 166 *see also* representation
imitsu (secret of the mind) 81 *see also* *sanmitsu*
imprints (types of signs) 12
incense smoke meditation 136–7
Indian philosophy of language xiii *see also* Buddhist philosophy of language
Indra's Net (model for the interrelation of all things) 25, 50, 67, 74, 115, 167
initiation *see* secret transmission
interpretation xiii-xiv, 29, 31–4, 119, 155, 183
interpretive apparatus 15, 104–15
In'yū (1435–1519) 67
Iron Stūpa in South India (Jp. *Nanten tettō*) 59
Iśāna 49
ishin denshin (mind to mind transmission) 188
isotopies (of meaning) xiv, 103, 112–15, 116–19, 142 *see also* *jisō-jigi*; *shijū hishaku*
Issaikyō kaidai 205
issatsu tashō ("to kill one so that many may live") 33–4
Itō Masatoshi 33–4

Japanese language 49, 175–9, 182–4, 193 *see also* Chinese language; Sanskrit
Japanese spirit (*wakon* or *yamato-damashii*) *see* *wakon yōsai*
Japanese superiority 177–8
ji (Sk. *akṣara*, linguistic signs) 64, 81, 85, 105
ji (phenomena) 9–10 *see also* *ri* (principle)
  as semiotic token 9–10
Jingang ding jing 28, 64, 168, 170
Jingang sanmei jing 209
Jingangding lianhuabu xin niansong yigui 215
jinpishaku ("profound interpretation") 15, 108, 111–12 *see also* interpretive apparatus; isotopies
Jinson (1430–1508) 36
jinzū (supernatural powers) 93
jisō-jigi xiv, 16, 73–4, 108–15, 116–17, 120–1, 124, 132, 201
jissō (true reality) 10, 81, 84, 87, 105, 120
jōshosachi ("wisdom that carries out completely what needs to be done") *see* five wisdoms
ju (spells) 7, 89 *see also* dhāraṇī; mantra; Shingon
Jung, Carl Gustav 61
jūroku genmon ("sixteen gates of obscurity") 106–7

kabun (result of religious practices) 10
Kada no Azumamaro (1669–1736) 176
Kakuban (1095–1143) 28, 48, 56, 65, 71–4, 81, 89–90, 99, 101, 110, 112, 113–15, 119–23, 133–6, 138, 139–51, 152, 156, 157, 160, 166, 169
kalpa 169–70

kami (Shinto gods) 28, 30, 31, 32, 174, 177, 178, 179
Kamo no Mabuchi (1697–1769) 176, 177, 178
kana (phonetic scripts) 97
Kangen ongi 206
kanjō (consecration or initiation rituals) 29–31
Kangyō gengi bun denzūki 204
karma 17
kaṣiṇa 71
Kawamura Minato 218–19
kechien kanjō (initiation establishing a karmic tie with a deity or mantra) 17 *see also kanjō*
Kegon (Ch. Huayan), tradition of Buddhism 15, 29
Keichū (1640–1701) 97, 175–6, 179
Keiran shūyōshū 30, 59, 162–4, 202, 206, 217, 218
kenmitsu fudōju 199–200, 211
kenmitsu fudōshō 204
Kharoṣṭha 48–9
kharoṣṭhi alphabet 49
Kinzoku (Indian King in Japanese texts) 59
Kissa yōjōki 57
Kishimoto Hideo 188
Kitabatake Chikafusa (1293–1354) 167, 168
Kōan xii, 189 *see also* Zen Buddhism
Kōbō Daishi *see* Kūkai
Kōfukuji temple 29, 36
Kohitsu shūshūshō 207
Kojiki 176, 178, 186, 218
Kokutai (national polity) 182, 189
Kokutai no hongi 180, 182–4
Kōmyō shingon (mantra of light) 17
Kongō busshi ("adamantine sons of the Buddha," monk signature) 34
Kongō hannyakyō kaidai 213
Kongōkai mandara (Kachiinbon) 120
Kongōchōgyō kaidai 203
Kōshū (early fourteenth century) 162–4
kotodama (spirit of Japanese language) 176–9, 182–3, 194
Kripke, Saul 76
Kūkai (774–835), founder of the Shingon school 6, 7, 8, 13, 16, 18, 28, 37, 38, 40, 41, 43, 45–6, 47, 48, 49, 50–3, 60, 61–2, 64, 67, 76, 84–7, 90, 97, 98, 103, 105, 106, 110, 111, 122, 126, 142, 153, 176
Kuroda Toshio 5
Kyōō jōjūin temple 28
Kyōōkyō kaidai 204
Kyoto School 180, 181, 188

Lamotte, Etienne 8
language
  constitutive dharmas of 79–80
  as fallacious 80, 89
  languages of beings 37
  ordinary, limitations of xi, 188
  origin of 46–50, 90
  sins related to 81
Lāṇkāvatāra Sutra (Ch. *Ru Lengqie jing*, Jp. *Nyū Ryōgakyō*) 82, 204, 209
Large Wisdom Sutra (Ch. *Da banruo boluomituo jing*, Jp. *Dai hannya haramitta kyō*) 211
Lincoln, Bruce 14, 54–5, 195
Li qu jing 205, 212
logic of yoga 35, 54, 168–9
López, Donald 94, 95, 156
Lotman, Yuri 68, 189
Lotus Sutra (Ch. *Miaofa lianhua jing*, Jp. *Myōhō rengekyō*) xii, xiii, 59, 206

macrocosm xvii, 53
macrosigns 14, 39, 41, 57, 59
Mādhyamika (Jp. Sanron or Chūgan) xiii, 15, 18–19, 29, 73, 80, 110
magic 1, 55, 68, 95, 141, 155
magical illocutionary acts 158–9
Magritte, René 171
Mahā-parinibbāna-sūtta 13
Mahāvairocana (Ch. Mohepilushena, Jp. Makabirushana or Dainichi) xvi–xviii, 3, 8, 14, 16, 40, 43, 50, 53, 56, 58, 67, 75, 85, 89, 93, 95, 103, 118, 119, 130, 143, 153, 166, 193 *see also* Dharmakāya
  as the mind 26, 44, 57, 112

samādhi 46, 47, 118
Mahāvairocana Sutra (Ch. *Dari jing*) 18, 28, 44, 45, 46, 64, 86, 90, 98, 138, 154, 204, 205, 207, 211, 212, 213, 215
Mahayana xiv, 11, 18
philosophy of language 8, 80, 105
Maheśvara 49
Maitreya, Bodhisattva (Jp. Miroku) 118
mandala xvi, 6, 14, 26, 32, 40, 45, 59–77, 98, 99, 117, 128, 129, 132, 144–8
conditioned (Jp. *zuien mandara*) 40
of the two realms (or twofold mandala: Jp. *ryōbu mandara* or *ryōkai mandara*) 42, 56, 62–3, 65, 71–5, 101, 162
unconditioned (Jp. *hōni mandara*) 40, 76
mandalization 30, 78, 101 *see also* esotericization
mantra xiii, 6, 13, 14, 16, 17, 47–8, 56, 81, 84, 87–96, 139, 143–4, 148–51 *see also* Tantric Buddhism; Tantrism
"imitation mantras" 89
performative aspects 155–8
mantric seeds (Sk. *bīja*, Jp. *shuji*) 64, 88, 89, 94, 101
Man'yōshū 176, 178
mappō (decline of the Buddhist Law) 9
Māra 163
mass culture (Japanese) 196
material substance (*tai*) 21, 57
materialism (Buddhist) xvii, xviii, xix, xx, 38, 164
matter, material objects (*shikihō*) 20, 51
māyā (veil of illusion) 10
medicine 56
meditation (Sk. *samādhi*, Jp. *sanmai* or *jō*) 20, 26
Meiji Restoration (1868) 173, 182, 196
mental image (Jp. *omokage*) 21
merit-making 1, 141
mesocosm 53, 66
metonymy 11–12
microcosm xvii, 53, 65, 69
mijin see atoms
Mikkyō see Esoteric Buddhism
Miller, Roy Andrew 183, 187
Mīmāṃsā school 85
mind 17–27, 52, 159–65
Misōde no shita 165, 217
mitsugo (secret words) 7 *see also dhāraṇī ;ju*; mantra; *Shingon*
mitsugō ("twilight language" or "intentional language," Sk. *saṃdhābhāṣa* or *saṃdhyābhāṣā*) 84, 89
Miyoshi, Masao 185
modernization of Japan 173
mon, *monji* (signs in the Shingon tradition) 16, 37, 49, 50–3, 84, 85, 86, 103, 205
as phonemes 79
moon-disk (Jp. *gachirin*) 132, 140, 147–8, 161
motivation 12 *see* remotivation
Motoori Norinaga (1730–1801) 176, 177–8
Mount Sumeru (cosmic mountain at the center of the human universe) xvii, 56, 129–30, 131
Mujū Ichien (1226–1312) 175
myōkanzatchi ("wisdom to observe the sublime aspect of things") *see* five wisdoms

Nāga 163
Nāgārjuna (second to third centuries CE) 18–19, 46, 59, 73, 75, 80, 110
Najita, Testuo 185
Namaḥ samantabuddhānāṃ aḥ vi rah ūṃ khaṃ (Jp. *nōmaku samanda bodanan a bi ra un ken*) 138–9
nāma-rūpa ("names and forms") 80
nāmu (Jp. *nōmaku*) 94
nativism (*kokugaku*) 175–9, 182, 193
nenbutsu 164–5
neo-Confucianism 173, 177
New Age obscurantism 61
Nichiren (1222–1282) xii, 62
Nihon bunkaron (discourses on Japanese culture) *see Nihonjinron*
Nihon ryōiki 43

Nihon shoki 206, 218
Nihonjinron (discourses on the Japanese) 184–90, 194
nine syllables mantra (Jp. *kujimyō*) *see Oṃ amṛta teizei hara hūṃ*.
nirmaṇakāya (Jp. *ōkejin*, conditioned manifestation body of the buddha) xvii, 9, 42–3
nirvana xviii, 11 *see also* enlightenment; transmigration
Nirvana Sutra (Ch. *Dabanniepan jing*, Jp. *Daihatsu nehangyō*) 76, 208, 213
Nishida Kitarō (1870–1945) xii, 180–1, 183
nominalism 19
nondualism (Sk. *advaita*, Jp. *funi*) xviii, 42, 58, 73–5, 111, 116, 219
non-hermeneutical dimension of Buddhism xiv, 82, 152
non-linguistic, direct communication (in Chan/Zen Buddhism: Jp. *furyū monji kyōge betsuden*) 83, 84
non-ordinary language (of Esoteric Buddhism) 83–4 *see also* mantra
no-self (Sk. *anātman*, Jp. *muga*) 18
nōsen (signifier) xiv, 116
nyogigo ("words that are identical to their meaning") 84
nyojitsu chi jishin ("know your mind as it really is") 18
nyūga ganyū ("[the deity] enters one's self, and one's self enters [the deity]") 126, 154 *see also* visualization

occultism, Western xvi, 4
offerings to the Buddha (Esoteric meaning of) 118
oṃ (Jp. *on*) 94, 100
oṃ amṛta-tese hara hūṃ (Jp. *on amirita teizei kara un*) 148–51, 152
oṃ maṇi padme hūṃ 89
Onkō Jiun (1718–1804) 97
ordinary knowledge (Sk. *jñāna*) 18
orientalism x, xi, 192
original enlightenment (Jp. *hongaku*) 26, 104, 108, 140, 202
Orzech, Charles 67
ostension (semiotic mode) 11–13, 14, 138

pansemioticism xvi, xviii, xix, 8, 13, 14, 37, 38–42, 104–5
pantheism xvii, xviii, xx
paribhogika (objects used by saints) 12
Pasolini, Pier Paolo (1922–75) xvi, 40–2, 57, 152, 153
Peirce, Charles S. 91, 101
pentaculum 68, 159
performative strategies and functions xi, xiv
perfuming (Sk. *vāsanā*, *abhyāsa*, or *bhāvanā*; Jp. *kunshū*: the production of new semiotic seeds in the store-consciousness) 24
phenomena as absolute xx
phenomenology (Buddhist) 20
philosophy of language, Buddhist 79–82, 84
phonosymbolism 90
"Pleasure of the Dharma" (Jp. *hōraku*) 45, 60
politics 69
Pollack, David 186
practice (religious) 18, 62, 99, 107
prajñā-pāramitā 92
"pre-transcendental" xii
proliferation and dissolution of sense 115–24, 138
pure consciousness (Sk. *amala-vijñāna*, Jp. *amarashiki*) 25, 26, 162 *see also* eight consciousnesses; store consciousness
Pure Land Buddhism xiii, 62, 129, 181

Raihō (1279–1330?) 25–6, 39, 42, 58, 107–8, 110–12, 116, 123–4, 127–8, 169–70
Raiyu (1226–1304) 28, 31, 44–5, 52, 126, 131
Reikiki shishō 201
relics 11, 12
remotivation of signs 14, 16, 69–74, 143–4, 166–8, 175
representation (theory, strategies, modes) xi, xvi, xx, 10–11,

64, 67–8, 98, 118–19 *see also* Aniconism
of the Buddha 10–13
rhetoric of immediacy xii, xvi
ri (principle) 9–10, 30 *see also ji* (phenomena)
as semiotic type 9–10
Rishukyō kaidai 204
Rishukyō shujisaku 214
ritual xiii, 26, 35, 65, 142
rokudai see six elements
rokudai hosshin (the six cosmic elements as the substance of the dharmakāya) 14
Ru Lengqie jing see Lāṇkāvatāra Sutra
rūpadhātu (Jp. *shikikai*, realm of pure forms) xvii
Ryōjin hishō, *Ryōjin hishō kudenshū* 206
Ryōjō 48–9
ryōkai shuji mandara 63

śabda (eternal words) 85–6, 98 *see also shō*
Said, Edward x
Saigyō (1118–1190) 175
Sakai, Naoki 186
Śakradeva 50
Śākyamuni xvi-xvii, 3, 9, 31
and polymateric communication 43–4
samādhi (meditation) 44, 64, 74, 76, 92, 104, 115, 126, 127, 129, 138, 154
saṃboghakāya (Jp. *hōjin*, "retribution body" of the Buddha) xvii, 9, 42–3
samples (types of signs) 12, 14, 58, 69
sandai ("three greats," i.e. the three modalities of the universe) 38–40 *see also* sōdai; taidai; yūdai
sangō (three karmic activities) 40, 80–1, 131, 168 *see also sanmitsu*
sanmitsu (three secrets, the salvific activities of the Dharmakāya) 10, 16, 40, 53, 56, 81, 104, 126, 131, 156, 167, 169 *see sangō*; soteriology
Sanskrit (Jp. *bongo*) 13, 47, 48, 49, 88, 92, 93–4, 96, 97, 105–6, 108–9
status of 82
santai (three truths) 109
Sanzhong xidi po diyu zhuan yezhang chu sanjie mimi tuoluoni fa 161, 205, 207, 217
sarīraka (bodily relics) 12
Sasaki Kōkan 95
satori see enlightenment
sat-samāsa (Jp. *roku rigasshaku*, "analysis of six combinations") 105–6
scholar monks (Jp. *gakuryo*, *gakuto*) 28–34, 113, 195–6
Schopenhauer, Arthur xi
Searle, John 156
secret (at the core of Esoteric Buddhism) 6, 101–4 *see also* Esoteric Buddhism
secret texts (Jp. *hisho*, *hihon*) 27 *see also* secret transmission
secret transmission (Jp. *hiden*, *denju*, *menju*) 17, 28–31, 58, 66, 75–7, 102
sekiten (Chinese examination system) 31
self-consciousness (Sk. *mano nāma vijñāna*, Jp. *manashiki*) 21, 22
semantics (of Esoteric signs) 81, 100–15
semiognosis 15–17, 55, 69–75
semiopietas 15, 17, 55
semiosis xvi, 20, 22
stop to 25
semiosophia 15, 17
semiosphere 68
semiotic
encyclopedia 68, 77–8
manipulation *see* semiotic, strategies
seeds (Sk. *bīja*, Jp. *shūji*) 22, 23–4, 79
strategies xiii–xiv, xx, 8, 127, 147, 151, 152, 170–1, 175
square 73–4, 124
semiotics, definition xv
semiurge 196
Senpo intonshō 207
senryakushaku ("abbreviated interpretation" 15, 108, 111–12

see also interpretive apparatus; isotopies
sense-consciousnesses (Jp. *rokushiki*) 22 *see also* eight consciousnesses
sense organs (Jp. *rokkon*) 22, 141–2
sentences (Jp. *ku*) 79
"Sermon of the flower" 83
Serres, Michel 44
sexual practices 164–5
shabyō ("decanting a bottle") 76 *see also* secret transmission
shajō ("elimination of passions") 107–8, 117
Sharf, Robert xii, 67, 68, 128, 181–2
Shi moheyan lun 199, 201, 203, 209
shijū hishaku xiv, 16, 116–19
Shingachirin hishaku 211
Shingon (Japanese translation of mantra) 6, 16, 89, 90, 92, 94, 95–6, 155 *see also* dhāraṇī; mantra
Shingon Buddhism xv, xvi, 2, 4–10, 25–6, 28, 40, 97
  Kogi branch 44
  Shingi branch 44
Shingon honmoshū 203
Shingon myōmoku 127–8, 199, 201, 202, 203, 213, 214, 217
Shingon naishōgi 167, 168–9, 217
Shingonshū kyōjigi 103, 213
shinjitsugo (truth words) 9
shinkoku (Japan as a divine land) 71, 174–6, 178
shinmitsu (secret of the body) 81
Shinto 5, 59, 62, 89, 174, 183, 193
shintō kanjō (secret initiation to Esoteric understandings of Shinto religion) 30
Shinzoku zakki mondōshō 202
shishu hosshin (four kinds of dharmakāya) 10
shishu mandara gi kuketsu 64–5, 207
shishu mandaragi 64, 65, 70, 207, 208
Shittan (Sk. *siddhaṃ*), script and graphs 13, 16, 28, 48, 81, 88, 96–100, 108–9, 119, 130–1, 140, 158–9, 187, 196
  visualizations of (Jp. *jirinkan*), 131–7
shittangaku (*Shittan* studies) 33, 97
Shittanrin ryakuzushō 212
Shittanzō 97, 204
shō (voice, sound, audible entities) 84–7, 105 *see also shōji*
Shōgei (1341–1420) 27
Shohō funbetsushō 58, 206
Shōji (phonic, linguistic signs) 51, 84–8, 105, 120
Shōji jissōgi 37, 41, 43, 51–3, 110, 111, 153–5, 176, 201, 203, 204, 205, 210, 213, 216
Shōji jissōgi kaigishō 205
Shōji jissōgishō 205, 209
Shoke kyōsō dōishū 203
shōmyō (Buddhist vocal music) 28, 67, 94
Shōrai mokuroku 200, 207, 212
shosen (signified) xiv, 116
Shoshū kyōri dōishaku 199
shōtai (substance/essence, also *taishō*) 38, 39
Shukaku, monk-prince (1150–1202) 28
Shutten daikō narabini jo 206
siddhaṃ script *see Shittan*
siddhi (supernatural powers) 4, 16, 74, 146
signified, signifier xiv
sign systems xiv
signless, signlessness (Jp. *musō*) 45, 123–4
  meditation (Jp. *musōkan*) 127–8
signs
  as absolute entities 10, 14, 77, 123–4
  Buddhist definitions 39–40 *see also mon/monji*
  in classical Buddhism 10–13
  and divination 55
  in Esoteric Buddhism 13–17, 69, 107
  of Japanese identity 185, 186, 190–2
  marvelous (*ryōi*) 204
  as microcosms 10, 14, 69
  as polymateric 14
  structure 87–8, 99–100, 112–13
  typologies 9–10
signs, status of xi

sincerity (Jp. *makoto*) 182, 184
six destinations (Jp. *rokudō*, *rokushu*) 56
six elements (constituting the universe, Jp. *rokudai*) xvii, 14, 38, 39
six kinds of objects (perceptual fields, Jp. *rokkyō*) 22, 51
sō (Sk. *lakśaṇa* or *nimitta*, signs) 21, 23–4, 39, 52, 123
sōdai (cosmic semiotic structure) 10, 16, 39–40, 64, 69 *see also* fourfold mandala
Sokuji nishin ("each phenomenon is the truth") xx
Sokushin jōbutsu ("becoming a buddha in the present body") 7, 8, 9, 10, 16, 75, 90, 101, 125–7, 147, 152, 168–9 *see also* enlightenment; semiotic strategies; soteriology
sokushin jōbutsugi 67, 125, 126, 203, 207, 214
Sokushingi gūsō 203, 214, 215
soteriology xi, xii, 1, 8, 16, 30, 36, 40, 56, 65, 69, 75, 78, 80, 88, 108, 112, 113, 125–7, 136, 143–55, 162
sotoba (funerary tablets) 98
sōyū (manifestations/operations) 38
speech acts 86–7, 156–8
  transitive 158
Spiro, Melford 1, 140–1
Staal, Frits 82, 90, 91, 92, 94, 156
store consciousness (Sk. *ālaya-vijñāna*, Jp. *arayashiki*) 21, 22, 23, 25 *see also* eight consciousnesses
Strickmann, Michel 4
Stuart-Fox, Martin 71
stūpa 12, 56, 58–9, 129–30
Śubhakarasiṃha (Ch. Shanwuwei, Jp. Zenmui, 637–735) 44, 46, 59, 75, 92
subject/object (distinction) 23, 180, 181
subjectivities 166–7, 182–4
suchness (Sk. *tathatā*, Jp. *shinnyo*) 19, 20, 21, 24, 27, 39, 53, 62
  "suchness words" (*nyogo*) 90 *see also* mantra
suffering (Sk. *dukha*, Jp. *ku*) 19, 23
sūnyatā (Jp. *kū*) *see* emptiness
sutra 31–2
  the universe as 45–6
Suzuki, D. (Daisetz) T. (Teitarō) (1870–1966) x, xi, xii, 180, 181–2, 190, 191
svāhā (Jp. *sowaka*) 94
symptoms (types of signs) 12
synecdoche 11

Tachikawa-ryū 56, 164
taidai (cosmic substance) 10, 16, 39, 55, 69
Taizō kongō bodaishingi ryaku mondōshō 104, 213
Taizōkai mandara son'i genzu shōshi 208
talismans 17, 89, 96, 98
Tambiah, Stanley 69, 91, 94, 95, 155–6
Tanaka Chiaki 85
Tanizaki Jun'ichirō 187
tāntra see Tantrism
Tantric Buddhism xiii, xv, xvi
Tantrism 3–4, 55, 75
Tendai school 6, 15, 29, 97
ten evils (Jp. *jūaku*) 81
ten worlds (Jp. *jukkai*) 37 *see also* four saintly beings; six destinations
Tenkai (1536–1643) 119
texts (Buddhist) 31–4
  as simulation of practice 152–5
textuality xiii–xiv, 29, 31–4, 152–5
three great kalpas (Jp. *san dai-asōgi kō*) 25
three jewels (Sk. *triratna* or *triśūla*, Jp. *sanbō*) 12, 65
three natures (Sk. *trisvabhāva*, Jp. *sanshō*), resulting from cognitive modes 20
three secrets *see sanmitsu*
three worlds (Jp. *sangai*) 198
"thundering silence" 83
tianfu ("heavenly talismans") 98
Tōdaiji temple 29
Tōji temple 60
Tokieda Motoki 178
tōtai jishō ("each specific material body is unconditioned") xx
Toyoda Kunio 178

tranformation of consciousness (Jp. *tenshiki tokuchi*) 24–5 *see also* eight consciousnesses; enlightenment; mind
translation 13, 82
transmigration (Sk. *saṃsāra*, Jp. *rinne*) xviii
true language (Jp. *nyogigo*, *nyogo*) 84 *see also* language, as fallacious; mantra
true reality (*jissō*) xi, 10
truth transcending language (Jp. *gongo dōdan*) 83
Tsuda Shin'ichi 35, 54, 55, 168–71
Tsukumogami ki 214
Tsunoda Tadanobu 188
Tucci, Giuseppe 60, 61
twelve factors of causation (Sk. *pratītya-samutpāda*) 80

uddeśika (illustrative or commemorative objects) 12
Ujike Kakushō 7, 92–3, 109
Uki, by Shukaku monk-prince 28
un 133, 137
unconscious 22
uncreatedness (Jp. *honpushō*) 47, 88
universal monarch (Buddhist ruler), (Sk. *cakravartin*, Jp. *tenrinshōō*) 69
Unjigi 110, 111, 142, 216
unobtainability (Jp. *fukatoku*) 73–5, 109–11, 113, 115, 116, 124
upāya (Jp. *hōben*), "expedient means" 13, 15, 34, 82, 83
Uṣṇīṣavijayā dhāraṇī (Jp. *butchōson darani*) 97
Uspensky, Boris 189
Ususama Myōō (Sk. Ucchuṣma vidyārāja) 137

va (Sanskrit syllable and mantric seed) 16, 109, 113, 141
vāc (Sk. for "word, language") 16, 85, 121, 141
Vaiyākaraṇa (Indian Grammaticians') school 85–6, 98
Vajra (diamond, thunderbolt, weapon) 3, 174
Vajra realm (Sk. *vajradhātu*, Jp. *kongōkai*) 27, 63, 101, 121, 122, 133, 144, 161 *see also* mandala; mandala of the two realms
Vajrabodhi *(Ch. Jingang zhi, Jp. Kongōchi*, 671–741), Chinese Tantric master 139
Vajrasattva 46
vaṃ (Jp. *ban*) 101, 119–23, 130, 131
vaṃ hūṃ trāḥ hṛīḥ aḥ 27
Vandermeersch, Léon 54
Vasubandhu (fourth to fifth centuries CE) 19
veridiction contract 139, 153–4
Vimalakīrti Sutra (Ch. *Weimojie suoshuo jing*) xiii, 82, 83, 204, 209
Violi, Patrizia 68, 69
vision 10
Viṣṇu 48
visual objects 52
visualization (Jp. *kan*, *kansō*, *kannen*) 4, 16, 26, 35, 45, 56, 65, 119, 127–37, 144–8, 159–65, 167, 169
voice 86

Waji shōranshō 218
waka kanjō (secret initiation on the Esoteric meaning of *waka* poetry) 30
waka poetry 17, 175–6
wakon yōsai ("Yamato spirit and Western technology") 180, 186–7
Washio Ryuki 60–1, 78
Watanabe Shōichi 187
Watts, Alan x
Wheelock, Wade 156
Wisdom Sutras (*prajñā-pāramitā*) xiii
womb realm (Sk. *garbhadhātu*, Jp. *taizōkai*) 59, 63, 101, 132, 148, 160–1, 174 *see also* mandala; mandala of the two realms
word of the Buddha 82–4
words (Jp. *myō*) 79

Yamaguchi Masao 219, 221
Yamamoto Hiroko 174
Yamasaki, Taikō 60

yantra 70
Yellow Emperor 49
Yijing (635–713) 44, 96
Yijing 50
yin-yang 55
Yogācāra xiii, 15, 17–27, 29, 51–2, 79–80
Yōsai (1141–1215) 57–8
Yōtenki 205
yūdai (dynamic aspect of the cosmos) 10, 40, 69
Yūkai (1345–1416) 164
yunzhuan ("cloud seals") 98
Yuqie jinggang ding jing shi zimupin 213

Zen Buddhism x–xiii, xvi, 173, 180
  modernist tendencies x, xii, 179–84, 188, 190, 191
  semiotics of x, xi, 83, 189
Zhenyan (Jp. Shingon) school 2
Žižek, Slavoj 194, 196